Madison Avenue and

Madison Avenue and the Color Line

African Americans in the Advertising Industry

JASON CHAMBERS

PENN

University of Pennsylvania Press

Philadelphia

Published by
University of Pennsylvania Press
Philadelphia, Pennsylvania 19104-4112

Printed in the United States of America on acid-free paper

10   9   8   7   6   5   4   3   2   1

A Cataloging-in-Publication record is available from the Library of Congress
ISBN-13: 978-0-8122-4047-4
ISBN-10: 0-8122-4047-2

Contents

Introduction

The most difficult and bewildering thing about the white world is that it acts as if blacks were not there.

—James Baldwin

In the early 1990s, Kay Lorraine, a Chicago-based advertising producer, assembled a cast and crew on location to film a commercial for a Cleveland grocery chain. She hired a multiracial cast to reflect Cleveland's diversity, but the client representative, after seeing the black actors at the taping, "had a fit and wanted them off the set." Lorraine refused. After several tense moments, he relented. "O.K.," he allowed, "they can push the shopping carts around in the back, but make sure they don't touch the food." So Lorraine filmed the commercial with the black actors in the back of the scene and not touching any of the products— quietly pretending that they were not there.[1]

Although Lorraine's encounter with a prejudiced executive took place late in the twentieth century, it could have happened in nearly any decade and in any place in America. For much of the century, to include African Americans in a commercial, even one aired in a city with a large black population, was anathema to many executives. Indeed, many of the people who decided the advertising and marketing direction for their companies simply acted as though blacks did not exist as consumers for their products. Therefore, they often gave them no place in their advertising, unless individuals like Lorraine, black consumers, or advocacy groups pressured them to do so.

Lorraine risked losing the account when she openly confronted the representative's prejudice. Advertising is a service business. Agencies exist to meet the needs of clients and those clients have complete power over where their advertising dollars go. That Lorraine, a white woman, took this stand was due in part to the hard work of numerous African Americans in the advertising and media industries. Over the course of several decades, these men and women stood up to the negative and denigrating treatment by advertising agencies and American corporations, and their hard work helped make the black consumer market visible. As this examination of the advertising industry will show, too few others acted with Lorraine's courage to include blacks in advertisements—or as employees in advertising agencies. Yet it was only through this sort of pressure that the advertising industry ever changed at all.

The struggle of African Americans for inclusion in the advertising industry is the central concern of this book: it connects the growing visibility of African Americans in advertisements with the increasing presence and hard work of African American advertising professionals. African Americans, both inside and outside the advertising industry, viewed advertising as an employment and financial opportunity *and* as a mechanism to effect cultural change in both the white and black communities. They actively engaged in defining the black consumer both for potential clients and for blacks themselves. They used advertising not only to promote images of consumption but also, within the advertisements, to promote positive images of black life and culture, from family life and academic achievement to religion and community.

Scholars like Marilyn Kern-Foxworth and Anthony Cortese have examined changes in blacks' representation in advertisements, documenting the transition from negative and disparaging stereotypes, through their virtual invisibility in advertisements, to the beginnings of genuine and realistic representations. But no one has fully explored the breadth of changes in the racial makeup of the agency world responsible for those advertisements. In fact, beyond a few brief references in historical works, scholars have ignored the experiences of black professionals in the advertising industry. In doing so, they have turned existing histories of the advertising industry into a story of white men and women only, and they have created the dangerous and inaccurate impression that African Americans have not fought for inclusion in this industry. This work shows that blacks contested discrimination in advertising employment much as they did in more recognized areas like politics, law, and manufacturing. Further, existing histories imply that the industry's racial homogeneity was simply a reflection of larger society, the result of a lack of interest from blacks or the absence of talented blacks. This work documents a history of active, systemic discrimination.[2]

It also documents the history of the pioneering African Americans who transformed the advertising industry in the face of that discrimination. It offers a broad historical examination of blacks' struggle for work in an industry that did not welcome them and examines their role as image makers for a market that that industry could not see. It shows how black advertising professionals—as sales representatives, as agency owners, and eventually as mainstream agency personnel—worked to develop corporate executives' appreciation of the black consumer market, and their advertising and marketing efforts targeting that market. Blacks' multifaceted development of this market directly led to the opportunities to advance into the advertising industry. This book thus provides a more complete picture of the history of advertising in the United States and contributes to the growing body of literature on the history of African Americans in business.

There are three major components to this book. The first examines how African American professionals in journalism, sales, and advertising changed the perceptions of black consumers among corporate executives and then used that interest as a foundation to gain wider participation in the advertising industry. Over the course of the twentieth century, African American advocates of the black consumer market gradually shifted from emphasizing the *presence* of black consumers to white business leaders, to stressing the *pressure* those consumers could create on a company or industry when they acted as a cohesive force. Second, I analyze how civil rights and government organizations used this pressure—specifically, through tactics of boycotts and selective purchasing campaigns, as well as legislation outlawing employment discrimination—to catalyze changes in the institutional culture of the advertising industry. These changes led to greater employment opportunities for blacks in mainstream agencies and as owners of independent firms. Finally, I show how black men and women, once they achieved power in the industry, used decision-making positions to present what they viewed as accurate, non stereotypical visions of African American life in advertisements.[3]

Beyond Salesmanship in Print

The first responsibility of any advertisement is to persuade. In the first years of the twentieth century one influential copywriter, John E. Kennedy, offered a simple, yet still suitable, definition of advertising: Advertising, he said, is "salesmanship-on-paper."[4] Whatever a salesperson might say to a customer on the sales floor, whether selling cars, clothes, automobiles, soda pop, or something else, that sales pitch is what an advertisement should communicate. Yes, advertisements are entertaining and their creators design them to grab and keep our attention, but their first job is to persuade us to take an action, to buy a product. But because of the ubiquity of advertisements, we sometimes fail to recognize the role advertisements have in persuading us about things beyond the particular product or idea they sell.

In the early twentieth century, advertisements told consumers of innovations in technology and interpreted the meaning of those advancements in their lives. In addition, their depictions of everyday life gave consumers an image of who they were and what the population of the country looked like. In presenting that vision, however, advertising personnel made no effort to be inclusive or even accurate. Instead, they addressed their work to the most powerful group: those consumers who had the economic power to buy, and thus uphold, the market society. Historian Roland Marchand theorized that advertisers worked in the framework of a "market democracy," in which one dollar equaled one vote. Within this structure those with more money had more votes than others, and those groups received more active attention from advertisers; in contrast, advertisers left those with little or no money or influence outside the system. Thus first years of the twentieth century, advertisers and advertising agencies did not recognize everyone as an equal citizen. Blacks were among those whose lowly status in advertisements confirmed their economic disenfranchisement, just as violence and Jim Crow laws confirmed their political disenfranchisement. But Marchand and other scholars have failed to account for how these "outsiders" reacted to the advertising vision of the consumer society. One way in which African Americans reacted to this economic exclusion was by fighting for changes in advertisements and employment in advertising agencies throughout the twentieth century.[5]

As both consumers and advertising professionals, blacks in the industry linked the ideas of consumer and citizen as understood by the broader African American population and expressed them in their work. They knew from their experience as consumers, and from their research as advertising professionals, that blacks fervently wanted recognition as full and equal members of society and that a key part of that definition lay in their status as consumers. They used this awareness not only to position themselves for jobs within the advertising industry but then also to work from the inside to change how others conceived of black consumers and to influence how advertisements expressed that view. Not every African American in the industry was a card-carrying advocate, pressing the case for inclusion or for targeting black consumers. But even those who did not do so found that white companies sought them out primarily for their expertise in this new market. By clarifying blacks' struggles for citizenship in the consumer arena, this study sheds important light on both their market activity and their broader quest for equal citizenship in all areas of life in America.

Consuming is not the same as voting. It does not provide tangible liberation or freedom in the same manner as extending political and civil rights. But scholars have shown that over the course of the twentieth century, consumption became a key aspect of citizenship, even, as McGovern argues, "a symbol of American social democracy." Therefore, advertising's positive and representative depiction of blacks fulfilling their role in the consumer society would be symbolic evidence of blacks' accepted status in society: stereotypes and subservient roles pointed to and justified discrimination, while positive or even simply accurate representations would point to their role as equal consumers and equal citizens. As one black advertising specialist observed, "Advertising plays an important role in demonstrating upward social mobility and is a yardstick in charting progress in the search for acceptance and recognition by the majority society."[6]

As Anthony Cortese has observed, "Ideologies are often latent or unrecognized; they are taken for granted as real, commonsense, or natural. The structure of ethnic, gender, and class inequality is justified as being profoundly destined by nature." Advertisements confirm to the viewer the current ideologies about race and the place of blacks in society. Yet, even in lieu of this sophisticated scholarly analysis of the sociocultural impact of advertising, African Americans' actions show that they recognized the utilitarian possibilities of advertisements. They knew that advertisements, with books, radio shows, music, and literature, formed one of the lenses through which others gained information about them. The increasing ubiquity of advertisements throughout the twentieth century made them one of the primary visualization mechanisms of that information. Specifically, blacks recognized that, because advertisements so effectively reinforced inequality, it might be possible to reverse their power to reinforce a message of equality. Positive and realistic images of African Americans could not only reflect the levels of their penetration into different areas of American life, that is; they could also ease white acceptance of them in those once closed areas.[7]

Advertisements maintain a vexed relationship to reality. Their world is one of myth and make-believe. In that world, everyone is beautiful, has ample leisure time, and has the time and money to buy and enjoy a bewildering array of goods. Additionally, if one looks at advertisements as documentaries, then the world for much of the twentieth century was one in which whites enjoyed the fruits of consumption and blacks, if visible at all, contentedly served them from the margins, just slightly out of view or focus. This reliance on myth has meant that advertisements have not challenged socially erected ideologies about race. Rather, they have reproduced those ideologies and in so doing helped to reinforce them. Instead of presenting Aunt Jemima (or anyone related to her) in a position of consuming the pancakes she made, advertisements depicted the portly black female joyfully serving them to whites. Historian Grace Hale noted, "Americans were people who could command the service of both blacks and consumer products." Blacks in twentieth-century advertising were subservient objects that served the cornucopia of products hawked in advertisements, but rarely subjects who used them. The explicit message that ads delivered with crystal clarity was that consumers were white. In picturing blacks in servant roles and whites in command, advertising images visibly upheld the assumed social organization of everyday society.[8]

Beyond their role as servants, advertisements in the late nineteenth and early twentieth century commonly represented blacks as lazy, ignorant, violent, or as little more than comic relief. Negative images of blacks also frequently circulated in the broader culture on trading cards, dolls, children's books, cooking utensils, and other products. Caricatures of African Americans advertised Niggerhead Tobacco, and coal-black children, the Gold Dust Twins, were symbols of a popular soap powder. Already the proliferation of degrading images of blacks in commercial and leisure items helped transmit ideas of black inferiority even as real blacks tried to claim the full privileges of citizenship in the early twentieth century. "The child growing up in the home of an average northern family may not have been taught to hate the black race, but more than likely the child caught the basic principle of prejudice from day to day living," noted one scholar.[9]

After the First World War, advertisements widely depicted blacks as cooks, porters, or agricultural laborers—a step up from items like Niggerhead Tobacco to be sure, but images that were nonetheless servile and demeaning. Advertisements used representations of black occupational skill and expertise to promote areas that existing stereotypes labeled blacks as naturally gifted in, such as cooking. Some advertisers used this ethnic shorthand as a testimonial of product quality and even, as archivist Fath Davis Ruffins has explained, as a metaphor for product authenticity. If a black cook like Aunt Jemima or a black waiter like Uncle Ben said the pancake mix or rice was good, then (advertisers assumed) consumers would accept their recommendation as authoritative.[10]

As in other areas of life, African Americans did not accept this subservient role. Rather, as historian Robert Weems pointed out in his pioneering study of black consumerism, *Desegregating the Dollar*, blacks tried throughout the twentieth century to use their economic power to gain respect. But they fought for a recognition of dignity that went beyond mere appreciation for their economic ability to buy consumer goods. For example, few whites are familiar with the embarrassing and painful daily experiences of segregation. Blacks who traveled around the country, especially in the South, carried guides that listed where they could find restaurants or hotels without facing discrimination; places where they could use the rest room or simply receive treatment as an equal citizen. As one black traveling salesman recalled, having these books

Figure 1. In the first years of the twentieth century, African Americans were little more than beasts of burden in the advertising landscape. Although at first glance, the image in this Cream of Wheat advertisement is representative of a child's game, the whip and the exhortation "Giddap Uncle" contributed to popular stereotypes about African Americans. Cream of Wheat advertisement, *Needlecraft* (September 1921): inside front cover.

"prevented some very serious racial incidents." Beyond their travels, even in their local communities blacks were also limited in public spaces: prevented from trying on clothes in stores, not seated at restaurants, and charged higher prices for lower-quality goods than other consumer groups. Thus, the repeated disrespect blacks faced in their consumer activities continually reminded them of unequal treatment within the larger society. By acknowledging the link blacks' made between their consumer activities other social goals, we illuminate their agency. In particular we can more clearly see their sophisticated linkage between consumption and their quests for rights in other areas of life. Those other areas, including political, civil, and social rights, as well as racial violence, understandably occupied blacks' attention throughout the twentieth century. But the images circulated in advertisements never completely disappeared from their purview.[11]

Indeed, blacks perceived these negative images as part of the collective whole of repression. So blacks, individually and collectively, expressed their displeasure with product advertisements through boycotts, selective purchasing campaigns, and other less formal measures. By voting with their dollars, blacks advocated for more positive representations in advertisements and for recognition of their involvement in the consumer society, and, by relation, their citizenship. As a result, because advertisements were one of the filters that distorted the reality of African Americans' lives, aspirations, and societal contributions, blacks could not leave advertisements and the industry that produced them unchallenged.

In *Making Whiteness*, Hale explained that the growth of consumer culture provided blacks with a host of physical spaces, such as stores or trains, within which to challenge their status as second-class citizens. This work takes her argument a step further. Just as consumer culture in general gave blacks spaces within which to challenge their social status, likewise, the ubiquitous nature of advertising gave blacks access to a visual space and a set of practices to challenge the existing images of themselves as a group and to present an alternative vision.[12]

Battle for the African American Image

In 1926, African American writer Langston Hughes described the efforts of black artists during the Harlem Renaissance to define their group and individual identity: "We younger Negro artists who create now intend to express our individual dark-skinned selves without fear or shame. If white people are pleased we are glad. If they are not, it doesn't matter. We know we are beautiful. And ugly too."[13] Throughout the twentieth century, blacks have sought to emancipate and rehabilitate the impression presented in advertisements and other forms of media. Communications scholars Jannette Dates and William Barlow characterized their struggle as a "war" over the African American image. Blacks' awareness of their invisibility and marginalization in advertisements made them more critical of advertisements. As one of the leading image-producing industries, advertising has been in the forefront of the industries presenting an effectively negative image of African Americans. Thus African Americans developed a more adversarial relationship with the advertising industry than any other racial or ethnic group in the United States.

"The definition and control of black images in the mass media," Dates and Barlow wrote, "has been contested from the outset along racial lines, with white cultural domination provoking African American [economic and] cultural resistance." On one side were white image makers who reproduced and maintained the negative, stereotypical portrayals of blacks. On the other have been the dual efforts of black consumers and black image makers. Black consumers responded to negative representations by avoiding the products advertised either individually or as part of collective boycotts or selective patronage campaigns. Black image makers in the advertising industry have responded to the humiliating depictions by creating their own versions of the African American image. In so doing, their work has often paralleled that of black artists. These black professionals in the advertising industry, heretofore overlooked contributors to the struggle to redefine and shape the African American image, were heirs of the tradition that Hughes described. For besides crafting art and copy to sell the product in question, they often created empowering and uplifting images representative of the goals and aspirations of the black population.[14]

Gaining Entry and Access to the Industry

Even when pressed to present positive images of blacks, white advertisers and agency personnel balked. Some protested that to depict positive images of blacks would offend white consumers and lead them to avoid the products so advertised. Others argued that white consumers would view positive images of blacks as a direct challenge to both white authority and obvious societal norms, and that such "social policy" stood outside the role of advertisements. Their strongest rationale was an economic one: advertisers and agency personnel did not believe blacks had the economic wherewithal to be an important consumer group. So advertisements did not need to appeal to black consumers for their patronage. Similarly, white advertisers and agency personnel saw no need to hire black professionals for their African American market expertise. This was more than a passive stance: most agencies actively enforced a policy restricting black participation at anything beyond a menial level. This has been, as one black advertising man put it, the advertising industry's "dirty little secret."[15] Thus for most of the twentieth century both advertisements and the advertising industry remained "lily-white."

The rejection of African Americans stood in marked contrast to the industry's acceptance of women. Indeed, the advertising industry was unique among professions in that it was fairly open to hiring and promoting women. During the early development of the industry, several major agencies actively sought out female employees and advanced them to professional or managerial positions. But compared to hiring African Americans, hiring women was both fiscally justified and socially acceptable. Many in the industry accepted the idea that women either made or influenced upward of 80 percent of all buying decisions. Thus, many executives had to admit, though begrudgingly, that white women had a potentially useful expertise and could help produce agency profits. Advertisers could readily see women as powerful consumers and, in search of workers with expertise in reaching them, agency executives recognized the need for a "woman's perspective." Given the paucity of consumer research in the early twentieth century these arguments were more anecdotal constructions than factually determined ones but they were, nonetheless, powerful rationales supporting the employment of women. Because executives lacked a similar opinion of the impact of blacks on purchasing, they had no economic reason to challenge racial conventions and pursue blacks for their marketing or advertising expertise. Moreover, men working in agencies had mothers, daughters, sisters, and girlfriends, so at a minimum they had a level of close personal interaction with women. Although the appearance of women in professional positions was new, their involvement in agency work lacked the visually arresting nature of a black face in the office. At best African Americans served or entertained the white advertising professionals; they did not work side by side with them. Finally, executives had little interest in upsetting the existing social fabric by hiring an African American for the intimate role of communicating with the white, middle-class women who were the targets of most advertising (or to work with the white women who crafted that advertising). As a result, for much of the twentieth century, racism and discrimination kept the doors of most mainstream agencies closed to African American professionals.[16]

In contrast to other industries, until the mid-twentieth century blacks overlooked the racism and discrimination in agency employment. This primarily resulted from two factors: industry size and visibility, and the educational pathway into advertising. In comparison to other large industries such as construction, manufacturing, or mining, the advertising industry is small. Therefore, for much of the century, black activists and the government pressed for equal opportunity in larger, more visible industries first. Also, although the products of the advertising industry, the advertisements, have long been widely visible, the actual creators of those advertisements have not. If asked, many Americans could name their favorite commercial or trade character but not the name of the individual or agency behind its creation. Thus the advertising industry, may be the most visible, yet most hidden industry in the United States. That invisibility has helped the industry avoid much of the public scrutiny and investigation that helped effectively diversify other areas of both white- and blue-collar employment.

The lack of a specific educational route into the industry also limited blacks' entry and advancement in the industry. While a college degree has often been a necessity for some jobs in the industry, there has been no consensus on what areas of study that degree should encompass. (Further complicating matters, some of the most recognized industry figures of the early twentieth century openly disagreed that a college degree was necessary.) The creative side of the trade, such as creating art, music, or copy, has the fewest recognized standards—other than the subjective measurement of "talent." In the absence of standard requirements, agencies sought people with experience in advertising or persons they could train for specific jobs within the agency. Many of the large agencies, such as J. Walter Thompson, developed agency-based "universities" in which they trained people for work in the company; that knowledge was transferable to other agencies. So, in contrast to aspirants to other professions such as accounting, law, or medicine, blacks were not able to look to the educational system for a guaranteed path into advertising. Racism and discrimination, combined with the aforementioned invisibility of the industry, made gaining the experience necessary for employment equally challenging. Nevertheless, over the course of the twentieth century, blacks gradually began to find positions in mainstream firms and open independent agencies.

As this book details, getting into the industry was not the end of the problem: black agency owners quickly found that, to many potential clients, their skin color and perceived advertising expertise rested solely in selling products to African Americans. As a result, this perception may have limited their business opportunities and the broader development of black entrepreneurialism in the advertising industry.[17]

An Economic Opportunity or Detour

As Juliet Walker brilliantly showed in her sweeping book, *The History of Black Business in America*, African Americans have a long history of business participation. An unfortunate aspect of that history, however, has been the limits placed on black business development by racism and segregation. In 1940, Merah Stuart published *An Economic Detour: A History of Insurance in the Lives of American Negroes.* He argued that throughout the late nineteenth and early twentieth centuries, racism and segregation drove most blacks businesses to operate in an "economic detour" where they served an almost exclusively black clientele (for example, barbershops, insurance companies, mortuaries, newspapers, beauty products manufacturers). Later, scholar Joseph Pierce extended Stuart's analysis and argued that black business owners faced a two-edged sword: segregation allowed them to set up profitable companies serving black consumers, but it also prevented most from having access to larger markets serving white consumers. While black-owned businesses never formed a totally separate economy, and they continually competed with white-owned companies, segregation gave them some shelter from significant white corporate intrusion. Although they were able to sustain, and sometimes economically thrive, in these segregated enterprises, black business owners lacked access to consumer groups and markets that might have allowed their firms to grow larger.[18]

Taken together, the work of Stuart, Pierce, and Walker demonstrates that black companies in segregated businesses sometimes had a finite lifespan. Eventually, larger white-owned corporations took over their areas of operation. These white-owned companies had the size and racial authority to deliver goods and services to black consumers, but usually black business owners lacked the capital and authority to do the same among whites. For example, two of the most successful fields for African Americans have been insurance and beauty products. Ignored by white-owned companies, blacks turned to their own race's enterprises for their needs. Black-owned companies like Supreme Life Insurance flourished by providing affordable insurance to black consumers. With beauty products, blacks found preparations more applicable to their skin tones and hair textures from companies, such as the Madame C. J. Walker Company, that were sensitive to their physical differences from white consumers. However, as awareness of the black consumer market grew among manufacturers and advertisers, so too did competition from white firms seeking the profits available in this niche. Black firms were often unable to compete because of their small size and relative lack of resources. As a result, once segregated but profitable companies gradually closed, merged, or sold their operations to white firms.[19]

Does the history of African American-owned advertising agencies fol-
 the same arc as these other areas of black business activity? That is,
 it fit Stuart's model of businesses working within an economic
 ir, or does it markedly diverge from it? As Judy Foster Davis pointed

out, black-owned advertising agencies may fit into at least the initial criteria of Stuart's theory. Several black entrepreneurs set them up in part because larger advertising agencies overlooked a possible area of service: the development of advertising campaigns specifically targeted to African Americans. Although some of these new owners initially sought to position their firms as general market agencies, they quickly found that their perceived expertise—and the best route to client accounts—was in the black consumer market. In other words, their clients' acceptance of their expertise in crafting advertising campaigns to black consumers did not usually evolve into significant opportunities to develop campaigns to reach non blacks. Certainly, white-owned agencies created advertisements to reach black consumers, but for most this was an intermittent area of activity. Therefore, as with black-owned insurance and beauty products companies, the economic detour in the advertising industry offered at least the potential for African Americans to carve out an area in which to operate. So one area explored in this book is how advertising has and has not been an example of an economic detour.[20]

Beyond the model of economic detour, another useful way to think about blacks in advertising is to compare their experience with that of blacks in white-collar professions. In fact, the experience of African Americans in the advertising industry parallels that of blacks in other white-collar professions, especially accounting and insurance. For blacks in mainstream agencies, their experiences mirror that of blacks in accounting, while for independent black-owned agencies, insurance companies are the closest parallel. For example, mainstream accounting agency executives claimed an inability to find qualified blacks.[21] When qualified blacks began to apply for positions, executives justified their continuing refusal to hire blacks by arguing that their clients would not want them involved in their financial affairs. These are precisely the evasive strategies that ad executives took, and as this book shows the structure and nature of advertising led them to argue that agency clients would not want blacks involved in the creation of their advertising campaigns.

When we combine the experience of blacks in the advertising industry with examinations of blacks' efforts to enter other white-collar professions, a disturbing historical continuity of racism and prejudice is evident. This prejudice often hampered blacks' ability to develop a career path in working for white corporations as well as limited their success in developing black-owned enterprises. Certainly other factors have been important in constraining blacks' success in advertising—inexperience, undercapitalization, mismanagement—but racism and discrimination, as well as the government's failure to adequately protect and encourage black business development, were the most damaging causes preventing greater development of black business enterprises. Further, one of the very things that could have enhanced blacks' chances to develop successful agencies—a broader range of agency experience—was also limited by existing racism and discrimination within the industry.[22]

Rehabilitating the African American Image

Once in the industry, African Americans combined their knowledge of consumers with their own individual experience as consumers. Those in black-owned advertising firms, advertising products mainly to black consumers, used their knowledge proactively to define the black consumer as one who shared the consumer values of the larger society but who had a unique history and social and cultural outlook that needed special expertise to target properly. Black media, sales, and advertising professionals actively countered the prevailing idea that black families were poor and unstable, redefined blacks as having the financial means to take part in the consumer society, and then actively promoted the idea that they had the aspirations to do so. They viewed consumption as a tool through which African Americans could express their goals and desires for social membership. Blacks created advertisements that represented blacks' need for social membership as equals within society as a whole, as well as membership in the imagined communities of middle-class homeowners and automobile buyers constructed by advertising.[23]

What types of images of blacks did they promote? One black copywriter answered, "People working productively; people engaging in family life, you know, people being well-rounded, and being thoughtful; people caring about other people; good neighbors, good parents, whatever the case may be; people with dreams and aspirations, people with ambition." Such images had three purposes: First, black professionals wanted and needed black consumers to buy the products of agency clients. Second, the images they created became part of the transformative social narrative of the definition of blackness and of the collective vision of blacks' identity as a group and as individuals. As Hughes charged black artists to do in the 1920s, these representations were part of reclaiming and rehabilitating the African American image. Finally, beyond satisfying the goals of agency clients, the images also helped satisfy the vision of how blacks wished to see themselves depicted. By ingeniously linking the financial and professional necessity of satisfying their clients with the aspirations of black consumers, they satisfied one by doing the other.[24]

Overall, African Americans used advertisements to project a vision of a racially diversified consumer market and of African Americans as a middle-class population. However, the images also sometimes closely mirrored ongoing developments within the broader African American community. For example, during the period of Black Nationalism in the late 1960s and early 1970s, some blacks in the industry used advertising to project a vision of pride and liberation and were part of the effort to redefine blackness. Black professionals like Vince Cullers used advertisements, especially for products made specifically for black consumers, to become involved in the ongoing narrative of what exactly it meant to be black.

African Americans in the advertising industry were in the unique position of being creators and interpreters of black life and culture. In these roles they actively defined the meaning of "black consumer" for both prospective clients and the public. Additionally, they presented conspicuous consumption to blacks as a means to both middle-class membership and equality with their fellow citizens.[25] Cast in this manner, securing the right to service and to receive equal appeal for one's patronage is but a little different from securing the freedom of choice in other areas of life such as housing, education, or vocation.

Throughout the twentieth century, African Americans strove for equality throughout all areas of American life. While most are familiar with their social and political efforts, only recently have scholars began to analyze blacks' struggles in the consumer realm. The black struggle throughout the century was about gaining equality in all of its forms and in all areas of life rather than just a choice few. To accept segregation and discrimination in any area was to raise the possibility of either not eliminating it or seeing it returning in another. Moreover, exclusion was especially painful and maddening in the market democracy, in which every dollar was supposedly equal to the other regardless of the hand that held it. So the pressures blacks generated against consumer industries like advertising—and their victories and struggles—are as important to the story of black advancement as the securing of other rights. Certainly extending consumer rights is dependent on others such as an end to racial violence and equal pay measures; but to reach full equality blacks not only had to be able to vote, but, on their way home from doing so, eat at a restaurant or shop in a department store that welcomed them and had also advertised for their patronage. Full citizenship meant full citizenship. Consumer rights formed an important part of that definition.

The Layout of This Book

Historical events, to the consternation of authors, do not simply occur in a neat, linear, or ordered progression. Instead, events and individuals, causes and effects, often overlap in time period and in effort. There are necessarily points of chronological overlap in this story; some chapters in this work share the same time period while addressing different themes. Chapter 1 examines the conversation between African American media publishers and executives and white businessmen that led major white-owned companies to their initial recognition of the black consumer market in the 1930s and 1940s. Chapter 2 details the role of black pioneers in the advertising industry in the period following the Second World War but before the racial revolution in the industry in the mid-1960s. As corporate interest in the black consumer market grew, experienced black professionals and entrepreneurs moved to take advantage of it to secure positions in advertising, marketing, and public relations. Much of this chapter details the emergence of the "Brown Hucksters," the African American marketing and advertising specialists in the 1950s who guided corporate clients in their efforts to reach African American consumers. Because of the multitude of changes ongoing in this period, Chapters 3 and 4 share the same chronological period, the 1960s, but each deals with a different theme. Chapter 3 devotes attention to the role of civil rights groups—the National Urban League, the Congress of Racial Equality (CORE), and the National Association for the Advancement of Colored People (NAACP)—in motivating changes within the advertising industry. The black consumer market reflected the social changes going on within the nation, and blacks used their economic presence to compel concessions from advertisers active both in the black and mainstream markets. Further, this chapter details the ways in which members of the advertising industry dealt with changes among black consumers. Chapter 4 analyzes the impact of state and federal government equal employment commissions on the advertising industry during this same period. The New York City Commission on Human Rights (NYCHR) and federal Equal Employment Opportunity Commission (EEOC) each focused significant attention on the advertising industry during the 1960s, and their efforts reinforced and extended those introduced by civil rights activists. The Civil Rights Act of 1964, which outlawed racial discrimination in employment, broke down many of the visible and invisible barriers to blacks in the advertising industry. As a result, many agencies began to lure black professionals from other industries and to recruit at black colleges. Chapter 5 analyzes the Golden Age for blacks in the advertising industry and examines the impact of the racial revolution on the industry. The chapter contains case studies of eight black-owned agencies that emerged between 1965 and 1975 and considers them in the light of Stuart's model of economic detour. The Epilogue examines how in the aftermath of the industry's short-lived racial revolution blacks' renewed their efforts to develop a presence in mainstream agencies as well the smaller, but stronger, black-owned agency niche.[26]

Several different sources support this work. A detailed, page-by-page examination of articles in *Advertising Age, Adweek, Ebony, Madison Avenue, Printer's Ink, Tide, Sponsor,* and *Sales Management,* most of which have not been indexed, heavily informs its content. Scholars of advertising have recognized the trade press as an especially important source because the articles provide insight into the ideas shared by the members of the advertising industry. The journals also contain revealing discussions about agency leaders and employees changing opinions of all consumers. Thus, they form my principal sources on understanding how the members of the advertising industry thought about both blacks in agencies and the black consumer market.

But the journals tell only part of the story. A review of the existing papers of former advertising personnel and organizations, specifically those of Barton Cummings, Caroline Jones, Moss Kendrix, the J. Walter Thompson Company, the Pepsi-Cola Company, the NAACP, and CORE were key to rebuilding the history of African Americans in the advertising industry. And interviews with Tom Burrell, Roy Eaton, Bill Sharp, and Chuck Smith, along with less formal conversations with a number of other black and white advertising professionals, offered insights, vivid detail, and perspective on these struggles for real people.

During initial conversations with former industry professionals, several often had the same reaction when I stated I was writing a history of blacks in the advertising industry: "Why?" There aren't that many." My interview subjects were neither sarcastic nor crass in asking this question; in their minds, the low number of blacks in the industry simply ruled out the subject as an area of study. However, the importance of blacks to the advertising industry lies far beyond mere demographic considerations. Just as the advertising industry as a whole has effects beyond its size, numbers say precious little about the actual influence and impact of black professionals on the industry as well as the broader consumer communication field.

I admit, though, that I began this undertaking with numbers in mind. I originally started this project with the notion that I would include every black person in advertising who was at any level above secretary and whom I could track down. I envisioned this book as a kind of joint biography of their work. But limitations of space and a desire to explore their historical context (as well as consideration for the patience of the reader) led me away from that to the present goal: an understanding of the key roles and fascinating experiences of these important social actors. This book focuses on blacks in two main roles: as professionals in mainstream (that is, white-owned) agencies and as owners of independent firms. In addition to those blacks who worked in black-owned advertising firms, an equally important segment of African Americans worked in mainstream firms. Although much of this work privileges blacks' activity in black-owned firms, the role of blacks in mainstream agencies is significant. When the doors of mainstream firms finally opened to greater numbers of black professionals, work in these agencies provided much needed experience and helped blacks create important networks of contacts that aided them when they created their own advertising agencies. Also, blacks in mainstream agencies fulfilled the key role of opening doors for other aspiring professionals and in countering stereotypes about blacks' abilities to work as advertising copywriters, artists, or executives. So, while the individuals in black-owned agencies often had a greater degree of latitude to use images of black life and culture, blacks in mainstream firms played a key role in developing a black presence in the advertising industry.

Regardless of whether in mainstream or black-owned agencies, African Americans have historically been underrepresented in the advertising business. Yet, as will be shown, that has not been the result of a lack of desire on their part. Instead, it has often been the result of a hostile industry where talent supposedly trumps other factors, including race, but it rarely has. Instead, African Americans have had to (and desired to) fight for their positions in the industry. Therefore this book is an effort to understand the role of the pioneers, to focus on specific individuals and their experience and impact on the industry. Of course that means that more than a few people are not present in this story in name. Yet it is my hope that this understanding of the larger story will honor their contributions to the industry's development as well. So, while the experiences of people like Keith Lockhart, Theodore Pettus, Joel P. Martin, Bill Richardson, Phil Gant, Joyce Hamer, Carol Williams, Don Coleman, R. J. Dale, J. Melvin Muse, Billy Davis, Kelvin Wall, and others are not detailed in this work, they are here in spirit.

In 1954, historian David Potter declared that as an institution advertising had no sense of any social responsibilities.[27] For African American practitioners of the advertising craft, this has proven false. Throughout the twentieth century, African Americans have struggled to gain control over their images and present their own vision of exactly what blackness represents. Given the depths from which advertising's image of African Americans needed rehabilitation, for blacks there was no question that advertising had a social role and that they had a dual responsibility: to their clients in selling their products, and to the larger African American population in working to change advertising's depictions of them from negative to positive. In turn, blacks created the opportunities for themselves in the advertising industry primarily by establishing the black consumer market.

Still, while the racial revolution in the advertising industry does not occur until the 1960s, the foundation of the changes in that period rest on work started by African Americans in the early twentieth century. The development of a black presence in the advertising industry rests on the corporate appreciation of the black consumer market. The initial catalysts in the establishment of that appreciation were black publishers. Two key factors, financial and symbolic, motivated the men and women who first began pressing corporate America to change its conception of black consumers. Financial interest led black publishers to press agencies and advertisers for increased advertising placements: ad revenues literally supported their publications. The second, symbolic, was part of the broader effort by African Americans to change the negative perceptions of them—that they were dirty, ignorant, poor, or ugly—that was so commonly represented in advertisements. Further, they communicated to the broader society that blacks were not, in fact, content to see them exist. Each factor supported the other: publishers needed the revenue, but to display their viability as an advertising medium, the advertised products needed to sell. To sell, however, publishers argued that advertisements to blacks could not feature the traditionally negative and pejorative images of them. As a result, black newspaper and magazine publishers were in the forefront of establishing a portrait of the black consumer that contradicted the prevailing definition. They were among the first to try to create advertiser and agency interest in African American consumers. It is with this group that our story begins.

Chapter 1

The Rise of Black Consumer Marketing

I am an invisible man. . . . I am invisible, understand, simply because people refuse to see me.

—*Ralph Ellison*, The Invisible Man

In the first decades of the twentieth century African Americans were emerging from what one historian described as their "nadir": the period following Reconstruction in which blacks were betrayed by the promises of the government and left to defend themselves against the violence and depredations waged against them. It was in these first years that blacks, especially in the urban North, began organizing themselves to wage what would be a century-long fight for equality. Blacks and liberal whites formed key organizations such as the National Association for the Advancement of Colored People (NAACP) in 1909 and the Urban League in 1911. And, while these two were among the largest and most easily recognized organizations, a host of smaller, but no less important ones, formed as well. A variety of business, fraternal, and religious organizations, with a multitude of purposes ranging from developing black business enterprises to organizing for local community development to providing information and news, were the backbone of more widely recognized groups like the NAACP.[1]

By the second decade of the century blacks also experienced growing opportunities for advancement through their racially segregated institutions. While some of these separate entities appeared before the turn of the century many found their fullest development during the First World War as millions of African Americans moved from the countryside to the cities in search of work and opportunity. Regionally, they migrated from the South to the North to take up residence in many of the nation's great urban centers and cities like Chicago, Detroit, New York, and Cleveland saw their black populations skyrocket. Once there, racial segregation combined with group affinity; many migrants sought to live near relatives, and they created visible and distinct black neighborhoods or sections. A portion of this affinity was that due to the natural affiliation of individuals of similar background or outlook. Much of it, though, emerged from the separate facilities in which blacks were forced to congregate. Prior to the turn of the century the Supreme Court had codified what was an already ongoing practice—separate facilities for blacks and whites—into law with the *Plessy v. Ferguson* decision. Racism and segregation forced blacks to establish something of a separate society outside the mainstream with facilities and services that met needs not met elsewhere. Blacks neighborhoods were, as one writer described them, a "city within a city." Certainly blacks were not always physically separate from their white fellow citizens, but they operated and patronized their own churches, banks, stores, barbershops, and newspapers. Such facilities eased the transition from a rural to an urban population and helped transform this group into a compact, measurable, consumer population.[2]

One key African American institution was comprised of the hundreds of independent newspapers that made up the black press. In the field of journalism, blacks had a history of operating their own periodicals. Long accustomed to having the events in the "darker nation" overlooked by the mainstream press, African Americans began operating their first newspaper in 1827 with *Freedom's Journal*. Alongside newspapers, blacks eventually founded and maintained successful magazines as well. While many of these organs remained small or local in terms of circulation, they nonetheless provided an important outlet for black writers and journalists, and they served as a source of pride and information for their readers.[3]

However, unlike other separate businesses operated by blacks, newspapers were unique in that, while they needed readers, the bulk of their possible revenue came from advertisers. Consequently, it is here that our story begins. The entry of African Americans into the advertising industry business has its beginnings in the related field of journalism. It was black publishers who, beginning in the second decade of the century, were the first to vocally and publicly press American corporations to recognize and patronize the black consumer market. Black publishers were key figures in the chain of events leading to an African American presence in the advertising industry. Some pressed for corporate recognition of black consumers in the interests of increasing revenue to their own newspapers. Others did so, though, while still recognizing the need for revenue, out of a belief that consumer goods were one additional aspect of full equality for African Americans. In other words, having blacks recognized as valuable consumers meant something more than just a capacity to buy. It meant that blacks were a valuable and recognized part of the consumer democracy in which everyone's dollar/vote was equal. Additionally, many publishers believed that if blacks were recognized as a viable consumer population, their papers would receive the revenue that came from companies eager to reach their readers with sales messages.

This chapter examines the development of African American media as a recognized vehicle to reach black consumers. Much like the development of advertising in the general marketplace, advertising in black-oriented media moved through the traditional progression from newspapers to magazines to radio in the pretelevision media landscape. Consequently, to understand the growth of the African American consumer market, we must first understand how blacks positioned that market and, simultaneously, their publications as sources to reach its constituent consumers. This chapter, therefore, analyzes the transitions between these media sources in terms of their perceived importance to advertisers interested in the black consumer market. It focuses on key individuals like Claude Barnett, William B. Ziff, and John Johnson as a window into the sometimes cooperative and sometimes independent efforts. In so doing, it sheds light on the actors in the earliest portion of the century-long effort to generate interest in the black consumer market. Historians have been too eager to privilege the years following the Second World War as the catalyst in which corporate attention first comes to African Americans. As a result, existing accounts fail to recognize that the success experienced in that period was built upon a foundation of work nearly three decades old. Consequently, this chapter begins with an examination of the work of Claude Barnett, one of the earliest advocates pressing American corporations to devote specific advertising and marketing attention to black consumers. The work of Barnett and other newspaper representatives provide the foundation that publishers like John Johnson, and station owners programming the Negro Radio format, build upon for significant revenue.[4]

Claude Barnett and the Associated Negro Press

When Claude Barnett returned to Chicago in 1906 he was likely thankful for a return to the moderate summers of the Midwest. Born in Florida but raised in Illinois, Barnett had recently graduated from Tuskegee Institute in Alabama. He had returned to the city of his youth in search of opportunity. As a graduate, Barnett admired the philosophy of Tuskegee founder Booker T. Washington and often echoed Washington's theories of self-help and economic advancement for African Americans. Additionally, like so many other southern blacks who made a similar journey, Barnett both sought to escape the daily threats of violence and humiliation of the South and to take advantage of the opportunities in the Midwestern city.[5]

Unlike other new arrivals to the city, Barnett already had existing contacts. As a teenager he had worked as a servant in the home of Richard Sears. Sears, one of the city's business titans, was cofounder of the Sears-Roebuck company and had taken a liking to the young man, offering him a job in his company. While Barnett had turned down the position in order to attend Tuskegee, his acquaintance with Sears helped him secure a job upon his return. Although he dreamed of becoming an engineer, his need for income led him to pursue something less grand, and he became a post office clerk. Although by his own account Barnett initially considered the position a "bum case," he quickly found that the position had distinct advantages. Most notably his clerkship brought him into contact with leading advertising trade journals. He voraciously consumed their contents. Doing so led him not only to consider advertising as a future career choice but also spurred the development of his own ideas as to what constituted good and bad advertising. The position also allowed him to learn the current advertising industry techniques, ideas he put into practice in later years.[6]

After several years at the post office, Barnett had the opportunity to use his advertising and marketing knowledge. During the fiftieth anniversary celebration for the Emancipation Proclamation he created a picture series featuring prominent African Americans. He sold it during the celebration, and then, at its end he created a sales brochure featuring the series and bought advertising space for it in black newspapers. After moderate success he started one of the first African American advertising agencies in the country: Claude A. Barnett Advertising.[7]

The slogan of the firm, "I reach the Negro," was the first of Barnett's many efforts to generate interest in the black consumer market. Like many other small firms in the still-fledgling industry the company was primarily a placement agency. Rather than focusing on creating advertisements in house, the firm placed owner-created advertisements for local businesses in the *Crisis* magazine, organ of the NAACP, and the *Chicago Defender*, a leading black newspaper. On a limited basis Barnett also did some advertising copywriting for small local African American businesses.[8]

Despite Barnett's efforts, his advertising company remained a small, local firm, and he earned money from other sources. In 1917, he and five other men formed a cosmetics business, the Kashmir Chemical Company. The other partners in the enterprise were established professionals who contributed most of the money to start the company. Barnett convinced his partners that his contributions to company advertising would equal their capital investments. At that time, three est-lished companies already dominated the field of black cosmetics: Poro College, the Madame C. J. Walker Company, and the Overton Hygienic Company. Though it was a new competitor, the Kashmir company began to carve a place within the industry brand of cosmetics. Barnett, perhaps immodestly, credited its success to the advertisements he created and to the quality of the product.[9]

In designing Kashmir advertisements, Barnett consciously sought to project a more positive image of African Americans than the ones other advertisers used. Advertisements from both black- and white-owned companies featured images of what Barnett viewed as unattractive black women with "ugly kinky hair." In contrast, for Kashmir advertisements he used images of attractive black women depicted in both everyday and luxurious settings.

The consumer response was "so astounding," he later recalled, "that the founder of the Poro system and Madame [C. J.] Walker herself expressed great interest in this new concept of advertising beauty products for the Negro market." He went on, perhaps in a bit of hyperbole, "soon the entire field had switched to the positive approach pioneered by Kashmir."[10] Exaggerating or not, Barnett was clearly onto something. When presented with attractive and credible representations, black consumers responded by supporting the product advertised. He concluded that to successfully market products to black consumers, companies needed to approach them respectfully with attractive advertisements. He carried this lesson with him the remainder of his professional life, and it became a central argument in his efforts to develop interest in the black consumer market.

In fact, the rapid success of the Kashmir company apparently led some in the black community to speculate that the company was secretly owned by whites. In 1918, Barnett placed a lengthy advertisement responding to the charge. Devoid of any imagery save for an enlarged version of the company name, Barnett responded to the three reasons detractors used in labeling Kashmir a white company: the quality of its products, sophistication of its advertisements, and its business efficiency. Barnett emphasized that, contrary to the seeming beliefs of some in the community, black-owned companies could operate with the same skill and efficiency of white-owned businesses. Further, he encouraged readers to both support Kashmir by buying its products or by becoming a sales representative for the company.[11]

Though he was finally experiencing a return on his efforts, the days of working in the post office and the hurried nights acting as an advertising representative had taken a toll on Barnett. On the advice of doctors he decided to take a break. Since he now had the time Barnett decided to take a trip west to see his mother. To help fund the journey, he con-

Figure 2. Although the Kashmir Chemical Company had offices only in Chicago, in some advertisements Barnett attempted to give the company an international image by claiming foreign offices in Paris, Tokyo, and Calcutta. Kashmir advertisement, *The Crisis* (November 1916): 44.

tracted with the *Chicago Defender* to work as an advertising representative. Along the way, Barnett sold advertising space for the *Defender* and crafted advertisements for some local companies. Despite his continued connection to advertising, Barnett increasingly found himself drawn to journalism. He met a number of editors and publishers of black newspapers, and each consistently related tales of difficulty securing national stories about African Americans. The entrepreneurial light in his head came on. What was needed, he surmised, was an organization to distribute national news to black newspapers around the country. When he returned to Chicago he proposed the idea for such an organization to executives at the *Chicago Defender*, the largest black newspaper in the nation.[12]

Even before he approached executives at the *Defender*, Barnett had decided to leave the post office in order to devote his time to the Kashmir Company and his fledgling newsgathering organization. In his initial meetings with *Defender* executives he found an enthusiastic response. Unfortunately for him, the founder and publisher, Robert S. Abbott, did not share their enthusiasm. Abbott believed that a national black news organization would damage the national circulation of the *Defender* and refused to invest in the venture. Disappointed but determined, Barnett again reached out to his network of associates. His partners at Kashmir agreed to provide financial support for the enterprise in exchange for advertising space in future member newspapers of his news venture. Now that he finally had the necessary funding, Barnett began to transform his vision into reality: he established the Associated Negro Press (ANP).[13]

Barnett envisioned the ANP as an information clearinghouse to deliver news items about African Americans to member newspapers around the country. Yet, despite his hopes and meticulous plans, the company struggled. Although black publishers were eager for the service, paying the subscription fees was something else entirely. Nearly all but the largest black newspapers operated with razor-thin profit margins. Excess money for subscription fees to add national news stories to their pages was difficult to justify when they struggled to pay existing labor and production costs. Once again Barnett found a way around the problem so that the ANP was compensated and newspapers received the service. This time, he linked the ANP with an advertising exchange, the Associated Publishers' Representative (APR). If publishers could not pay the subscription fees, they would compensate the ANP with "white space," the unsold advertising space within their newspapers. Through the APR Barnett then sold the previously unused space to advertisers. In addition to placing advertising for others, Barnett attempted to position the APR as an advertising agency. He solicited black cosmetics manufacturers by offering APR services in creating advertising copy, as well as in placing and verifying advertisements.[14]

Barnett's brief time as an agency owner provided him some limited experience in the advertising field. And years at the post office examining advertising trade journals, as well as work creating advertisements for Kashmir, gave him clear ideas about advertising creation and placement. But shortly after creation of the ANP, the Kashmir company became embroiled in a trademark dispute with the larger, more powerful, Cashmere Bouquet company. To settle the case, Kashmir executives agreed to change the name of the company to Nile Queen cosmetics. Advertisements for the renamed company and brand stressed that the only change at the firm was its name. Unfortunately, the name change proved too difficult to overcome in the already crowded black cosmetics field, and declining sales forced executives to close the firm. After its demise, Poro College became the major client for the APR. Barnett himself designed and placed advertisements for the firm and constantly implored the company founder, Annie Turnbo-Malone, to increase her advertising efforts. More, more, and still more advertising, Burnett urged.[15]

In a nod to Booker T. Washington's philosophy, Barnett recognized that black businesses operated in a segregated economy. He reasoned that if blacks were to have segregated institutions, then companies like Poro College should get the benefits of that segregation via business from black consumers. However, he did not expect racial solidarity to trump good consumer sense. If consumers were unaware of a company's products, considered them inferior, or were unwilling to pay the price requested, a company would not be successful. Therefore, in repeated letters, he urged Malone and other black business owners to increase their advertising schedules in the black press. But in seeking advertising work from companies other than Poro College, Barnett was rebuffed. The companies most able to pay for his services, like the Madame C. J. Walker company, operated in-house advertising departments and had no interest in external consultants. As a result, he often scrambled to find advertisements to fill the white space he could access, and he had only moderate success at making the APR a significant newspaper representative. Still, though he had twice failed to establish a successful advertising agency, by the early 1920s the ANP and APR placed Barnett in a unique position as a solicitor for advertising for black newspapers throughout the country. In this capacity he became a leading figure pressing American corporations and their advertisers to take note of the growing consumer power of African Americans.[16]

Barnett was a journalist and a businessman, not a population specialist. Yet he could see that since he had first come to Chicago there had been a large influx of other African Americans. Indeed, in the first two decades of the twentieth century the black population in Chicago had more than doubled. Attracted by job opportunities during the First World War, over fifty thousand blacks moved to Chicago between 1916 and 1920 alone. The movement to urban areas placed more blacks in wage-earning positions, and the overall income of the black population began to rise. As a rapidly expanding but geographically concentrated group, this population formed a compact consumer target, one whose purchasing power men like Barnett would seek to tap in future years. By the early 1920s African Americans in both the South and the North had more money to spend than ever before. The purchasing power of these locally based black consumer markets passed beneath the gaze of national corporations, but local merchants, both white and black, began to recognize their growing importance.[17]

At the same time, coincidentally, the nation's corporations had begun an unprecedented increase in advertising spending. The Committee on Public Information (CPI), the publicity and information distribution arm of the federal government's war effort during World War I demonstrated the power of advertising and public relations to impact public opinion. The success of the CPI in generating public support for the war effort alerted corporate executives of the potential power of advertising. Many reasoned that if advertising could help turn public opinion about American participation in World War I from one of opposition to support, it could definitely help sell their products in peacetime. Additionally, the possible implementation of an excess-profits tax encouraged many companies to begin spending much of their extra income on advertising. As a result, from 1918 to 1920 the volume of annual advertising spending in America jumped from $1.5 billion to just under $3 billion annually. This was a financial windfall tempting every publisher, especially black publishers whose organs had always lacked a satisfactory level of advertising funding.[18]

As the de facto advertising representative for many papers, Barnett moved to take advantage of the rising advertising outlays. His access to advertising space throughout the country meant little, however, without advertisers to pay for it. To secure the necessary buyers he repeatedly sent out sales letters to the nation's major advertisers. In these letters, Barnett provided a concise portrait of African American consumers and advised advertisers how to reach them. He emphasized that African Americans spent over $1 billion on various consumer goods, their greatest expenditures being food, clothing, and household goods. Yet blacks also chose products for reasons beyond quality or price. Advertisers could win consumers by paying attention to three important additional factors: image, distribution, and product awareness. First, companies needed to appeal to African American racial pride via their advertising. Second, they had to be sure that they advertised products that black consumers could find within their segregated communities. Third, the advertising appeals must appear in a medium in which blacks had confidence, and here, of course, Barnett pointed to the black press. He noted that this third fact was actually connected to the first factor, the question of image, as blacks viewed placement of advertisements in the black press as a visible appeal for their specific patronage. Finally, Barnett often incorporated the words of Paul Cherington into his letters. Cherington, a research expert at the J. Walter Thompson advertising agency, argued that if a similar market "were suddenly opened to American manufacturers on the other side of the ocean there would be commissions and council and surveys to tell us of its value. But this one we grew up with, so we do not find appreciation easy."[19]

During the 1920s, Barnett repeatedly solicited editors of advertising periodicals like *Printer's Ink* and *Tide* to examine the value inherent in the black consumer market and the black press as an advertising vehicle. In addition to the trade press, he pursued a multifaceted approach, targeting manufacturers and advertising agencies to get each group to devote attention and money to the black consumer market. If successful, he not only would produce revenue for black newspapers, but also for his companies. Yet there was only so much that a man operating two companies could do. If the effort to promote the black consumer market were to succeed he needed some help.[20]

In 1929, Barnett wrote to J. B. Bass, editor and publisher of the *California Eagle,* and to other editors of black newspapers around the country. He enthusiastically spoke of executives at three companies—the Kellogg Company, American Tobacco Company, and Louis Meyer and Son— who had conditionally agreed to start advertising in black newspapers. The caveat was that each company wanted information about the circulation coverage of the recommended newspapers. In addition to the circulation numbers, Barnett also asked Bass and other editors to cooperate in underwriting an advertising effort in advertising trade journals. Although individual newspapers sometimes advertised in the trade press, Barnett envisioned a central campaign that would highlight the newspapers that participated. The advertisements would also stress the size and value of the black consumer market and the power of black newspapers in reaching that market. Barnett also sent requests for black employment figures and income to the Urban League. He planned to combine these figures with the newspaper circulation numbers into a strong picture of black purchasing power that could be submitted to corporate executives and advertising agencies, as well as featured in the trade press advertising campaign.[21]

Some executives responded enthusiastically. Robert Balderston of the National Dairy Council told Barnett: "Every time that I have an opportunity to survey the American market field I am renewedly impressed with the promotional possibilities of the Negro market. I feel as if we had somewhat neglected the cultivation of a group of people who are liberal spenders insofar as they have money to spend. We have found . . . that we can increase the consumption of dairy products among the Negro portion of the population very substantially by making the right kind of appeal and through the proper channels."[22] This response was exactly what Barnett wanted and needed, a corporate executive who appreciated both the value of the black consumer and the black press in reaching them. Other executives, however, did not share Balderston's enthusiasm. When Balderston wrote his enthusiastic letter to Barnett, the nation was mired in the Great Depression. Precious few dollars were available for advertising to the general market, so companies earmarked even fewer, if any, for a consumer group most corporate leaders overlooked. Even among those executives who recognized the value of black consumers to their product lines, many responded to Barnett's queries by arguing that their existing advertising campaigns sufficiently attracted black consumers. Therefore, some understandably asked, since blacks were already buying their products, why spend extra funds to advertise specifically to them? Still other companies never signed on with Barnett because he never fully compiled black newspaper circulation figures. He was able to provide them an estimate of weekly circulation figures for these organs, but it was backed only by "sworn statements" from publishers. Most black newspapers did not have their circulation numbers independently audited. Hence, to the already cautious executives, there was little motivation to spend money advertising in the periodicals Barnett recommended.[23]

By the end of 1931 Barnett's professional fortunes had declined significantly. Unable to maintain both the ANP and the APR, he chose to focus his energies on growing the newsgathering service and sold his interest in the ANP. But since the success of the ANP was inextricably tied to the success of black newspapers, Barnett remained active in efforts to create corporate interest in the black consumer market. However, he bitterly concluded that black newspapers would continue to "get practically none of the millions of dollars poured out into white publications for the advertising of the necessities which white people buy" unless companies recognized blacks as a legitimate consumer group worthy of reaching through black newspapers. Also, though another entrepreneur continued the APR service, other newspaper representatives outpaced it. Especially prominent at this time was the white-owned William B. Ziff company, the clear leader in the field.[24]

The William B. Ziff Company

When he entered the field of advertising solicitation Claude Barnett had two central concerns: First, he sought to use the APR as a revenue source to help sustain the ANP. Second, he wanted to enter the "white-monopolized field of national advertising for black newspapers," and break the stranglehold of companies like that owned by William B. Ziff.[25] Barnett viewed white-owned companies like Ziff's as an impediment to black business development because they, rather than black entrepreneurs, got the largest share of the profits from blacks' segregation. Barnett recognized that some segments of black-owned business profited from their relationship with these companies, in this case newspapers, but he believed that they also hampered the growth of the broader black business community. "If we are to have segregated institutions," Barnett passionately argued, "we ought to get whatever economic values go with such forced solidarity."[26]

William Ziff founded his company in Chicago in 1920 as a solo, one-room operation. From the beginning he wanted to publish topically based magazines in areas he foresaw a growing public interest. Like many idealistic entrepreneurs, however, his ambitions conflicted with his financial wherewithal. As a result, he kept his fledgling publishing company afloat by acting as an advertising representative for black newspapers. Ironically, after his magazine publishing ventures brought Ziff financial success and he and a partner formed the Ziff-Davis Company, he refused to acknowledge this part of the company's history.[27]

As an advertising representative, Ziff placed considerable demands on his newspaper clients. Not only did he require them to carry inserts, he also charged high commission rates. These rates ranged from 35 to 50 percent, considerably higher than the industry standard 15 percent. He was able to demand such rates because of his unquestionable success in drawing national advertisers to his client's papers. Additionally Ziff guaranteed payment for the advertising placed, a crucial service for publishers used to dealing with local merchants who did not always pay for services rendered.[28]

By the mid-1930s several major companies and brands could be found in black newspapers, including Camel cigarettes, Lifebuoy, Chevrolet, Pepsi-Cola and Seagrams. These advertisements were simply replications of those found in mainstream newspapers; advertisers made no effort to use African American models or develop advertising copy to attract black consumers. Ziff's firm gained the attention of these clients by placing ads in the advertising trade press and distributing information pamphlets about black consumers. In 1932, for example, he published a forty-one-page booklet entitled *The Negro Market* describing the overlooked black consumer and presenting blacks as a separate and distinct market. The pages of *The Negro Market* illustrated the separate banks, churches, fraternal organizations, and newspapers that blacks maintained. It also provided pictures and descriptions of blacks' social and leisure activities. Further, turning the conversation to blacks as consumers, it argued that if advertisers used the black press to issue specific and directed advertising appeals, they could generate more sales among black consumers. Blacks were willing and able to buy a variety of products, but they reserved their loyalty for companies that appealed for their patronage. Blacks "regard advertising in their newspapers as a direct invitation to buy the merchandise advertised [and] it makes them feel their patronage is desired and appreciated and they respond with wholehearted enthusiasm," the booklet argued. For example, Gold Medal flour was the leading brand in its category, but research suggested that tens of thousands of black housewives and domestics were unfamiliar with the brand. Thus the company lost sales in two areas—in black families where African American women did the bulk of their family's purchasing, and in white families where black domestic workers did the purchasing and influenced consumption. As one white matron told *Tide* magazine, "Advertisers probably don't realize how often choice of a brand for household work depends not on the lady of the house but on her Negro houseworker." Therefore, African Americans were an important market segment with a greater means to purchase and a greater influence on buying among whites than commonly assumed.[29]

In *The Negro Market*, Ziff also assured potential advertisers of something else—confidentiality. This was important to those executives interested in increasing their sales but concerned that making specific appeals to blacks would negatively impact sales to white consumers. To assuage their fears he told readers that a key benefit of black newspapers was that they had few white readers. He asked them to consider: "Do you ever see a picture of the commencement exercises at Lincoln, Howard or Wilberforce Universities in the rotogravure sections of our metropolitan dailies? Do you ever find mention made of the annual Tuskegee Relays or the National Negro Tennis Tournament in the Daily sport pages? Do you see a photo of a Negro wedding or a prominent Negro Club-woman on any daily's society page? Of course not."[30] In other words, executives should expect their white consumer base to have the same awareness of the content of black newspapers as they did, that is, very little. As a result, advertisers could reach out to the black consumer market without fear of losing existing sales.

But *The Negro Market* was more than just a call for increased advertising schedules in black newspapers. Echoing the words of economist Paul Edwards, the booklet also encouraged readers to develop racially specific advertisements for black consumers. Companies that placed advertisements in the black press already had an advantage over those that did not because blacks viewed these ads as recognition of their importance as a consumer group and as a specific invitation for their patronage. To that invitation, though, Ziff recommended that companies craft messages in a manner that appealed to blacks' racial pride. He argued that black consumers wanted advertisements that used natural language rather than dialect, avoided condescending explanations of product use, and only used slang in an appropriate context. When advertisements used those rules, he concluded, black consumers would react with "wholehearted enthusiasm" for the product or brand.[31]

While actively pursuing more advertising schedules, Ziff also pressed black publishers to alter some of the content of their newspapers. He knew that the lack of advertising placed many black newspapers in a nearly perpetual economic crisis and that many accepted advertisements from any company or person with the ability to pay for them. As a result, many papers contained advertisements for psychics, charms, or other similarly ludicrous offers that lowered their stature in the mind of potential national advertisers. Further, many black newspapers had their origins as protest organs, or they contained negative articles or editorials against some of the very companies Ziff sought as prospective advertisers. The effect was that among potential advertisers the majority of black newspapers had a dismal reputation, and revenue to black newspapers suffered. If black newspapers could alter that reputation, however, greater attention from national advertisers would presumably follow and lead to better overall quality within the field. As one black newspaper manager remarked, "If at least a half dozen of the big advertising agencies would pay attention to the buying power of our group [black consumers] we would have much better newspapers than we have."[32]

Ziff believed that one important way to improve the reputation of black newspapers was to have the Audit Bureau of Circulation (ABC) verify their circulation figures independently. These numbers, he reasoned, would provide him with conclusive evidence that he could take to advertisers to show influence of his client newspapers within the black community. Ziff told Robert Vann, publisher of the *Pittsburgh Courier,* "The future of the race field exists only upon the possibility of proving to the general advertiser that here is a large group of people well worth merchandising to and ably represented by capable newspapers."[33] Ziff knew that the estimates or statements about circulation numbers like those Barnett once compiled were far from enough to sway hesitant advertisers. Instead, the only way to develop a broad appreciation among advertisers about the power of black newspapers as an advertising medium was to prove it with figures conclusively showing their reach among black consumers.

Unfortunately, the tenuous economic situation of many black papers left them unable to pay for the yearly verification conducted by the ABC. Moreover, many publishers felt that, Ziff's arguments notwithstanding, even with verified circulation figures they would remain unable to attract national advertising (a concern aptly demonstrated by John Johnson's inability to obtain advertisements in *Ebony* even after independent verification). To most black publishers, advertiser prejudice against using the black press was something that no amount of statistics could overcome. Therefore, few black newspapers contracted with the ABC verification service—and national advertising in most remained limited.[34]

Researching African American Consumers

In researching the habits of black consumers, publishers and newspaper representatives were largely working untilled ground. There had been some examinations of black consumer activity, but most were limited in scope. For example, in 1928, the National Negro Business League (NNBL) had conducted a study of blacks' participation in business. Alongside the positive assessment of black business efforts came recommendations about the black consumer population. The authors of the study suggested that national advertisers work more diligently to cultivate the black consumer market, a potential source for companies to increase their revenue stream. Additionally, it implicitly suggested that blacks had an untapped economic strength that could be used in various ways to improve their standing in America.[35]

Among academic researchers, only Paul Edwards had investigated the purchasing habits of black consumers. Further, no writers in the advertising trade press had taken any interest in the NNBL's study. In fact, in the trade press, a set of articles, one published in 1928 and another in 1930, were the only significant analyses of the black consumer market until the 1940s.[36]

In 1928, H. A. Haring, an editorial contributor to the trade journal *Advertising & Selling*, published one of the first analyses of blacks as consumers. In these examinations, based on his own observations, Haring reinforced existing societal stereotypes about blacks' purchasing habits. In so doing, he provided the foundational analysis for future trade reporters. Haring was harsh in his description of black consumers. He concluded that blacks lacked the educational background to make independent product selections. Instead, he argued, blacks often mimicked whites in their purchases. If the necessary white examples were lacking, blacks simply bought the lowest cost items available. Additionally, he argued that blacks had poor memories for detail, and that advertisers should use pictures rather than words to motivate them. In short, he reasoned, blacks were imitative, impulsive buyers of low- to medium-cost products.[37]

Two years after his initial article, Haring revisited his study of black consumers. This time he compared black consumers in both the North and the South. He argued that southern blacks were too illiterate to be moved by advertising and too poor to buy most goods even if so swayed. Blacks in the North, however, were a different story. The migration of blacks to the North had led not only to a more literate population but one with well-paying jobs and a desire to buy consumer products. Further, as two-income households, some black families had an income that approached, and sometimes surpassed, that of white families. Though, as was the case with many whites, the Depression limited blacks' purchasing power, he estimated they could become a valuable consumer population. Haring also argued that northern blacks were receptive to advertising, especially if it came in black newspapers. Also, he considered northern blacks a possible market for high quality goods, finding that as a group they were loath to accept substitutes. He concluded, "Now they have the money to spend, they are potentially a market such as they never were before."[38] Haring's position was unique: this was the first time a white researcher advocated blacks as a viable consumer population in the pages of a trade journal. Because of the Depression, however, few company executives took significant action to reach out to black consumers.[39]

Soon other researchers followed Haring's lead. In 1932, a white Fisk University professor, Paul K. Edwards published a book entitled *The Southern Urban Negro as a Consumer*, the most detailed examination of black consumers then available. In this primarily statistical analysis, Edwards concluded that southern blacks controlled hundreds of millions of dollars in disposable income. Companies that were willing to make the suitable requests for black consumer patronage could tap that income, he reasoned. Blacks were brand conscious, a practice many had adopted to avoid being cheated by unscrupulous merchants or salespeople. In contrast to Haring's 1928 article, though, Edwards found black consumers particularly adroit at dissecting advertising. He pointed out that blacks consciously avoided buying products whose advertisements they considered offensive. His research found that blacks clearly disliked advertising trade characters like Aunt Jemima or the Gold Dust Twins that depicted blacks in positions of servitude or as figures for ridicule. Respondents to Edwards's questions about the characters stated that they were "disgusting" and "not a true picture of Negroes." Thus, companies that wanted to receive black consumer dollars needed to first avoid offending them.[40]

Yet Edwards wished to do more than provide statistical and anecdotal evidence on black consumers. He wanted company executives to take action to reach out to them. So a short time after his book was published, he distributed a summary of its contents to executives around the nation in hopes that they would launch an advertising or marketing program among black consumers. He found a positive reception from several white executives who responded that they were giving "careful thought" to an active solicitation of black consumers. Moreover, executives at the Rumford Baking Company planned to go beyond theoretically supporting and, instead, set up an experimental marketing program among black consumers. The question for Edwards, though, was how best to ensure to success of this groundbreaking effort. For help he turned to Barnett.[41]

Although the two men did not know each other, Edwards was aware of the ANP, and he knew of Barnett's connections with newspapers throughout the country. Therefore he believed Barnett could be a valuable ally in generating national attention about the Rumford program. For Barnett, the Rumford program had the potential to support his efforts to generate corporate attention to the black press and the black consumer market. By using the press to create awareness of the Rumford experiment, it could demonstrate its ability to move the black consumer population to action. Further, if black consumers responded by buying the company's products, the program also showed the value of black consumers to the Rumford company, and, potentially, others in the baking products industry.

The two men enthusiastically planned the details of the effort in a series of letters. The program called for the employment of four black sales representatives (two men and two women). Over a period of eight months, the quartet would travel throughout the major cities in the South, demonstrating Rumford products to black consumers. While Edwards kept close contact with the four representatives, Barnett would publicize the Rumford program among black newspapers. To do so he would send out press releases about the program to ANP member newspapers. He also would personally contact editors in cities where the representatives were to appear and request that they announce the presence of the representatives in the city. Additionally, he would encourage editors to publish the findings of Edwards's book as a way to help gain more advertisers in their pages.[42]

Both Edwards and Barnett believed that, if successful, the program would have three important consequences for African American professionals, publishers, and consumers: First, it would show the impact of black sales personnel on motivating black consumer purchasing. Thus, it had the potential to open a new avenue of employment to blacks. Second, the publicity carried out in black newspapers would clearly demonstrate their influence in catalyzing black consumers' purchasing and could lead to increased advertising lineage. Third, a successful program would result in greater appreciation for the black consumer market among corporate executives and their advertising agencies that could also mean additional professional opportunities for African Americans.[43]

At the end of the experiment, the two men's hopes came to fruition as Rumford executives judged it a success. The demonstrations that the four representatives carried out in black grocery stores, churches, and fraternal organizations had led to increased sales. As a result, the company hired some black sales representatives onto its permanent staff. The success of the program also helped Edwards get one other company, the L. C. Smith & Corona Typewriter Company, to hire a black sales representative. The accomplishments of the Rumford program may have also influenced other companies to follow a similar course. For example, during the Rumford program, the Helms Bakeries company in Los Angeles conducted a similar experiment using black sales representatives that also resulted in permanent positions for black sales representatives.[44]

Corporate recognition of the black consumer market notwithstanding, the actions of African American consumers demonstrate that they understood their economic power could either enhance or hinder sales. By the late 1930s, there had been several instances of African American consumers actively using their economic power to press for better treatment and employment. Blacks found that they could not only use their buying power to ensure success in programs like that developed by the Rumford company but also to achieve other employment and economic goals. Long the victims of the "last hired, first fired" phenomenon, blacks now had the economic clout and geographic concentration to try and fight back. In chain and department stores in cities throughout the North, black newspapers organized "Don't Buy Where You Can't Work" (DBWYCW) campaigns and effectively pressed companies doing business with black consumers to employ them as well. These campaigns also encouraged blacks to spend their money with black merchants in order to enhance their growth. They appealed to race pride and argued that spending money with black merchants and manufacturers kept more money within the community. Said one black minister: "All of that money goes into the white man's pocket and then out of our neighborhoods. It is used to buy white men cars and homes and their wives mink coats and servants. Our money is being used by the white man for being his cook, his valet, and his washwoman."[45] This is not to say that blacks did not support black businesses. But the argument that came to dominate discussions of how best to direct black consumer power emphasized using it to attract attention from white corporations. Albon Holsey of the Colored Merchants Alliance wrote, "At this particular time the proper use of our buying power is so closely related to our economic liberation and is such an important factor in our civic adjustments that it transcends in potential power all other defensive tactics."[46]

By the mid-1930s most analysis of black purchasing power centered on them as a revenue source for white-owned corporations rather than for black businesses. An editorial in the *Chicago Defender* argued:

Large white corporations could accelerate this movement [black consumer support] by making the proper gestures for these 'acres of black diamonds.' Timid experiments, as white financial magnates call them, will not bring the results in either volume of trade or sustained loyalty. Large corporations which now enjoy the accidental patronage of the Race could, with bold recognition of the market and the proper selection of leaders and personnel from the Race, increase their sales to the exclusion of all of their competitors. Any large corporation which starts such a program of definitely catering to the Race, and uses imagination and capable Race leadership and counsel will find its money and time well invested and the yield a thousand fold.

In contrast to the early twentieth century when Booker T. Washington argued for using black buying power to enhance black-owned businesses, that power was now more broadly conceived. Yet the turn that Barnett, Edwards, and others advocated in the 1930s was less than a rejection of Washington's philosophy than an evolution of it. Barnett and other black leaders did not reject the Washington philosophy as much as they recognized that the interest in blacks' consumer power could effectively lead to both an enhancement of their stature in America and the further development of some black-owned businesses, especially newspapers. As a result, black newspaper representatives increased their efforts to compile research information about black consumers in an effort to interest corporations in the positive impact blacks' spending could generate.[47]

Additional Newspaper Representatives

By the mid-1930s Ziff's attention to his duties as a newspaper representative had waned. He began to experience more success in the publication of magazines and, beyond that, some of Ziff's major black newspaper clients terminated their use of his services. In 1934, he lost the *Pittsburgh Courier*, one of the largest black newspapers of the period and a high-profile client, after publisher Robert Vann had gotten fed up with Ziff's high commission rates. Also, Vann believed that some of the material in the supplement that Ziff forced his clients to carry offended his readers. Therefore, Vann severed his ties with Ziff and turned to another advertising concern, the H. B. Chron Company, which he later bought and reorganized into Interstate United Newspapers (IUN). Initially IUN had difficulty attracting both national advertisers and black newspapers, many of which remained with the Ziff company. Fortunes began to turn in the early 1940s, though. First, Ziff fully withdrew from the field of newspaper representation to focus on magazine publishing, and many of his clients came to IUN. Second, Vann hired William Black as IUN's sales manager. Black was a tenacious and skilled manager who led IUN to impressive growth during the 1940s.[48]

Before joining IUN in 1941, Black directed advertising for several black newspapers, so he was acquainted with the problem of securing national advertisers. At IUN, like Ziff, he urged black publishers to upgrade the reputation of their papers by getting rid of the ads for fortune-tellers, home remedies, charms, and other similar ads that made it difficult to convince advertisers and advertising agencies to use black newspapers. The quandary for publishers, as it was when Ziff and Barnett made similar recommendations in the 1930s, was that these ads provided much needed working capital. However, the changes brought on by World War II briefly made black newspapers more attractive to advertisers. Threatened with an excess profits tax similar to that in existence during World War I, companies used the extra funds to buy ads in black newspapers.[49]

Black also directed IUN onto an aggressive advertising and research course. He commissioned studies of the national black consumer market to determine black purchasing habits and income. In addition, IUN consistently ran advertisements for their services in the trade press. Though the ads usually lacked all but the most rudimentary graphics, they always featured a bold headline in large, eye-catching type. These headlines varied, but the central idea remained the same: investment in the Negro market was a sound business idea. In contrast to *The Negro Market*, nowhere in IUN's advertisements were there arguments for creating racially specific advertisements for African Americans. Instead, the ads assured readers that placing advertisements in the black press was enough to ensure loyal black patronage.[50]

In 1944, Associated Publishers (no relation to the earlier Claude Barnett–owned firm) joined IUN in the newspaper representation field. Together, the two firms represented nearly all of the black newspapers in the country. Though they were competitors, they shared a common need to increase advertiser interest in black newspapers and the black consumer market. The executives of each company knew that a broader

acceptance of black newspapers as an advertising medium would help
both companies and their clients. As a result, the two firms sometimes
cooperated to produce information about black consumers.

In the 1946, for example, the two firms cosponsored a booklet profil-
ing black consumers entitled *City Within a City*. The book analyzed the
impact of segregation on the purchasing choices and habits of black
consumers, concluding that it made blacks a geographically confined
market and one best reached by black newspapers. As Ziff argued in *The
Negro Market* a decade earlier, the book posited that placing advertisements in black newspapers was the only invitation blacks needed to
make the desired product choice. An advertising schedule in black newspapers was therefore an enhancement to existing advertising programs
for the general market instead of a redundant application of them.[51]

However, in contrast to *The Negro Market*, the *City* booklet did not recommend the creation of specific advertisements for black consumers.
This likely was a conscious decision. Black, as well as the leaders of Associated Publishers, knew that national advertisers were hesitant to incorporate black newspapers into their advertising programs. Therefore,
rather than reduce their chances of getting advertisements from those
companies or their advertising agencies, they did not encourage them
to take the additional step of crafting new advertisements. Instead, they
only recommended that companies place the advertisements in black
newspapers and allow that placement to carry the message that the product was intended for black consumers.[52]

By the late 1940s, black publishers and their representatives were the
leading organizations in analyzing black consumer habits and promoting the black consumer market. Both groups sponsored local and
regional studies of groups of black consumers and promoted their findings in the advertising trade press. As a result of the efforts of Barnett,
Ziff, Edwards, and other advocates of the black consumer market, several national companies, primarily alcohol, soft drink, and food manufacturers, began using the black press as an advertising source. Further,
some companies took the additional step of including black models or
different copy for black consumers than that used to reach whites. Still,
for most companies, these groups found that research information often
was not enough to convince executives to develop advertising campaigns
among black consumers. Instead they had to deal with a prejudice
among some advertisers and agencies about the value of the black consumer market and the viability of black newspapers in reaching them,
prejudice that sometimes appeared to even trump the prospect of revenue.[53]

Complicating the advertising goals of black newspaper publishers and
their representatives even further, new media options broadened adver-

tiser access to the black consumer market. In the mid-1940s a new magazine quickly became the leading vehicle for advertising to black
consumers. The black consumer marketplace had never had a stronger
or more publicly successful advocate. But outside of a brief spike in
advertiser revenue among black newspapers following the Second World
War, its arrival led to an even greater decline in advertising revenue for
black newspapers.[54]

A New Media Vehicle: *Ebony* Magazine

In November 1945, John H. Johnson launched *Ebony* magazine.
Although other black-oriented magazines had been attempted in the
past, Johnson's innovatively modeled his black magazines on successful
white magazines. For example, the *Negro Digest*, his first magazine, replicated *Readers Digest* and like that publication offered condensed versions
of stories available elsewhere. The key difference was that *Negro Digest*
focused on stories about African Americans. Following his success with
Negro Digest, Johnson modeled his new periodical on *Life* magazine. Johnson's second major innovation was that he imagined an audience of people like himself. Before becoming a publisher, Johnson was headed for
a career as a successful insurance executive. Therefore, when designing
his flagship magazine, he focused on reaching blacks who had similar
accomplishments: those in the middle class, the ones who had secondary
educations, cars, houses, and some leisure time but did not see those
interests reflected in existing magazines.[55]

Similar to Barnett's effort to fill an information gap among black
newspapers, Johnson created *Ebony* to fill the gap in black periodicals.
He believed that black newspapers, while a valuable source of information, focused too heavily on the important, but nonetheless negative,
issues blacks faced. In contrast, he positioned the editorial course of
Ebony to "mirror the happier side of Negro life," and it featured richly
illustrated stories of successful blacks and their accomplishments. These
stories were lushly illustrated with images of their lifestyle and its material accompaniments. Advertisements in the trade press for the magazine explicitly stated that *Ebony* represented the black version of *Life*
magazine and that it was not a "protest organ." While Johnson did not
want to wholly avoid "serious" topics, he reserved *Negro Digest* for their
coverage. In the inaugural editorial he set the magazine's tone for the
next four decades: "We're rather jolly folks we *Ebony* editors. We like to
look at the zesty side of life. Sure you can get all hot and bothered about
the race question (and don't think we don't) but not enough is said
about all the swell things we Negroes can do and will accomplish."[56]
Sales quickly proved that Johnson had hit upon a winning formula:

Ebony circulation numbers reached well over two hundred thousand within a few weeks. The rapid success, however, presented Johnson with a problem as his production and distribution costs rapidly began to exceed his income.[57]

To keep the magazine afloat, Johnson had to find a way to secure advertising revenue.[58] He chose to be selective in the advertisements he accepted, and this caused some problems for him. Although he had not been in the black newspaper field, Johnson knew that they types of advertisements many papers accepted damaged their reputation among national advertisers. Therefore, he insisted that ads for lucky charms, psychics, and patent medicines had no place in *Ebony* and instead took a calculated risk. Rather than pursuing advertisements for the initial issues he waited until circulation of *Ebony* crested one hundred thousand issues and then approached agencies for advertising schedules. With this high circulation, he believed he would have a much better chance to secure the large four-color ads for *Ebony* that he saw in *Life*. Yet despite the circulation numbers he learned that *Ebony* agency executives did not view the new magazine as a useful source. Traditionally, agency executives were wary of suggesting any new or unproven publication for advertising. The fact that *Ebony* was both new and black-oriented only compounded Johnson's problems, as few executives were willing to chance recommending a black publication for their clients' products. This forced him to temper his expectations and he began accepting advertising schedules from small companies and mail-order firms.[59]

Despite these difficulties, *Ebony* gradually began to receive some advertisements for national-level products. In 1946, the advertisements for Chesterfield cigarettes and Kotex appeared in *Ebony*, the first full-page color advertisements ever placed in a black magazine. But these ads were placed on an experimental basis in order to test the magazine's effectiveness. Further, the revenue they generated was far below what Johnson needed to keep up with production costs. At one point revenues were so low that Johnson started a mail order company and advertised a variety of products in the magazine. "I sold vitamins, wigs, dresses, and hair-care products. I sold anything that I could sell in order to get enough capital to keep *Ebony* going," he recalled.[60] Although the revenues from that company kept the magazine solvent, they were still not enough to fund the growth he envisioned. Finally, in 1947, after stretching his credit with lenders to the near-breaking point, he decided to bypass agency executives to approach their clients directly.[61]

Johnson was not the first black publisher to attempt circumventing advertising agencies. Barnett and Edwards had done so in the 1930s with limited success. Yet Barnett and Edwards's efforts had been limited by the wide-ranging impact of the Depression while Johnson operated in a period of growing prosperity. Thus, if only for the reason that money was available, he found a different climate in the executive suites. And the executive suite was his firm destination. He knew that he could not afford to risk delivering his message to a midlevel manager who lacked the power to change company policies. Working through acquaintances, Johnson secured a pivotal meeting with Commander Eugene McDonald of Zenith Radio. With no input from Zenith's advertising agency, McDonald committed to an advertising schedule in *Ebony*. Further, he directly assisted Johnson in securing advertising schedules from other major corporations. In fact, for the next several years the number of advertising pages in *Ebony* increased, sometimes to the point that Johnson rejected ads due to a lack of space.[62]

The success of *Ebony* magazine with advertisers and readers alike gave Johnson an unprecedented level of authority among those who professed to be experts on the black consumer market. He had access to an expanding body of research from his own employees, outside research into black purchasing habits, and a growing publishing empire. He was also a tireless advocate of the profits available among black consumers for companies adroit enough and bold enough to reach out to them.

With individual advertising schedules in place, Johnson moved into the second phase of his advertising and marketing plan. He wanted to make *Ebony* the leading advertising vehicle for reaching the black consumer market. During the 1950s, he initiated a total marketing campaign. He continued to solicit advertising directly from corporate executives, and now he also wrote articles in the trade press featuring marketing advice on black consumers. In addition, he spoke before trade organizations, organized a research center that compiled information on black consumers, maintained a merchandising program that placed endorsements from *Ebony* in stores with products advertised in the magazine, produced marketing films on black consumers, and maintained a regular advertising schedule in the trade press. "This was not sociology," he argued, "this was hard boiled marketing . . . We had to change the perceptions of corporate America." This multifaceted approach gave Johnson and his employees a level of authority in marketing and advertising to black consumers greater than that of any other black-owned company.[63]

Though his actions may be read as a self-serving effort to increase revenue to his own companies, Johnson's importance in generating corporate interest in black consumers can scarcely be overestimated. Additionally, it is important to understand the factors underlying his success. First, Johnson recognized and was able to fill an unmet need by directing *Ebony*'s editorial focus toward the "great middle group" of African Americans who fit neither in the category of genius or criminal.

Instead, they were not sports stars or entertainers but were a large population of African Americans interested in the same kinds of articles and photos on success, celebrities, and self-help as other Americans. Through *Ebony,* Johnson successfully presented this group to advertisers as a major middle-class consumer group who owned their homes, had money and time for leisure activities, and were a significant potential target for an array of consumer products. Also not to be overlooked is the factor of timing. *Ebony* first emerged in the years following World War II, when African Americans had more money to purchase goods and when researchers were compiling more information about black consumer habits. That information, combined with the circulation and editorial content of the magazine, provided Johnson with convincing arguments for why companies should advertise in *Ebony.*[64]

Johnson was also keenly aware of the role of consumer products in African American culture. Like Barnett he believed that African Americans were particularly brand conscious, buying the best that they could afford in order to be assured of product quality. He argued that such habits were not solely the result of a desire to display conspicuous consumption. Although blacks were not immune from these desires, their emphasis on brand names was also the result of past abuses by merchants who short-weighted their purchase or tried to pass poor-quality goods onto them. Thus buying brand-name goods was one way to guarantee some measure of confidence and fairness in the marketplace. However, in addition to issues of quality, in Johnson's view brands were symbols of class status among blacks in a way that differed from that among whites. The ability to purchase the number-one brand of liquor, soap, or automobile was a sign of affluence and standing within the black community. In 1949 these ideas were summarized in a widely reprinted *Ebony* editorial entitled "Why Negroes Buy Cadillacs." It is worth quoting at length:

Just as to white America, the Cadillac is a sign of wealth and standing, so to Negro Americans the Cadillac is an indication of ability to compete successfully with whites, to maintain the very highest standard of living in this nation. It is more than just "keeping up with the Joneses," more than just a matter of caste and class. To a Negro indulgence in luxury is a vindication of his belief in his ability to match the best of white men . . . It is a worthy symbol of his aspiration to be a genuinely first class American . . . Long ago they [African Americans] found out they could not live in the best neighborhoods or hotels, eat in the best restaurants, go to the best resorts because of racial discrimination. But in their own neighborhoods luxuries have never had any restriction.[65]

Johnson carefully distinguished between those blacks that could and could not afford the expensive car. Those who could not he chided for their "misplaced values." As for those who could afford the automobile, though, he believed they should no more be expected to buy less car than they could afford than would be the white person of similar financial circumstance. He concluded, "To berate colored Cadillac owners for not spending their money instead on good race causes is to deny Negroes the right to reach for equality *on every level* [emphasis mine] of U.S. life."[66] To Johnson, in a world of segregation and discrimination, it was impossible not to view the purchase of number-one or luxury brands as part of the struggle against the discrimination that had engendered it. Instead, consumption of luxury goods was evidence of success and a necessary part of blacks' broader quest for civil, social, and political equality. "It is part of the uphill fight for status," he argued.[67] However, although money and conspicuous consumption were not the end goal of African Americans' struggle for rights, they were key tools to reach those goals. As he bluntly offered in another editorial, "Money talks . . . it is power."[68]

Johnson's observations on money and consumption drew the ire of some readers, but he did not sway from his original editorial course. And while his editorial direction may not have endeared him to critics, among agency personnel it proved appropriate. "When *Ebony* came along, with its clear, factual, frank approach, we decided to use it," stated one agency man.[69] As advertising pages in the magazine grew, it became evident that black newspapers lacked the power to challenge *Ebony*'s position as the vehicle to reach black consumers. Johnson's aggressiveness in meeting the needs and desires of advertising and marketing executives helped ensure this continued dominance. One major issue that continued to plague advertisers interested in the black consumer market was the lack of reliable statistics. Advertisers and agencies accustomed to consulting statistical factors such as population distribution, income, and purchasing habits found few such sources available regarding black consumers. While there had been studies of local black markets during the 1940s, information about the national picture was lacking. So if a company was interested in reaching the national black consumer market, the lack of information forced its executives to rely on estimates rather than concrete figures. Fortunately for black consumer market advocates, the 1950 census promised new information on the national black market, and corporate executives eagerly awaited its figures. But because *Ebony* reporters had access to a broad range of black professionals, Johnson was uniquely positioned to deliver the new figures in advance of other sources.

In April 1950, editors at *Ebony* scooped every other source and published a detailed preview of the census report. The magazine was not simply estimating the figures. A staff writer had interviewed Joseph R. Houchins, head of Negro statistics at the Census Bureau. Houchins had been with the census for ten years and was one of the leading African Americans in the federal government. For that reason alone, editors had decided to do a personality feature on him. During the course of the interview, however, the writer discovered that Houchins had access to the completed statistical figures soon to be made public. What editors originally planned as feature article on Houchins alone became a five-page summary of census predictions. They reduced the attention on Houchins's life and career to a few paragraphs in a text box set within the article. Prior to publishing the report in *Ebony*, editors sent the predictions to selected members of the advertising press. The prerelease access to the figures made Johnson and his staff seem almost omniscient about black consumers and further solidified *Ebony*'s reputation among reporters.[70]

The *Ebony* preview and the census itself revealed a number of key facts about black consumers. The black population had topped fifteen million, nearly a 17 percent increase since 1940. African Americans were reproducing at a faster rate than that of whites as their death rate continued to decrease. Most importantly for *Ebony* and its advertisers, income for blacks had increased nearly 300 percent since the last census, and now approached $1,400 annually. The rise in income was accompanied by a rise in black homeownership, thrusting more blacks into the category of purchasing agents of the multitude of products necessary for home maintenance. A likely source of increasing incomes was their changing occupational status, with a rising percentage of blacks in white-collar occupations. Figures also indicated that blacks continued to move into well-paying blue collar occupations. Finally, statistics conclusively demonstrated a geographical shift among the black population from the South to the North and to urban areas. Therefore, if companies hoped to see product success in several of the nation's major cities, the writer concluded, they had to begin taking black consumers into greater account in advertising campaigns.[71]

Beyond its anticipatory release of the census figures, *Ebony* was also an advertiser favorite because independent research indicated that its readers were a lucrative target market. Over 25 percent of *Ebony* readers earned in excess of $4,000 per year, 36 percent owned their homes, 40 percent owned new cars, and 27 percent had attended college. So, *Ebony* readers had the disposal income and consumer habits that made them a solid target market. Advertisers and agencies responded by placing advertisements in *Ebony* in numbers unprecedented for a black-oriented publication.[72]

The 1950 census was the first of an array of studies researchers completed on the black consumer market. Black newspapers and black-oriented radio stations compiled a host of local analyses and complemented studies coming from the federal government. Researchers also published two book-length studies that analyzed the growth of the African American market. First, in 1952, Joseph Johnson published *The Potential Negro Market*. Six years later, William K. Bell's work, *15 Million Negroes and 15 Billion Dollars* expanded on Johnson's study. Throughout the 1950s, a variety of sources conclusively demonstrated that blacks were rapidly improving their capacity to purchase consumer goods. As a result, individuals within the publishing and advertising industries began using blacks' changing consumer visibility to argue for more nuanced programs to reach the black consumer market.[73]

Johnson was in the forefront of research on and access to the black consumer market. His entry into the research aspects of the African American market was not limited to scooping the census figures. Instead, Johnson continually increased his information cache and published the results in his magazines. Through his staff at Johnson Publications, he compiled figures on black income, brand preferences, purchasing habits, and other categories. His reports were paramount in helping shift the opinion that blacks were a market for low-cost goods only. Instead, he continually informed advertisers and agencies that, regardless of the cost of the product, a segment of black consumers could afford it and could be reached through his publications.[74]

The wide circulation of *Ebony* combined with Johnson Publishing's continued compilation of research information made the company the dominant force in the black consumer market. Meanwhile, Interstate United Newspapers' share of the market continued to dwindle. In 1954 the widow of Robert Vann sold the firm, and it ceased to be a competitive factor in the marketplace. Associated Publishers' involvement with the African American market continued, but its fortunes worsened alongside those of its clients. In contrast to *Ebony*, during the 1950s the circulation of black newspapers declined. But, as the plight of black newspapers fell, Johnson's role as an expert on black consumers and the stature of his publishing company continued to grow.[75]

Johnson's position of leadership was not solely due to the promotion of his own ventures. He actively recruited the best reporters and editors he could find and he often did so by hiring them away from black newspapers. Also, in contrast to the largely amicable relationship between IUN and Associated Publishers, Johnson used his statistical research as weapon in his drive to build his company. For example, in 1952 *Jet*, a magazine within his publishing conglomerate, featured a report entitled "Circulation and Cost Comparison, Negro Newspapers and Magazines." The primarily statistical survey compared the advertising costs and circulation numbers of black newspapers with the magazines controlled by Johnson Publishing. The report argued that circulation numbers of black-owned newspapers had declined nearly 20 percent since 1947 while the cost of advertisements within their pages had risen over 20 percent. In contrast to newspapers, though, black magazines (which implicitly meant Johnson publications) experienced positive growth. Based on lineage and page estimates, costs of advertising in magazines was one-third lower than that of newspapers. Further, the report claimed, blacks were shifting their reading habits to include more time with magazines and less with newspapers. So the long-range view was of a continued decline in newspaper circulation with a corresponding rise in magazine circulation. While in cities with more than one hundred thousand blacks, circulation of the leading black-owned newspaper exceeded that of any single magazine, the combined circulation of the four Johnson magazines dwarfed its numbers. Defending the figures as "impartial," the authors were quoted in *Advertising Age*, "Markets cannot be profitably expanded in terms of increased sales, when at additional cost, media coverage shrinks."[76]

The impact of the report would probably have been negligible had it not been for the publicity it received in the trade press. Major trade journals reprinted excerpts from the report and one reporter characterized it as a "slashing attack" that indicated that the cooperative spirit among black publishers was "headed for the ashcan." In response, Johnson challenged the characterization of the report as an attack. One week after *Advertising Age* reprinted portions of the study, the magazine also published Johnson's letter to the editor. Somewhat disingenuously he argued that the report was not meant as an attack but as an impartial compilation of facts. He also emphasized that cooperation between black newspaper and magazine publishers was "functioning at its highest and most effective level." He asserted that his staff continued to recommend black newspapers as advertising vehicles and that newspaper publishers did the same for his magazines. His letter concluded with the optimistic observation that publishers of various types of black-oriented periodicals continued to work together to secure recognition of the black consumer market.[77]

Although Johnson characterized the *Jet* report as routine, black newspaper representatives were not as charitable. Letters from D. Arnett Murphy, head of Associated Publishers, and Earl V. Hord, general manager of the *Pittsburgh Courier*, appeared in *Advertising Age*. Both men vehemently disagreed with the conclusions of the *Jet* report and Johnson's claim of impartiality. Writing separately, the two men argued that the report deliberately misstated facts on black newspaper circulation. Murphy conceded that the circulation of black newspapers had declined, but he argued that the long-term outlook indicated a future rise. Additionally, the actual penetration of the four Johnson magazines into the black community was not as great as their circulation numbers indicated. Instead, the "hidden factor" was that the four magazines had a large number of white readers. Therefore, while numbers were indeed high, the Johnson magazines were not as great a tool for reaching blacks as numbers alone indicated. Murphy also reasoned that it was contradictory of the report to criticize the sales power of black newspapers while Johnson Publications continued to advertise in them. Therefore either Johnson was voluntarily wasting money in an ineffective medium, or the selling power of black newspapers was greater than the report allowed. Both Murphy and Hord criticized editors at *Advertising Age* for uncritically accepting the report and contributing to the negative impression of black newspapers.[78]

Despite their protests, future developments confirmed the accuracy of the *Jet* report's predictions. The circulation numbers of black newspapers continued to decline while that of black magazines rose. The era of black newspapers as the primary medium to reach black consumers was coming to an end. Black-owned newspapers found themselves outside of advertising programs as advertising agencies increasingly chose to reach black consumers through magazines. Also, the rapid growth of black-oriented radio stations further hampered black newspaper's use as advertising mediums to reach black consumers. Nevertheless, Johnson's claims notwithstanding, the *Jet* study was far from simply routine. It was, as Murphy and Hord recognized, a direct attack upon black newspapers as a sales vehicle. Johnson recognized that advertisers and agencies often spent only secondary funds for the black consumer market while reserving primary spending for the mainstream market. Since the dollars available to black media were limited, the *Jet* report was clearly an effort to ensure that the lion's share of those dollars went to Johnson Publishing. In that respect his efforts paid off. By the mid-1950s *Ebony* reporters in trade press routinely described the magazine as the "key national medium" for advertising to black consumers.[79]

The public disagreement between leading figures of the black publishing field is evidence of the tremendous growth of the black consumer market in the postwar years. Prior to the war, when publishers were competing for limited advertising dollars and no single entity received an amount far in excess of the others, they maintained amicable relations. When the available dollars stretched into the millions, however, the once genial, if not cooperative, effort to generate interest in the black consumer market disappeared. The advertising revenue available in the 1950s helped turn a once amicable effort into one in which the needs of competition outweighed the spirit of cooperation. The rapid growth of the infant medium of Negro radio in the 1950s only further energized the media competition.[80]

Negro Radio

While members of the black publishing arena argued over the sales effectiveness of magazines versus newspapers, the field of black-oriented radio (commonly called Negro radio) grew tremendously. The first black-oriented radio programs went on the air in the late 1920s, but were confined to their local region. A few advertisers bought airtime on these programs but as a medium, Negro radio did not experience growth as a national medium until after World War II. In fact, it was the growing body of research on black consumer habits that first raised advertiser awareness of the penetration of radio into the African American community. In 1949, Edgar Steele of the Research Company of America, a prominent research firm, released a study detailing the rate of African American radio ownership. His results indicated that in major cities African Americans owned radios at a rate in excess of 90 percent saturation. Further, of those blacks who did not currently own radios, a significant number planned to buy them in the near future. Radio was a medium that could potentially reach more blacks than either newspapers or monthly magazines.[81]

Writers in the trade press were especially laudatory of the prospects of Negro radio. In article after article they described the "tremendous psychological forces" of the medium. Radio provided a more intimate way to speak to black consumers. Rather than the message coming in static print or image, the medium allowed for the message to come "from within the community." The use of black deejays to deliver advertising messages also gave listeners the impression that the advertiser had black employees, a useful benefit. Also, appealing to blacks through radio allowed for the removal of vestiges of discrimination. "The very fact that a station [talks] directly to him [the black consumer] is almost enough to guarantee that he will spend his money on the products and services advertised on that station." That is, through the trade press radio executives extended the argument developed by black publishers. To sell to black consumers and receive their patronage one simply needed to extend the invitation for them to purchase. Such appeals, it was argued, implied recognition of the market and its people.[82]

Beginning in the late 1940s, Negro radio expanded from a little-known medium to one increasingly recognized for its sales potential. One executive recalled how few people were aware of the Negro radio in the mid-1940s: "One of our biggest food accounts was worried because sales had slipped and their overall share of the market was down. All afternoon we discussed ways and means of reaching every possible segment of U.S. housewives. Finally, I suggested: 'Why don't we buy some Negro radio as part of the campaign?' I can still remember the blank looks I got."[83] While the executive's account did not detail the impact of the purchase of Negro radio space on the campaign, the "blank looks" of his coworkers could have been duplicated in most advertising agencies during the decade. This lack of knowledge was in part based upon the limited number of stations programming content to black listeners. The number of such stations was small during much of the 1940s, but by the mid-1950s over four hundred stations were directing at least part of their daily programming to African Americans. Additionally, major advertisers began flocking to local Negro radio stations in larger numbers.[84]

The rapid expansion of Negro radio following World War II was due in no small measure to the groundwork laid by black publishers. Executives in the radio industry drew upon nearly two decades of work by black publishers to generate models of black consumer purchasing, income, and other consumer information. This information base, combined with the prosperity generated by the war, allowed the far-reaching medium of radio to eclipse much of the black publishing establishment. While magazines like *Ebony* were able to maintain and even increase their advertising schedules in the face of Negro radio's growth, black newspapers were the ones feeling the brunt of its impact. Not only did advertisements on radio have the advantage of repetitive frequency over the weekly black newspapers, but many radio stations also engaged in extra merchandising efforts to aid campaigns. Radio deejays appeared at stores, and as locally famous celebrities they drew crowds that newspaper columnists could not hope to duplicate. Stations also helped set up product displays, sent out promotional items to stores, and often contacted store owners to maintain the relationship between the merchant and the advertiser. These added-value efforts led to higher sales and increased the possibility that agencies would use the station again in the future. In the meantime, advertising prospects for black newspapers dimmed even further.[85]

Stations active in Negro radio provided advertisers and agencies with research statistics that only publications in the Johnson Publishing family could match. Station executives commissioned local studies of black consumers that supplied agencies with extensive population, income, and brand-preference information. Although agency executives continually emphasized the need for additional statistical information on the national black consumer market, these local and regional studies helped further develop that picture. Admittedly, black newspaper representatives commissioned similar studies, but they had failed to offer continual updates like those coming from radio stations. Also, many of the studies completed by radio stations provided the specific sales numbers that advertisers desired and, as such, gave agencies specific figures to utilize when approaching black consumers.[86]

By the late 1950s advertisers and agencies had the choice of targeting black consumers through one of the hundreds of local radio stations throughout the country or choosing a national-level approach on one of the existing network organizations. Yet despite this access and the numerous success stories of campaigns targeting black consumers, many stations continued to struggle to attract national advertisers. This difficulty did not escape the attention of the trade press. In 1955 the editors of *Sponsor* conducted a series of investigations on the seeming reluctance of agencies to recommend the use of Negro radio.[87]

In the study *Sponsor* received input from some of the leading radio advertising agency executives in the nation. Although there were different opinions among those surveyed on the actual sales potential of the Negro market, respondents recognized its size, spending power, and potential impact. Still, even though the executives surveyed agreed that blacks had sizable spending power, most professed no desire to target African Americans. Their reasons for this varied but most cited their fear of alienating white consumers and of the lack of enough research information about the national black consumer market. Several executives also lamented the lack of national programming options to reach several markets with a single campaign. Too often, some argued, agencies had to approach stations on an individual basis and, though those who had done so had developed successful campaigns, the time and cost required was more than that needed to reach the general market. Consequently many them simply refused to recommend the increased costs to their clients. One agency man maintained that, although his research indicated differences between the buying habits of blacks and whites, he was unclear how to use Negro radio to influence black purchasing choices. In the end, for most of those *Sponsor* surveyed, the risks and costs of reaching black consumers through radio simply outweighed the possible results. But the author of the report concluded that while several of the criticisms of Negro radio were valid, the potential results were worth the risks.[88]

In spite of the reservations of individual executives, advertising from national companies slowly increased on Negro radio. In the process, those active in the medium added even more nuance to the formula for the optimum approach to black consumers. Specifically, station executives and black deejays argued that advertisements on radio needed to be even more carefully conceived than those appearing in print. Lacking that careful consideration, and in some cases restructuring, advertisements could alienate or offend black consumers. Further, some products, despite their popularity among blacks, should not be advertised on radio. For example, station representatives cautioned that advertisements for hair straightening products and skin bleaching creams were inappropriate for radio. While these products were regularly advertised in black newspapers and magazines, placing them on radio increased the possibility that whites would hear the ads as well as blacks. As William Ziff informed readers of *The Negro Market* almost twenty years earlier, in a black publication the number of white readers was negligible, so the person reading the advertisement was almost assuredly black, and there was little fear of embarrassment. Placing ads for these products on the airwaves, however, meant that whites might hear them and in the process confirm that blacks really wanted to be white. Black consumers would not accept this type of image-damaging affront, and makers of these types of products responded by not placing advertisements on radio.[89]

Through radio, advertisers also could speak to consumers in a manner that could not be duplicated in the world of print. But, in this more intimate setting, agency executives learned that they could not speak to black consumers in the manner in which they spoke to whites. With guidance initially coming from radio deejays and executives, agencies learned that it was often better to have a black deejay read their copy than a white person. Additionally, black deejays were sometimes given the latitude to change the copy and deliver it in a manner they felt was more appropriate for their listeners. Or, if agencies were unwilling to have their advertising copy altered, they directed to not use the same copy among blacks that they did among whites. Few went as far as the advertising representatives of one drug firm who planned to advertise their hair care product with the pitch: "Attention Negro women! Now you can have hair that's *just as attractive as that of white ladies* [emphasis mine]." This company's error was not in marketing their product to black women, station managers cautioned, but in assuming that its key point of comparison and appeal should be the opportunity for black women to be like white women. This emphasis was an affront to blacks' pride and should have been altered to simply emphasize how the product enhanced the hair of black women. Yet, even among those who avoided the obvious gaffes, Negro radio advocates cautioned that agency men had to be careful lest they repel rather than attract black consumers. To be sure of attracting rather than offending blacks, the best thing to do was to get the input of an African American advertising or marketing expert (or at least a deejay) before running a campaign. As one executive noted, "Nobody sells the Negro like a Negro who knows how to sell."[90]

As the number of national advertisements on Negro radio increased so to did requests for the alteration of copy. On repeated occasions sta-

tions received advertising copy that managers felt was either inappropriate or likely to be ineffective among their consumer population, and
they pressed for changes. In the process radio executives helped engender an important shift in the targeting of black consumers. For several
years African American publishers had argued that there was no need
to alter the advertising copy from the general to the black consumer
market; simply placing the ads where blacks could see them was enough.
Now, companies interested in using Negro radio were increasingly told
to get the advice of black experts on marketing to blacks.[91]

The need for a new level and type of knowledge in reaching black
consumers that leaders in Negro radio and publishing continually advocated, helped open opportunities for blacks to act as consultants and
"special marketers" for advertisers and agencies involved in the black
consumer market. The most famous of these early black consultants was
James "Billboard" Jackson, a representative of the Esso Standard Oil
Company.

Hired in 1937, Jackson had a history of individual firsts. He was one
of the first black intelligence officers in the military and the first black
bank clerk in the state of Illinois. Later he became the first black member of the American Marketing Association. At Esso, Jackson's responsibilities involved promoting company products to black consumers
through advertisements, appearances at organizational conferences,
and various other promotions. During the 1930s other firms had hired
black marketing representatives including Pepsi-Cola, Beech-Nut,
Anheuser-Busch, and Philip Morris, but it was not until the 1950s that
their numbers began to appreciably increase. Alongside these external
representatives and marketing consultants, blacks gradually began to
find limited opportunities in the nation's advertising agencies.[92]

Conclusion

By the end of World War II a set of assumptions about black consumers
was in place. Blacks were an urban, brand-conscious group that made
them a compact target for advertising and marketing campaigns. Moreover, because racial segregation closed certain areas of living and recre-
ation to them, blacks often spent more for food, cars, clothing, and
personal care products than whites in the same income bracket. Also
blacks were brand loyal. Brands assured them of quality and provided a
measure of conspicuous consumption. Blacks were keenly aware of the
link between their purchasing power and choices and employment. In
the panels and trade journal articles that began examining the black
consumer market, both blacks and whites argued consistently that the
racial consciousness of African Americans mandated the need for black

Figure 3. James "Billboard" Jackson, one of the first black special markets representatives. "Appointments," *Opportunity* (August 1934): 254.

sales agents to be used to reach them. Later, this argument would expand to include the employment record of companies beyond just their hiring of sales personnel. Although the combination of Depression and war may have slowed corporate interest in black consumers, among some executives there was growing appreciation about its possibilities.[93]

African American newspaper publishers and representatives were at the forefront of opening corporate interest in the black consumer market. The slow-growing interest and careful extension of experiments like

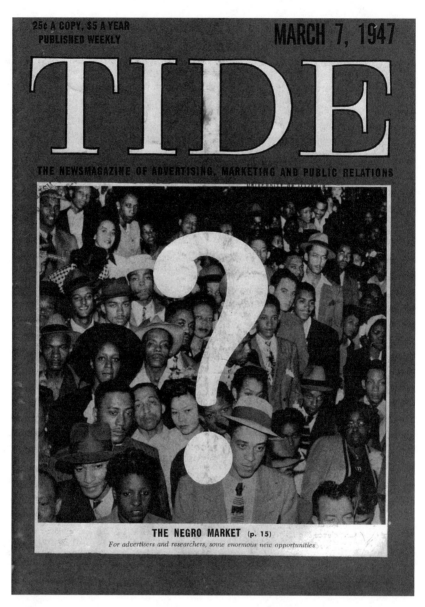

Figure 4. In 1947, *Tide* magazine published one of the first major stories in the advertising trade press about the growing Negro market. *Tide* (March 7, 1947): front cover.

that conducted by the Rumford company led to increased advertising lineage for some of the larger papers. Over time, however, black newspapers did not receive as much of the revenue that their efforts had helped produce as did other segments of media. Low circulation numbers and the poor reputations of black papers among potential advertisers worked to limit their use. Also, the critical position of some papers led to limited advertising. One observer noted, "You can't kick a company on the front page for not hiring Negro employees, then expect the same company to buy an ad on the inside of the paper."[94] Although some papers briefly experienced increased advertising lineage during the Second World War, that trend did not hold. Instead, black newspaper publishers found their position eclipsed by the growth of *Ebony* magazine and Negro radio.

Ebony and stations programming Negro radio lacked much of the protest spirit that had long been the hallmark of black newspapers, but their impact went beyond greater advertising content and revenue. In the case of *Ebony*, for example, it was through working at the magazine that blacks gained access to spaces into which they had previously been unable to enter. In many corporate offices throughout the country, *Ebony* space salesmen were often the only black faces to be seen and their professionalism may have helped convince some companies to open employment opportunities to other blacks. Also, through working on the writing, content, art, and design of the magazine, blacks gained professional experience unavailable elsewhere. Through this unprecedented access, many blacks gained the experience that they would later use to open their own businesses. Though it would be inaccurate to say that Johnson singlehandedly developed the black consumer market, the impact of his publications went far beyond their viability as advertising mediums.[95]

The growth of African American–oriented magazines and radio programming led to the decline of advertising revenue for black newspapers. But they led to opportunity in other areas. When station executives, trade reporters, and black publishers each began encouraging the use of African Americans to provide the expertise to reach black consumers, they helped open employment opportunities for African Americans in marketing and advertising. A black consumer population that began to be vocal in their displeasure about advertising depictions supported their arguments. Blacks also were growing more willing to withdraw their spending from companies whose advertising messages they found displeasing. As one reporter noted, "Negroes, more perhaps than most minority groups, are considerably touchy about the elements relating to the Negro race in advertising copy and directed to them particularly."[96] Although the progress of blacks in major advertising agencies was agonizingly slow, it began in the early 1950s with the arrival of the first "Jackie Robinsons" of the advertising industry.

Chapter 2
The Jackie Robinsons of Advertising and Selling

Nothing counts but pressure, pressure, more pressure, and still more pressure through broad organized aggressive mass action.

—A. Philip Randolph, 1941

As a nation, America in the 1940s faced a host of challenges. Still emerging from the crisis of the Depression, Americans also confronted the chaos of a world war. Within the country, the departure of men and women for military duty led to significant labor shortages in key industries. But wartime also brought opportunities. Rising wages were one immediate result of the conflict, and African American leaders like A. Philip Randolph used the labor shortages to demand better treatment of black workers. In a bold move Randolph, once labeled by Attorney General A. Mitchell Palmer as "the most dangerous Negro in America," threatened to lead over ten thousand blacks in a march on Washington to protest discrimination. Some African American leaders viewed his proposed march as being too aggressive in tactics and tone. The *Pittsburgh Courier*, the largest-circulation black newspaper, went even further, calling the idea "a crackpot proposal." There had been other protest marches to be sure, but those were local protests confined to the city or issue immediately related to the precipitating event. In contrast to other protest efforts, Randolph proposed a direct confrontation with the highest office of government during wartime. Undaunted, Randolph pressed further as the proposed march triggered a wave of support from the average black American. In response, he increased his original call from ten thousand to one hundred thousand blacks. That was enough for President Roosevelt to act. To forestall the march he capitulated to demands and signed Executive Order 8802 banning employment discrimination in companies with defense contracts and establishing the Fair Employment Practices Commission.[1]

The signing of Order 8802 was a major victory for African Americans, and it foreshadowed a rising wave of militancy against discrimination. For example, blacks continued their protests to eliminate segregation in the military. Activists also began calling for a Double V campaign to emphasize the need for victory against fascism abroad and against racism and discrimination at home. All of these efforts foreshadowed a postwar world in which blacks would expand their pursuit of equal rights across a wide spectrum of society.[2]

The presence of African Americans in the advertising industry is the direct result of pressure like that which Randolph brought to bear on Roosevelt. In the history of the industry, very few agencies proactively sought to hire African American professionals. In the postwar period, those mainstream agencies that did hire blacks did so either out of a need for their expertise on reaching black consumers or because the talent of the applicant was undeniable regardless of race. In fact, in the employment of African American professionals, advertising agencies followed rather than led their clients. Rather than actively seek out black employees as many major corporations had begun to do, most agencies waited until the needs of a particular client necessitated blacks' expertise on the black consumer market. When such recognition occurred, as when Branch Rickey decided to make Jackie Robinson a member of the Brooklyn Dodgers, agencies sought their own black firsts.

Executive Order 8802 generated tremendous employment opportunities for blacks. Firms with government contracts opened their doors to black employees, giving blacks access to opportunities they could not have imagined just a few years before. Additionally, the number of black civilian workers in the federal government increased to over two hundred thousand. In defense plants, blacks earned as much as ten to fourteen times their prewar earnings. For example, one black domestic worker recalled that her earnings increased from $3.50 per week in Oklahoma to $48 per week as a riveter at an aircraft plant. "When I got my first paycheck, I'd never seen that much money before," she noted, "not even in the bank, because I'd never been in a bank too much." Although they still faced a wage imbalance with white workers, many African Americans had more money to spend than ever before. After the war, blacks' rising wages helped bring them to the attention of the advertising trade press.[3]

Writers in *Advertising Age* and other trade journals encouraged their readers to view blacks as a key underdeveloped market and one that would help strengthen the economy. They found a fertile reception for these arguments among American corporations, which looked for ways to maximize profits in the United States and to expand internationally. In alerting companies to this untapped market in their midst, trade journals argued that it was in many companies' best interests both to hire black sales representatives and marketing professionals and to begin to alter their traditional approaches to black consumers. And, albeit slowly, the leaders of some of the nation's largest companies began to listen. The number of advertisements in *Ebony* magazine continued to increase, and stations programming Negro radio found increased interest from both national and local accounts in their advertising services. Also, as Claude Barnett and Paul Edwards anticipated in the 1930s, blacks interested in pursuing careers in the sales and marketing fields found greater opportunities to do so. However, the recognition of the need for black sales and marketing professionals proceeded faster among the clients of advertising agencies than it did within the agencies themselves.[4]

This chapter examines the experiences of the black pioneers in the advertising industry. The presence of these early pioneers was in part tied to the growing recognition of the black consumer market among consumer product companies. Corporate leaders of soft drink, alcohol, tobacco, and office-machine companies were among the first to hire black sales and marketing professionals. Additionally a number of these companies retained black public relations consultants to help enhance their image among black consumers. Therefore, the chapter begins by discussing the professional and organizational lives of some of the first black sales and marketing professionals hired by major corporations.

The central portion of the chapter analyzes the occupational experiences of the pioneer black agency owners and blacks in mainstream agencies. These eight men represent the two arcs of black participation in the industry that found fullest development during the industry's racial revolution in the 1960s. Their experiences illustrate the stark contrast between when these men worked at their own firms versus the latitude some blacks had as employees of mainstream agencies. Anticipating the struggles that black agencies faced in the 1960s and '70s, when they operated their own firms, they worked on campaigns solely to reach black consumers. In contrast, as employees of mainstream agencies, some blacks had the latitude to work on campaigns to reach the general marketplace. Accordingly, the activities of these men offer the first opportunity to evaluate the advertising industry in light of Merah Stuart's classic theory of economic detour.[5]

The chapter concludes with a discussion of the NAACP protest against the *Amos 'n' Andy* television program and the sponsorship difficulties of the *Nat King Cole Show*. Blacks' protests against the image portrayed of them in the *Amos 'n' Andy* program foreshadowed their battle against their representation in advertisements and against the advertising industry in the 1960s.

In the employment of black professionals, advertising agencies fol-

lowed, rather than led, their clients. Preceding any significant employment of African Americans in mainstream advertising firms were
growing numbers of black sales and marketing representatives in other
industries. Several companies followed the lead set by Esso Standard Oil,
Lever Brothers, and Pepsi-Cola, hiring blacks to serve as sales and public
relations representatives from their employer to the African American
community. It was these "Brown Hucksters" who helped to pave the way
for the expansion of black-owned advertising agencies and for blacks to
gain professional-level employment in mainstream advertising firms.

The Brown Hucksters

Using African Americans to sell to other African Americans was not a
wholly new technique in the 1940s. Companies like the Fuller Brush
Company employed black salesmen to handle black territories as early
as 1922. However, Fuller's was a local effort in Oklahoma and the
employment of national black market representatives did not occur
until the 1930s. James "Billboard" Jackson was the dean of these
national black special-markets men. By the end of the Second World
War he had worked for Esso for almost ten years. His success in generating sales and goodwill among black business owners and consumers had
led a few other companies to hire their own black sales and merchandising men during the 1930s and early '40s. In the postwar period their
number exploded. Further, a number of firms, including Philip Morris,
Lever Brothers, and Pepsi-Cola, began to support the efforts of these
black salesmen by initiating advertising campaigns specifically directed
at black consumers. In a 1948 article, an *Ebony* writer labeled this group
of men the "Brown Hucksters," taking a cue from the popular book and
Clark Gable film *The Hucksters*.[6]

By the early 1950s, over forty blacks worked in a special-markets capacity for American corporations. Some companies, like Pabst Brewing and
Pepsi-Cola, went so far as to establish a specific office of special markets
within their corporate structure. Others, like Coca-Cola, contracted with
blacks that owned independent marketing or public relations firms. The
activities of these men varied, but regardless of their employer, they had
three primary responsibilities: First, to generate sales among black business owners and consumers. They made sales calls, did store merchandising, and engaged in any other conventional or unconventional
methods possible to produce sales for their employers. Some, like Moss
Kendrix, leader of Coca-Cola's special-markets efforts, developed marketing campaigns used around the country. Others, such as Major C.
Udell Turpin of office-machine giant Remington-Rand, were one-man
sales forces that traveled throughout the country hawking the com-

pany's products to small business owners. Indeed, all of these men traveled extensively, a process that for blacks in the 1940s and '50s was rarely simple. Racism and segregation made travel challenging and blacks had to constantly be aware of where they were and were not welcome. One former sales representative recalled: "Airplanes and railroads were not a problem. It was when we got to our destination that the impact of the restrictive social patterns brought about by prejudice and discrimination became real. . . . Wherever we went we tried to find the best possible public stopping place where Blacks could find accommodations. In same places we had to stay at the local Black YMCA or with friends. There were isolated occasions where we had to stay in roach infested, dimly lit places where one could hear down the hall the hourly "time's up" call. Since we were never sure where we were going to end up, we found it extremely wise to carry with us things like light bulbs, toilet paper, soap and extension cords."[7]

Beyond their travel concerns, the second responsibility of many Brown Hucksters was to compile research information about black consumers. Therefore, several of these men worked together with black media organizations to compile data regarding buying habits, brand preferences, and purchasing motivations. While much of this information only covered local markets, along with the growing body of research from the government, black media organizations, and Negro radio stations, all of it helped to broaden the national picture of black consumers.[8]

Their final responsibility was to act as public relations agents and generate goodwill among black consumers for their employers. In many cases this took the form of advocating corporate support for black organizations. For example, Coca-Cola's representative, Moss Kendrix, often recommended that Coke sponsor local groups such as the Boy Scouts or black religious and fraternal organizations. Sometimes this support came through direct contributions to the organization, but more often, through providing needed materials like uniforms or beverage stations to refresh thirsty convention attendees.[9]

Sometimes these men had to go beyond generating goodwill to preventing the spread of negative publicity about their employers. In 1955, Kendrix became involved in a dispute between the Coca-Cola company and the NAACP. Precipitating the conflict were statements a South Carolina bottler made in an interview with the *New York Amsterdam News*, a black newspaper. In response to blacks' circulation of a petition supporting school desegregation, the bottler (who was also the mayor of Orangeburg) ordered his bakery and ice and fuel companies not to sell blacks that had signed the petition. Also included on his list of targets were members of the NAACP. Beyond these actions, the mayor also implied that violence was a possibility. "I have checked with the 30 or more nigger employees that I have working for me, and if I catch any of them joining that NAACP, or signing the petition, they might as well leave town," he growled. In response, NAACP officials requested that the parent Coca-Cola organization, as a national company, either encourage the bottler to promote blacks into responsible positions or cancel his bottler agreement. When Coke executives refused, the NAACP publicly announced that they were removing the Coke vending machines from their national headquarters. The organization did not take the step of calling for an actual boycott of the company's products. However, Wilkins viewed it as a display of "self respect" and a way to show solidarity with blacks in the South who faced reprisals for their open support of the recent *Brown v. Board of Education* decision. Kendrix's concern, as well as that among Coca-Cola management, was that the removal of Coke machines from the national office would lead to an avalanche of negative exposure for the company.[10]

To forestall a major outbreak of negative publicity, Kendrix wrote directly to Roy Wilkins, head of the NAACP. He explained that the local bottler was an independent operator and that the parent company could not sway him to a particular action. Next, he wrote to black newspapers and provided them with a similar explanation. In a release sent to black newspaper editors and publishers he stressed that Coca-Cola could not "control the political, social and other activities of the men and women who bottle Coca-Cola." Kendrix also provided them with information about the "positive programs" the company maintained in the black community, including the employment of black sales personnel, support of black fraternal organizations, use of black entertainers on radio programs, and sponsorship of African American sports tournaments and beauty pageants. Many black newspapers, while sympathetic to the NAACP's goals, echoed the words of an editorial writer for the *Houston Informer*: "It doesn't seem to me that the Coca-Cola Company can be blamed for the individual actions of this mayor. . . . Since there is not the slightest indication that they have inspired him to do it, or that they have condoned the action." Kendrix's efforts helped ward off a potential public relations nightmare. While not all special marketers had to perform in this crisis-response manner, they had to be ready at all times to generate support for their employers.[11]

By the early 1950s there were enough blacks operating in special-markets positions to support establishment of a national organization. In 1953 a group of five men: Walter Davis, H. Naylor Fitzhugh, Moss Kendrix, Samuel Whitman, and Herbert H. Wright, created the National Association of Market Developers (NAMD). During the 1950s and '60s, the NAMD became the central organization through which blacks active in public relations, special marketing, and advertising promoted the black consumer market. Among the five cofounders, Kendrix was recognized as the catalyst behind the effort. "Without Moss Kendrix there would not have been an NAMD because he supported the organization by supplying the needed resources," Fitzhugh recalled.[12]

Kendrix could lead the creation of the NAMD because he had ample resources to draw on. In addition to working with Coca-Cola, he owned a public relations firm in Washington, D.C., and he was also a consultant for the Carnation company. In addition he did public relations work for a variety of civic, religious, and private organizations. Prior to opening his firm, he had worked in both government service and as a journalist, which, combined with his various public relations efforts, gave him with a broad network through which to promote the black consumer market. Similar to Claude Barnett, he was a strong advocate of the market because he believed that corporate interest in black consumers likely meant more business for his company. Also, alongside self-interest, Kendrix astutely realized that if blacks were recognized as a distinct consumer segment that it would likely mean more job opportunities for young black professionals overall. Therefore, like *Ebony*'s John Johnson, he took every opportunity to convince companies and advertising agencies that it existed and they should market to it. The author of one article enthused, "It cannot be gainsaid that much of the advertising, merchandising and goodwill which is exchanged between the Negro market and industry today stems from the activity and influence of Moss Kendrix in the field."[13]

In part, the NAMD was the child of the frustration of a growing number of black marketing and public relations men. The racial politics of the time meant that company training on new marketing or sales techniques sometimes did not include them. One early NAMD member Chuck Smith recalled that "You weren't a part of anything real within the company marketing program or organization. You didn't participate in the meetings where they would discuss what's going on and what the new strategies were . . . I don't think many of those company managers really gave a damn about anything more than the fact that they were going to have somebody out there identified with the Negro market." While not all special marketers faced the difficulties that Smith described, some were in fact employed for no other reason than so that the company could use them as an example of their enlightened hiring policies. As a result, black professionals often lacked access to the training and development opportunities made available to their white counterparts. These men were often victims of the collision between the stated ideals of corporate leaders and the realities of day-to-day business operations. So, rather than finding white middle managers or marketing directors supportive of their efforts, black professionals like Smith found that they were to be seen, but not necessarily heard.[14]

The NAMD was a direct response to this kind of prejudice and its resulting frustration. The group acted as a support organization for blacks in commercial communication fields and, until the mid-1960s, was often the only consistent source of networking and training in new marketing techniques and research information. Additionally, in contrast to the individualized efforts of newspapermen like Barnett and Robert Vann, in the postwar era the NAMD became an important organizational voice advocating for greater recognition of the black consumer market and for black employment opportunities in sales, advertising, and public relations. Consequently attendance at NAMD conventions often included many professionals who were not special marketers but who were active in the black consumer market, including *Ebony* publisher Johnson. Additionally, white executives from companies active in the market routinely attended NAMD conventions.[15]

But the NAMD was more than simply a training and networking group. Members of the association helped initiate the shift in advertising and marketing used to reach black consumers. Workshops at yearly conventions often featured panelists who examined the black consumer market and advocated more creative and systematic ways to reach it. Moreover, executives at the conventions heard firsthand of changes among black consumers. As their companies then adjusted their approaches to African American consumers, their sales jumped—and their competitors copied their successful efforts. In this way, some of the techniques and ideas advocated during NAMD workshops supplanted the traditional advertising and marketing paradigm regarding the black consumer market.[16]

Traditional advertising efforts to the Negro market had required very little from companies. Since the late 1920s, black publishers consistently articulated what many in the postwar era considered to be a conservative approach to the Negro market. Specifically, they had told advertisers and agencies that they simply needed to place their advertisements in black media in order to receive the patronage of black consumers. *Ebony* publisher Johnson often informed advertisers "the fact that you're in a Negro publication is enough to inspire loyalty." There was no need, Johnson and other publishers argued, to create special advertising copy or to use black models in any but the most intimate or familial scenes. Now, in contrast, members of the NAMD, like those active in Negro radio, counseled advertisers to create special appeals that spoke to black consumers in the manner those consumers desired. In addition, they advocated that advertisers use black models throughout advertisements directed at blacks regardless of the situation depicted. Postwar black consumers, NAMD members argued, were more likely to purchase when they felt that companies appreciated them for their patronage. Further, members of the NAMD strongly recommended that, in order to achieve the best possible results, companies hire black experts who could create the advertisements and marketing programs necessary to generate maximum appeal among black consumers. Supporting the advice of NAMD members were articles in the trade press listing "seek guidance from a black consultant" as the number one thing to do when pursuing sales among black consumers. "Do not invest one dime in a marketing program for Negroes without first securing proper guidance. This may take the form of a sales promotion and marketing member on your staff, or the services of a private organization. *But do it* [emphasis in original] or, with the best intention in the world, you may not get your product off the ground," a reporter cautioned.[17]

In the parlance of the postwar trade press, "proper guidance" was a euphemism for guidance from a black professional with experience or expertise. While that perception may seem anathema in the twenty-first century, it must be remembered that blacks were routinely referred to as a "nation within a nation," "a city within a city," or an "undiscovered" market. These colonial metaphors reveal the widely held perception that whites knew next to nothing about African Americans. Recall, for example, the question William B. Ziff asked readers in his 1932 booklet *The Negro Market*: "Do you see a photo of a Negro wedding . . . on any daily's society page?" White business leaders accepted this logic (primarily because it carried a strong measure of truth), but blacks also cultivated these characterizations (also because they were often true), which gave them entry into previously restricted job opportunities.[18]

However, both the NAMD and the trade press routinely cautioned that skin color was no guarantee of advertising or marketing prowess. In other words, companies should not hire someone to guide sales or marketing programs solely because he was black. Members of the association knew that this sense of racial insight could be carried too far and become a haven for con men who masked their lack of expertise with their skin color. If such individuals became widespread, the overall goal of promoting the black consumer market and black sales, advertising, and public relations professionals would suffer accordingly. As a result, the NAMD consistently argued that companies interested in black consumers should employ one of the many blacks who had gained experience through work for a black newspaper, for Negro radio, or in special marketing. These men would know how to act as liaisons between companies and the black consumer market, communicating about products in ways that customers would respect and respond to while knowing how

to inform the company, in turn, about the tastes and practices of consumers.

Special marketers were well aware of the importance of race to their
employment and the tenuous hold they had on these white-collar jobs.
Specifically, it was because of their race that most of their employers
originally hired them. But racism matched whatever advantage race gave
them: any failures they had would not be easily forgiven. Or, put more
simply, they knew that as black marketers they had few chances to prove
their worth to their company. If they were to keep their jobs, and if any
blacks were ever going to be hired after them, they had to succeed. Yet
for those early black pioneers in white corporate America, even success
itself could be a double-edged sword. On one hand, it meant that they
were a shining example of their race and could open the door to the
hiring of others, that they were lesser-known "Jackie Robinsons." On
the other hand, observers might ascribe their failure as evidence of
blacks' inability to compete and flourish in white-collar positions, which
would lead to fewer opportunities for future blacks. Every individual
black professional carried the weight of the race on his back.[19]

The overwhelming majority of the Brown Hucksters worked for the
corporate clients of advertising agencies. Regardless, in the early 1950s,
a few agencies took the bold step of hiring an African American to work
directly in their firm. Still, while only a handful of blacks found positions
in the industry in the 1950s and early '60s, their success laid important
groundwork for the expansion of black employment in advertising in
later years. The first significant blacks to operate within the industry
were those who used the postwar corporate interest in black consumers
to become the owner-operators of their own advertising agencies.

African American Advertising Agencies

Blacks operated their own advertising firms starting in the second decade of the twentieth century. Most were small, local firms that lasted little more than a few years. Many, like Claude A. Barnett Advertising,
operated on the periphery of the advertising business serving local clients and placing advertisements in the black press. Few actually created
any original advertising copy, however; instead, many simply retooled
advertisements that were created by mainstream agencies for black newspapers. The limited size and longevity of black firms in this early period
was due to several factors. Prior to World War II, the Depression hindered black agency development as firms of all sizes cut back on advertising expenditures. Another major factor was that the primary outlets for
black advertising, black newspapers and magazines, often either operated their own advertising departments or engaged newspaper represen-

tatives to solicit advertisements. More important, though, was that there was a limited pool of potential clients for such firms. Black agencies had virtually no chance to produce advertisements for large consumer-products firms, the leading advertisers in the country. Instead, such agencies were limited to producing work for local black-owned businesses. The development of broader-based, full-service, black-owned agencies needed the prosperity generated by the war and the wider corporate interest in the black consumer market. With those factors realized, some blacks parlayed their experience as advertising representatives or marketing consultants into independent agency ownership. The first African American to do so was marketing and sales expert David Sullivan.

DAVID J. SULLIVAN ADVERTISING

Although *Ebony* publisher John Johnson became the recognized national expert on the black consumer market during the postwar era, in the years preceding the war David Sullivan occupied that role. Sullivan had a broad range of experiences before entering the advertising agency business. Like other blacks who entered the industry, Sullivan once worked in the newspaper business; he had been the advertising manager for the *New York Amsterdam Star-News*. He was also in retail sales, as a store manager for General Electric, and had managed the black consumer market program for the Wilson Distilling company. Yet he first came to national attention as an author and researcher through articles in the trade press. Two of his most well-known pieces, in which he provided guidelines on targeting black consumers, appeared in *Sales Management* and helped inaugurate a spate of "how to" articles in the trade press, putting Sullivan in the limelight.[20]

In a 1943 article, Sullivan described the advertising and marketing practices some firms used, making it clear that black consumers found them offensive. He filled the article with descriptions of companies that had produced offensive products or company literature that demeaned or offended blacks. His examples ranged from the American Tobacco Company's Nigger Hair Tobacco to Whitman Candy's Pickaninny Chocolates. He told how both companies had felt the ire of black consumers after their release of the products and had subsequently issued public apologies. These firms had not set out to purposely offend blacks, he noted; they simply had not accounted for them in any way.[21]

The racist offenses Sullivan described in the article were not limited to products. For example, the offending action of Noxzema Chemicals took place in company literature. Noxzema manufactured an all-purpose skin cream that was popular among blacks. In the early 1940s the company had sent out a letter to merchants encouraging them to bring

Figure 5. David Sullivan. "The Negro Market: An Appraisal," *Tide* (March 7, 1947): 17.

their delinquent accounts current. To illustrate the point, readers were reminded that maintaining an unpaid account was like having a "nigger in the woodpile," meaning that it was a not-quite-visible but not-quite-hidden problem. The letter also featured a drawing of a black man peeking out from behind a pile of lumber. It is unclear whether the letter was sent to white and black merchants, but reporters somehow became aware of its contents. Aware of the impending release of news stories about the letter, Sullivan and his staff made an informal survey of Noxzema sales in drug stores and beauty salons with primarily black clientele. Prior to the release of the story, sales were brisk. But after the local black newspapers publicized existence of the letter, sales of Noxzema products slowed considerably. In response, company executives issued an apology and began an advertising effort in black newspapers featuring black models. The intensive effort helped the company through the public relations crisis and helped it regain its leading sales position among black consumers. Corporate executives may or may not have had great appreciation for blacks as a group, but they definitely recognized their value to the company's bottom line. The lesson, Sullivan cautioned, was to avoid the demeaning extremes of the companies in his story, to approach black consumers respectfully, and, when necessary, issue a public apology and engage in efforts to generate goodwill.[22]

In the article, Sullivan went beyond simply providing anecdotal evidence and overall warnings. He also offered readers specific tips on what not to do when approaching black consumers. He presented the following advice, which gives us another sense of the range of advertisers' ignorance:

- Don't exaggerate Negro characters with flat noses, thick lips, kinky hair and owl eyes.
- Avoid Negro minstrels. Avoid even the use of white people with blackface and a kinky wig for hire to depict a Negro.
- Don't constantly name the Negro porter or waiter "George." Nothing makes Negroes angrier than to be called George.
- Avoid incorrect English usage, grammar and dialect . . . get away from "Yas suh," "sho," "dese," "dem," "dat," or "dat 'ere," "gwine," "you all."
- Don't picture colored women as buxom, broad-faced, grinning mammies and Aunt Jemimas.
- Don't refer to Negro women as "Negresses."
- Avoid, even by suggestion, "There's a nigger in the woodpile," or "coon," "shine," and "darky."
- Don't illustrate . . . any . . . advertising piece showing a Negro eating watermelon, chasing chickens, or crap shooting.
- Don't picture the "Uncle Mose" type. He is characterized by kinking hair and as a stooped, tall, lean and grayed sharecropper, always in rags.
- Avoid using the word "Pickaninny," or lampooning illustrations of Negro children.
- Don't insult the clergy.[23]

Sullivan's list of "don'ts" illustrated how *not* to approach black consumers and what actions to avoid. Sullivan even provided readers with the rationale behind his advice. For example, he knew that in the Pullman cars then in operation on the nation's railways, whites did not learn individual porter's names but, instead, referred to each of them with the generic moniker of George. Thus, referring to blacks as George in an advertisement was to continue an insulting practice that failed to recognize blacks' individuality.

But Sullivan failed to provide the same level of guidance on what *to* do in approaching black consumers. Simply put, what to do was not necessarily the opposite of what not to do. In fact, Sullivan was implicitly positioning himself as a consultant. Although he did not expressly advertise for his services, the laudatory words of executive editor Philip Salisbury neatly did so for him. In a separate box embedded in Sullivan's article, Salisbury strongly encouraged readers to take Sullivan's words seriously. The exact size of the black consumer market was, admittedly, unknown but it was one that "no manufacturer can afford to ignore." It was a large market with considerable buying power and influence. Accordingly, it was not a market that advertisers and agencies could afford to ignore, either. Moreover, if advertisers were going to solicit black consumers they needed to do so in an acceptable manner—or the manner that Sullivan suggested in describing unacceptable methods. After all, Salisbury concluded, "he knows his markets as few whites know theirs."[24]

The article, combined with other public appearances before marketing and advertising groups, gave Sullivan a platform to tout black consumers and his own expertise in reaching them. Also, his often-reprinted advice came on the heels of one the first major public discussions on the black consumer market. In the summer of 1942, the *New York Amsterdam Star-News* had sponsored a forum on the black consumer market, replete with experts on the market discoursing on its meaning to advertisers. Participants concluded that the black consumer market represented fifteen million customers with a potential spending power of over $6 billion annually. Further, they argued that black consumers represented a market larger than most of the nation's export markets and that they needed cultivation now and in the postwar period, whenever that might come. John Hagan, an advertising-space buyer, argued that companies needed to employ black marketing experts in order to properly cultivate the black consumer market. White advertising buyers, Hagan reasoned, lacked the interest and expertise to give the market proper attention, and "all have infantile notions about Negro buying habits."[25] Forums like this, albeit of smaller scope, were held around the country during the 1940s as local radio stations or black media organizations sought ways to generate attention to black consumers. Sullivan sensed that he was on the verge of an opportunity, and in 1943 he opened an advertising firm.

The name of the Sullivan's agency, the Negro Market Organization, silently expressed the goals and expertise of the agency to prospective clients. Sullivan sought to create an entirely new niche within the agency field, an agency dedicated solely to the black consumer market. With the capacity to run an advertising campaign from conception to placement, conduct market research, and develop public relations and marketing programs, Sullivan's was the first full-service black agency in the country. What separated Sullivan's venture from preceding efforts, like those of Barnett in the 1920s, was that he sought clients from large white-owned corporations as well as black-owned firms. Sullivan, like Johnson in his development of *Ebony*, knew that growth in agency revenue required large blue-chip clients. These firms, in contrast to their small black-owned counterparts, had the money to maintain advertising campaigns and to pay him the industry-standard fifteen percent commission for his work. Sullivan, while not quite a thunderous success, was able to keep his agency open for six years. Although a small agency, the Negro Market Organization serviced accounts for several large clients including Sacony-Vacuum, Beech-Nut, and the General Baking Company. He also acted as an advertising and marketing consultant for mainstream advertising agencies such as the J. Walter Thompson company. As an independent agency owner, Sullivan's focus and assignments were squarely within the Negro market. Advertisements for the company asked readers: "Are you selling them [blacks] effectively?" Assuming the answer was no, the ads teased readers with the prospect of a "$7 billion Negro market" that Sullivan could provide them with the "expert counsel" to reach.[26]

Throughout the 1940s, Sullivan maintained his agency and wrote articles for the trade press. Aside from his "do's and don'ts" pieces, Sullivan's focused on compiling research statistics on Negro consumers. As a former newspaper advertising manager and as operator of his own firm, he knew that agency executives based their first point of resistance to turning their attention to black consumers on the lack the available research information. Therefore, a number of his articles provided statistical information on black consumers.

In a 1945 article, he estimated the national income of African Americans and provided an eight-category breakdown of how they spent their money. His goal was to provide a national overview instead of the local estimates that black newspaper publishers developed over the years. He estimated that outside of housing, blacks spent the largest portion of their income on food, clothing, drugs, and cosmetics. Further, blacks spent a larger percentage of their income than whites on products in

ARE YOU SELLING THEM EFFECTIVELY?

•

*You should have expert counsel
on how to reach the growing
$7 Billion Negro Market. Consult—*

•

DAVID J. SULLIVAN
Negro Market Organization
Marketing • Advertising • Research
545 Fifth Avenue • New York, N. Y.

I OUT OF
EVERY 10
AMERICANS
IS A NEGRO

Figure 6. Advertisement for David Sullivan's advertising agency. Sullivan's advertisements encouraged readers to recognize the size and value of the Negro market. The Negro Market Organization advertisement, *Advertising Age* (February 21, 1944): 54.

these categories, making them an especially valuable market. Yet Sullivan's article contained within it the seeds for refusal on the part of advertising executives. For they could validly point out that not only were Sullivan's figures estimates, but they were estimates based on data nearly ten years old. So on one hand he was providing valuable analysis, and on the other executives could reasonably question its accuracy because of the sources on which he based his conclusions. At the very least, the lack of reliable, measured data kept agency executives from giving the same level of credibility to the arguments of black consumer market advocates like Sullivan that they did their mainstream counterparts.[27]

Nonetheless, Sullivan's research efforts brought him to the attention of advertising and marketing practitioners. In addition to writing trade journal articles, his work also appeared in academic marketing journals, and he also continued to speak before marketing and advertising organizations. His skin color made his presence conspicuous, and his expertise drew the attention of conference attendees; his was often the lone voice urging them to pay greater attention to Negro consumers. Sullivan also appeared at meetings of black newspaper publishers and, similar to Barnett and Ziff in the 1930s, counseled them on ways to attract advertising revenue. He strongly urged them not only to improve the stature of their papers by devoting more space to news and less to horoscopes and gossip columns but also to allocate more money to researching local consumers. He also advised them to provide merchandising services to companies that advertised in their publications. These extra services would require them to devote resources to working directly with merchants to enhance product sales. Admittedly these were costly and time-consuming efforts, but they were an additional way to enhance the reputation of black newspapers as an additional source.[28]

Eventually Sullivan was unable to financially maintain his agency and he closed it in 1949. His many articles and public appearances had brought him some acclaim, but they did not translate into enough consistent opportunities. Though people were willing to hear his opinions and analysis, too few were willing to pay him for it as well. Curiously, given his experience and stature he was unable to find work in any mainstream advertising firms. It took him fifteen years and over twelve hundred resumes to find work in a mainstream firm (see Chapter 3). In the intervening years, he worked as a freelance Negro market consultant and researcher. In 1959, he briefly reopened a marketing and public relations agency, but it remained open for only a short time. He also continued to write articles on the Negro market for various trade publications. Despite his failure, though, other black entrepreneurs followed his example and opened advertising agencies.[29]

BRANDFORD ADVERTISING

Not all blacks that opened agencies came out of the newspaper trade. In fact, one notable agency owner of the period, Edward Brandford, began as an artist. Brandford arrived in New York City in 1924 from Jamaica with plans to continue his studies as an artist. Before he could do so, however, he needed to accumulate enough money to cover the costs of his schooling. After two years of work and four years of art school, he graduated from the Cooper Union Art school in 1930. After graduation, Brandford faced the typical difficulties of any aspiring professional artist. But, as a young black artist beginning his career during the Great Depression, Brandford would have been forgiven had he simply given up and tried to make a living via other means. As luck would have it, despite the economic downturn, Brandford found just enough work to continue pursuing his goal of being a professional artist. He completed two covers for the Urban League's *Opportunity* magazine, and he found a job with a printing company. While the magazine covers brought him some attention, it was his work at the printing company that had the most lasting impact. Specifically, working on client advertising designs and layouts piqued his desire to pursue a future career in advertising. Bradford left the printing firm after a few years and worked as a freelance artist creating images and designs for magazines, books, and posters. His success provided him with just enough capital to open his own commercial art firm and hire a small sales and office staff.[30]

By 1946, Brandford's freelance work for various publications and advertising firms convinced him of the need for a central location for advertisers and publishers to find black models. There was no black modeling agency in operation and aspiring black models found existing agencies less than welcoming. "Negro women [models]," he concluded, "always have been neglected." A black modeling agency could ease the struggles experienced black models had in finding work, give advertisers a source of black models, and train aspiring models. Therefore, with two partners, Barbara Watson and Mary Louise Yabro, Brandford organized the first modeling agency for African American women.[31]

Brandford announced the opening of the agency during a lavish ceremony at the Astor hotel in New York City. Canada Lee, a black actor, was master of ceremonies and made an appropriately laudatory opening speech. The agency, he concluded, was "the beginning of something we Negroes have known should have existed for a long time."[32] The ceremony drew the attention of both black newspapers and the advertising trade press, and pictures of Brandford and his models were widely reprinted.

Similar to the importance of *Ebony* magazine as a media outlet to reach black consumers, the Brandford agency provided advertisers or mainstream agencies looking to rework campaigns for the black consumer market a central location from which to select black models. By providing this access Brandford not only helped open professional opportunities for black women, he also helped further streamline the process for reaching the black consumer market with racially specific advertisements. Soon after opening models with the "Brandford look"—slender, with medium skin tone and height, and long hair—were a sought-after commodity for companies designing campaigns specifically for the Negro market. Although they appeared in advertisements for a variety of products, the models were particularly popular for companies advertising beauty products. In fact, in some advertisements, the women were specifically identified as being Brandford Models. Thus, for a time Brandford succeeded not only in developing a thriving modeling agency but also in turning his models into brands whose association with the agency conveyed positive qualities about the products they advertised.[33]

Shortly after creating the modeling agency, Brandford announced the opening of his full-service advertising firm. The two firms were linked in that Brandford often used models from the agency i   h:-
advertising work. Further, he had reason to expect success as an a
owner. Several companies already used his models in campaigns a

Figure 7. Commercial artist and advertising man Edward Brandford. "Edward Brandford—Commercial Artist," *The Crisis* (January 1947): 12.

at the Negro market, he had become known as the "foremost Negro commercial artist" in the city. Additionally, he staffed his small firm with experienced artists and public relations counselors. Brandford, like other pioneers in the black-owned agency niche, positioned his firm as a specialist on the Negro market: "Negroes represent vast spending power in America, and yet never have had their wants or tastes consulted," he observed. He hoped that companies interested in the black consumer market would select his advertising firm to create an entire campaign. After all, his was, he believed, a unique and valuable role. "Advertising agencies," he noted, "have not been able to sell the Negro market properly, and since their copy lacked the punch of message directed specifically to Negroes." He represented himself and his firm as having the insight and expertise to provide the "punch" those current advertisements in the black consumer market lacked. Additionally, he believed that the comprehensive structure of his two companies gave him an advantage over other black firms. In particular, he stressed to potential clients there was no need to go to multiple agencies to acquire the expertise to reach black consumers, for the models, artists, and public relations experts were in his firm. Unfortunately for Brandford, while executives were willing to use his models for campaigns to black consumers, he found that they were less eager to hire his advertising agency. At this time clients active in the black consumer market thought that simply changing the race of the models was enough for racially specific targeting. Therefore, they found little need for the more in-depth guidance that Brandford offered. As a result, like other black-owned agencies of the 1940s, Brandford Advertising never secured more than a local client base looking to place ads in black media. Although he was able to keep the agency open into the 1970s, it remained a small firm. Like David Sullivan, Brandford was a few decades ahead of his time. Thus, in spite of some success as a commercial artist and his innovations in modeling, leadership in the black-owned agency fraternity of the postwar years went to another firm.[34]

W. B. Graham & Associates

Among the best-known black agencies of the postwar years was the W. B. Graham agency. The firm had many elements supporting its success that other black-owned agencies could not match. First, the agency founder, William B. Graham, had extensive marketing and public relations experience. Additionally, when he opened the firm he already had a roster of national-level, blue-chip clients. Graham had vaulted to fame in the late 1930s with a marketing and public relations campaign for Pabst beer. In a four-month period, Graham increased Pabst distribution among outlets catering to blacks in Cleveland, Ohio, from 7 percent to over 90 percent. After that brilliant success, Pabst executives made Graham a company troubleshooter with a mandate to travel throughout the country developing ways to increase Pabst sales among blacks. He promoted the beer to stores and bars, and he raised awareness of the brand among black consumers in the Midwest significantly. His efforts led to sales increases among blacks—and also in service areas in which blacks

Figure 8. William B. Graham. "Joe Louis Punch," *Tide* (August 23, 1946): 20.

serviced white customers. In particular, his promotion of Pabst to black train porters was so successful that on some trains they automatically served customers Pabst unless they specifically requested another brand.[35]

His most widely known accomplishment for Pabst, though, came in 1941 in Harlem. Company executives sent Graham to the city because Pabst sales among blacks lagged behind those of its competitors. Before making any recommendations, Graham made an informal survey of the area by talking to bar owners and patrons about their opinions on Pabst beer. He found that feelings toward it were no more or less favorable than toward other brands. He learned that Pabst was equal to other brands but neither the beer nor the company had top-of-mind awareness. So he decided that one way to make the company stand out was to change the area salesman. He removed the white salesman from the Harlem territory and replaced him with a black salesman. Graham also developed a series of company-sponsored contests and promotions involving black musical artists. These changes had tremendous results. Less than a year after he arrived in the city, nearly as much Pabst was sold in a single month (twelve thousand cases) as had been sold in the entire preceding year (fifteen thousand cases). Further, the success of his management efforts led the company to hire two full-time black salesmen for the area and sponsor a radio program featuring black entertainers. In the process Pabst became the leading brand among blacks in Harlem. He later delivered similar results for the company in other cities around the country.[36]

Both the advertising and beverage trade press reported impressive sales Graham generated for Pabst. Thus, when Graham and fellow Pabst sales representative, Henry Parks, Jr. (who later became a famous sausage manufacturer), opened an advertising firm in 1944, he brought a proven capacity to increase a company's profit margin among black consumers. Further, the experience had given Graham concrete ideas on how to advertise to the changing African American population. As he pointed out to an interviewer, blacks were becoming "fed up with the dice game-watermelon-chicken coop tag."[37] Instead, respectful, consistent, and reasoned advertisements and promotions were the way to generate sales, as he had proven in his time at Pabst.

When he started his agency, Graham had advantages other black agency owners did not. First, he retained some responsibility for Pabst marketing and promotions efforts in the Negro market. So, Graham's firm, unlike other black-owned agencies, had at least one primary account that it could look to for revenue. The Pabst account also gave him a visibly successful base from which to approach other major companies to solicit interest in the Negro market. Second, Graham routinely engaged in public relations through distribution of *News of the Negro Market*, a promotional pamphlet describing its marketing efforts. Third, Graham's proven success in generating sales allowed him to charge fees for his services more in line with those charged by mainstream agencies. Finally, Graham's firm was solely responsible for the promotion of Joe Louis Punch, a soft drink.[38]

In fact, Joe Louis Punch was Graham's idea. He persuaded Joe Louis to lend his name and, along with musicians Duke Ellington and Cab Calloway, to finance the venture. The marketing and advertising materials featured Louis, the most popular black athlete of the period, as the sole figure alongside copy testifying to the drink's quality.

Ellington and Calloway composed a theme song for the drink played on radio stations. Combining the efforts and celebrity of the three men with his own advertising and marketing acumen, he promoted Joe Louis Punch throughout the United States, Central America, and the Caribbean. Radio programs and newspaper, magazine, and billboard advertisements, as well as a variety of promotional ventures, briefly made Joe Louis Punch a success in the beverage industry. Unfortunately, over time it developed quality issues that no amount of advertising or promotion could overcome. A former salesman for Joe Louis Punch recalled that when exposed to sunlight the soda pop lost its color, and when combined with ice it lost most of its aroma. The financial difficulties of the former heavyweight champion compounded these quality problems because the company lacked the resources to make the proper quality-control changes. As a result, by the early 1950s the drink was a forgotten part of beverage history. However, its initial success increased the visibility and client base of Graham's agency.[39]

Graham's success demonstrated that survival as a black-owned agency required more than perceived expertise on the black consumer market. It even required more than the ability to provide full agency services, as Sullivan's and Brandford's agencies did. Instead, a black-owned agency needed major clients and, most important, the proven capacity to increase a client's revenue in order to keep its doors open. The Graham agency was also the only agency that had a real opportunity to prove its services to major clients. Other black-owned agencies of the decade were forced to compete over the limited roster of local and national clients interested in black consumers, especially in New York City.

VINCE CULLERS ADVERTISING

Like the mainstream agency businesses, the leading black-owned firms were in New York City. But, in the mid-1950s, hundreds of miles away in Chicago, a black war veteran, Vince Cullers, decided to try his hand in the agency field. Eventually his firm, Vince Cullers Advertising, would become one of the leaders of the black advertising agency sector in the 1960s and 1970s. For years, though, the firm remained a small agency with a local client base. In these early years, the firm did not appear capable of lasting through the end of the decade, let alone through the end of the twentieth century.

Cullers began his advertising career as a Marine combat artist in the Pacific theater during World War II. When he returned home, Cullers sought ways to translate his artistic skills into paid work, just as Brand-

Figure 9. Graham often used the image of the "Brown Bomber" to promote Joe Louis Punch to consumers and potential bottling partners. Author's collection.

ford had in New York. Accordingly, he and two partners started an advertising agency, a precursor to his solo company. This early firm secured some work from local businessmen, but the billings were not enough to support three partners and the firm closed. But Cullers was determined to succeed in the business. Out of work, he tried to find a job with a mainstream advertising agency, but racial discrimination made that virtually impossible. Fortunately, like Brandford, he found enough work as a freelance artist to keep him financially solvent.[40]

For a short time in the early 1950s, Cullers worked as an art director at *Ebony* magazine. Although his time there was brief, it had a profound impact upon his career plans. Working with the magazine's advertising layouts, he noted that images of blacks, even those designed for a black-oriented publication, needed alteration in the layout or touch-up work on the color of the models. Or, in many cases, in the ads submitted by agencies to reach readers of this black-oriented magazine, the models and copy were the same as they were for the white consumers. Echoing the position held by Brandford and other blacks in the industry, Cullers believed that many of the ads done by mainstream agencies approached black consumers as if they wanted to be white. Agencies that placed ads in *Ebony* often gave them no special creative attention other than replacing white faces with black ones. He recalled that "there was no effort to make the ads appealing to blacks . . . and there was nothing particularly creative being done." Therefore, after leaving *Ebony*, he resolved to use his own artistic skill and experience to change the ways in which advertisements portrayed blacks. To fulfill that goal he founded the Vince Cullers advertising firm.[41]

The agency began in a small office and secured clients from local black businesses, including black insurance companies and a local snack-food company. Cullers also developed programming for Negro radio, now much more of a presence than it had been ten years before. In the late 1950s, for example, the agency staff created a Sunday morning musical program for a local savings and loan. The firm also picked up some minor fee-based work from mainstream agencies, though Cullers found crossing racial barriers to be difficult. On one occasion a white client canceled a project after finding out that Cullers was black. Those whites who did want to work with him had to do so from behind the scenes, telling him, "I'm going to help you, but don't tell anybody . . . here is something you can do for me." The racial politics of the times, however, prevented such solicitation from coming openly, and in effect they limited the growth of the agency. Although cross-racial work helped keep the agency solvent, the lack of public recognition for it could not help generate any additional work. Unlike William B. Graham's agency, which could boast of a client like Pabst in order to attract new business,

Cullers's firm had only invisible, covert white clients and small, local black ones.[42]

Fortunately, the agency survived long enough to be a beneficiary of changing attitudes. When the civil rights protests of the 1960s forced advertisers and agencies to begin changing their approach to black consumers, Cullers's firm began to achieve appreciable growth. Other black-owned agencies founded during the 1950s, despite high expectations, were not as fortunate.

BLACK ADVERTISING AGENCIES IN POSTWAR AMERICA

Black-owned agencies founded in the postwar era tried to capitalize on expertise in reaching the black consumer market. Unfortunately, the appreciation of that market by most corporate executives had not reached the point where a firm could grow on accounts only directed to black consumers. As a result, during the 1950s, black firms had difficulty in securing clients on a national level. In comparison to mainstream advertising agencies, black-owned agencies remained small, local concerns until they eventually folded. It would not be until the late 1960s and early '70s that African American-owned agencies began to achieve noticeable growth and a recognized presence within the industry.

Like other black-owned businesses in the segregated society of the 1940s and '50s, black advertising agencies were restricted in their list of potential clientele. At the same time, as Cullers's experience demonstrates, it was outside the realm of possibility for black-owned firms to land significant accounts for products aimed at whites. The fact that some potential clients cancelled assignments after learning of Cullers's race or that some white clients felt comfortable accepting his work while he remained in the shadows, anticipates the difficulties black agencies during the Golden Age had in receiving assignments in the general marketplace. That is, while working as independent agency owners, their racial background commonly trumped their possible contributions to advertising work in the general marketplace.[43]

Still, despite their limited size and length of existence, black-owned agencies gave African Americans the all-important opportunity to develop experience in the advertising field. Certainly their numbers remained small, but the men and women in these agencies were among the first professional-level blacks in the agency field, and as such they disproved the myth that blacks did not have the intellect or creativity for advertising work. Further, for some blacks, the experience they gained in black agencies provided them with opportunities when American corporations began welcoming black professionals to their ranks. For example, Pepsi-Cola hired Harvey Russell because of his involvement with the sales and marketing of Joe Louis Punch. Russell later went on to become a vice president at the company, one of the first blacks in such a position in any major U.S. company. Thus, although these agencies were small, they were important actors in the future of blacks in the advertising industry and other areas of corporate America.[44]

However, that black agencies found client acquisition difficult did not necessarily mean blacks were wholly unwelcome in the agency business. In fact, during the 1950s and early 1960s advertising agencies made a few high-profile hires of black professionals. Some were hired by agencies in search of experts to help guide clients with an interest in the black consumer market. Others, though, were the result of some exceptionally talented and creative people seeking agency employment—and finding that, in contrast to the experience of black agency owners, at least at some firms the color of their skin was secondary to their talent.

African Americans in Mainstream Agencies

Although the trade press did not recognize the presence of blacks in mainstream agencies until the high-profile hires of the 1950s, there were some blacks in these agencies in the 1940s. Most worked as clerks, porters, secretaries, or in print production areas, but a few were artists or space buyers. While the record is silent on the activities and experiences of many of these men and women, a few went on to prominent careers. By understanding the careers of a few of these men, we are provided a window into the experiences of that pioneering group of black executives operating in the still very white world of advertising agencies. Although agencies only hired a few blacks to work in a professional capacity during the 1940s and '50s, they helped lay an important foundation for the expansion of black employment in coming decades.[45]

The 1950s was a time of unprecedented prosperity for the advertising industry, as well as for the country as a whole. By the end of the decade nine of the top ten agencies had annual billings in excess of $100 million. The first agency to reach that number, J. Walter Thompson, had not done so until 1947, but within the decade eight other agencies were also members of the $100 million club. By the end of the decade the top four agencies in the country billed in excess of $200 million annually. Three factors fueled the industry's growth. First, the rapid expansion of television advertising in the postwar years provided access to consumers on a heretofore unimaginable scale. Second, the American public, eager to spend the income that rationing forced them to save during the Second World War, bought consumer products on a massive scale. Their desires led to a boom in postwar home construction that in turn helped power the sales of automobiles, appliances, and packaged goods all of which needed to be advertised. As a result, postwar spending on advertising campaigns exploded. Within this rapid industry expansion new opportunities opened in the advertising industry. As black consumers drew mounting attention from researchers and trade press writers, some agencies began to hire African American professionals. The first of these men entered these agencies as specialists on the Negro market. In the mid-1950s, however, some agencies took the revolutionary step to hire blacks based on their talent, rather than skin color.[46]

As far as many in the industry were concerned, the center of the advertising universe was New York City. After all, even those not in advertising commonly used Madison Avenue in the city as a euphemism for the industry. Many in the industry believed that if it did not happen in New York that it really did not matter. As a result, sometimes the trade press and agency people overlooked advertising news from other areas of the country; in particular, there were several reports of a mainstream agency's hiring of the "first" African Americans. To many, the first African American executive in a mainstream agency was Clarence Holte, hired in 1953, but in fact, Holte's executive role was predated by four years by the employment of Leonard Evans of Chicago.

W. LEONARD EVANS, JR.

Leonard Evans, Jr., had a unique educational and professional background. In contrast to other black professionals in the postwar era, he worked in both the black-owned agency segment as well as in mainstream agencies. Like other blacks in the business, he was a college graduate; unlike many, he had an extensive professional and sales background in both insurance and cosmetics. In the 1940s he was a member of the Associated Publishers newspaper representatives. While with the company, he participated in one of the first extensive studies to examine the purchasing habits of black consumers in Baltimore, Philadelphia, and Washington, D.C. After leaving Associated, he briefly set up a small advertising agency in New York. Like other blacks, he viewed the growing attention from corporate advertisers and the trade press toward black consumers as an entrepreneurial opportunity. What separated him from others, though, was that he was given the chance to work in a mainstream agency. In 1949, a short time after he opened his firm, he joined Arthur Meyerhoff & Company, a mainstream advertising firm in Chicago, as an expert on the Negro market. Although Evans wanted his own firm, he did not want to pass up the chance to gain the experience of working in a mainstream agency. Unfortunately the record is silent as to the reasons behind Evans's employment at Meyerhoff. Exactly how he came to the attention of executives at the firm is unclear.

One possibility rests with Meyerhoff's major client, the Wrigley Chewing Gum company. The major competitor for Wrigley, Beech-Nut gum, had been active in the Negro market for several years, so it is possible that Wrigley executives wanted a similar presence in the market.[47]

Evans's experience in the advertising business also anticipated those of future blacks in the industry. In the future, like Evans, most black agency entrepreneurs would first gain experience working in mainstream agencies, rather than in advertising sales for black media outlets, and use it to open their own firm. At Meyerhoff, Evans received much of the experience he had hoped for when he left his fledgling New York agency. He reached the level of account supervisor, the first African American to hold that title and responsibility at a mainstream firm. From this position he worked on accounts for black-owned companies like the Supreme Liberty Life Insurance Company and studied blacks' purchasing habits and motivations. For example, he argued that any company that targeted the black consumer market needed to do so with a specialized, targeted approach to reach black consumers. That meant avoiding the use of white models, as well as copy that implied that blacks' buying motivations simply mirrored those of whites.[48]

After nearly four years at Meyerhoff, Evans reduced his role at the firm and opened a second agency in Chicago. His experience and reputation as an authority on the Negro market, combined with his relationship with Meyerhoff, gave him access to national advertisers that his fellow black agency owners lacked. Evans's firm created Negro market campaigns for companies such as Pet Milk, Philip Morris cigarettes, Wrigley gum, and Armour meat products. His relationships in the black media, built during his time at Associated Publishers, also led major clients to his firm. For example, in 1957 executives at Pillsbury wrote to Claude Barnett, who was still part of the Associated Negro Press, seeking his opinion of an agency they were considering hiring to initiate a campaign in the Negro market. Barnett responded that the agency under consideration lacked the expertise to craft the campaign the company needed. Instead he recommended Evans, a "capable and experienced man in the field of public relations in the Negro market." Thus Evans's experience and connections gave him a decided advantage over other black agencies. There were few black-owned agencies at this time, and none could genuinely claim a significant degree of experience over the other, but Barnett's recommendation anticipated the growing competition between black agencies over accounts to reach the black consumer market. However, this competition did not find its fullest expression until the 1960s when the number of black-owned agencies appreciably increased.[49]

Ultimately, several factors limited the growth of Evans's firm, both external and internal. Externally, the slow growth of attention directed to the Negro market hampered the increase in firm size and billings. Although a handful of firms had major blue-chip clients, like those of Evans, W. B. Graham, and Sullivan, these were still only single accounts. No black agency had a full client roster of blue-chip clients and, instead, existed on a combination of billings from blue-chip national accounts and smaller local and regional ones. Unless black agency owners could successfully generate additional major accounts (and their billings), the increase in firm growth, as in Evans's case, would remain stagnant.

Internally, Evans' attention to projects beyond advertising campaigns hampered his ability to grow his agency. In 1954, Evans turned his energy to creating a network of stations devoted to programming Negro radio. At that time many considered network-level programming for blacks audiences to be the last hurdle in the complete development of Negro radio. With the creation of a network, agencies and advertisers that wanted to initiate a national-level ad campaign targeting the Negro market could do so through a single source, rather than approaching stations on an individual basis. Evans created the National Negro Network (NNN), which linked forty-three already existing stations throughout the country that together (he estimated) reached over 80 percent of the black population. The network offered news programming as well as a soap opera, *The Ruby Valentine Show*, sponsored by Philip Morris and the Pet Milk Company. The news programs focused on information of interest to blacks, and the soap opera featured black characters and used blues and gospel music. While the soap opera was a success and both sponsors reported increased sales where it was aired, the network did not attract additional sponsors. Evans believed the reason for this rested solely with agency reluctance to recommend the network to their clients. He recalled, "Agencies are aware of our existence and watch our growth closely, but . . . are still reluctant to come right out and make a recommendation [for using] Negro radio, preferring to keep campaigns at a 'test' level while watching to see what others do." As Johnson found when he was developing *Ebony* magazine, the most interest in black-oriented media came from agency clients, but this was not enough to keep the network on the air. Lacking consistent advertising support, Evans disbanded the network after just over a year.[50]

Evans's attention to the NNN, combined with his ongoing account work at Meyerhoff, limited the growth of his firm. In 1965, Evans left the advertising field entirely and reentered newspaper publishing through the creation of a newspaper supplement. But he had helped open the door for other blacks to enter the industry. Despite the fact that he was the first African American hired in a professional capacity at a mainstream agency, Evans's visibility as the first, or original Jackie Robinson, went unrecognized in the trade press. That title, as well as the industry visibility went to one of his contemporaries in New York City, Clarence Holte.[51]

CLARENCE HOLTE

In the early 1950s, executives at Batten, Barton, Durstine and Osborn (BBDO) decided that they needed to hire an African American to guide their existing clients interested in the Negro market and to attract new ones. Lyle Purchase, director of merchandising and research, came to this realization while completing a study of black drugstores and realizing exactly how little the company knew about the Negro market. As a result, he concluded that BBDO could become a pioneer in Negro market research and advertising and he convinced the company search for a black specialist. There were few black professionals in American corporations in the early 1950s, and hiring one was a major step for any company. Therefore, the twenty men who applied for the position faced more detailed interviews and examinations than would a white applicant for a similar role. What BBDO executives wanted was their own version of Jackie Robinson—specifically, a man not only who was supremely qualified but who they also believed could withstand any negativity based on his race without responding aggressively.[52]

After extensive interviews, executives settled on Clarence Holte, a black sales representative with Lever Brothers. Holte had worked for Lever for over ten years and at one point was the only African American on the staff, so he was familiar with both the Negro market and the pressures of being one of the few black faces at the professional levels of a major company. He also had the advantage of being acquainted with leaders of some of the newly independent nations in Africa, in particular Nnamdi Azikiwe, the governor general of Nigeria. While at Lever Brothers, Holte had used his association with Azikiwe and other African leaders to improve the company's image among the people of West Africa. Thus, when Holte applied for the BBDO position, his experience and international contacts successfully elevated him over the other applicants.[53]

It is worth mentioning that the historical record is silent as to whether or not David Sullivan applied for the historic opening at BBDO. Both he and the agency were in New York, and Sullivan had enough connections in the industry to have been aware of the opening. Also, his trade journal articles and conference presentations would have at least made BBDO executives aware of his involvement in the Negro market.

In contrast to Evans's hiring at Arthur Meyerhoff in Chicago, Holte's appointment attracted significant attention from the advertising trade

Figure 10. Clarence Holte, the "Jackie Robinson" of the advertising industry. "Clients Seek Advice on Negro Market," *Sponsor* (July 25, 1966): 40.

press and black newspapers. Several factors played into the attention paid to the hiring. First, company executives planned it that way by sponsoring a luncheon to which they had invited several reporters. Second, BBDO was one of the largest agencies in the nation, so what happened at the firm naturally drew interest from the trade press. Third, BBDO announced that it was not only hiring Holte as an executive at the firm but also creating a Negro Markets group under his guidance and development. Thus, in announcing both items, BBDO was publicly betting on the growth potential of the Negro market. All of this was an important break from the traditional agency practice of hiring freelance Negro market consultants to guide them on the market. Both black reporters and the advertising trade press warmly greeted Holte's appointment, and they quickly labeled him the "Jackie Robinson of advertising's major leagues."[54]

At the luncheon, Purchase introduced Holte and made a point of saying that his employment was a voluntary choice by the agency, not a response to outside pressure or social activism. "I'm not a crusader," he declared. "This is a cold calculated move on my part for the dollar sign only. I was not pushed. I was not shoved. I was only moved by the dollar sign. We feel that by taking direct aim at the target with a rifle instead of a shotgun we may be able to score more bulls eyes." In short, Holte was not a token hire, but the agency desired his expertise and felt he would make a genuine contribution. Still, Purchase's careful emphasis on the voluntarism of the hire suggests that, while he may not have been pushed, he may have felt compelled to hire a black professional. In the wake of the passage of Executive Order 8802, the state of New York passed its own fair employment laws and established a Fair Employment Practices Commission (FEPC). In the early 1950s, the state FEPC began to increase its investigation of charges of employment discrimination in the state. While no advertising agency had yet faced such charges, Purchase and other business leaders could scarcely have been unaware of their existence. Further, groups like the Congress of Racial Equality had recently engaged in street-level demonstrations in Chicago to press the case for employment opportunities. Thus, Holte's hire, while voluntary and based in larger part on BBDO's efforts to lead in the Negro market, may have also been motivated by other concerns.[55]

In addition to Holte's employment, Purchase announced, BBDO also planned to add 450 black families to its national consumer panel of 3,000 families. These families were the basis for Holte to compile research information on the tastes and purchasing habits of black consumers. Purchase concluded by noting that BBDO sought nothing less than to become the leading agency for the Negro market, a goal to which Holte's appointment was only the first step.[56]

Despite the less-than-altruistic reasons behind Holte's appointment, several writers in the advertising press viewed it as evidence that agencies were opening their doors to African Americans. Because the advertising industry was an imitative one—what worked for one agency or advertisement was likely to be copied by others—reporters assumed that other agencies would follow by developing Negro market divisions. This assessment proved wrong. Although more blacks eventually joined major firms, it was not until the late 1960s that another agency created an office specifically to handle ethnically focused advertising. At the time of Holte's appointment other agencies continued to utilize outside black consultants when designing campaigns for the Negro market. As the decade wore on more agencies hired professional blacks into their firms, but only BBDO had a special division within the corporate structure.[57]

Reporters in the advertising trade press were not alone in their high expectations for the possible impact of Holte's appointment. Black reporters also viewed Holte's employment as a major step; a perception spurred in part by the fact that Holte's employment was announced in a manner that assured widespread coverage in the black press. The BBDO luncheon included invitations to representatives from the three largest black newspapers, the *Chicago Defender, Pittsburgh Courier,* and *Baltimore Afro-American.* Accordingly, the three papers simultaneously announced BBDO's selection. Headlines included: "Purchasing Power Recognized: Major Ad Agency Hires First Tan Executive," and "Batten, Barton, Durstine and Osborne [*sic.*] Makes a Really Sound Move." To reporters, Holte's appointment was clear evidence of the growing respect for black consumers and their purchasing power—a point of no small concern to black publishers. Moreover, the employment of a black man in an executive capacity at a major agency was viewed as evidence of a growing racial diversity within the advertising industry. One year later editors of the *Chicago Defender* placed BBDO on their honor role for "extending the area of democracy" by employing a black executive.[58]

While all reporters saw Holte's appointment as a major step, one saw his position as having even deeper implications. Conservative black columnist George Schuyler waxed poetic about Holte having entered "the advertising Valhalla." Beyond the Nordic imagery, Schuyler viewed Holte as positioned to influence how corporate America—and eventually all of America—felt about black Americans. The client roster of BBDO ensured that Holte could present the value of the black consumer market (and blacks) to the executives of major firms. Further, he would be able to demonstrate the tremendous social and economic progress blacks had made within the preceding years. In Schuyler's estimation Holte was part of a "quiet revolution" that would "change the minds of the people who own and run America." Further, once minds had changed about blacks in an economic sense, that improved perception would filter to thoughts about blacks within the social, political, and cultural senses as well. "A man with a large Negro market for his high-class product is not easy prey for propaganda about Aframerican barbarism or impoverishment," Schuyler remarked. Instead, when people saw blacks as good customers, he assumed that they would eventually begin to view them as good and equal citizens as well.[59]

As the public attention calmed, Holte began his work at BBDO. He crafted campaigns directed at the Negro market, hosted leaders from Africa, appeared at various conferences, and wrote articles for the sales and advertising press. In addition, on occasion he represented BBDO clients in their negotiations for development in West African nations. He was also a member of the NAMD, at one point sitting on the executive board. Because of his status at BBDO and the research information his department generated, Holte's opinions appeared in nearly every major article on the Negro market published during the mid- to late 1950s. Thus, his was a very public position that garnered attention from those both inside and outside of the advertising industry. Holte recognized the importance of his position as well, and he knew that in some ways the future of blacks in the advertising industry—at BBDO and elsewhere—depended on his performance. Holte clearly realized that he was one of the first blacks in any agency with the decision-making power to shift the approach to the Negro market. He used that influence to urge clients to deal with blacks in a more respectful manner and to encourage agencies and their clients to hire more black specialists and representatives. Echoing the arguments of others active in promoting the black consumer market, Holte argued that if more blacks were involved in the creation of advertising, then the traditional approach to black consumers would eventually change for the better.[60]

Holte was intimately familiar with the manner in which black consumers were approached in the past. As both sales representative and black consumer, he knew of the negative and stereotypical representations commonly used in advertisements. So he actively used his position within BBDO to strive to change the perception of the Negro market and how blacks were depicted both within the agency and among the firm's clients. He and his staff were consulted on BBDO campaigns to the Negro market, ensuring that the ads used suitable imagery and struck the proper tone to attract rather than repel black consumers. An avid collector of books on African and African American history, amassing over seven thousand by the end of his life, Holte drew on these materials to craft advertisements that brought attention to the positive contributions of blacks. One award winning series, "Ingenious Americans," developed for Calvert Distillers, called attention to the contributions blacks had made that were ignored by textbooks, including the work of Benjamin Banneker, Harriet Tubman, and others. The series demonstrated a technique that became popular in advertising to the black consumer market, using elements of African American history in sales campaigns. This technique appealed to blacks eager to learn of their historical accomplishments, and it gave advertisers an almost effortless way to demonstrate their insight into blacks' role in America. Copies of Holte's series were reprinted and distributed to schools and community groups, and they performed the dual purpose of attracting consumer attention to the product and social attention to the historical information they contained.[61]

Beyond creating advertisements, Holte led the industry in the analysis of the Negro market. From the information he generated using the families in BBDO's national market panel, Holte crafted a more nuanced portrait of black consumer purchasing. In a 1958 article in *Printer's Ink*, for example, he anticipated two arguments that developed about the black consumer market in the 1960s. First, Holte argued that directing advertising campaigns to black consumers would not harm sales among whites. Not only was there considerable history of companies such as Pepsi-Cola, Beech-Nut, Calvert Distillers, and numerous others doing so with no negative impact, but statistical surveys supported that history. In the article, Holte described a survey completed among blacks in the North and whites living in both the South and North. Results showed that over one-third of blacks could name a company that gave some recognition to the Negro market, while less than one-fourth could not. Additionally, blacks often consciously avoided buying products of companies that did not extend such recognition. Among whites living in the South, less than 10 percent could name a company known for extending advertising recognition to blacks. Further, among that percentage, less than half said that they would consciously avoid buying such a company's products. Among northern whites, less than 5 percent could name a company whose advertisements recognized black consumers, and less than 1 percent indicated they would avoid that firm's products. Holte concluded, "In short, the whites don't care, but a good many Negroes do." Thus, should a company have the courage to do so, it could confidently direct advertisements to the Negro market without negatively impacting sales among black consumers.[62]

Second, in the *Printer's Ink* article, Holte offered one of the first descriptions of socioeconomic stratifications within the Negro market. There had been efforts in the early years of the decade to present segmentations within the Negro market, but none had attracted much attention. Agency executives and their clients had enough difficulty accepting the existence of the Negro market as a true consumer segment; an understanding of more complex, smaller pieces eluded most. Holte argued that the black social structure was shaped like a triangle (versus a diamond for the general market). African Americans had a small upper class, a slightly larger (and growing) middle class, and a large lower class. Members of each of the three classes had specific purchasing motivations that could be tapped via advertising. Within the upper class, education and respectability were the primary characteristics. Members had attained high educational and employment levels but resented the impact that racism had on their social and economic opportunities. The middle group contained persons with lower educational achievements than the upper class, but this group had well-paying white-collar jobs. This subgroup emulated the purchasing tastes and lifestyles of upper-class blacks. The largest group, the lower class, was composed of working-class blacks with low educational levels. Members of this group were more likely to practice conspicuous consumption and were more product loyal than the other two classes. Like the middle class, members of this lower-class group mimicked the tastes of the upper class. He concluded that advertisements that indicated leading members of the community used a particular product would increase sales within the other two segments.[63]

Some companies with a lengthy history in the Negro market already utilized this technique. One of the most widely reported Negro market campaigns of the late 1940s was the Pepsi-Cola company's "Leaders in Their Field" program. Led by Edward F. Boyd, who had been hired by the company to head up its special-markets division, Pepsi designed the Leaders campaign to increase its sales and create a positive product image among African Americans. Rather than emphasizing price, which was standard throughout the country, Pepsi used advertisements to link itself to leading African American figures. The ads contained a large picture of a prominent black figure such as Ralph Bunche at work in his professional surroundings. The picture was accompanied by a description of the subject's achievements, with an emphasis on how he or she overcame discrimination. Below each picture was a Pepsi bottle, which, though never stated explicitly, implied that prominent blacks drank Pepsi. Though no study was ever made of the sales impact of the campaign, the company and the members of the soft drink industry considered it a success. Other companies targeting the black consumer market in the 1940s and '50s would copy the Leaders campaign and its tactics of "implied emulation" in their own marketing programs. Harvey Russell, former vice president of special markets, later recalled that the company's marketing program to African Americans was so successful that the company would later make efforts to distance itself from them. At a convention in the 1950s company president Walter Mack stated that the company needed to shed its image as a "nigger Coke" if it were to grow in the future.[64]

Holte's stratification of the black community challenged existing perceptions of one mass Negro market in which all members could be reached with the same appeal. Instead, he reasoned that agencies must recognize that what attracted one group of blacks might repel another. For example, the use of radio advertisements voiced by hard-driving rhythm-and-blues deejays might attract one segment of the black consumer market but not others. Further, he illustrated not only that blacks wished to acquire goods commensurate with their current economic level but also that they aspired to achieve a higher economic status. In other words, contrary to images of smiling blacks happy with their position in America, many blacks had unrecognized consumer aspirations that could be tapped through advertising. Holte's analysis helped initiate a discourse on changing the marketing efforts toward blacks because he credibly explained that black consumers were a more complex group than heretofore understood. His analysis also illustrates the contributions that he and other blacks brought to the advertising industry. They did far more than change the negative characterizations of blacks within advertisements, for they also provided a more nuanced and complex picture of the Negro market. Moreover, because they worked within the industry rather than as freelance consultants or publishers, they had no fear that presenting a complex picture of black consumers would lead to the loss of business. Whereas publishers like John Johnson had to be concerned that too complex a picture would lead to agencies simply choosing to avoid the market and his magazines, Holte had no such fears. Instead of simply placing advertisements where blacks could see them, Holte demonstrated that, to sell to black consumers, campaigns had to appeal to as many different aspects among blacks as they did among whites. In short, placing advertisements in black publications, while important, was no longer enough; instead, critical research and careful approaches were the way to sell to the Negro market. These suggestions were only slowly implemented in the 1950s. In the 1960s, though, they found renewed currency as black consumers began actively demonstrating that approaches that were once enough to secure their patronage were no longer sufficient.[65]

ROY EATON

Although Holte quickly became the most famous African American in the industry, he was not the only black professional in a mainstream agency in New York. In 1955, Young & Rubicam (Y&R) hired Roy Eaton, and together he and Holte became the two highest-profile blacks in the New York advertising community of the 1950s.

Eaton entered the advertising business with a list of qualifications impressive for a person of any color. At the age of sixteen he had simultaneously enrolled in the City College of New York (CCNY), where he studied history and languages, and the Manhattan School of Music, where he studied the piano. He was later inducted into both Phi Beta Kappa and Phi Alpha Theta (a history honor society) and he simultaneously graduated from both schools, earning magna cum laude from CCNY. Eaton went on to win fellowships to study music in Europe, win major awards in musical competitions, and teach music in the United States and abroad. After completing his studies in Europe, Eaton earned master's degrees in music from Yale and the Manhattan School of Music. But in the military he first encountered the advertising industry.[66]

In 1953, Eaton was drafted and for two years worked with the Armed Forces Radio Service. Responsible for writing and producing various programs, his duties brought him into contact with representatives from Dancer-Fitzgerald-Sample, the Army's advertising agency, and he learned the basic points of creating advertising copy. After leaving the military, Eaton came to a crossroads in his life when he realized that he was tired of teaching and that he could not continue to make a living as a pianist. One day, while listening to the radio, he heard a piece of music that changed his professional life. The song so intrigued him that he wrote a note to the network to ask about the composer and title of the piece. Fortuitously, instead of the network, someone from Y&R, the agency responsible for the piece, wrote back to Eaton with the information. Weeks later, while walking in downtown New York, he remembered the agency's response and thought: "Why don't I go up to an advertising agency and see what they may have for me?" In making this snap decision Eaton set in motion the chain of events leading him to a new career.[67]

Eaton decided to look for work at an advertising firm largely on the spur of the moment. Quite simply, he was out of work and needed a break. Therefore, when he looked up Y&R's address in the phone book and found that it was only a short distance away, he decided that he had little to lose by applying for a job with the firm. So, he went to the agency, filled out the necessary paperwork, and was granted an interview. The personnel director, Harvey Fielder, gave Eaton a cursory interview in part because it was a slow day and he was not occupied with other work. Additionally, he was undoubtedly curious as to why someone with Eaton's background (not to mention skin tone) was applying for work in the agency. Regardless of his reason for granting the interview, Fielder told Eaton that the agency did not produce music for radio programs but instead contracted the work to an outside production house. Therefore, there was no position in the firm like that responsible for creating the music Eaton originally found so intriguing. Disappointed, but still curious, Eaton asked "Well if you don't provide music, what do you do here; you have 12 floors?" After explaining the basic workings of an advertising agency, Fielder invited the young man to try his hand writing some advertisements. That weekend Eaton pulled ten advertisements from *Life*, wrote new copy for them and took them back to the agency the following Monday. His efforts earned him an interview with Charles Feldman, Y&R's creative director. Feldman then invited Eaton to try another practice effort, this time at writing advertising jingles. After returning with the jingles, the pleased Feldman confessed that he had an ulterior motive in having Eaton go through the extra practice efforts. "The reason I had you write the jingles is that, though you obviously have creative talent, if you were white you would have been hired immediately, just on the basis of the commercials you wrote. But I want a Jackie Robinson. I want someone who is not only good, but superior!" He then hired Eaton as a commercial writer to work on advertising accounts to the mainstream market and to write advertising jingles, making him the first African American professional hired at the firm.[68]

Eaton found success relatively quickly at Y&R. He crafted jingles for a variety of products including Chef Boy-Ar-Dee, Cheer, and Kent cigarettes. For Texaco he was part of the team that crafted the well-known slogan "You can trust your car to the man who wears the star." Also, because he spoke several languages, he drew on that knowledge to create foreign language ads. Yet it was his background in classical music that led him to bring a different outlook to his creative efforts. Eaton believed that, used in conjunction with the words of the advertisement or jingle, the music could convey important aspects of the product. For example, in one of his early efforts for Chef Boy-Ar-Dee, whose brand image was built around the authenticity of the Italian recipes used to make the product, he used music based on Italian folk forms. Thus the authentic Italian musical form supported the authenticity of the product. It was a multilayered approach to the advertising process that linked the art, copy, and music together. He argued, "Using music creates an attitude, a message, and a concept that gels with whatever the concept is that you want to further about the product." Further, "Music is its own language." Eaton used this outlook throughout much of his advertising work, but by far his greatest early success was in crafting the jingle for Kent cigarettes.[69]

In the early 1950s executives at P. Lorillard, parent company of Kent cigarettes, like others in the tobacco industry, were concerned about mounting reports of the harmful impact of tobacco use. In response, company scientists invented the "Micronite Filter" that, when incorporated within the cigarettes, lowered the amount of tar smokers inhaled. With the new innovation in hand, executives approached Y&R for an advertising campaign to reflect the new technology. The task for creating the jingle for the campaign fell to Eaton. He recognized the filter's innovation and he sought music to convey the sense of newness and creativity through the advertising. He crafted a jingle based on the modern jazz then being introduced by artists like Miles Davis, Charlie Parker, and Thelonius Monk. The words to the jingle said:

> Smoke Kent . . .
> Smoke Kent . . .
> Smoke Kent with the Micronite filter.
> It is the mild, mild cigarette
> It's got the freshest, cleanest taste yet
> It is the mild Kent cigarette
> Smoke Kent with the Micronite filter.

This music was different from anything else in use at the time, and it conveyed the sense of uniqueness inherent in the filter. The public response to both the product and the jingle was tremendous. A number of jazz musicians and deejays wrote to the company praising the song. The jingle was also replayed on radio programs across the nation. Eaton also later wrote a popular song based around the jingle. Executives at P. Lorillard were similarly impressed and increased the billings to the company by over $1 million annually.[70]

The success of the Kent jingle brought significant praise from Eaton's superiors and coworkers as well as attention from trade reporters. Shortly after the release of the Kent song, however, he experienced a horrific personal tragedy. Vacationing in Utah with his new wife, the pair was involved in an automobile accident that left his wife dead and him in a coma. After a lengthy hospitalization and difficult recovery, Eaton eventually returned to New York and resumed his advertising career at Y&R. Though he had been with the agency only a few years at that point, the agency paid all of his medical bills and kept him at full salary during his nine-month recovery. The young man was, regardless of his skin color, treated as part of the Y&R family.[71]

After five years at Y&R, Eaton took a post as an associate creative director at MusicMakers, a leading music production firm. Though he was loathe to leave his comfortable position, the new position nearly doubled his current salary, so he switched jobs. Unfortunately, creative and personal differences led him to have a short stint at the company. Eaton was the victim of office politics, in which his superiors took credit for ideas he had created without extending him due credit or compensation. Two months after taking the job he left the firm. Due to his reputation he quickly obtained a job at the Benton & Bowles advertising agency, remaining there until he left to start his own musical production company in the 1980s.[72]

Eaton recalled, "I left advertising [agencies] because the guys in charge were only looking at the bottom line, and they felt someone who could just administer musicians contracts could perform the job just as easily . . . They had a total non-recognition of what it was that I was doing."[73] Eaton worked in the industry in the 1950s, '60s, and early '70s, when musical artists routinely labored in the advertising trade and as professional artists. Like other musicians in the business, Eaton had written for his advertising clients and crafted popular songs. Although he eventually left the trade, Eaton was one of the ones who created a path for other blacks in the profession.

Although press reports labeled Holte as the "Jackie Robinson" of advertising, Eaton's appointment was no less groundbreaking. Eaton was one of the first African Americans to work in a mainstream agency on campaigns for the white market. Because Eaton was a classically trained musician with four degrees and years of experience, he worked on campaigns to reach the general market. When Eaton was hired at Y& R, and later Benton & Bowles, it was for his expertise and talents. Having a skill that was unique and needed by the agency insulated him from the glass ceiling experienced by other blacks. In other words, as a multilingual, award-winning, classically trained musician with extensive experience in both writing advertising copy and creating advertising jingles, he was not easily replaced. In fact, his skill and expertise allowed him to be "dictatorial" in his approach and demands of his coworkers. His musical talent allowed him to thread his way around obstacles that other blacks in the industry faced. Additionally, as a musician, being an African American was sometimes a positive factor. As a member of a group stereotyped to be musically and rhythmically inclined, Eaton was perceived as an expert. For some clients, if an African American musician said that a piece of music worked in a commercial, that was enough. After all, some reasoned, they certainly knew more about it than some "square" white executives from the suburbs. In short, Eaton did not find himself locked into the same types of creative boxes as did other blacks they entered mainstream advertising firms.[74]

Along with writing advertisements Eaton also appeared in them. In 1963, he was in an advertisement for Chemical Bank New York. Standing prominently in the front row holding a loan check, he was part of an integrated crowd of other bank patrons. As one of the first integrated advertisements in the country, the ad was considered an example of an acceptable way to use whites and blacks in the same advertisement. Additionally, the Mayor's Committee on Job Advancement in New York City gave the advertisement an award for placing Eaton in a conspicuous position in the advertisement rather than obscuring him behind rows of white customers.[75]

Like fellow black advertising executive Georg Olden, Eaton was also featured in an alcoholic beverage advertisement. In 1969, Eaton appeared in an advertisement for Gordon's Gin. Pictured in the studio at B&B, Eaton was shown directing the taping of a commercial. Above his picture were a list of his professional accomplishments as well as his product testimonial: "Getting music to sound right in a studio is a matter of getting a perfect balance of elements. The same thing applies to getting a great gin . . . a perfect balance of elements . . . dryness, flavor, the works. That's what I find in Gordon's Gin."[76] The advertisement, along with his other professional accomplishments, confirmed Eaton's status as one of the most prominent black executives in the city.

As one of the early black professionals in the New York advertising community, Eaton was acquainted with the few others in similar positions. He lived a short distance away from Holte, and the two men sometimes discussed the future of blacks in the advertising business. Yet despite the similarity of their own professional status, the two differed on their future visions of blacks in the business. Holte believed that for the immediate future the most opportune path for blacks in advertising was in selling products to other blacks. Further, he felt that special-markets groups within agencies were the only avenues for most blacks to gain agency employment. For if agencies were not involved with clients active in the black consumer market, Holte believed they would have little reason to hire black professionals. Eaton's experience of broad professional opportunity, Holte reasoned, was the exception, not the rule. In contrast, Eaton believed that blacks should operate throughout all areas of advertising. He feared that the continued expansion of special-markets groups would lead to blacks being pigeonholed into selling only to blacks rather than to the general market. This virtual internal economic detour would lead to a cadre of black professionals with limited potential for advancement.

The paths the two men had taken into the industry obviously impacted their viewpoints. On the one hand, Holte began his career as a sales representative in the Negro market. He had maintained a living and advanced professionally at Lever Brothers, while witnessing other Brown Hucksters advancing in a similar manner. Holte was among the first black professionals to be in position to be hired in a white-collar role in a mainstream company, and that experience shaped his outlook. In his lifetime a veritable sea change of employment opportunities had taken place for African Americans. Therefore, he logically extended the benefits he associated with Negro market sales work to his assumptions about future opportunities for blacks in advertising. In contrast, Eaton's education, intellect, and broad range of experience gave him opportunities that few people in the industry of any color could match. Those qualities in turn allowed him to work in areas beyond those of virtually any other African American in the industry and, like Holte, he extended his personal experiences to his projections for future black employment in the industry. Despite their ideological differences, though, the two men were active in efforts to expand opportunities for other blacks in the industry. Holte worked with the NAMD in this regard, and during the 1960s Eaton lent his knowledge and expertise to groups who sought to open positions for blacks in the industry.[77]

The experiences of Holte and Eaton illustrate the state of race in the advertising industry during the 1950s and anticipated the future questions blacks faced. Expressly, should they seek to enter the industry as an expert on the black consumer market or not? In the 1950s that question seemed impossible to conclusively answer. For an African American to find a place in a mainstream agency he (or rarely, she) either had to enter an agency with clients who had an interest in black consumers or had to have a list of qualifications and experience matching or exceeding those of whites. The problem facing blacks at that time is that there were few companies or people in either category. Neither Evans's nor Holte's employment led other agencies to establish internal special-markets units and few blacks interested in advertising work could match Eaton's qualities. As a result, the issue went unsettled. The number of blacks in mainstream agencies remained small, with most black professionals entering the industry to work on products or campaigns to reach black consumers. However, in the early 1960s, blacks slowly began to occupy more positions in mainstream firms. The highest-ranking black executive, however, Georg Olden, lacked the racial consciousness of other blacks in the business.

GEORG OLDEN

Like many others in the industry, Georg Olden did not seem destined for a career in the advertising industry. Born in Alabama in 1920, he was the son of a Baptist preacher and grandson of a former slave. As Olden grew up, the family moved to Washington, D.C.; after graduation from high school, Olsen enrolled at Virginia State College. After the nation entered World War II, Olden dropped out of college and went to work as an artist for the Office of Strategic Services (OSS). During his time at the OSS, he worked with some of America's leading artists, designers, and writers and made the contacts that opened significant professional opportunities after the war.[78]

Olden's graphic talents had always led him to spaces occupied by few other blacks. After the war he was a successful freelance artist and graphic designer. In 1945, he also participated in conference that formed the United Nations where he was responsible for many of the graphics that were produced, including maps and charts. Also, his wife, Courtnaye, was one of the famed Brandford models. Olden, a writer in the Urban League journal *Opportunity* argued, was a young man on the rise. He had flourished in his position at the OSS. So, when the head of the Communication division, Lawrence Lowman, returned to CBS after the war and asked a former OSS colleague for a recommendation of someone who "had a full grasp of the whole range of commercial art techniques," he named Olden.[79]

Working at CBS placed Olden in the unique position of being near the top of a new industry. Though at the time no one could have predicted that television would become the central communications medium throughout the nation and the world, Olden was nevertheless in a unique professional role for a black man in postwar America. He rarely had to get his work or ideas approved, and it was nearly impossible for him to break the rules of television because people in the industry made them up as the medium developed. In fact, in terms of television graphics, it is fair to say that Olden helped develop many of the rules. A former colleague recalled, "He solved many of the initial technical problems of presenting graphics and type on television. He invented many of the techniques that we used." Among the graphics men at the network, Olden was a leader. He was considered to have a strong intellect and, as one of his contemporaries noted, "one of the most fertile imaginations in television today."[80]

While at CBS, Olden was a successful and recognized art and graphics director. In his private time, Olden drew cartoons, several of which were published in the *New Yorker* (during which time he had dropped the "e" from his first name in order to garner more attention). He also had the distinction of being one of the first blacks featured in an integrated advertisement: In 1951, he was featured in the "Men of Distinction" series for Calvert Distillers. The series featured black executives and showed them in action in the workplace and consuming Calvert whisky in their leisure time. The advertisement featuring Olden showed him at work at CBS with white colleagues, in a position showing him as their equal, and at home sitting in a plush chair wearing a smoking jacket and ascot. Olden was a man for other black consumers to emulate professionally if possible, but, if not, then definitely in their choice of beverage.[81]

Aside from being featured in an advertisement, before leaving CBS Olden had shown no interest in the advertising industry. So, the record is silent as to why he chose to leave his position in 1960 to pursue work in an industry in which he had no experience. It is possible that as a man of varied interests Olden had simply grown bored at the network after having worked there for nearly fifteen years. Or, it is possible that the potential for a salary increase proved irresistible. Regardless of his motivations, Olden found agencies readily welcomed his talents. Within a few hours of making his desires known to a friend in the industry he had received offers from three agencies. He chose to join BBDO as the Television Group Art Supervisor. Despite the presence of Clarence Holte and the special-markets division, Olden appears to have had no connection with that group. Instead, he was involved in all facets of the agency's commercial production. His role gave him a degree of creative freedom that few blacks in the industry could match. He worked on accounts for clients such as Lucky Strike, Bromo Seltzer, Pepsi-Cola, Chrysler, General Electric, and U.S. Steel. Olden was involved in various stages of commercial production with few limitations on his involvement and output. The only other black in the industry approaching this level of freedom was Eaton. Yet even he lacked the wide degree of influence within his agency that Olden wielded. Both men shared the distinction, though, of having a level of skill, creativity, and experience common to few others of any racial persuasion. As a result, the two men had a level of freedom and access to the types of campaigns that no other blacks in the industry could match.[82]

Under any circumstances Olden was a rising star at BBDO. In fact he was rising so rapidly that he was actually recruited by other advertising firms. In 1963, he accepted an offer to move to the McCann-Erickson agency to become vice president and senior art director. He was also part of the agency's exclusive Professional Advisory Council (PAC). The PAC was a think tank, a "creative task force" whose members did not focus on single campaigns. Instead members moved among the campaigns being run by the agency and offered input and expertise as they saw fit. As he had at CBS and BBDO, Olden flourished in this position. He won several Clios (the "Academy Award" of the advertising industry) for his work throughout the 1960s and first prize in the Cannes Film Festival in 1967. In fact some have argued that he was the actual designer of the Clio award. He also repeatedly won medals from the Art Director's club of New York. Additionally he had several high-profile projects that occupied his time, including the design of the commemorative stamp for the Emancipation Proclamation. Among both his internal peers at the agency and external observers, his work was consistently viewed as outstanding, and he experienced all of the success and privilege that came with his position. An article on Olden in *Ebony* showed him living in an expensive home set on several acres, complete with a swimming pool, kennels, and private stream.[83]

Despite his executive position and the mounting pressure on the advertising industry to increase the number of black employees, Olden was not involved in any efforts to increase the number of blacks in advertising. His record on racial progress is in some ways contradictory. On the one hand, he was involved with the Urban League, designing the organization's symbol of an equals sign on a black background. On the other, he argued that race was not the mitigating factor against success that others claimed. "Acceptance is a matter of talent. In my work I've never felt like a Negro." His disinterest in race was not lost on other blacks who described him as arrogant and standoffish. One black contemporary argued, "He was not interested in being seen, identified with, or helping other black people in the business." Rather than emphasizing race, Olden argued that his success had come as a result of his talent and hard work. Therefore others, regardless of color, who desired a position in advertising, would have to exhibit a similar degree of talent, skill, and work.[84]

The factor that Olden overlooked was that his talent was combined with a degree of opportunity and timing that many others, especially blacks, lacked. In the early 1940s his talent had led to his position at the OSS. And, when the war ended and people returned to their civilian occupations, his connections from the agency led to the position at CBS. So, at only twenty-five years of age, with no experience in broadcasting, he was placed in charge of the artwork and graphic designs for a major network. From this position, talent and hard work carried him through promotions at CBS and to those in the advertising industry. Yet without his connections he may have remained an overlooked and frustrated artist.

Still, while criticizing what Olden could have done to open opportunities for other blacks, the precarious nature of his position must be taken into account. He may have very well been the arrogant and standoffish man some described, but he was also one of only a handful of blacks at CBS and later BBDO and McCann-Erickson. Certainly he was the only one of his professional rank at any of the three companies. A coworker recalled that at CBS Olden was one of only twelve blacks during the 1940s—and all of the others were porters. Olden had few chances for error. He could scarcely be the standard-bearer for racial progress when he knew that pressure for racial change might lead to his own dismissal. Further, in his professional life, he believed color had never been a particularly restrictive issue. "My own experience," he mused, "has been entirely removed from race." In some interviews he noted that his experience as a black man in the 1940s and '50s was unique and that perhaps he had been "lucky."[85]

Additionally, once he had moved into the advertising industry he was part of a culture that even at the time of his arrival had only just begun to employ ethnic whites in professional capacities. The racial tradition within the industry was primarily a White Anglo-Saxon Protestant one in which he was conspicuous by his skin color. But, his professional recognition never translated into him taking action on matters of racial progress; on those issues he remained silent. Admittedly, he may have envisioned himself as a leader by example. A biographical entry he penned for *Who's Who* indicated his outlook: "My goal was the same as that of Jackie Robinson in baseball: to achieve maximum success and recognition by my peers, the industry and the public, thereby hopefully expanding acceptance of, and opportunities for, future black executives in American business." Despite his seeming explanation of his silence on racial issues and emphasis on "leading by example," any appreciation of his arguments is limited by the fact that the entry was penned after he had left the advertising industry and fallen on hard times.[86]

Ironically, while he had long argued that race had not been a factor early in his career, it became one late in his professional life. In 1970, he was laid off from his position at McCann-Erickson, a move the agency credited to the economic downturn then affecting the industry. Olden rejected their explanation. He sued the firm for wrongful termination based on the belief that he was the victim of racial discrimination. The PAC that he had been part of had been dissolved and its members terminated. Some at the agency argued that the group was not giving the agency the return on the investment equal to the high salaries of its members. It "fell apart of its own weight," said one former McCann employee. In his lawsuit Olden did not contend the reasons behind McCann's dissolution of the PAC; instead he charged that upper executives had consciously prevented him from moving out of the group. Executives, he charged "managed to deny me, *because of my race* [emphasis mine], positions for which I was qualified. This made me vulnerable to dismissal." He argued that a pattern of discrimination kept him near the professional level he occupied when he initially joined the agency. As a result, rather than being promoted to an upper-level executive position that would have placed him outside the scope of potential layoffs, he argued that agency leaders purposely restricted him from advancement. The explanation McCann leaders offered was simple: Olden never requested a transfer out of the PAC into a position leading to promotions to the upper levels of management. The Equal Employment Opportunity Commission (EEOC) agreed with McCann that Olden's termination was valid and not racially motivated. Although the commis-

allowed that race may have prevented Olden's advancement, his
al dismissal was consistent with company layoffs of similarly placed
executives. Thus, while commissioners felt that the small numbers of
blacks and Hispanics at the agency was likely indicative of a discriminatory hiring policy, Olden lost his case. In the end, a man who had
claimed never to have been impacted by his race believed he had lost
his position because of it.[87]

After losing his EEOC case, Olden moved to the West Coast where he
worked in a variety of positions, including television director and freelance artist, until his death. He filed a class-action lawsuit against
McCann-Erickson on behalf of himself and other blacks who were allegedly victims of discrimination, but he was killed a few days before the
opening of the case. For one whose professional life had began with so
much promise, by the end Olden was largely forgotten by his contemporaries, and he died still bitter over his dismissal from the advertising
industry and loss of stature. A man who had once dined with the U.S.
president and designed images and copy seen by millions of people, he
reached the end of his life tragically in poverty, failure, and violence, as
he was shot to death by a live-in girlfriend.[88]

Nonetheless, Olden was one of the last black professionals who gained
his position in advertising before civil rights groups and government
organizations turned serious attention to the industry. In the coming
years, blacks would continue to be hired on the basis of their talent or
expertise, but their hiring came at a very slow pace. Although by the late
1950s African Americans had become more confrontational with issues
of racism and discrimination, the advertising industry avoided their scrutiny. Still, blacks' pressure on the television industry foreshadowed their
growing attention toward their image as represented in the media and
their impending attention to the advertising industry.

Advertising, Television, and Black Consumers

Television presented the advertising industry with an unprecedented
reach into the lives of all consumers. In terms of black consumers, however, the medium met with an entirely new set of problems. In 1951, the
Blatz Brewing company wanted to reach out to black consumers
through sponsorship of the *Amos 'n' Andy* show, a program about blacks
living in Harlem. Blatz executives thought they had a surefire winner on
their hands, given that the show had been an enormously popular radio
program for over twenty years. Moreover, the television program was to
be cast with black actors, rather than with the whites that had starred as
the voices of the characters on radio. Although company leaders felt
that a televised version of *Amos 'n' Andy* would vault them to leadership

among black consumers, the show ran into immediate difficulty. The NAACP openly criticized the Blatz company for sponsorship of the program. Though the group applauded company officials for reaching out to black consumers, they deplored the vehicle used. Walter White, executive secretary of the NAACP, called the show "a gross libel on the Negro and distortion of the truth." The show's portrayals of bumbling African Americans were heightened further by the images of sophisticated, attractive whites drinking beer on Blatz commercials during program interludes.[89]

The NAACP was carrying on a fight against the *Amos 'n' Andy* program that had gone on since the show originally appeared on radio. In 1931, Robert Vann, publisher of the *Pittsburgh Courier* wanted to have the show banned from the air. Also Nannie Helen Burroughs, head of a prominent school for black girls in Washington, D.C., argued:

Amos and Andy have piled up millions for two business concerns and two white men. Amos and Andy broadcast subtle and mischievous propaganda against Negro business. They tell the world that when it comes to business the Negro is a huge joke and a successful failure. Millions of children are getting their first impression of the Negro from Amos and Andy. But there is another Negro in America. Do the American people want to meet him on the air? He keeps a clean cab, does not steal money from his organization, is not a blusterer, a braggart, nor a sham. He has social standards and high ideals and lives up to them. He should be given the same "break" on the air that Amos and Andy have had.[90]

With several years of preexisting opposition to the radio show, NAACP leaders were disinclined to allow a distortion of blacks, even one that had existed for two decades, to transfer over to television without a fight. Leaders were concerned that the transfer from an aural to a visual medium would do even further damage to the image of blacks in America. Given the larger struggle against racism, discrimination, and segregation with which they were engaged, they did not want the most powerful communications tool ever invented to carry a negative image of blacks, especially with no programming to counter that image. If shows existed that "portrayed Negroes as normal human beings and as an integral part of the American scene, a series such as *Amos 'n' Andy* or *Beulah* could be taken in stride," allowed NAACP head White. The NAACP tried to utilize economic pressure to force cancellation of the program, but they lacked the critical mass to do so. Further, the show was defended in the advertising trade press as "a frank bid for the Negro trade" by Blatz and indicative of the desirability of black consumers to the company. Additionally, no major African American newspaper took up the issue and most African Americans were unaware of the NAACP's objections. The *Amos 'n' Andy* show remained on network television until

1953 and was then run in syndication with full sponsor support until 1966.[91]

The growing civil rights movement also brought challenging issues before the advertising industry. After the outbreak of violence in Little Rock, Arkansas, over the integration of Central High School, agencies became wary of associating client products with African Americans. For example, Pillsbury executives, although they actively sought help from Leonard Evans to develop the Negro market for their products, were concerned that too close an association with blacks would damage sales among whites. As one advertising executive commented, "If it gets out that we were pushing Negro talent on a Pillsbury program, the next thing you know, it would be branded a 'nigger flour' and it would never move." Advertiser fears over association with blacks were only heightened with the spread of television. The appearance of some blacks on some programs had resulted in newspaper petitions, boycott threats, and the cancellation of franchise agreements. Just as it was no small thing to integrate an office or restaurant, it was equally so on television programs broadcast into the private spaces of American homes. Advertiser fears of an association with blacks are best exhibited with the case of the *Nat King Cole* show.[92]

In early 1956, singer Nat King Cole became the first African American to have his own television show. The National Broadcasting Company (NBC) initiated the program as a way to give advertisers access to the black consumer market. The *Nat King Cole* show began as a quarter-hour program sponsored nationally by Carter Products (parent company of Arrid deodorant and Rise shaving cream). Cole's show was later expanded to a half-hour, but after its initial contract ran out, Carter Products refused to renew its sponsorship. Although the show found some local sponsors, no national sponsor was found, and the show was canceled after sixty-four weeks.[93]

The sponsorship difficulty faced by the *Cole* show illustrates the dilemma that advertisers faced during the late 1950s. Some companies, like show sponsor Carter Products, may have wanted to reach out to black consumers, but they feared doing so because of racial prejudice. Advertisers and agencies did not want to risk alienating groups of white consumers, and so they capitulated by avoiding most signs of African American use of their products in mediums other than those with a primarily black audience. So, while companies continued to run advertisements in black-oriented publications, they did so for the same reasons they had since the 1930s—profits and black readership. Therefore, advertisers were sure that they would not antagonize the growing black middle class by not reaching out to them or fall prey to backlash from white consumers by admitting that they were doing so. Thus in media with a primarily white audience, blacks were invisible in nearly all advertisements. In ads where they were present, it was in the traditional role of maid, servant, butler, or cook.

However, the irony that *Amos 'n' Andy* did not have trouble in securing sponsors while the *Cole* show did was not lost on some observers. For over two decades two white men who pretended to be black were used as spokesmen for a number of products. *Amos 'n' Andy* stars Correll and Gosden appeared in character as the black stars and out of character as themselves and acted as spokespersons for Pepsodent. As television developed, however, live blacks were not used to sell any products, not even those who played the characters in *Amos 'n' Andy*. In a letter to the NAACP, one man reflected, "Isn't it strange that the *Amos 'n' Andy* television show had no difficulty in obtaining sponsors? Was it because the show low-graded the character of Negroes? As long as Negroes can play parts that tend to be stereotyped, everything is all right." Others wrote into NBC in support of the *Cole* show: "To coin a word, your show was super-sensational. Best wishes in getting a sponsor. If he sells toothpaste, I'll buy it. If he sells beauty, I'll try it. If he sells a broomstick, I'll fly it." In another letter a salesman wrote, "I understand that you've had trouble selling this show. Well, I'm a 'white' salesman myself and I just wished I had Nat selling my product for me. Everyone I talked to thinks he's terrific regardless of race or color. The ad boys are all wet on this one." Upon leaving his program, Cole argued that the problem was not with racial prejudice but with national advertisers based in the supposedly enlightened North and, especially, advertising agencies. "After all, Madison Avenue is in the North, and that's where the resistance is. I think sometimes the South is used as a football to take some of the stain off us in the North. Madison Avenue still runs television, and there is a certain amount of reluctance on its part to sell my show," he contended. Moreover, he reasoned that of all the sponsors that the program had on a local basis (Continental Baking Co., Gunther Beer, Folgers Coffee, Rival Dog Food, Weidman Brewing, Gold Brand Beer, Commercial Solvents, Wilen Wine, Swan Cleaners, and Coca-Cola), none had lost any sales in any region of the country. "Ad Alley thinks it's still a white man's world," Cole observed. "The Nat King Cole show put the spotlight on them. It proved who dictates what is seen on TV: New Yorkers and particularly Madison Avenue."[94]

Conclusion

Although the struggles to end the *Amos 'n' Andy* television program and to find sponsors for the Cole show failed, they foreshadowed developments in the coming decade. The twin struggles anticipated the pressure that blacks would soon bring to bear on the nation's communications and image-producing industries. Nightly advertisements and television programs continually illustrated to blacks the disparity between their lives and those of others. Moreover, as employment options opened for blacks, on a daily basis they saw the contrasts between their communities and those of their white contemporaries. "A Negro laborer living in Harlem and rarely peering beyond the boundaries of his ghetto might be reasonably content; but if he gets a good job downtown, mixes with white people on a more or less equal basis and then in the evening is forced to go home to a miserable house in Harlem, he will be bitterly discontented."[95] Simply put, the black population and black consumers were increasingly resistant to the traditional approach to them. Instead, blacks wanted realistic portrayals of both who they were and of who they aspired to be. Advertising agencies, though, were reluctant to provide this recognition in fear of what it might do to the brand identification of their products. Still, social and legislative developments provided blacks with the foundation to mount an offensive against the advertising industry.

The wartime FEPC set the stage for individual states to pass fair employment legislation. Additionally, the integration forced by FEPC considerations proved that whites and blacks could work side by side without violent results and that existing presumptions about blacks' technical or professional work were wrong.[96]

In terms of hiring, it is evident that advertising agencies were not going to change their practices without pressure. Of course men like Eaton or Olden might be hired, for they had talents that exceeded those of most agency applicants of any color. Or, an agency might follow the lead of corporations and hire blacks like Holte for clients interested in the black consumer market. But most agencies, like companies in other industries, were unwilling to take the chance of upsetting the racial ideals of either customers, existing employees, or tradition and hire blacks for professional-level jobs. In fact, when it came to hiring policies, advertising executives were no more radical or conservative than most white executives in other industries. In a 1955 interview a prominent management consultant candidly admitted that "most businessmen are not bigots, but they are cowards."[97] What that cowardice translated to during the postwar period was executives that protested that their firms practiced color-blind hiring policies in which blacks had to meet the same standards as whites. What that passive action translated to in reality, however, was few blacks in white-collar positions in mainstream corporations.

For blacks with hopes of developing independent advertising agencies, the story was somewhat different. The growth of the Negro market provided them with an opportunity to position themselves as "experts" and allowed them some entry with American corporations where none existed before. However, the majority of corporations active in the black consumer market either continued to favor the services of their major advertising agency, employed black freelance market consultants, or maintained a sales force of black men and women to help their sales in the black community. As a result, black agencies in the years following the Second World War remained small operations with few employees. In contrast to their counterparts in other segregated industries, such as insurance, black advertising agencies lacked even the possibility to become large firms with multiple employees and significant revenue and operating capital. Those companies, like Chicago Metropolitan Assurance or Supreme Life, could appeal directly to black consumers and be the immediate beneficiaries of their product choice; a person either sent their premium to the company or they did not. Black advertising agencies were no less reliant on the support of black consumer purchasing, but in most cases to reach it they first needed the support of a client (usually white owned) with the motivation to do so. Lacking that motivation, they either subsisted on local accounts, or in most cases, closed.[98]

Nonetheless, these agencies represent the first examples of the economic detour blacks faced in the industry. None of the agencies examined in this chapter appears to have made a significant effort to develop accounts in the general market. But that hesitancy speaks as much about the potential profits they saw in developing advertising campaigns to black consumers as it does the futility with which they viewed pursuing accounts to reach white consumers. Admittedly, four of the five black agency owners gained their first introductions to the advertising industry through segregated media enterprises; Sullivan and Evans at black-owned newspapers and Cullers at *Ebony* magazine. Also, Graham and Holte worked as Negro sales representatives for large, white-owned companies. Therefore, when these men moved into agency ownership, pursuit of the Negro market may have seemed the most intuitive and profitable option. Regardless, their experiences foreshadow those of black agencies during the racial revolution of the 1960s and '70s: black agencies that competed with one another over the relatively meager allotment of advertising billings for the black consumer market. Of course by that time the size of the black consumer market had grown appreciably larger, as well as the potential billings available to reach it. But as later chapters will show, at the same time, blacks' opportunities to develop campaigns outside of that market remained disturbingly similar to those faced by black agency owners almost two decades earlier.[99]

By the early 1960s, the issue of equal employment opportunity drew the attention of civil rights organizations. These organizations were key actors in changing the landscape of employment opportunity as it helped draw the attention of legislators as well as the American public. Additionally, their involvement evidenced blacks' changing definition of employment opportunities or breakthroughs in racial progress. In the 1940s and early '50s, blacks hailed the hiring of an African American in a white-collar position as a breakthrough. Blacks like baseball player Jackie Robinson or adman Clarence Holte were symbols of African American achievement and of crumbling barriers to black advancement. By the early 1960s, these hirings were criticized as "tokenism." Rather than being breakthroughs, blacks viewed them as evidence that companies planned to hire only one, and they refused to give the expected gratitude to corporations for having done so. Instead of accepting the hiring of just one black, civil rights organizations wanted more. Specifically, they wanted advertising agencies and other companies not only to hire blacks without advanced degrees or the ability to speak multiple languages, or simply on the same basis and with the same qualifications as white applicants, but also to actively find, train, or promote black professionals. As a result, true change began to develop in the early 1960s as civil rights groups and government officials turned their attention to the advertising industry.[100]

Chapter 3

Civil Rights and the Advertising Industry

As a people, we must remember that we are not as weak as we have allowed ourselves to be painted, and we are not as strong as we can be.

—John E. Jacob

For African Americans, the 1960s seemed destined to become a decade of momentous changes. Near the end of the 1950s, activists won victories in local protests throughout the South, and the Civil Rights Act of 1957 became the first piece of federal civil rights legislation in nearly eighty years. While this legislation lacked significant enforcement measures, it signaled that the federal government was taking the first halting and long overdue steps toward ensuring equal rights for all citizens. Alongside legislative victories, black students integrated public schools (sometimes forcibly); black families moved into previously all-white suburbs; and the nation narrowly elected a new, young, vigorous president, who seemed sympathetic to even further measures of racial advancement.

But these were not victories without cost or pressure. Blacks continued to be victims of racial terrorism and violence, and each victory they won came as the result of their direct action. Direct, nonviolent action was their tactic of choice, and marches, sit-ins, and pressure for legislative redress were the order of the day. Throughout the nation, African Americans organized themselves into groups to press for desired changes. American corporations and advertising agencies could no longer look at the civil rights movement as a strictly southern phenomenon. Instead, the pressure not only came northward, it soon came right into their boardrooms.

In protesting to receive equal treatment and to change existing practices, civil rights activists had more individual foes than allies. While racism stood at the root of much of this opposition, it also sometimes came from a general malaise or unwillingness to change traditional methods. In the case of the advertising industry, blacks faced entrenched ideology that said that blacks and whites should not appear together in advertisements. This kind of imagery supposedly alienated both black and white consumers and, instead, ads should separate the two races with ads featuring black models reserved for ethnically targeted media. In contrast, activists realized that, for whites to view blacks as equals, blacks had to become part of the visual consumer landscape that advertisements depicted. Therefore, not only did they demand more blacks in advertisements in general, civil rights groups pressed agencies and advertisers to place them in integrated scenes with whites in mainstream media sources rather than just black-oriented ones. Civil rights activists wanted nothing less than for advertisements to become tools in the larger fight against racism and discrimination. A writer for *Sales Management* observed, "For a Negro to see a Negro on television or in an ad is for him to see a visible man. And that has never happened before." What he overlooked in his otherwise perceptive analysis is something that activists understood and intended—whites would see that visible man as well.[1]

This emphasis on a black presence in advertisements mirrored the larger civil rights goal: that African Americans be able to be present in various spaces in American life. Black children and white children should go to school together, blacks and whites should sit together on buses, and they should work side by side at equal pay in offices and factories. Once those goals were reached the casual interactions between the two groups would help to break down historical walls of racism and prejudice. As those walls fell, activists believed that even greater opportunities for development and advancement would emerge. In this sense, advertising and media were another public space in which blacks challenged their current status. The pressure on the advertising industry to employ more blacks in agencies would help activists fulfill the goal of placing blacks in responsible white-collar positions with the power to influence change. Simultaneously, pressure on the industry for integrated advertisements would both feature blacks as a visible part of the consumer landscape and help change the negative and pejorative image of them held by some in the larger society.

This chapter examines blacks' organizational efforts to change the advertising industry in the 1960s. Three major civil rights organizations, the National Urban League, Congress of Racial Equality (CORE), and National Association for the Advancement of Colored People (NAACP), worked separately but almost simultaneously in a multifront attack on discrimination in advertisements and in the advertising industry. The three groups shared information and tactics among themselves in this common struggle in a way that allowed for more far-reaching victories than if each had been working alone. What they wanted was simple: expanded employment opportunities and a visible change in the way advertisements incorporated black models. Additionally, each group placed a strong emphasis on the creation of racially integrated advertisements in media directed at the general market. However, this organizational struggle against the advertising industry did not begin in the 1960s. Instead, the Urban League, CORE, and the NAACP built on the work initiated by the National Negro Congress in the years following World War II. What united these groups across the intervening years and across organizational lines was that each of them viewed advertising as a tool, a tool that could help change the negative image of African Americans and that could present them as equal citizens and consumers in the commercial landscape and thereby enhance their efforts for equality in America.

The pressure on many of America's largest advertisers formed a second but equally important element of activists' campaign against their media image. Like Claude Barnett and John H. Johnson, the civil rights organizations recognized that agency clients were the ultimate authority over the location and content of their advertisements. Moreover, that the largest advertisers had considerable influence over agency business practices. Thus they knew that getting the support of leading advertisers could give them more influence in forcing changes in advertisements and in agency employment. Specifically, the support of corporate clients of agencies prevented agencies from refusing to change based on fears clients would move their accounts if blacks appeared in their ads or worked on their campaigns.

An explosion in the number of boycotts and selective patronage campaigns demonstrated blacks' willingness to use their consumer dollars to achieve socioeconomic and political goals. These efforts greatly bolstered activists' appeals because they threatened economic loss to the companies affected and drew negative publicity against the targeted companies. This economic pressure helped to motivate advertisers and agencies to take action when lethargy or flat rejection had been their past responses. In fact, without the public and economic pressure generated by black consumers, it is unlikely that the campaign against the advertising industry would have experienced the success it did. Therefore, that activism is the first point that must be explored.[2]

More Than a Hamburger

In February 1960, four black students at North Carolina A&T University decided that they had suffered indignity and discrimination long enough. After days of careful consideration, four young black men gathered their schoolbooks, went to the local Woolworth's, and sat down at the lunch counter. They did not receive service at the counter, instead they sat quietly and completed their homework assignments; blacks could shop in Woolworth's but could not eat at its lunch counter. Within the local store, executives of the national chain accepted local Jim Crow practices that separated the races. The students' direct action at the lunch counter signaled that blacks were becoming more active and confrontational in their tactics, and their efforts encouraged similar protests around the region. As A. Philip Randolph had during World War II, these young activists perceived that real change would not come by waiting on government legislative action or a change of heart among their opposition; genuine change only came when they directly confronted the racism and discrimination that dominated their lives.[3]

The sit-in at the North Carolina store catalyzed activists across the country. It also aroused the anger of local white citizens in the following days as more students joined the protest. Whites routinely poured mustard, ketchup, salt, or sugar onto protesters, and jeered at them verbally in a pitiful attempt to elicit a response that they could respond to with violence. Yet, even under the painful and denigrating assaults, the protesters waited for service, sat quietly, and did not react to the taunts and threats. After six months, the lunch counter was desegregated and blacks could eat their hamburgers and hot dogs alongside other citizens. And with this move the young men ignited a sit-in movement that inspired students across the country of various racial backgrounds. Activists picketed national chains that supported segregation policies in their southern stores, eventually integrating hundreds of consumer spaces like Woolworth's.[4]

Black consumers in Greensboro faced a double standard; they could spend their money in some parts of stores but not in others. For example, in Woolworth's blacks paid for their store purchases a mere two feet away from the lunch counter that denied them service. In other stores, black shoppers could not try on clothes before they purchased them, as store managers feared whites would reject clothes blacks had worn even temporarily. In still other cases, blacks could eat in the same restaurant as whites but they had to do so in a separate section, usually cordoned off by a wall or curtain. Thus it was within these consumer spaces, where daily activities brought blacks and whites into proximity with one another, that activists launched some of their initial battles in the civil rights movement. Activists reasoned that in these spaces, the equality of dollars should have guaranteed equality of treatment but usually did not. For example, blacks did not pay a different price to ride the bus in Montgomery, Alabama, but they were forced to sit in a separate section or gave up their seats if there were no space in the "whites only" compartment. Thus, when blacks in Montgomery launched a bus boycott in 1955, they did so with the goal of matching the equality of treatment with the equality of cost. In Montgomery and elsewhere, activists used this visible black consumer power to compel change, on the local, and eventually national, level.[5]

While the black consumer actions in Greensboro and Montgomery drew more public attention, the selective patronage campaign in Philadelphia provided a different, but no less effective, model. In 1961, a group of four hundred black ministers in Philadelphia organized a campaign to motivate area companies to employ more blacks in white-collar positions. To describe the effort they consciously selected the term "selective patronage" rather than "boycott." Selective patronage, they felt, conveyed a more positive image because participants would continue to spend their money but would do so with selected merchants. Together the group of ministers reached nearly 250,000 people every Sunday, and they used their pulpits to inform congregants of the program. The local black newspaper also covered the effort so even those blacks that did not attend church services were aware of its goals.[6]

The focus of the Philadelphia campaign was not on securing general employment for blacks—A. Philip Randolph had pressed that case for years—instead it was about finding white-collar and executive positions for blacks. Additionally, the campaign targets included companies that had a history of soliciting black consumer patronage and of having open hiring policies. Also, by targeting companies in a northern city, the campaign brought the protest to the front doorstep of American corporations. Executives could no longer talk about the shame of the open racism in the South. The Philadelphia campaign forced company leaders to confront the hidden prejudice that singer Nat King Cole had argued was ever present in the North and had doomed his television show to failure.[7]

Blacks comprised nearly 30 percent of the population of the city but held less than 1 percent of the white-collar jobs in private industry. Leon Sullivan, one of the ministers involved in the effort observed, "You could walk Walnut Street and Chestnut Street in Philadelphia and you would hardly see a colored girl walk out of an office building with a job of any sensitive nature. Just a handful hired as tokens of some symbol, an effort of some company to appease its conscience." Ministers wanted real, lasting changes, and they refused offers that involved only a single high-profile hiring. They also turned down company executives who tried to mollify them by buying tickets to church fund-raisers or other kinds of "get off my back" contributions. Over a one-year period, the campaign targeted companies that had black employees in production areas but lacked them in professional areas such as sales or the secretarial pool. Companies included both those that had resisted similar employment campaigns in the past and those who had a history of actively courting black consumers. Thus even companies like Pepsi-Cola, whose policies had seemingly made them "friends of the Negro," did not escape scrutiny.[8]

In campaigning for professional jobs for blacks, the ministers emphasized that they did not want white employees displaced or denied advancement. Instead, they requested that blacks receive either currently open jobs or newly created positions. Some company executives initially refused to work with the ministers. But the withdrawal of local black consumer patronage usually convinced even the staunchest opponent to reconsider. In fact, most companies, especially those with a history of actively soliciting sales in the Negro market, voluntarily cooperated with the effort and increased the numbers of blacks in requested areas. By the end of the program, ministers reported that over one thousand new positions were made available for blacks throughout the city. Also, the success of the Philadelphia effort led to similar programs in Detroit, Baltimore, and New York City. What separated these campaigns from other consumer boycotts was that they sought to develop a specific level of employment opportunities. Jobs were certainly important, but activists in Philadelphia and elsewhere now pressed corporations to open opportunities for blacks to fill professional-level positions. In doing so, they targeted companies with a history of activity and interest in the black consumer market.[9]

But what did this developing black consumer activism mean for the advertising industry? For the industry, the new black consumer activism meant that black consumers had gone beyond accepting the presence of advertisements in black publications as motivation for patronage or brand allegiance. The Philadelphia campaign signaled to agencies and their clients that black consumers now took note of their employment policies as well as their advertisements. "If an employer has an unfair employment policy, and it's known to Negroes," Clarence Holte warned a *Wall Street Journal* reporter, "he can advertise, he can promote, he can do anything he wants to, and he won't sell merchandise." Harvey Russell, vice president of special markets at Pepsi-Cola, went even further in the *National Bottlers' Gazette*, calling a company's employment policies the "fourth dimension" of their marketing program. "Negroes tend to support companies which employ Negroes," he observed, "and no matter how great your advertising budget for a special market may be, you won't get that market unless there is concrete evidence that employment opportunities are available." Thus, blacks directly linked racially inclusive employment polices with favored companies and brands. As part of this broad quest for white-collar employment and for altered representations in advertisements, activists soon set their sights on the often-overlooked advertising industry itself. As one reporter observed,

"Though advertising has traditionally assumed that it could divorce itself from the nation's social issues, the Negro revolution has proved otherwise." To activists, the use of servile images of African Americans made advertisements a central actor in maintaining the racial status quo in which white society considered discrimination and black exclusion normal.[10]

Joining the Affluent Society

The pacifist but determined black protests in Philadelphia, Greensboro, and other cities were evidence of changes within the larger black consumer population. The black population rose steadily throughout the 1950s, climbing 25 percent versus 16 percent for the white population. Not only had blacks become more active in using their consumer power to press for desired change, as a market they had also become more affluent. The value of the black consumer market had risen, with estimates topping $19 billion per year. In terms of their location within the country, more than half of all blacks lived in 78 major cities and over one-third resided in the 25 largest cities in the nation. Within these 25 cities, black residents accounted for over 60 percent of all retail sales and 90 percent of all wholesale sales. Therefore, activists, Negro market consultants, and black publishers emphasized, black consumers had the market power to ensure the success or failure of many sales efforts. In short, devoting attention to black consumers through advertisements was becoming more than simply good community relations; it was becoming an economic necessity.[11]

The growth of ethnically specific media eased advertisers' reach into the black consumer market. The era of the black newspaper as a major ethnic advertising medium was over, but, in the world of print, *Ebony* magazine continued its impressive growth. Negro radio mirrored *Ebony*'s rapid development. Between 1961 and 1966, advertising revenue on stations programming Negro radio increased by nearly 300 percent. With over seven hundred stations devoting at least some content to attract black listeners, advertisers had many choices to reach blacks with the intimacy of radio broadcasts. A growing number of advertisers took advantage of this access to black consumers.[12]

In advertising agencies, the growing interest in market segmentation—breaking down the mass market into smaller, more efficiently targeted segments—established the theoretical framework for ethnically targeted marketing. Writers in the trade press argued for creating products and promotions to reach specialized markets and to create advertising that would tell those in the market why the product was for them. The wealth and geographic concentration of African Americans made them a textbook market segment, one that trade writers described as "the least understood, most controversial, and yet most promising consumer group in the nation." Thus the question of the day was, in light of the rapid social changes ongoing among blacks, how to successfully reach them as a market segment without alienating white consumers in the process.[13]

While advertising executives weighed the challenges of the increasingly vocal but potentially profitable black consumer market, activist pressure was unrelenting. Although protestors considered a company's profit needs in their demands, civil rights groups saw the ads as symbolic. Ads illustrated for blacks (and whites) exactly where blacks were not welcomed (or respected). Material goods and appeals to purchase the goods were symbols of where blacks stood in their quest for full status. As civil rights leader Ella Baker noted in the wake of the Greensboro protest, it was "crystal clear that the current sit-in and other demonstrations are concerned with something bigger than a hamburger . . . The Negro and white students, North and South, are seeking to rid America of the scourge of racial segregation and discrimination—not only at the lunch counters but in every aspect of American life."[14]

The Negro market that David Sullivan and John Johnson introduced to corporate America in the years following World War II was one in transition. The interpretations of the market that Johnson and other recognized market experts provided now included the kinds of nuance and complexity they had only hinted at during the early 1950s. "What Negro consumers want now is recognition of their humanity and an industry wide respect for the Negro image," Johnson surmised. "No Negro consumer asks for more; few, if any, Negro consumers are willing to accept less." Blacks were unwilling to accept advertisers ignoring their purchasing power or taking it for granted. Instead, a new, aggressive black consumer was on the rise. And this new consumer was "no Uncle Tom shuffling down to the corner store for grits and chittlins," but was instead "trim, well-groomed, and militant." These new black consumers wanted see their desires accounted for by advertisers, or they would use their consumer power to show their displeasure. Thus the new black consumer expected more than the traditional "invitation" to purchase a company's products represented by an advertisement in a black magazine or newspaper. Instead, black consumers filtered their actions through the lens of race. As a result, Johnson and others warned, advertisements now needed to position products not only as symbols of status but also of racial progress.[15]

During the 1950s, many advertisers and agencies assumed that blacks wanted to be white and that they mimicked whites in their habits and tastes. They had the same tastes and desires and, therefore, advertisers simply needed to use black media to extend them an invitation for their patronage. John Johnson had used this argument to significant financial success, but the model that had proved so profitable for over a decade was quickly becoming irrelevant. Now, instead of even implying the same advertisements could reach whites and blacks, or that changing the models from white to black was enough, he and other black consumer market experts urged agencies to envision a different black consumer model. As Leonard Evans caustically noted to a white marketing manager, "We [blacks] have no great desire to become white. In fact, we tend to have more pride than ever in being Negroes. Integration does not mean the elimination of Negro culture." Advertisers and agencies needed to adjust to the new sense of racial pride that blacks felt or face sales repercussions. Specifically, they had to accept that blacks' consumption of expensive cars or liquor was not indicative of their desire to be white but of their efforts to own the goods symbolically representative of societal leadership. In fact, it was whites who had ascribed a racial categorization to consumer product choices, while blacks placed an economic one on them. So, to whites, consumption of a particular product was as an indication of blacks' desires to be white, but to blacks it simply demonstrated their desire to be middle class. Johnson, Holte, and others explained that it was an appeal to these middle-class aspirations and racial pride that blacks demanded to see in greater number.[16]

Ironically, at least some of the discontent that African Americans expressed could be laid at the feet of the advertising industry. Through the words and pictures created in advertisements, blacks received a daily reminder of just how deeply their second- (if not third-) class citizenship ran. In an article directed to advertisers, one writer noted, "Every time you [advertisers] buy a spot on television . . . you advertise the benefits of white society." Advertisements provided blacks with a daily reminder of their forced exclusion from areas of American life, of what opportunities and choices were available unless you were black. So, while the ubiquity of advertisements made them below the conscious view of most whites, to blacks they were a constant reminder of their status in America—something no Cadillac or bottle of expensive scotch could erase. "Nearly any movie, almost any page of *Life* magazine, the advertising on the billboards and in the newspapers, most of what we see each day on television—all of these constitute a kind of torture to many Negroes. For they know that this, or something like it, is what awaits the American who is willing to work for it—unless he is a Negro. American advertising is responsible for much of the Negro's current demand that he, too, be allowed to participate in the fulfillment of the American dream," observed Myrlie Evers. Blacks, Evers and others argued, wanted the opportunity to participate in the consumer lifestyle inherent in the

American dream. "Negroes want to share this life. They want to join the affluent society, not overthrow it."[17]

Pressuring the Advertising Industry

The various consumer-based protests in the South and North caught the attention of market researchers. In 1963, the Center for Research in Marketing, a private research firm, conducted a study of the potential impact of a national black consumer boycott. After surveying 180,000 blacks in 15 states, researchers concluded that almost 90 percent of African Americans would support a product boycott if asked to do so by leaders of one of the major civil rights organizations: the National Association for the Advancement of Colored People (NAACP), National Urban League, Congress of Racial Equality (CORE), Student Non-Violent Coordinating Committee (SNCC), and Southern Christian Leadership Conference (SCLC). The study indicated that, given the success of local campaigns such as that waged in Philadelphia, a black consumer boycott nationally could inflict significant profit losses on a targeted company. This was a key finding for activists because it demonstrated that they not only could use moral outrage to foster their goals but also could use potential loss of black consumer dollars to compel economic and other changes.[18]

By the early 1960s, the advertising industry had ceased using most of the pejorative and derogatory images that had been popular in the early portion of the century. But rather than featuring more realistic images of blacks, the industry simply eliminated blacks from most of the advertisements in mainstream media, rendering them invisible. In turn, that invisibility helped perpetuate the belief that blacks were not equal to whites. As one black advertising executive noted, "The advertising industry did not create discrimination, but is one of the most powerful influences for continuing it." It was this power that activists expected to challenge and, eventually, change. Certainly blacks could open an *Ebony* magazine and see blacks enjoying the material comforts of the consumer lifestyle; finding similar results in *Life* or the *Saturday Evening Post* was nearly impossible. Those few blacks that were present in ads in general interest media were either sports stars like Jackie Robinson and Joe Louis, or unnamed porters or domestics happily serving white clientele. To replace those images, activists wanted representations of the broader spectrum of black life. Not all blacks were doctors, lawyers, or executives, but neither were they all butlers like Uncle Ben (rice) or cooks like Aunt Jemima (pancake mix).[19]

The push against the advertising industry was part of a broader effort for job opportunities waged by the major civil rights organizations in the

1950s and '60s. Somewhat like the Double V campaign during World War II when blacks fought for victory abroad against fascism and at home against racism, blacks in the industry would perform a double duty: An African American presence there not only meant more blacks in white-collar positions but that they could have a direct impact on how blacks were pictured in the nation's consumer communications. Working independently but almost concurrently, the Urban League, CORE, and the NAACP pressed the advertising industry and their clients for what they defined as appropriate changes. But they were not treading new ground. In the years following World War II, one civil rights group, largely defunct by the 1960s, targeted the advertising industry and other media trades for just the changes sought by those active in the current struggle. Uniting the struggle across the years were the twin goals of opening job opportunities for blacks in the advertising industry and altering the depiction of blacks in advertisements. So civil rights groups of the 1960s were heirs to the battle started by the Cultural Division of the National Negro Congress (NNC).

THE NATIONAL NEGRO CONGRESS

The National Negro Congress first met in 1936. The interracial group of organizers envisioned the NNC as the umbrella organization for existing groups fighting to improve blacks' position in the United States. At the first meeting over 800 delegates from 28 states and representing nearly 600 separate organizations met in Chicago. Future March on Washington organizer A. Philip Randolph became the organization president with the overarching principle that any single political faction should never dominate the group. Unfortunately, group members failed to maintain that principle, and a few years later the group became affiliated with the Communist Party. Still, in the late 1940s the group became the first civil rights organization the draw attention to the racial hiring practices of the advertising industry.[20]

By 1947, the NNC was an organization in decline. Regardless, enough interest and energy in the group existed to support the creation of a new organizational division, the Cultural Division. This division was part of a larger effort to foster black employment in the arts and to use the arts to improve the images of blacks to whites, which the group viewed as the necessary first step to changing their behavior toward and treatment of them as well. The group's Statement of Principles concluded, "For generations in this country, the arts have been prostituted to help foster discrimination, the dangerous illusion of 'white supremacy' [and] to make the Negro people an object of scorn and contempt. . . . It is to root out these falsehoods that we are dedicated." So, alongside the fields of music, radio, theater, literature, and motion pictures, activists focused on black employment in the advertising industry and their image in advertisements. In agency executives, though, activists faced opponents with entrenched ideas about the proper role of blacks in advertisements. "You'd lose your audience if a colored man appeared in the ad. However, in a picture of the Old South, whiskey ads and so forth, one puts in an Uncle Tom for atmosphere," one advertising executive observed. While the industry may not have been the bastion of "anti-Negro" feeling that some observers charged, it was one whose companies had seemingly little interest in opening their firms to black employees. The NNC's guiding principles focused on achieving "full freedom" for African Americans. That freedom, however, went beyond political, economic, or social goals to include issues of image and representation. Specifically, group leaders wanted to use the arts to as a way to eliminate racism and discrimination against blacks and other minority groups.[21]

Membership in the Cultural Division of the NNC included some of the leading figures in the artistic world of the 1940s. At the meeting to organize the group, over three hundred people wedged themselves into the Murray Hill hotel in New York City. As its specific mission, the division had a twofold role that future civil rights groups eventually mirrored: First, to increase black employment in seven artistic fields: music, radio, literature, theater, film, advertising, and art. Second, they wanted to change the manner in which each of the aforementioned fields incorporated images of blacks. For activists, artistic representations that featured blacks as objects of scorn and ridicule were too much the norm. But the group firmly believed the arts could be a source to motivate active changes, and they established specific goals to measure success. For example, members wanted a set number of black musicians employed in theaters by a specific date. They placed careful emphasis on reaching specific goals within a limited amount of time and on compiling detailed research information to guide their plans. To ascertain the status of blacks' employment in advertising, the division commissioned an industry study by the Biow advertising agency. Biow was also charged to examine the use of blacks in advertisements.[22]

Agency founder Milton Biow had a history of nondiscriminatory employment, but it is unclear if he had a prior connection to the NNC. Biow did not fit the traditional mold of an agency executive or owner. He lacked the Ivy League educational background, had no relatives in the industry, and when he entered the business had not even graduated from high school. In fact, he recalled that his only outstanding quality was the intense desire to enter the agency business and to find someone to give him the opportunity to do so. Despite his lack of a traditional education, Biow created one of the leading advertising agencies of the

1940s. Further, because of his own nontraditional entry into the industry, he established a hiring policy that interviewed people based upon desire and talent rather than racial, economic, or educational achievement. "My belief in giving Negroes the business opportunities to which they are entitled is not a matter of 'tolerance,'" he argued. "It's just a better way to do business. It gives you that many more people from which you can choose the best." Biow later worked with NAACP head Walter White to find black applicants for his agency, telling him, "Send me applicants for jobs and I'll judge them side by side with applicants of any other color, on their merits."[23]

Biow revealed the results of his agency study at a meeting of the Cultural Division. The finding that there were few blacks featured in advertising surprised few, but the study went further. Specifically, Biow concluded the low number of blacks in advertisements was due to agencies' reliance on "snob appeal." The emphasis on this approach led to an imagined world in which affluent settings dominated and blacks were little more than servants. This "white world" was one in which blacks had a specifically proscribed place and "that advertising, in its most representative statements presents a subtly biased picture of the world, the effect of which is to tell us, our children, and the Negro for that matter, of the Negroes second-class citizenship."[24] Beyond showing blacks in menial roles, advertisements failed to depict blacks as existing in even the most public scenes. For example, an advertisement set on a busy New York street included no blacks. Those involved in the Biow study did not expect that blacks would appear in advertisements in socially integrated situations depicting close involvement between the races. What they did expect was for them to appear in public scenes where their presence made sense. Where the NNC and the Biow study pioneered was in viewing advertisements as more than "salesmanship in print," but as a source of information and education that visually locked blacks outside American life and helped to maintain a discriminatory status quo.

Further, the study argued that advertising agencies replicated the white world depicted in advertisements in their employment policies. "This [snob appeal] has been such a potent factor in sales that the agencies have extended its use to their own mahogany-paneled precincts and to their selection of genteel, white [employees]." The Biow study was the first to make a case for racial diversity in advertising agencies and to estimate the current number of blacks in the industry. Across various advertising fields (including agencies, art service companies, department stores, and publications), Biow estimated there to be only a handful of blacks out of 20,000 employees in the New York advertising community. The *Advertising Age* report of Biow's findings erroneously put the number of blacks in agencies at 36. In fact, within advertising agencies the number was even lower. The Biow study found only 21 blacks, 11 of whom were messengers, clerks, receptionists, or janitors, spread across ten agencies: Biow Advertising, Chernow, Albert Frank-Guenther Law, Grey Advertising, Duane Jones, McCann-Erickson, Red-field-Johnstone, Sterling, J. D. Tarcher & Company, and Young & Rubi-cam. Only a few of the dismally small number worked in production areas, with the others in administrative roles. One was a secretary to an art director, and the remainder worked in various roles as assistants. Thus, the remaining number of blacks doing anything connected to advertising in New York City was 15. Biow's analysis was admittedly "incomplete." However, in decision-making or executive-level positions, it is likely there was no black presence in mainstream New York agencies in the 1940s. Laughably, and perhaps sarcastically, however, writers for *Advertising Age* hailed the report as evidence of blacks' significant prog-ress in advertising.[25]

To increase the low number of blacks in agencies, the Cultural Divi-sion crafted ambitious plans. Their strategy included: to establish a placement service to find qualified blacks; to set up a training program for blacks to gain experience in advertising; to publicize the advertising industry among blacks as a viable career; to maintain public pressure on the advertising industry to prevent discrimination; to award public marks of "honor" and "dishonor" for agencies' treatment of blacks as employees and advertising subjects; and to establish a code of fair prac-tices for the industry.[26]

As part of the NNC and an advocate of equal employment opportu-nity within his own firm, Biow could have become an important voice in motivating change within the advertising industry. Unfortunately, by the early 1950s, health problems forced Biow into a reduced role at his agency. He was the sole owner of the firm and, true to his organizing principles (that he always be part of any firm bearing his name), he closed the agency in 1953 rather than have it continue without him. As a result, blacks lost a potentially important advocate for increasing their presence in the advertising industry. Had he remained in advertising, Biow could have hired African Americans and led others to a similar path by his principled example. Still, Biow continued working on issues of employment discrimination in advertising and other industries throughout the country. In recognition of this work, Wilberforce Uni-versity, a historically black institution, awarded Biow an honorary doctor-ate in 1958.[27]

The NNC proposed nothing less than making the advertising industry more inclusive of African Americans and advertisements reflective of the nation's population. The group set an important model for future activ-ists in that they directly linked black employment in the advertising

industry with their image in advertisements. Further, that linkage anticipated that of the coming spate of how-to articles in the trade press about
reaching the black consumer market. Market advocates from John Johnson and David Sullivan to the men and women of the NAMD linked successful selling efforts among blacks to securing the advice of black
consultants. While their arguments were often more economic than
social, taken together with those of the NNC, they demonstrate how different, disconnected groups made parallel arguments correlating
blacks' employment in advertising and their image in advertisements.
Unfortunately, resistance to change and outside pressure limited the
impact of the NNC efforts. Further, as a group, the larger NNC was
weakened by the allegations of communism that had dogged the group
for several years. When that pressure exploded in the McCarthy witch-
hunts of the 1950s, the group disbanded.[28]

Following the demise of the NNC, the fight for black employment and
representation in advertising lay dormant for much of the 1950s. In the
early 1960s, led initially by the National Urban League, civil rights
groups began building on the framework set by the NNC. Although
there were no evident connections between the organizations, the goals
of the Urban League, as well as those of CORE and the NAACP, greatly
reflected those established by the NNC.

RENEWING THE FIGHT: THE URBAN LEAGUE

By the early 1960s, the Urban League had been active in issues of black
employment for several decades. Working primarily through its local
chapters, the group effectively waged protests for employment opportunities. Although their victories did not often gain national attention,
they were, nonetheless, important steps toward ending employment discrimination. Also, in the 1940s, one chapter actively campaigned against
the negative and derogatory images of blacks. An article in *Business Week*
on the Los Angeles chapter described it as "an organization set up to
guide advertisers and advertising agencies in their treatment of Negroes
in copy, pictures, package labels, trademarks and radio programs."
Floyd Covington, executive secretary of the Los Angeles chapter, inter-
mittently acted as an adviser for local companies by examining their
advertising copy for images and phrases offensive to blacks. Further, he
played an active role in convincing a local baking company to target the
Negro market by hiring black sales agents. Despite the limited success of
Covington and the Los Angeles chapter, by the 1960s League pressure
on the advertising industry had shifted east. Activists in the New York
chapter led the struggle to increase the black presence in the advertising
industry. In contrast to the future efforts of the CORE and the NAACP,

the Urban League focused solely on the issue of black employment in the industry.[29]

In 1963, the Urban League of Greater New York released the findings of a three-year study of the hiring practices of the ten largest New York-based advertising firms: J. Walter Thompson; McCann-Erickson; Young & Rubicam; Batten, Barton, Durstine and Osborn; Ted Bates and Company; Foote, Cone & Belding; Benton & Bowles; Compton Advertising; Grey Advertising; and Kenyon and Eckhardt. These ten agencies employed more than twenty thousand people combined, but fewer than twenty-five blacks were in "creative or executive positions." In fact, three unnamed agencies employed over one-fourth of all the blacks that held these positions. Also, over one-third of the top-ranking blacks worked in areas related to the Negro market, a practice the League frowned upon. To them, restricting blacks to accounts directed at black consumers was "a form of segregated integration." Consequently, the League made two demands: First, they wanted agencies to work proactively and increase the number of blacks in more than menial positions. Second, they wanted agency leaders to guarantee that blacks would be able to participate throughout the agency structure, including working on campaigns designed for white consumers as well as black ones.[30]

Although Urban League members viewed special-markets work negatively, some black admen disagreed. For example, both former agency owner David Sullivan and Clarence Holte, head of BBDO's special-markets group, argued that working on the Negro market was an opportunity for black professionals. Sullivan had long believed that special markets work was not a mark of discrimination, but, instead, was valuable recognition of the unique attributes of black consumers. Echoing Sullivan, Holte argued that special-markets groups were a way to generate black employment in the industry. Moreover, if done appropriately, this targeted advertising responded to the desires and aspirations of the black community. To Sullivan, blacks working in special markets helped create campaigns that gave black consumers a sense of belonging and of being "a recognized member of society." Hence instead of being the "segregated integration" the League charged, blacks who worked on Negro market campaigns filled an important industry niche in crafting effective campaigns and using images of blacks (albeit in black-oriented media) that were realistic and appealing to black consumers.[31]

Sullivan and Holte's criticisms notwithstanding, the League presented its findings to agency executives and advertising organizations. In response, the American Association of Advertising Agencies (AAAA) initiated an employment survey of all agencies with more than 500 employees. In contrast to the League's findings, the AAAA survey found 100 blacks working in agencies. While the figure was higher than that found by the Urban League, the AAAA survey also counted blacks working as maids, mail clerks, and janitors, groups the League had not included in its tally. With those numbers removed, AAAA researchers had in fact found few additional blacks in creative or executive positions. Regardless of the number, whether 100 or 25, it was dismally small in an industry with more than 20,000 employees in New York City alone. More importantly, it was not a significant gain from the number the Biow study found over a decade earlier. Unfortunately, the League seems to have been unaware of the Biow study and did not use its findings to demonstrate the slow rate of black employment in the industry.[32]

Urban League members had limited their study to New York City, surmising that, if the agencies could not find qualified blacks working there, they would be highly unlikely to find them elsewhere. But in reality advertising firms did not actively seek out black employees. The League knew that agencies did no recruiting on black college campuses, nor did they reach out to attract black applicants to existing agency-based training programs. Therefore, rather than simply listen to AAAA members opine about the lack of qualified black applicants, League members took the proactive step of forwarding the resumes of twenty-seven blacks with advertising experience to the AAAA with the expectation that the group would help the applicants to find jobs. But the AAAA considered only five of the men to have the experience needed for advertising work. When League members questioned him about the quick elimination of twenty-two candidates, AAAA president John Crichton protested the group had "gone out of its way" to set up interviews for the five that it did. Further, that, since the League emphasized positions in either art or copy, the AAAA eliminated any candidate that did not fit those categories. He did not say whether or not any of the other candidates were suitable for other positions in the industry, just that they did not fit into the aforementioned categories.[33]

Aside from professional qualifications, implicit in Crichton's statement was the centuries-old argument that blacks should be happy with what they got. Further, Crichton cautioned League members to lower their expectations because of the extremely competitive nature of the advertising business. Agencies, he said, often had more applicants than they had jobs available, and personnel managers could afford to be selective in whom they hired. And, rather than assume the race of the League's twenty-seven applicants had anything to do with the AAAA's rejection, they should recognize that "color is no barrier to talent" and advancement. Activists viewed Crichton's comments as specious and condescending. Although the industry was different, they mirrored arguments that League members had heard for years: color was not the issue; the number of qualified black applicants was the problem. In contrast to Crichton's assumption, the League was not asking him to find positions for which people were not qualified. Indeed, they argued that black hires needed exceptional qualifications. They knew that any individual black integrating an all-white environment would stand as a representative of their entire race. If he or she failed, they knew observers, though they might not say so publicly, would argue that it was because blacks could not succeed in accounting, engineering, advertising, or whatever the particular field happened to be. The League did not imply that there were legions of experienced African American professionals available. Rather, what they wanted was for Crichton and others in the industry to recognize the dearth of black employment as a problem and enter into a constructive dialogue on how to change it. Thus what irritated them about Crichton's response was that he seemed unwilling to enter into that conversation. Unbowed, they moved forward with a plan to approach advertising agencies directly and get them to either justify their lack of black employees or to hire more black professionals.[34]

Some executives retreated to the traditional argument that there were simply no qualified blacks available. Edward Stern, owner of an agency staffing firm, condescendingly noted, "I have yet to meet a competent copywriter or account executive who is a Negro. There just aren't any. I don't feel there would be any discrimination on the executive or creative ends. It's just a complete lack of available talent." The record is silent as to whether the interviewer asked Stern how many Negroes he had ever met. When approaching individual advertising agencies, the experience of chapter activists mirrored that of the average black applicant—a cordial reception followed by a complete lack of action. Executives were more than willing to meet with the League to discuss their concerns but not to follow up with concrete steps to address them. "All the agencies we met with agreed discrimination is wrong, that Negroes should be hired. And yet they've done nothing."[35]

Other executives professed that they lacked any personal racial prejudice, but their clients and white consumers were far less enlightened. One creative director observed, "If an agency has a bias, it's because the client wants it that way."[36] So "if" prejudice existed in an agency, it was in deference to the bigotry of others that they had to maintain their position on black employment. The shifting of blame and responsibility by agency personnel was maddening, as one League member noted: "Most advertising executives regard themselves as enlightened, thinking people who are above such primitive attitudes. For them prejudice is a psychological, emotional factor that leads to irrational acts. On the other hand, however, the same unprejudiced executives enforce a covert policy of discrimination in employment, because it is the custom in the advertising industry."[37]

Thus, according to advertising executives, the lack of blacks in the industry and in advertisements was due to three causes (all of which were seemingly out of their control): First, there were no qualified blacks available. Second, even if they found qualified black applicants, they had to bow to the wishes and desires of their prejudiced clients and white consumers. Third, the dearth of blacks in the industry was, as the Biow study argued following World War II, an unwritten tradition that, outside the case of the most superqualified blacks, (like Roy Eaton or Georg Olden), executives were unwilling to break.

Not all those within the industry found the League's charges of discrimination and prejudice unfounded. Charles Davis, a white agency owner, wrote to *Advertising Age* in support of the League's efforts. He realized that the most serious impact of excluding black employees went beyond the walls of agencies. In particular, he saw that a lack of positive and realistic representations of blacks within advertisements went hand in hand with the lack of black agency professionals. Incorporating blacks into the largely all-white agency world would be admittedly difficult, but it was a clear necessity. He passionately argued, "The hiring practices of a relatively small employer group are minor compared with the harm of systematic exclusion of over 10 percent of the population from representation or reference in most advertising purporting to depict American scenes. The public is thus educated to accept such exclusion as normal and proper, and group prejudices are enforced."[38] Whites in the industry had not created racial discrimination, but their hiring policies and the racial homogeneity that was present in their work ensured its continuation. As much as League members may have appreciated Davis's support, within the industry his position was in the minority. Unfortunately, among the executives the League met with, innocence and indifference were the common response, and no firm offered to change its hiring practices.

But the League and advertising executives agreed on one point: blacks with significant advertising experience were few. That part of the low number was because of the discriminatory Jim Crow hiring patterns of most agencies went seemingly unmentioned in meetings between the two parties. Black employment specialists did not have such hesitancy or myopia. "Do I think there's discrimination in advertising? There's discrimination under every rock," one specialist concluded. Still, rather than angry rhetoric or large-scale street protests, League members adhered to their traditional organizational practice of trying to work with recalcitrant employers: They encouraged agencies to develop a pool of black personnel, to begin recruiting black college students, to enroll blacks in agency training programs, and to consider offering permanent positions to experienced black freelancers. The results from this reasonable and organized program were minimal. Rather than finding executives willing to work out a plan within their agencies, the League met with the apologetic, but firm, argument that they would not alter their traditional employment practices.[39]

In response to the lethargy and disinterest they received from advertising executives and the AAAA, the League turned up the heat. They gave their statistical findings, as well as information from the AAAA and agency meetings, to the New York City Commission on Human Rights (NYCHR), the New York State Commission Against Discrimination (SCAD), and the President's Committee on Equal Employment Opportunities (PCEEO). They also sent the report to other civil rights organizations, black newspapers, corporate advertisers, and labor groups. On this step Urban League president Frederick Richmond said, "We have gotten nowhere after trying all the persuasion we could. It is now time for publicity and a little stronger action than persuasion." Like the NNC, the Urban League did not use the threat of boycotts or selective-purchasing campaigns by black consumers as motivation. They did, however, recognize the value of those tools, and they shared their information with groups, like CORE and the NAACP, that used them as part of their efforts to bring forth change.[40]

During the four-year period between when League members began their study of the industry and their public release of their findings, their efforts had frustratingly little impact. After all the meetings, phone calls, and letters, only one agency responded to the League's requests. Foote, Cone & Belding hired an African American into its research department. Unsurprisingly, one new black researcher out of twenty thousand agency employees was not something that excited League members. As a result, the League hoped that involving additional government and civil rights organizations in the effort would begin to catalyze greater changes within the industry.[41]

The broader civil rights activism that was part of the 1960s almost ensured that something would happen on black employment in advertising. In previous decades, advertising agencies might have been able to deflect activists' criticism long enough to avoid making any significant changes in their employment patterns. Yet what they found in the 1960s was that, as had been the case in Greensboro, Montgomery, and elsewhere, black consumers and civil rights organizations were willing to maintain their pressure until significant employment changes occurred. Hiring a token was far from enough to get blacks to reduce their pressure or attention. Although the members of the New York chapter turned their attention to employment issues in other industries in the mid-1960s, other civil rights organizations and equal employment opportunities committees filled the void. These groups, building upon the information they had received from the Urban League, continued to press advertising agencies to take concrete steps toward racial inclusion.

PRESSURING ADVERTISERS: THE CONGRESS OF RACIAL EQUALITY

Founded by a group of interracial activists in Chicago in 1942, the Congress of Racial Equality (CORE) believed in using nonviolence and maintaining an interracial membership. In a variety of local instances during the 1940s and 50s, the group demanded equal employment opportunities and fair hiring policies. Like other civil rights organizations, CORE's long-range goal was an equal and integrated society. CORE activists linked the program that targeted the advertising industry directly to this larger organizational goal. The national organization became involved in the effort at some points, but, like the Urban League, the New York chapter primarily directed the effort. Led by chapter president Clarence Funnye, the group launched the TV Image Campaign in 1963. Funnye believed that part of the resistance to black participation throughout American life was the popular image of African Americans that presented them as either a nonexistent or barely human group. The goals of the campaign included providing a true and humane portrait of black life, promoting racially integrated commercials, and obtaining jobs for blacks in advertising and other media industries. Like the NNC and Urban League before them, CORE activists consciously sought to use advertising to change blacks' image in the nation and to create a more favorable depiction of black life in America.[42]

Funnye wanted racial integration to be the standard in all forms of advertising. But, rather than spread their attention too thin, they focused on a single area for improvement—television commercials. As a communications tool, television was the most intimate medium available. Unlike radio, newspapers, or magazines, television ads had the power to speak to consumers and present them with a visual image. Moreover, in their short history television commercials had replicated existing advertising patterns and presented blacks with images of their exclusion from mainstream society. One observer argued, "When the Negro looks at your TV commercial for a detergent . . . he has one eye on your product, but his other eye is on the background against which that product is displayed. The dishwasher, the freezer, the manicured lawn in Westport, the crystal clear swimming pool, the power mower, and all the other paraphernalia of what is considered the good white life today. Negroes want to share this life." But, beyond sharing in the consumer visions displayed in advertising, activists wanted the secondary discourse of ads—the message behind the sales message—to communicate that blacks were equal citizens in America. In other words, like the NNC, Funnye and other CORE members believed that advertisements could do more than represent material culture and offer sales messages; they could also communicate the racial diversity already contained, yet overlooked, in American life. As black adman Leonard Evans critically observed, "You put Negroes on TV to educate the white man that the Negro is part of America."[43]

Before launching the Image campaign, CORE members developed an unscientific but dramatic experiment to illustrate the low number of blacks within television commercials and the roles they played. On a Harlem street corner, they set up seven television sets with each one tuned to the seven major New York stations. Over the course of six Saturday afternoons they offered a silver dollar for every black face (outside sports stars) participants found. After six weeks and hundreds of participants, they gave away only fifteen dollars. While the program was not a controlled study, it attracted the attention of the community and the media and gave Funnye a point of departure in the first phase of the program.[44]

In contrast to the NNC and the Urban League, CORE activists focused their efforts on the clients of advertising agencies rather than the agencies themselves. Because agency clients ultimately controlled their own advertising budgets, they had the final control over their agencies' output and some influence over television networks. Therefore, if activists were ever going to get beyond executives' arguments that there were few blacks within television advertising because clients wanted it that way, they had to work with those very clients. Further, as Johnson had initially done when soliciting advertisements for *Ebony* magazine, Funnye chose to appeal to the top executives of each company—the people with the power to make immediate policy changes. Starting at the top also ensured that CORE expressed its goals in person rather than in a memo from a middle manager's desk. With the results of the street study in hand, he initiated a round of meetings with three of the largest advertisers in the country.[45]

In the early 1960s, the largest packaged-goods advertisers in America were Procter & Gamble, Lever Brothers, Colgate-Palmolive. Together the three firms spent nearly $300 million annually for advertising and over $100 million on television alone. Funnye believed that if he could convince the largest advertisers to comply with CORE requests he would have greater success among smaller firms.

During the Image campaign, CORE had organizational allies among other civil rights groups, religious organizations, and labor groups. The hammer in their hands, though, was a series of selective-purchasing committees throughout the nation that the national CORE organization could mobilize a community against any company unwilling to work to with the organization. So, when activists met with leaders of these three large consumer-product companies, whose sales relied on black consumers' dollars, they stressed the existence of these groups so executives knew the potential impact of a refusal to negotiate. Moreover, the cohesive and effective selective-purchasing campaigns waged in Philadelphia and elsewhere strengthened the threat these committees posed. Although CORE did not lead these protests, their existence and success demonstrated their potential. Consequently, when activists mentioned the possibility of a selective-purchasing effort they were doing much more than spouting empty rhetoric; they were providing a tangible threat to company profits and public image.[46]

The first company to meet with CORE was Lever Brothers, a firm with a long history of black professional employees and of maintaining advertising campaigns to black consumers. In the late 1940s Lever had announced that they were expanding advertising in black newspapers. Also, the so-called Jackie Robinson of advertising, BBDO's Clarence Holte, was a former employee at Lever Brothers. Therefore, CORE had ample reason to expect more than just a cordial reception at Lever; they expected action. What they encountered were upper-level executives already prepared to address the goals of the Image campaign. However, not all of that cordiality came solely from egalitarian feelings in the executive suite. Both the Urban League and the NYCHR had already approached the company about their advertising program. So, when CORE activists reached the company, executives had already begun establishing specific polices about the use of blacks in commercials. Before hearing CORE's requests, Lever executives had directed their six advertising agencies to submit plans for a more inclusive usage of blacks in their commercials. The company also took the proactive step of publicly announcing their new policies so no agency executive could claim ignorance of their plans. The directive included not only the ads from Lever Brothers but also those of all affiliate companies. Yet Lever executives did not stop at these measures: they also told their roster agencies to develop plans on using blacks in commercials and to report on the number of blacks at their firms and any supporting companies they used. The agencies for Lever Brothers included some of the largest in advertising, so the impact of such a directive from a major advertiser reverberated throughout the industry.[47]

The sweeping Lever announcement signaled a new level of action and interest in black employment and advertising imagery among agency clients. Further it was a key public relations victory for CORE. Although Lever executives initiated their plans in advance of meeting with Funnye and other activists, reports in the trade press associated their decision to the meetings with CORE. Thus CORE was given credit beyond that which it may have deserved. Regardless, the front-page coverage of the meeting in the trade press and Lever's response served as immediate evidence that, as Funnye and others originally hypothesized, the actions of major advertisers could cause a powerful ripple effect of change among advertising agencies and other major advertisers.[48]

The first racially integrated Lever commercials appeared a few months after the initial announcement. Television host Art Linkletter asked a black woman in his studio audience about using a Lever detergent to take care of her family's laundry. He did not ask her for political commentary, a stance on civil rights, or any other potentially controversial matter, he asked for a simple testimonial about the product. This was exactly the representation that CORE could accept and that Lever executives wanted. It was a depiction of a naturally integrated scene and the black woman had a key role in the commercial. As one Lever executive noted, the firm wanted to use blacks only in scenes where it was "natural, but not controversial." "We are not trying to create change," a Lever executive cautioned, "we're trying to reflect it." Undoubtedly relieved, Lever executives proudly reported that they had experienced no adverse reaction from white consumers. This was an important finding because CORE, trade reporters, and other firms monitoring the effort believed the reaction of white consumers to these first ads would likely dictate the immediate future of integrated imagery in advertisements. As one executive admitted, "Everyone is afraid of repercussions in the South and is looking over their shoulders at their competitors."[49]

After meeting with Lever executives, the Image campaign moved on to its other targets. In mid-1963, Funnye's committee sent a letter to Colgate-Palmolive chairman George Lesch calling the company "one of the most flagrant offenders" of racial discrimination in advertising. As they had with Lever, CORE asked the company to begin using more blacks in its commercials, black actors on sponsored television programs, and black models in print advertising directed to the white consumer market. In closing, CORE requested that Lesch make a "good faith" effort to achieve these steps within thirty days. Lest he fail to take their concerns seriously, Funnye stressed the presence of CORE's selective-patronage committees and the potential impact of a boycott by black consumers.[50]

CORE activists walked a fine line between presenting the selective-patronage committees as an encouragement to executives to change their policies versus a threat to intimidate those who resisted their demands. Funnye's actions demonstrate that he believed the way to gain concessions was not through antagonizing company executives but in steadily altering their view. Moreover, Funnye and CORE wanted integrated advertisements to be the beginning of a growing trend rather than an initiative that burned brightly in response to intense pressure and then quietly died. Like the ministers in the Philadelphia Selective Patronage campaign, Funnye and CORE wanted real, not token, changes. The ultimate goal of the Image campaign was that television, in commercials and, eventually, programming, reflect an accurate picture of the nation's racial diversity. Funnye reasoned, "What we want is for television to show things the way they are—all the way, in the shows and in commercials. We think it's unrealistic the way advertising is now. Now wouldn't it be nice if now and then on television a little Negro girl came running in shouting, 'Look, Ma, no cavities.' That's what we want; just ordinary things. We're not asking for anything revolutionary."[51] Therefore aggressively threatening company executives was a tactic of last resort. Instead activists preferred that executives listen and grow to understand the social and economic benefits of integrated advertising.

As they had with Lever Brothers, Funnye found Lesch and other Colgate executives to be willing to listen. Executives argued that, even before they had received CORE's letter, they had begun an internal study of integrated advertising. Further, like Lever Brothers, they requested that their agencies begin utilizing more blacks in their commercials. Also, they had increased their advertising budgets on stations programming to black listeners.[52]

The trade press lauded the immediate steps taken by Lever Brothers and Colgate. Two huge advertisers had agreed to take active steps to incorporate blacks into their advertisements and to go even further by trying to influence personnel changes within their advertising agencies. "[They] should be applauded and followed by other advertisers, many of whom have been dragging their heels," a reporter observed. Furthermore, if this new positive trend were to expand, "American advertising may, after all these years, begin to mirror American life reasonably faithfully, instead of presenting an idealized picture of American life as a handful of cloistered romanticists would like it to be."[53]

Funnye and the rest of the New York chapter were justifiably elated when the last of the initial three targets, Procter & Gamble, agreed to begin integrating their advertisements. In fewer than eight months the Image campaign achieved its initial goal—the three companies Funnye called the "giant killers" agreed to integrate their advertising. Also, each had gone beyond CORE's emphasis on blacks' role in advertisements to at least inquire about blacks' employment in their advertising agencies and to put some pressure on television networks to incorporate more black actors in their television programs.[54]

CORE used the momentum from the initial three companies to per-

suade other major companies to meet with them and discuss their advertising polices. In contrast to the individual meetings with the first three
companies, CORE now met with company representatives in groups
rather than individually. During these meetings, CORE described how
companies at the meetings used blacks in past advertising campaigns
and then explained how they expected them to use them in the future.
The leaders of some selective-patronage committees were also present
at this round of meetings. Also, CORE reinforced the impact of nonco-
operation with their goals. They ensured that meeting attendees
received results from the updated survey from the Center for Research
in Marketing showing that nearly 90 percent of blacks would participate
in a consumer boycott and that almost 10 percent would permanently
stop using the products of the company being boycotted. In response,
representatives at this second stage expressed a willingness to cooperate
similar to that of CORE's first targets. After attending the CORE meetings, representatives told reporters that their firms would begin to look
for more ways to include blacks in their advertising work. Perhaps even
more revealing, none expressed any sentiment that the group's objec-
tives were excessive or would be difficult to implement.[55]

By the end of the first two phases of the Image campaign, CORE had
met with representatives from thirty-six major advertisers. Companies
including Coca-Cola, Kellogg's, Gillette, and Philip Morris had sent representatives to meet with the group and the parties had reached a
mutual agreement. These agreements called for each company to begin
to integrate its advertisements to the general market. CORE activists
were specific that rather than seeing more whites in advertisements in
Ebony and other black publications, they wanted more blacks appearing
in white publications and on television shows. An agreement between
CORE and a company was not a written contract. Instead it was an
understanding that the company would begin to craft integrated advertisements within the CORE-established time frame of ninety days. During the ninety-day period, advertisers were asked to submit progress
reports every thirty days. CORE members contacted any advertiser
whose report was more than three days overdue and requested an immediate update. Companies fulfilled their side of the agreement when they
could produce either advertising storyboards or completed commercials
featuring black characters. While this did not guarantee production of
the advertisements, these agreements brought the issue of racial integration to the forefront. Moreover, the agreements were evidence that, on
the client side, the tide had shifted toward a greater incorporation of
racial diversity in advertising than ever before.[56]

In September 1963, forty major advertisers announced that they had
begun preparing integrated advertisements. The impact of the pressure

"Dig up <u>42nd Street?</u>"

Yep. We're digging up <u>42nd Street</u>. But only because we have to. Take a look down that famous thoroughfare. The UN stands at the eastern end. Skyscrapers line both sides. And renewal projects are changing the face of the West Side. All this progress brings the need for more electric energy. So, we'll be digging up 42nd Street, east to west, during the next few months.

We're bringing in new high-voltage cables to deliver more electricity to the new substation on W. 42nd Street between 10th and 11th Avenues. "Dig we must" for the growing West Side of a growing New York.

A big job like this is bound to get in somebody's way. But we'll do our best (and we've had lots of practice) to work fast and safely and get out of the way as quickly as possible.

We've spent months planning the job with City agencies, stockpiling materials, selecting the most direct route. We found other, narrower, cross-town streets would affect traffic even more. And along 42nd Street we can use abandoned trolley lanes to save time.

POWER FOR PROGRESS

Figure 11. An "acceptable" form of integration in advertisements, two men discussing street construction within the context of their daily routines. Con-Edison advertisement, *Advertising Age* (September 23, 1963): 115.

brought by CORE and the Urban League had clearly done more than generate meaningless agreements between executives and activists. In fact, things had progressed so steadily that Funnye optimistically observed that integrated advertising would become "commonplace by the end of 1964." While history shows that he was overly sanguine in this prediction, by the end of 1963 anecdotal evidence convinced Funnye and other activists that there had been a considerable increase in the number of integrated advertisements. In television, print, and on billboards blacks discussed typical consumer problems with detergents, toothpastes, vacations, or public utilities. With the successful second phase complete, CORE moved on to the next part of the campaign.[57]

During the third portion of the Image campaign, CORE met with the final sixty-four companies that made up the one hundred largest advertisers in the country. As in the first two phases, they largely found willing representatives. One representative noted, "Their requests are not unreasonable. This [integrated advertising] is coming, and you didn't have to go to that meeting to figure it out. The soaps [companies] have shown us the way; now for us, it's just a matter of when and how." Continuing their initial model, CORE secured agreements with the remaining firms. Importantly, during this stage executives learned that failure to fulfill their agreements meant direct action by CORE and that the organization did not play favorites among targeted firms. During a brief "misunderstanding" between the group and the Pepsi-Cola Company, activists began preparations for a selective patronage campaign against the cola giant.[58]

On the surface, Pepsi's actions signified that its leadership implicitly agreed with CORE's goals: They had a highly placed black executive, Harvey Russell, and a special-markets group staffed with black representatives; they also produced phonographic records on black history and funded scholarships for black students. Yet, for all of their support of African Americans and the black consumer market, Pepsi did not use black models in advertisements to white consumers. Although the company did use black models, they only appeared in advertisements in black magazines and newspapers. That segregation aside, what precipitated the present conflict with Pepsi-Cola was the company's failure to submit a progress report. In response, Funnye contacted company president Donald Kendall and set a deadline for receipt. This action was an unambiguous message that history had little to do with CORE's present expectations. In his letter, Funnye warned Kendall that Pepsi had two weeks to submit its report or face a selective-purchasing campaign. The matter never got that far. Within a week, Russell phoned Funnye with Pepsi's verbal agreement to use blacks in advertisements to all consumers and defused the potential conflict. Nonetheless, the developing rift between the two sides illustrated to other companies (whose history on black employment and within the black consumer market was often far weaker than Pepsi's) the seriousness with which CORE took their effort to alter advertising practices.[59]

The Image campaign was tremendously successful in reaching its original goals. Major advertisers agreed to begin increasing the number of integrated advertisements, and the campaign helped initiate a discussion in the trade press about blacks' presence in commercials and within advertising agencies. After the campaign's success with advertisers, Funnye planned to move on to advertising agencies to press for expanded black employment, which he and fellow activists knew would be a much tougher prospect. "We feel many companies will concede on the advertising issue. But such progress will still be only relatively token. Real progress comes with jobs," observed one CORE member. After gaining compliance from advertisers he wanted to use that power and publicity to force changes within agencies. In 1965, Funnye began conducting preliminary research into discrimination in the advertising industry. But, as the national CORE organization took a Black Nationalist turn in the mid-1960s, Funnye found his influence within the organization waning. CORE began to move away from integration and interracial cooperation as organizational goals, and organizational support for the Image campaign (as well as those connected to it) dwindled. Tragically, Funnye died in a plane crash in 1970.[60]

Fortunately for those interested in the issues the Funnye and CORE raised, the struggle for integration in advertisements and a broader black presence in the advertising industry had other organizational advocates. Alongside CORE, the NAACP also addressed the issue of black representation in advertisements. Further, it incorporated the original goals of the Urban League to increase black professional employment in the advertising industry. Thus, by combining the two goals into one organizational push, the NAACP mirrored the work started by the NNC as well as complemented and extended that done by the Urban League and CORE.

IMAGES AND EMPLOYMENT: THE NAACP

Like to the NNC campaign, the NAACP action against the advertising industry was part of a broader effort to increase the number of blacks employed in three media industries: television, radio, and motion pictures. Specific to advertising, it wanted to get advertisers and agencies to agree to include more blacks in their sponsored television shows and the accompanying commercials. Like CORE, the organization met with advertisers to convince them to use their power to compel agencies to include more blacks in advertisements. And, like CORE, the primary weapon went beyond moral suasion to threats of boycotts or selective-purchasing campaigns. However, in contrast to CORE and the Urban League efforts, the national organization, rather than local chapters, led the NAACP's program. Before meeting with representatives from advertisers or advertising agencies, it established a list of eight major demands. Of these demands, the one related to the advertising industry was the third: "Negroes *must* [emphasis mine] be used on television commercials." The NAACP initiative against the advertising industry developed out of this single overarching demand.[61]

In August 1963, the NAACP met in Los Angeles with 125 representatives from radio and television stations as well as advertising agencies. The media industries, it charged, were "flagrantly and openly discriminatory to blacks," and worse they had made "pitifully few indications of even token hiring." Roy Wilkins, executive secretary of the NAACP, informed the group that he expected blacks to receive the same opportunities as whites. Directing his comments to representatives from ad agencies, Wilkins expanded on the NAACP's initial eight demands. He asked representatives to return to their agencies and develop training programs for blacks and to increase recruitment efforts among them. He cautioned that agencies should not hire blacks as "tokens" or as a way to appease protest groups. Instead, he recommended selecting qualified and promotable hires. As the Urban League had done, he cautioned executives to either find already qualified blacks or to be willing to provide the necessary training but not to lower their employment standards to do so. "Hiring any unqualified Negro," activists cautioned, "can be quite as bad as hiring none. More importantly, it convinces those who want to be convinced that 'Negroes aren't ready to be advanced.'" Wilkins also reminded the audience that agencies had a responsibility to present a realistic depiction of life in and the racial makeup of the United States. Bringing more blacks into advertising agencies, he reasoned, would lead to reminders of the nation's racial diversity being present on a daily basis and that awareness would be communicated in advertisements.[62]

One month after the Los Angeles meeting, NAACP officials met with officers from the AAAA and representatives from leading agencies. The purpose of this second gathering was to discuss the specific issue of black employment within agencies and the images of blacks in advertisements. Afterward the AAAA agreed to assemble a larger body of agency representatives to hear and discuss the NAACP's concerns. A few weeks later the AAAA called a meeting of representatives from the fifty-six largest advertising agencies in the country. In front of more than one hundred agency executives, Herbert Hill, national labor secretary of the NAACP, charged the representatives with maintaining a vision of blacks lagging far behind that of the rest of society. He pressed the body to return to their firms and begin to present blacks in a more positive and realistic manner. James Tolbert, president of the Beverly Hills NAACP, told the agency men that their own apathy and prejudiced actions had led to the organization's demands. It was the "unawareness, habit, apathy and a few instances of out and out racial prejudice" that had led the organization to this point. "No segment in America has done so much to make Negro Americans the invisible men as the advertising industry." Beyond rhetoric and accusations, the NAACP presented the representatives with a five-point program designed to lead to increased black employment in agencies and better representations in advertising:

1) Recognition of "the simple truth" that 20,000,000 American citizens are Negro consumers, and therefore ads in basic media must reflect the fact that Negroes are represented in every walk of life. 2) Sponsorship of TV and radio programs and commercials that eliminate all racial barriers and permit the unrestricted use of Negro performers. 3) Ad agency employment based upon merit, with Negroes participating in on-the-job training and/or apprenticeship programs. 4) Use of Negro models in national and local campaigns for general media, not only for Negro appeal media. 5) Formation of a Four A's committee to help implement this program and resolve present and future problems.[63]

The NAACP designed its program specifically to force advertising agencies to become part of the "fundamental alteration" of the black image. While recognizing that only a limited number of blacks currently had advertising experience, the organization knew there were potentially thousands more with the desire and interest to work in agencies and in commercials. Therefore, it focused upon both training and creating positive images of blacks alone and in integrated scenes in all forms of media. Officials also cleverly placed responsibility for monitoring compliance of their demands at the feet of the AAAA. For that reason, if the program faltered, activists had a central organization to deal with rather than the leaders of individual agencies.[64]

Following the meeting, AAAA's president Crichton announced that several member agencies had already agreed to maintain antidiscrimination policies. However, as he had done during meetings with the Urban League, he cautioned the NAACP and other observers that an immediate increase in black employment levels was not possible. Crichton argued that the hiring of professional blacks in a wide variety of industries had made it difficult for agencies to find qualified black applicants. Although some agencies maintained an active recruitment policy among black college students, they were in the minority. Instead, he observed that most firms searched for black employees through the traditional channels of employment agencies or employee referrals. What he failed to acknowledge was that in the past these channels had located precious few experienced black candidates. But simple statements of a desire to do better were no longer enough to satisfy black activists, especially if they were accompanied by the protest that there were no qualified blacks available. Instead activists viewed such declarations as a preemptive declaration of failure before any program of remediation even began. Accordingly, as CORE had done in its dealings with major advertisers, NAACP activists insisted that their satisfaction was dependent on evidence of concrete action by the AAAA and its member agencies. Lacking that evidence, the organization would maintain their pressure on the industry.[65]

In November 1963, the AAAA held true to its agreement and invited the NAACP to address a body of advertising representatives. The occasion was the eastern meeting of the AAAA during which a special day-long session was held on the Negro market. The meeting was unprecedented and one reporter hailed it as evidence that "the color line has been irrevocably splintered in national advertising." While more of an overstatement than an accurate assessment, the sentiment mirrored that of other observers. New York was the center of the advertising universe and, accordingly, the eastern meeting was the largest regional assembly held in the country. Placing the Negro market as the subject of a keynote session at the meeting conveyed the importance of the subject and Wilkins's presence demonstrated how seriously the NAACP viewed the meeting.[66]

Wilkins was the keynote speaker for the eastern conference, and two advertising executives joined him on the dais. Wilkins painted a picture of the black community seething in disillusionment and anger over the current conditions and slow pace of change in America. However, Wilkins did more than just describe current conditions: he laid the responsibility for the white perception of blacks and resistance to granting them full equality at the feet of the communications industries. Part of what blacks were struggling to alter was the "white man's image of the Negro" as lazy, morally deficient, ignorant, or happy with his current status in America. "What we in the Negro protest movement ask is realistic treatment of the Negro in the roles he actually plays in American life today. Only recently, and still too rarely, has the viewer of television commercials had any reason to believe that the United States is populated by any persons other than White Anglo-Saxon Protestants . . . Only when one turns to *Ebony* magazine or to the Negro newspapers is one made aware of the existence of Negro consumers," Wilkins asserted. He challenged the gathered body to return to their agencies and change their current depiction of blacks. Reinforcing the NAACP's prior list of demands, he urged them to place ads featuring blacks in both white and black publications. This subtle but important action would fulfill the corporate goal of revenue generation and of black consumers' demands for evidence of change and of a desire to see a realistic image of them as a people. "Not all [are] doctors and lawyers and businessmen, to be sure. But, also, not all [are] menials and clowns and criminals." Further, opening employment opportunities for black models and others connected to advertising production work would lead to more disposable income in the general economy. "Negroes," he observed, "do not enjoy a reputation as hoarders of money." Thus more jobs for blacks meant more spending power for goods and more purchases of goods meant more jobs for all American workers. To Wilkins, employing more African Americans not only made good social sense but good economic sense as well.[67]

In summation, Wilkins warned that the changes that he and the NAACP were requesting were nearly inevitable. So the actions of the people in the room could dictate the future outcome. Change could either come through summits and negotiations or through protests and pickets. He warned, "The NAACP and other civil rights organizations are prepared to mobilize the Negro's considerable purchasing power in the fight for jobs and freedom."[68] Black consumers were already consciously choosing to spend their money with firms that projected a positive image of blacks or had a nondiscriminatory hiring policy. All of this was without the direction of a national organization or structured boycott. What was possible with that organization, he implied, was even more dangerous to the clients of the agencies at the conference.

Other speakers echoed and supported Wilkins's comments. Each reasoned that advertisers and agencies should seek out black employees because they brought a degree of insight and creativity currently lacking in agencies. One white executive, from C. J. LaRoche Advertising, argued that blacks could help fill the overall scarcity of young creative talent facing the industry. "I often think what a matchless copywriter James Baldwin would have made," he mused. "Baldwin is almost the sum total of the good copywriters I have observed. He would have been hell to get along with, but my, oh my, what campaigns he would have turned out."[69] Not all aspiring black copywriters would have Baldwin's literary skill, he allowed, but they could still ably contribute to developing advertising campaigns.

Within a few days of the meeting, the AAAA placed a full-page advertisement in the *New York Times* with the heading "An Invitation to All Bright Young Men and Women to Consider Advertising as a Career." The newspaper's publishers offered the space free of charge as a gesture of concern for the racial crisis. Above the copy was a drawing of a group of young persons including a black man and woman. The copy assured readers that the only requirements for an advertising career were "intelligence . . . enthusiasm . . . common sense . . . and persuasiveness."[70] It concluded that experience was not as important as potential and that a college education was not a requirement. Over the course of the next few weeks, forty other newspapers reprinted the advertisement. The AAAA advertisement was a direct response to the session held at the eastern meeting and the agreement the group reached with the NAACP. Admittedly it was a passive step since it required people to contact the organization, but, nonetheless, it was an initial effort to attract black candidates to the industry. It was also the first time any advertising organization had published a recruitment advertisement featuring an interracial cast, and it was a small step toward countering the image of advertising as a whites-only industry.

One week after the AAAA regional meeting, the Association of National Advertisers (ANA) held its annual conference. Some of the largest advertisers in the country were members of the ANA, and the group discussed the issue of blacks in advertisements. Several of the gathered members had already participated in meetings with either CORE or the NAACP. Their consensus was that there was no longer any question about whether to include blacks in advertisements; the question was now how best to incorporate them. Executives from companies that had already run integrated advertisements spoke and reported no significant adverse response from white consumers. While the national ANA stopped short of taking an official stance on the inclusion of blacks in advertisements, the implication was that they supported the practice.[71]

Despite public pronouncements of support or plans for change, among major advertising agencies, the use of integrated scenes for the general market had a mixed reception. Most agencies deferred to the wishes of clients rather than establishing an internal policy. The CORE Image campaign was ongoing but the transition from an advertiser's agreement with CORE to a visible impact on its advertisements moved slowly. Some agencies, like J. Walter Thompson, developed a policy of actively seeking ways to use blacks in their advertisements with the only stipulations being that such scenes fit the needs of the client and be natural, rather than forced.[72]

Regardless of the agency, the use of integrated scenes held to the practice of avoiding intimate social scenes. Agency leaders viewed interactions between blacks and whites as acceptable as long as it took place within a public space such as baseball stadiums, airports, or busy city streets. Intimate social scenes in private spaces such homes or bars, especially when using noncelebrity blacks, were not. Blacks like John Johnson supported this approach. "To be believable," he argued, "you should not contrive an ad, you should not show as integrated something that is not. If it is normally integrated, then show it; if it is not integrated, then don't show it as such. Tell the truth." As the decade wore on, however, Johnson's arguments became those of the minority. Black activists began challenging agencies not only to use blacks in "natural" scenes depicting current reality but also in social scenes showing how things could become.[73]

Activists with the NAACP were among those who viewed advertising as another tool to speed African Americans' elevation to first-class citizenship. Carol Taylor, president of Negro Women on the March, felt that many of the new images coming from advertisers had not gone past the tokenism of earlier decades. She argued, "As far as I'm concerned, big business will have to take the stand that they should help lead the country, even in TV commercials. Sure they may find themselves portraying social scenes with Negroes in commercials that are not quite normal, but they should take a chance and do so." Harvey Russell, one of the few blacks at the executive level with a mainstream firm, viewed advertising as having the potential to lift blacks out of "cultural isolation." Advertising, if used appropriately, could present to blacks an image of the United States that not only included them, but also welcomed them to become a part of the national life. Advertising could improve both the white majority's image of blacks and blacks' image of themselves. As a writer for *Sales Management* explained, "For a Negro to see a Negro on television or in an ad is for him to see a visible man. And that has never happened before." An American Civil Liberties Union (ACLU) study echoed this point, noting that advertisements "should go further and portray the Negro not only as he is, but as he should be as an equal member of a culturally and racially-mixed society in which Negroes and Caucasians work together, play together, go to school together and live as neighbors." But social integration within advertising scenes was a powder keg with which no advertiser or agency wanted to experiment. Most believed that both whites and blacks would reject scenes of social integration, possibly even to the point of boycotting products. Consequently, what integrated advertisements appeared were carefully constructed in broad public spaces.[74]

The NAACP continued to monitor the presence of blacks in television commercials and in agencies, but, like other groups, found their attention drawn to other pressing social issues in the mid-1960s. Activists could hardly devote attention to blacks' representations in advertisements after several consecutive summers of urban riots by blacks fed up with continued racism and discrimination against them. In 1967, the NAACP issued its last major pronouncement on the issue. Leaders criti-

cized the continued lack of blacks on television, especially during programming with a high number of minority viewers. Although they
agreed there had been improvements, the current state of minority participation seemed little more than tokenism. The group concluded that
if advertisers and agencies continued to move at a glacial pace, the only
remaining alternative was for the government to become involved.
Beyond this final pronouncement, however, the NAACP's involvement
in matters of black employment in and depiction by the advertising
industry had peaked. In the late 1960s, the organization briefly returned
to the issue of blacks' depictions in advertisements, but this attention
never matched that which they displayed earlier in the decade.[75]

A View of Reality from David Sullivan

By the mid-1960s some advertisers and agencies had taken visible steps
to change the portrayal of blacks in advertisements, to develop integrated advertisements, and to increase their employment numbers in
the advertising industry. However, despite the celebratory pronouncements of the AAAA and other organizations, one man viewed the results
with a more critical eye. In 1964, black advertising veteran David Sullivan
wrote to an open letter to AAAA president Crichton. He sent copies of
the correspondence to Whitney Young, head of the National Urban
League, and Wilkins, head of the NAACP. Editors at *Advertising Age* also
printed a portion of the letter, but its unclear whether or not Sullivan
sent them a copy of the entire letter. In this bitter but heartfelt statement, Sullivan chronicled his own experiences in the industry. There
had been strides toward racial inclusion, he charged, but there was still
a long way to go.[76]

Sullivan's topic was black employment within the advertising industry,
and his central theme was that hypocrisy filled the advertising business
industry. On one hand, agency leaders complained about the lack of
qualified, employable personnel, but on the other, they refused to hire
an experienced African American. Sullivan had carefully followed the
developments of 1963, especially as they related to increasing the number of blacks in agencies. He owned one agency for six years, briefly
opened a second, and had once been a nationally recognized expert on
black consumers. But, when he closed his first agency in 1949 he was
unable to parlay his experiences into a job with a mainstream firm. After
looking for over fifteen years and distributing twelve hundred resumes,
he had only been able to secure one "nearly firm" offer. His lone offer
then vanished as the company hired a freelance black consultant rather
than bring him into the firm as a permanent employee. Although several in the industry had told him that he was a "better than average

copywriter," none were willing to give him a job. One agency executive went so far as to tell him that, although he was "quite sure you [could] contribute to any agency in the country," there were no jobs at his firm. Therefore, rather than finding permanent employment, financial necessity forced him to accept the role of consultant and freelancer.[77]

He argued that even for those blacks able to find positions in mainstream firms, their experiences were more difficult than those of their white counterparts. Blacks had fewer opportunities for job mobility, and they often had to accept lower pay. This was particularly troubling, he pointed out, because job mobility was a key source of gaining experience on multiple account types that led to promotions and higher salaries. Racism and discrimination barred them from the primary avenue through which they could increase their salary, responsibility, or professional advancement. Even those who had won awards for their work found their salary falling behind those of less recognized white employees. "My work salary range has been around $20,000, sometimes a bit lower," one of Sullivan's colleagues angrily recounted, "but I've seen my white colleagues go up to $30,000 with far less to offer." This experience, as well as Sullivan's own, was, unfortunately, far from rare. Instead, he argued that the experiences of some of the more documented and celebrated blacks in the industry like Clarence Holte, Georg Olden, and Roy Eaton were unique. Although Sullivan's experiences only represent those of one man, his story is instructive, whether or not his contemporaries believed his tale. He was an experienced advertising man looking for work in New York City, the center of the American advertising community, to no avail. Even more distressing, the reasons that he had been turned down by multiple agencies had less to do with his talent or experience than with his skin color. To Sullivan, the AAAA should do more to aid the multitude of less celebrated black figures, among whom feelings of frustration and disillusionment were more common than were ones of professional satisfaction.[78]

Sullivan's purpose in writing the six-page letter was not to lament his career, but to prod his recipients to further action. He feared that the AAAA and individual agencies would eventually fail to meet the agreement they had reached with civil rights groups or that agencies might point to the existence of training programs as evidence of their desire to hire more blacks and stop there instead of pursuing creative recruitment measures. Instead of passivity, Sullivan wanted consistent action. "To wave blithely at the trainee recruiting program as an action in being, at this time and tide of events is a travesty of the first order." He emphasized that agency leaders needed consistent prodding to increase minority employment. For they had the power to compel personnel directors and account managers—the front line of most employment decisions—to increase the number of minority employees. Should such action be lacking he predicted that public pressure on the advertising industry would increase. "In the circumstances," he concluded, "it is small wonder not that the 'pressures outside' have been put on the industry of advertising and marketing, but, rather that it was so late in coming on the one hand, while being as gentle as it is on the other hand."[79]

In fact, Sullivan's arguments foreshadowed growing pressure on the advertising industry in the mid-1960s. Although the New York chapter of CORE, like the NAACP, turned its attention to the urban crises, the national organization took up the cause. As the Image campaign faded in the mid-to-late 1960s, the national CORE organization partnered with a local black consumer organization in a direct action campaign against selected advertising agencies.

CORE and Consumer Information Services

In 1966, the national CORE organization and the media information arm of Consumer Information Services (CIS) launched a joint protest. CIS was an urban-based organization whose stated mission was to improve the relationship between corporate America and urban consumers. CORE and CIS joined forces to protest the "high cost of Jim Crow advertising and the segregated media." The joint campaign targeted the Benton & Bowles (B&B) agency, the lead advertising agency for Procter & Gamble (P&G). The stated basis for their protest was that P&G made considerable revenue from black consumers but did not invest directly into the black community. Although the firm had agreed a few years earlier to begin using integrated advertisements, this new campaign sought direct community investments from the company and an increase in the number of blacks working at B&B. While the Image campaign pursued the goal of increasing the use of integrated advertisements, the CORE/CIS campaign centered on improving the lives of underclass blacks. Activists pressed for lower prices for urban residents and training programs as a way to open employment choices for the black underclass. Also, they viewed the Image campaign something that only aided the black upper and middle classes who had the professional flexibility or education to take advantage of new employment choices. In contrast, the new campaign also focused on jobs, but it stressed poor blacks as its beneficiaries, an effort deemed worthy of CORE's emphasis on aiding the black underclass.[80]

Flo Kennedy led the CIS portion of the campaign. Known for her aggressive and flamboyant tactics, Kennedy had a long history of battling consumer products companies for greater investment into the black community. After graduating from high school, she organized a success-ful boycott against a Coca-Cola bottler who refused to hire black truck drivers. Later, she forced Columbia Law School to admit her after she threatened to file a discrimination suit, and she became one of the first black women to graduate from the school. Kennedy developed her tac-tics to grab attention and was unapologetic about her methods. She believed that any successful protest against a hesitant corporation depended upon generating the public attention that forced executives to the bargaining table. "When you want to get in the suites, start in the streets," she reasoned. "Be patient. It may take thirty years, but sooner or later they'll listen to you, and in the meantime, [you] keep kicking ass." Often clad in a cowboy hat or pink sunglasses, Kennedy was easily conspicuous within a crowd. With her strong sense of political theater, Kennedy was a difficult adversary for those who stood against her chosen causes. B&B executives faced an opponent who was willing to wage a boisterous publicity campaign designed to shame the company into negotiations. Unlike the years of the Image campaign in which oppo-nents gathered quietly in meeting rooms and later announced their agreements to the press, Kennedy and CIS waged their battle against B&B on the sidewalk in front of the agency in full view of television cam-eras.[81]

Kennedy and CORE argued that P&G should return a portion of their $250 million annual advertising budget to the black community in one of two ways: either through a hiring policy that increased the number of blacks at the company or a graduated pricing structure that lowered prices for blacks living in urban ghettos. However, the call for graduated pricing was a feint masking the primary goal. The primary goal of the CORE/CIS protest was to convince B&B to sponsoring a training pro-gram for blacks interested in entering the advertising industry. It was a manipulative, but clever, strategy. Picketers lined up outside B&B with placards reading: "Have you got a bigot in your shopping bag," and "Black buyers can't afford Madison Avenue parasites." B&B was the tar-get because Kennedy considered them a "liberal, modern agency with a neat complement of Negroes on its payrolls." The agency was the home of Roy Eaton, easily one of the highest-ranking blacks in advertising at the time, and had a host of blacks working in other capacities. In fact, Eaton, unaware of the hidden reason for the choice of B&B, confronted the protesters one day telling them that they had chosen the wrong agency. B&B, he argued, was an agency with a strong policy of hiring blacks and placing them in important positions in the agency. Unwit-tingly the frustrated Eaton was simply confirming what protesters already knew. Kennedy knew of B&B's hiring policies but smartly rea-soned that "if we got nowhere with them, we had no reason to believe other agencies would treat us any better." Hence, in this way the CORE/ CIS tandem used Funnye's tactics although he did not participate in the protest against B&B. Where the two efforts differed was that CIS now focused specifically on agencies and wanted B&B to agree to train what they and protestors called the black "underclass." CORE and CIS targeted a single representative company with hopes that a successful action against them would lead to other agencies following its policies, this time on the agency side. The only reason Kennedy even mentioned P&G was to raise the possibility of a product boycott in the minds of B& B executives and convince them to meet with the group rather than face negative publicity.[82]

The larger advertising community and reporters in the trade press recognized the shift in CORE's strategy. CIS was a newcomer to protests against the industry, but the reporters had met with CORE activists during the Image campaign and reported favorably on their goals and strategy. In contrast to the near-universal support for the Image campaign, opinions differed on whether the CORE/CIS effort was appropriate. While some argued picketers' motives were correct, but that they were unfair in marching outside B&B, others went further, calling the protest a "mild form of extortion" or evidence of black "bigotry." Among those in the trade press who agreed that there was a need to involve more blacks in the advertising business, they differed on the route through which it should take place. On one side were those who argued that protesters should let individual agencies develop their policies voluntarily. Protesters anticipated and countered that position by arguing that voluntarism had been in practice since the inception of the industry and had effectively failed to increase the number of blacks in the industry. On the other side were those who viewed marches and demonstrations as the only alternative available. One writer summed up the sentiment against protestors noting, "More Negroes should be brought into agency work, and more should be employed as models and actors in advertising. Many agencies are bending over backwards to do just that. But bending over is different from being sledge-hammered over."[83]

The public debate had no impact on Kennedy and CORE's tactics. In fact, if anything it strengthened their resolve that they were on the right track. The letters and articles, even if they were against the protests, demonstrated that many in the industry recognized the need to employ more black professionals. The problem, as Kennedy and CORE viewed it, was that little action had accompanied that realization. Instead, they believed that if agencies were going to address the issue of black employment in the industry voluntarily, they would have already done so. Madison Avenue, Kennedy charged, had no genuine desire to see blacks gain positions of power and control in advertising. The tactic of voluntarism was a failure and consistent pressure was the only true means to ensure changes.[84]

With pickets arrayed outside B&B, company executives agreed to meet with Kennedy and other activists as a sign of their willingness to hear her demands. B&B leaders also asked them for an outline of their demands and proposed solutions to the issues in contention. The meeting was held inside the agency. What Kennedy brought to the meeting was an outline for a Media Workshop Institute in Harlem. With an expected $5 million first-year investment from B&B, the Institute could provide training for blacks and other minorities interested in working in advertising. Further, the plan called for executives from B&B and other interested agencies to serve as instructors for the various classes. After successful completion of the six-week workshops, interested students would enter the industry.[85]

The proposed workshop may have surprised B&B executives, but it complemented CORE's broader organizational focus on community organizing. A training program that incorporated poor blacks into their own uplift fit squarely within this broader goal as well as President Lyndon B. Johnson's ongoing War on Poverty and, if successful, gave blacks a way out of their economic deprivation. Also, apart from the necessity of having white instructors for the program, it was a program organized by blacks for blacks, another part of CORE's shifting focus. In the past the group's guiding ideology emphasized racial integration with whites and blacks working together, but the new organizational direction emphasized militancy and nationalism to the exclusion of significant white involvement. While this did not extend to complete racial separation, it did stress blacks helping blacks without the direct control of whites.[86]

During the initial meeting between B&B and the CORE/CIS group, the agency balked at providing the $5 million for the Institute, but they agreed to work with the group to set up a training program. They also agreed to interview anyone that CIS recommended who had the qualifications to work in an advertising firm. Executives concluded, "It is our earnest hope that out of these activities will emerge recognizable progress for the people you represent. You may be sure that we shall for our part see that this comes about."[87] With the agreement for a training program reached, the demonstrations around B&B ceased.

Much to the consternation of B&B executives, four months after reaching the agreement with the Kennedy and CORE, protesters returned. Agency leaders were surprised by their sudden return because they felt they were in compliance with the original agreement they had reached with Kennedy. Executives had worked directly with Kennedy and James Haughton, head of the Harlem Unemployment Center, on the initial planning for the training program and in the interim hired three black youths into the agency as clerks. While these were not the professional-level positions that protesters wanted, part of that responsibility was theirs as they had failed to send B&B the names of any blacks with greater qualifications. Further, instead of protesting the hiring rate for blacks or the current state of the training program, Kennedy and the protesters appeared figuratively with their hands out asking for more money. However, this time it was to have the agency sponsor a local black television show. Even in light of this additional request, executives met with the group and agreed to recommend to clients that they buy time on the program. Kennedy was unwilling to stop there, however. She unwisely pressed even further and insisted the agency underwrite all the production costs associated with the program. Even supporters of the original goals found her request outlandish. After this new request, B&B executives withdrew from the discussion.[88]

Instead of taking their withdrawal as an opportunity to alter her approach and renew discussions with the firm, she wrote to some of B&B's clients and later carried the same demands to other advertising firms. Warning both agencies and advertisers of possible "direct consumer action against your company, its image, service and/or products," Kennedy overplayed her hand. Her threats drew little response. Over the next few weeks she met with advertising agency executives, as well as client-side advertising managers, but all refused to support the program. Though she had once dealt with executives sympathetic to her larger goals, this time they ignored her. In his time, Funnye had the backing of the selective-patronage committees, but in her renewed battle against B&B, Kennedy lacked the support of CORE and its committees. It is unclear why CORE severed ties with CIS, but its absence meant that Kennedy was, at best, able to organize a local boycott against the company but that she had little power to mobilize the national campaign that would have drawn the attention of B&B or its clients.[89]

By choosing to press B&B for more funds, Kennedy and CIS may have lost a genuine opportunity. In B&B they had an agency with an existing liberal hiring policy and a willingness to go even further. Executives at the agency took CIS and CORE seriously and admitted that their work with the group led to "intensive soul-searching" and a recommitment to an open hiring and promotion policy. Further, at the time when the final round of meetings took place between B&B and CIS, black and white advertising professionals in Chicago were in discussions for what became the Basic Advertising Course. Thus, had B&B and CIS been able to continue making strides in the development of their original training program, an effort similar to the Chicago course may have been possible in New York. Unfortunately, because the two groups chose to diffuse their efforts into developing community television programming, rather than the agency work, they missed an effort that might have generated significant changes.

Conclusion

Although the CORE/CIS effort eventually fell apart it foreshadowed more aggressive tactics against advertising agencies and professional organizations. To his credit, AAAA's president Crichton did not shy away from meeting with civil rights organizations or with using his position to publicly advocate industry support for their goals. He used his office to press for greater employment of blacks in the advertising industry. Crichton also continually urged advertising agencies to establish training and recruitment programs for blacks and to incorporate them into integrated advertisements where possible.[90]

Still, during the 1960s the media were a contested battleground. Not only did agencies face the demands of civil rights activists, they also faced southern whites displeased about programming that depicted "all white Southerners as ignorant, degenerate and villainous and all Negroes as straight out of Oxford."[91] An executive with the Ted Bates agency likely summed up the thoughts of many others in the industry when he lamented to an interviewer, "You must understand that the businessman does not wish to antagonize anybody—even the bigots."[92]

The grassroots activism blacks maintained in the early 1960s was a key component in supporting civil rights organizations' agreements with major corporations. Whether in the case of the protest at Woolworth's, against companies in Philadelphia, or, eventually, the equally successful campaigns waged by Jesse Jackson's Chicago-based Operation Breadbasket, black consumer activism was directly responsible for the expansion in employment opportunities in the advertising industry and elsewhere. Without these supportive efforts, civil rights groups would have undoubtedly had a much more difficult time convincing corporate leaders to meet their demands.[93]

Collectively, the efforts of the Urban League, CORE, and the NAACP each enhanced the other. On one side was CORE, working with advertisers to convince them to utilize more inclusive advertising policies. On the other side was the NAACP, working with advertising agencies to foster employment and image changes. Both of these organizational campaigns benefited from the earlier work of the Urban League and the NNC that had combined issues related to both advertisers and agencies. Additionally, although their protest eventually foundered due to poor strategic decisions, the CORE/CIS protest foreshadowed a growing interest in the experiences of poor consumers. Further, each these groups gained results within a short period of time. These organizations successfully encouraged the business community to embrace the concept of immediate action as a way to make up for the impact of historic discrimination and to generate immediate results. Additionally, the use of black models in advertisements in general-market media sources increased, and several agency executives expressed an interest in increasing their numbers of black employees.[94]

Civil rights activity alone was not responsible for all the changes realized in the industry during the 1960s. The attention from civil rights groups directly helped bring about that of state and federal legislators and commissioners. As these local and federal government organizations became involved in equal employment opportunity programs they complemented activists' efforts and led to important measures of legislative redress and protection to ensure fair employment policies. Their involvement insured that agencies had to comply not only with agreements reached with private organizations but also with the dictates of public laws. In addition, the combined action of civil rights organizations fostered a major shift in public opinion to one of support for an end to discriminatory hiring practices. Thus, equal employment opportunity became not only a matter of compliance with the law but also a legitimate expression of social responsibility.[95]

Chapter 4

Affirmative Action and the Search for White Collars

> *If we do not now dare everything, the fulfillment of that prophecy, recreated from the Bible in song by a slave, is upon us: "God gave Noah the rainbow sign. No more water, the fire next time!"*
>
> —*James Baldwin*, The Fire Next Time

By the mid-1960s, the disillusionment and pent-up anger that many blacks felt were ready to explode. Obviously the nation had made strides with some of the recent civil rights victories in the South, but they had slight impact outside the region. For black residents in northern cities, the victories against bus companies, hotels, and department stores were an important symbol of racial progress but little more. African Americans in most northern cities could already freely vote, experienced few instances of overt racial violence, and already received mostly equal treatment in consumer spaces. In contrast to their southern brethren, the primary focus for northern blacks was economic. As one resident of Harlem bitterly remarked, "The black cat in Harlem wasn't worried about no damn bus—he'd been riding the bus for fifty years. What he didn't have was the fare." As a result, blacks in the North not only continued the fight for job opportunities that they waged since World War II but also expanded their demands to include a special emphasis on professional- and management-level opportunities. The growing problem, however, was that not all African Americans were willing to wait for the ongoing protests to bring the changes that addressed their needs. As writer and poet Langston Hughes passionately warned whites over a decade before the cities exploded:

Negroes,
Sweet and docile,
Meek, humble and kind:

Beware the day
They change their minds![1]

This chapter examines the intense period of investigation and scrutiny in which state, local, and federal government organizations echoed
the ongoing work of civil rights activists and demanded changes from
advertising agencies in both hiring and creative practices. The twin pressures from private and government organizations captured the attention
of the industry as leaders realized agencies now faced not only the possibility of negative publicity and boycotts of their clients' products but also
possible prosecution for discrimination. The story and chapter begin at
the state and local levels, as government investigators explored industry
hiring practices as well as how agencies used blacks in advertisements.
The chapter continues as federal EEOC later joined the fight and called
executives to answer charges of discrimination and to explain the dearth
of minorities in the industry. Commissions at all three levels of government pressed agencies to do more than develop open hiring policies,
including training and recruitment of blacks for professional-level
agency work. Further, commissioners at all three levels echoed the arguments of civil rights groups in linking the issue of minority employment
in advertising agencies with the depiction of minorities in advertisements. If agencies had more black and minority employees, activists and
civil servants argued, then the interconnected faces of discrimination,
industry diversity, and advertisements would be altered. Specifically, if
blacks were routinely present in advertising agencies, their presence and
influence would help lead agencies to question their traditional use of
blacks in advertisements.

In advance of the riots of the mid-1960s, the federal government
began taking reluctant but decisive steps demonstrating a more active
involvement on employment discrimination. In 1961, John F. Kennedy
issued Executive Order 10925 stipulating that companies with government contracts should set up affirmative action hiring policies. This
order strengthened Roosevelt's Executive Order 8802 that had banned
employment discrimination in companies with defense contracts. The
new order also established the President's Committee on Equal Employment Opportunity (PCEEO), a group with the mandate to actively investigate discrimination complaints in companies with government
contracts.[2]

After Kennedy's assassination, Title VII of the Civil Rights Act of 1964
expanded the legal requirements of fair employment even further and
added an investigatory and administrative arm, the Equal Employment
Opportunity Commission (EEOC). Further, the passage of fair employment legislation in several states, as well as rising activity from state and

municipal employment commissions, broadened the impact of these federal developments. Also, the progressive spirit and economic support of Lyndon B. Johnson's War on Poverty only enhanced the earlier legislative victories. This comprehensive program, like the New Deal during the 1930s, sought ways to involve poor and low-income citizens in their own education and advancement. Johnson knew personally what it was to be poor and he recognized the soul-destroying impact that poverty often brought. But he was also a self-described "son of the New Deal," and his experience with that program helped convince him that any efforts at individual uplift needed the direct involvement of the individual in need. By giving the poor the support of the federal government and proposing alternative approaches beyond direct handouts or neglect, Johnson raised the possibility of real change in the economic well-being of thousands of people. He called on the rest of the nation to take part in this massive effort, especially business leaders. They had the capacity for the most immediate impact on poverty because they could help develop new job opportunities.[3]

Business leaders, however, often still resisted change. For example, civil rights groups repeatedly found that executives were almost always willing to meet with them but not necessarily to meet their demands or follow through on agreed-on changes. Thus, the power and attention of local, state, and federal government were key because they helped intensify the light of public scrutiny on discrimination as well as compelled businesses to adhere to the law. And, though small in comparison to some of the major industries in the country, the advertising industry began receiving attention from government commissions. Agency heads found that commissioners usually agreed with civil rights activists about the unique broad social and economic impact of advertising. Advertising agencies, commissioners argued, had the twin responsibilities of ensuring fair employment like that of any other business as well as presenting a fair and racially diverse image of America through their advertising work. As a result, the period from 1963 to 1970 was one of intensive scrutiny and change in the industry unlike any it had witnessed before.[4]

Still, even with this investigatory and legislative foundation, history shows that it was the urban violence of the long hot summers of 1964 through 1967 that forced government and corporate leaders into greater levels of action. The industry responded with what trade reporters described as a "tremendous push" of training and recruitment programs that began to increase the number of blacks working in mainstream agencies. The government scrutiny that helped engender that "push" began in New York.

The New York State Commission Against Discrimination and the
Mayor's Committee on Job Advancement

By the early 1960s, the city and state of New York had had a long history
with human rights commissions. In 1945, the state was one of the first to
pass its own fair employment legislation and to set up an independent
committee to investigate charges of discrimination, the New York State
Commission Against Discrimination (the name was later changed to the
New York State Commission for Human Rights [NYSHR] and hereinafter will be referred to by that name). For nearly the next two decades,
the NYSHR was the only agency in the state with the authority and juris-
diction to investigate discrimination complaints. The New York City
Commission on Human Rights (NYCHR) eventually became the leading
government body in the nation examining discrimination in the advertising industry, but it was the NYSHR that launched the first governmental inquiry in the early 1960s. However, despite its mandate to look into
employment discrimination, the commission's first concern was with
how advertisements incorporated blacks.[5]

The flurry of boycotts and selective-patronage campaigns by civil
rights activists in the early 1960s galvanized the NYSHR's inquiry into
discrimination in advertising. Also, the investigations and public pressure brought first by the Urban League, and later CORE and the NAACP
(see Chapter 3), laid important groundwork for analysis of industry hiring practices and use of minorities in advertisements. In mid-1963, the
Urban League released results of its study of agency employment discrimination. Almost simultaneously, the NYSHR released findings from
a five-month study examining the ways in which networks, advertisers,
and advertising agencies dictated the use of blacks in television programs. Before the investigation, some networks, like CBS, had issued
statements on the need to increase the number of blacks in their programming. Michael Dann, vice president of programming at the network, informed his staff that there are "many Negro doctors, lawyers,
school teachers, engineers, policemen, nurses, and jurymen in life
today" and that they should "maintain realism about having them
appear as such in our dramatic programs." Some individual television
producers declared a similar willingness to use more black actors regularly, but they often did not actually do so because they feared program
rejection by networks or advertising agencies. As for advertisers, the
committee assumed that they followed the recommendations of their
advertising agencies about how best to appeal to consumers and had little impact on the models in their advertisements. At a minimum, advertisers often shied away from any association with controversial racial
topics. During broadcasts of the 1963 March on Washington, for exam-

ple, the lack of sponsors forced major networks to broadcast hours of coverage of the event without commercials.[6]

So, since networks and producers were open to more black actors, and advertisers followed agency recommendations, the NYSHR concluded (as Nat King Cole had done in the 1950s) that advertising agencies were the primary stumbling block. Their study revealed that even in the rare instances in which blacks appeared in advertisements, they usually did so in an institutional role as an employee of the advertiser rather than as spokespersons. Agencies included them as evidence of an integrated employment policy within the company sponsoring the advertisement. To be fair, this was a direct response to the arguments from black marketing and advertising professionals who stressed the need for firms to display their fair hiring policies as a way to reach black consumers. To commissioners, this institutional approach, while not problematic by itself, unfairly limited the roles blacks could play in advertisements.[7]

Fortunately, in part because of the continuing work of civil rights organizations like CORE and the NAACP, NYSHR commissioners were well aware of the shell game-like arguments networks, advertising agencies, and advertisers routinely used when questioned on the use of blacks in advertisements. They knew that it was easy for the networks to pass the responsibility for blacks' invisibility on television onto advertising agencies and for agencies to pass it back to networks or onto their clients. Commissioners focused their attention on advertising agencies, therefore, for two primary reasons: proximity and influence. The television and motion-picture industries were mainly based in California and beyond the effective reach of the committee. In contrast, forty of the largest fifty agencies in the nation had offices in New York City, well within the range of the committee. Thus, once investigations evolved beyond advertising images to include agency hiring policies, the NYSHR could threaten agencies with more than moral suasion, that is, with prosecution under state fair employment laws. Additionally, because advertising agencies were the link between networks and advertisers, they had the influence to change the policies of both parties about the use of minorities. Commissioners believed that agency executives could reassure networks that they would in fact recommend sponsorship on integrated shows and at the same time reassure clients that white consumers would not reject their products because their ads included African Americans.[8]

In New York City, an advertising study by the Mayor's Committee on Job Advancement (MCJA) echoed the conclusions of the NYSHR's advertising study. Like the NYSHR examination, the MCJA study analyzed the influence of advertisers and advertising agencies and concluded that agencies had the greatest potential impact on increasing the use of minorities. Advertisers certainly had to be willing to allow such images, but commissioners believed that they would do so if the recommendation came from their agencies. The tone of the report was hopeful. Commissioners believed that if agencies understood the social and economic benefits of incorporating images of African Americans and other minorities into their advertisements, they would do so. Therefore, the MCJA planned to work with the American Association of Advertising Agencies (AAAA) and the Ad Council, the public-service arm of the advertising industry, to develop a presentation to advertising agencies explaining the positive impact of minority inclusion in advertisements.[9]

Although the CORE Image campaign and the investigations by the MCJA occurred simultaneously, the two groups did not work directly together. Still, the pressure from two groups, one private and one from the government, mutually reinforced each other. Further, by the start of 1964, both Clarence Funnye of CORE and members of the MCJA agreed that agencies had made a "breakthrough" in their use of blacks. In early 1964, the MCJA released "The Racial Revolution in Advertising," a page-by-page survey of advertising in the four largest circulation magazines. The examination found that the number of ads with identifiable black faces had grown from a mere two in 1962 to more than eighty-five by the end of 1963. Further, of the five hundred companies the MCJA contacted, seventy-three could show definite plans to craft integrated ads. Although the report failed to provide any evidence of the role that blacks played in the ads, commissioners viewed their mere presence as being valuable. At that point, they stressed the quantity of racial portrayals rather than their quality. At a minimum, they viewed the statistical increase as evidence that agencies and advertisers were trying (albeit slowly) to make changes. Viewing the developments, New York mayor Robert Wagner enthused that he was "extremely pleased at the cooperation" displayed by advertisers and agencies. Beyond the report, the MCJA announced the creation of a job center to place qualified minorities into the media industries. And, while this was a valuable step in increasing the availability of qualified minority employees, it was the last major effort by the MCJA to alter advertising industry practices.[10]

The MCJA was limited by the fact that it was a political creation of New York mayor Robert Wagner. Although focused on employment, the committee had no enforcement power to compel companies to action. Instead, the most it could hope for was to secure "binding agreements" with business leaders to recruit and hire minority employees. Therefore, the influence of the MCJA never grew to a level equaling that of the NYSHR and eventually the NYCHR.[11]

For its part, the interests and involvement of the NYSHR with the advertising industry did not extend much beyond its initial investigation.

In fact, for the next several years the commission's only involvement with the industry came in developing a series of commercials to illustrate the psychological damage resulting from discrimination. The commission worked with veteran black advertising executive Roy Eaton, music director at the Benton & Bowles advertising agency to develop the series "How Would You Feel?" But as the MCJA ceased to be an important factor and the NYSHR continued its work on discrimination in other fields, the mantle of government leadership on investigations into the advertising industry shifted to the New York City Commission on Human Rights (NYCHR). The NYCHR not only continued the two groups' investigations into the use of blacks in advertisements, it also investigated blacks' employment in advertising agencies, something neither commission had significantly addressed.[12]

The New York City Commission on Human Rights

Similar to the state government, the city of New York set up its first race relations commission in 1943. During the 1940s and '50s, that early commission morphed into the interracial Committee on Intergroup Relations (COIR), but, beyond an impressive name and list of supporters, it lacked strong investigatory powers. Especially during the McCarthyite era of the 1950s, city leaders feared giving any group unchecked investigation authority and, as a result, the group had little tangible impact on city policies. Additionally, until the early 1960s the power to explore charges of discrimination rested at the state, rather than city, level. Instead of investigation, then, the COIR stressed racial tolerance on two counts: tolerance among all for people of different ethnicities and tolerance by minorities fed up with the slow pace of change. The group also developed programs to educate the public about the harmful impact of discrimination. But as the civil rights movement's nonviolent protest tactics brought the intense light of public scrutiny onto discrimination issues, the passive "conciliation and compromise" approach of the COIR changed as well. In the early 1960s, in a nod toward the vision of its new chairman, Stanley Lowell, the group took on the new name New York City Commission on Human Rights (NYCHR).[13]

The newly named NYCHR emphasized equality in three major areas: housing, schools, and employment. Of the three, however, Lowell believed employment discrimination to be the foundation on which discrimination in the other two areas rested. If the NYCHR could effectively challenge discrimination in employment, he reasoned, changes in racial practices in the other two areas would undoubtedly occur. The interracial committee also had a history of working with private organizations like CORE or the Urban League to research discrimination. As a result, when the Urban League forwarded information from its meetings with advertising industry representatives to the NYCHR in April of 1963, they found a willing partner (see Chapter 3). The NYCHR worked in concert with CORE and/or the Urban League to increase black employment in the industry and in advertisements. The organizations shared information, and both civil rights groups, especially the Urban League, looked to the committee to force compliance when moral suasion and boycott threats failed to produce desired ends. However, until 1965 the power to prosecute cases of employment discrimination remained with the NYSHR. Jurisdictional infighting between the two organizations meant that the NYCHR's only weapons to compel changes in hiring patterns came in two areas: First, if investigations revealed employment discrimination, it could refer cases to the NYSHR for prosecution. Second, like civil rights groups, it could use threats of negative publicity to encourage an employer to alter its policies.[14]

Nevertheless, working with the NYCHR was an important relationship for civil rights activists. As a formal government organization, the investigations from the commission at least put the issue on the agenda of city administration. Whether changes would actually occur remained unknown, but commissioners, especially Lowell, could walk in corridors of power that activists could not and present their case. Fortunately, Lowell was a strong advocate of the role of government in guaranteeing equal opportunity. He argued, "The protection of human rights needs the *fist* [emphasis mine] of government." So the information the two civil rights groups provided the NYCHR about their meetings with various advertisers and agencies gave Lowell and the rest of the commission an important foundation for their own first public meeting with advertising agencies.[15]

In early 1964, the NYCHR sent invitations to ninety-nine advertising agencies to meet with them to discuss the question: "What are agencies doing about equal job opportunity, and can they do more?" Over eighty agencies accepted the invitations, but only thirty-one made it to the meeting because of a snowstorm. The meeting took place just a few days after the MCJA's glowing report about incorporating minorities into advertisements. Although that became a future area of concern for the NYCHR, the focus this day was on employment. Richard Scheidker, senior vice president of the AAAA, provided the most detailed report of the day. He opened by noting that the AAAA board of directors had developed a statement on minority employment that it circulated to member agencies and high school and college guidance counselors. The employment statement clarified the organization's belief that it was "vital to seek out, recognize and employ the best talents available wherever they may be found, regardless of race, color, religion or national origin."

Following issuance of the statement, eighty-five agencies sent in written commitments in to the AAAA reiterating their support for job equality, and several jointly issued a public statement on antidiscrimination in agency employment. These agencies agreed to "take affirmative steps toward the end that minority-group performers are cast in all types of roles so that the American scene may be portrayed realistically." To lend weight to the developments, he quoted the formerly bitter Nat King Cole (see Chapter 2), who now cautiously allowed that the television networks had adopted a new "forward thinking attitude toward Negro performers." The group also published a booklet for students that described opportunities in the advertising industry illustrated with pictures of minority employees. The organization placed several advertisements highlighting the nondiscriminatory nature of agency employment in several major newspapers.[16]

Scheidker took care to point out that the AAAA was doing more than simply placing advertisements and issuing statements. Instead, it was encouraging agencies to actively seek out minority employees by recruiting black college students or black professionals with skills transferable to the industry. In addition, as part of the agreement the group made with the NAACP at the landmark eastern conference meeting in late 1963, the organization directed agencies to involve local civil rights groups in recruitment efforts. The advertising industry, Scheidker concluded, clearly wanted to address the concerns (or demands) of civil rights groups and of the NYCHR.[17]

But in his report Scheidker also cautioned the committee to temper its expectations about the pace of change. Specifically, he warned them not to expect a deluge of black employees in advertising agencies because securing a job in the industry was difficult for anyone. In 1962, the six largest New York agencies received over twenty-three thousand applications, nearly four times their number of employees. The agencies then interviewed more than eighteen thousand of the applicants and hired an unspecified number. The advertising business was small and competitive, and most agencies searched for experienced personnel rather than recruiting beginners from colleges and universities. So, one of the areas where they might find black recruits went unexplored. Additionally the large pool of available hires often meant that a lack of experience in the industry made nearly any applicant unemployable. Kenneth Laird, president of the Tatham-Laird agency, argued, "If you take one big agency here and set out to find where an executive came from, you'd probably find he didn't come fresh out of college. He had prior experience with a smaller agency, or with an advertiser. In the art department, the director worked for a studio before, and with a department store before that. The account executive came from a smaller agency, and you can trace him back sometimes to the ad department of a client where he was a brand manager, assistant product manager or a marketing director."[18] So, inexperienced people, regardless of color, could not simply be thrust into professional work simply to meet the demands of activists or government commissions. Instead, unless blacks began to get agency experience, or agencies adjusted their hiring practices, any increases in black employment would be slow to occur.

However, what Scheidker and Laird did not allow was that the surplus resulted from industry-wide policies that made it a mostly White Anglo-Saxon Protestant (WASP) preserve. So the training grounds that Laird described as leading to the valued experience were ones that racism and discrimination had made almost all white. Moreover, as David Sullivan articulated in his open letter to AAAA president John Crichton, even for blacks with the necessary experience, their skin color sometimes trumped their knowledge and experience, and they were not hired. As Sullivan concluded, if the industry was going to find black talent, agencies had to change their passive policies in which they did not look for black employees. Additionally, they would need to change their discriminatory policies that kept experienced black professionals like Sullivan unemployed.[19]

Some advertising representatives, like Laird, at least in theory, recognized the need for an evolution in hiring practices. "There must be a much broader effort or this program (job opportunity) will touch only a few of the people we hire," Laird argued. Based on Scheidker's testimony, some industry and agency leaders were taking steps to address the issues of advertising representations and minority employment. And although agencies continued to prefer experienced applicants, the AAAA issued constant reminders for them to work with employment agencies, civil rights groups, and black colleges and universities to find potential black employees. These special efforts had in fact begun to lead to a slow influx of black employees. But Scheidker wanted to ensure that commissioners knew that if the trickle did not develop into a flood, it would not be for lack of effort by agencies or the AAAA.[20]

Further, he suggested that agencies were also using more black talent in client advertisements and television programs. This new racially inclusive activity had not gone unrecognized and the Scheidker again quoted from Nat King Cole's recent praise of the television industry for "living up to its public responsibilities." To Scheidker, Cole's praise, as well as that of Mayor Wagner and the MCAD, was clear evidence of an industry sympathetic to the demands of activists and the goals of the commission. He closed optimistically: "None would claim that all of the problems have been entirely met and solved. But we believe that this summary is enough to show that helpful forces have been set in motion by advertising agencies, not only with respect with their own employment of Negroes, but also with the employment of Negroes in advertisements and programs on behalf of their clients." Lowell offered tentative praise for Scheidker's report. He also cautioned the representatives that the NYCHR planned to continue watching industry progress to ensure that its actions matched its rhetoric. But when the frustration of urban blacks repeatedly exploded over the next several summers, it forced the nation to confront the crisis of the cities. If industry representatives expected the government focus on them to wane, they were mistaken.[21]

Burn, Baby, Burn!

The riots changed everything. From 1964 through 1967, a series of urban rebellions (or "riots," depending on your perspective) gripped the nation. The violence was costly in terms of both life and property. Over the four-year period, the violence resulted in over 130 deaths, 5,000 injuries, and over 20,000 arrests.[22] Estimates of damage to property stretched into the hundreds of millions of dollars, and in some cases entire blocks of commercial and residential life disappeared. The destruction forced the issue of fair employment back to the forefront of consideration. These violent street uprisings convinced many business leaders that they must play an active role in relieving the causes behind the unrest. Many, like W. P. Gullander, head of the National Association of Manufacturers, resolved that "The problem of Watts is not a Negro problem; it is our problem as a nation." Others agreed with the less grandiose, but more direct observation of the head of the Neiman-Marcus department store: "Once a man sees his investment in a community going up in smoke he is going to act." As a result, an immediate demand to "do something" to produce results replaced plans that once emphasized slow growth and careful progress. Instead of just looking for college students and other qualified or experienced blacks, dozens of companies developed training and educational programs among the group reporters labeled the "hard-core unemployed." In 1967, the National Alliance of Businessmen was founded to link the federal government with private business and coordinate the business communities' response to the crisis. Thus even companies that were not dependent on black consumer buying became actively involved developing responses to the urban crises. By late 1968, a *New York Times* report noted that a listing of the number of companies with outreach and training programs in urban ghettos "would read much like a stock-market table and run just about as long."[23]

Similarly, the riots forced government organizations to renew their interest in addressing the problems of employment discrimination. In early 1968, the federal EEOC held hearings on discrimination in white-collar employment in a variety of industries, including advertising. Shortly after that, the NYCHR renewed its interest in the industry and launched one the most in-depth investigations of agency employment in history. Both commissions mirrored the rising militancy of minority citizens for greater tangible progress and each looked for ways to play a more vigorous role to end discrimination. Thus, New York agencies again found themselves the focus of attention from the local and federal government on the twin issues of minority employment and representation within advertisements.[24]

The Equal Employment Opportunity Commission

Title VII of the Civil Rights Act of 1964 banned employment discrimination based on race, color, religion, sex, or national origin. Title VII also established the EEOC, which had investigatory and enforcement powers. The act equipped the EEOC with the power to launch an investigation of discrimination complaints, regardless of whether the company in question had a government contract. Commissioners also had the power to compel employers to work with the party introducing the complaint to achieve remediation. If the employer was unwilling to work with the commission or satisfactorily settle the mater, the EEOC could recommend that the U.S. Attorney General bring criminal charges under Title VII. However, commissioners viewed actual charges as the tactic of last resort. Instead, as they would with the advertising industry, commissioners preferred to work with companies to develop lasting policy changes rather than prosecute them. EEOC chairman Franklin Delano Roosevelt, Jr., stated that the commission wanted companies to do more than simply agree to invite black applicants for open positions. "We are asking management for more than fair hiring practices," he said. "We are suggesting creative recruitment policies that actually seek out qualified employees among minority groups."[25]

In January 1968, the EEOC conducted a series of hearings to examine discrimination in white-collar employment. They chose New York City as the site of the hearings because it had the nation's highest concentration of white-collar employees. Also the city was the headquarters for many of the nation's leading corporations and, in the case of the advertising industry, agencies in the city placed 50 percent of all national advertising. Each day's hearings began with a report giving a review of the employment statistics of the industry under examination. Prepared witness statements and questions by members of the committee followed the reports. The statements from company representatives accompanied those from blacks who had sought work in the industry in question. Not

TABLE 1. NEGRO PARTICIPATION: ALL WHITE-COLLAR BY INDUSTRY PERCENTAGE

City Average	5.2%
Radio and Television	3.9%
Book Publishing	3.7%
Newspaper Publishing	3.0%
Periodical Publishing	2.9%
Advertising	2.5%

Source: Equal Employment Opportunity Commission, *Hearings before the United States Equal Employment Opportunity Commission on Discrimination in White Collar Employment* (Washington, D.C.: GPO, 1968), 336.

surprisingly, the testimony of the job applicants often contradicted that of the representatives explaining their company's stance on equal employment opportunity.[26]

Representatives from the communications industry testified on the third day of the hearings, including advertising agencies, book and magazine publishers, and radio and television broadcasters. The commission grouped these industries together in part because they felt individual advancement in each of them rested on creativity and verbal skill, rather than on educational background or specific technical knowledge. Also, these industries each had a high degree of job mobility with people moving both within the industry and across the different industry groups. Most important, however, the commission viewed communications as having an "awesome influence" on the public. "These industries play a role more significant than all others in reporting and interpreting events, molding public opinion, and creating popular tastes and attitudes. It is they who can most readily establish the intellectual climate for significant social change," it argued. Employment in the communications industry had to become more reflective of the nation's racial diversity, or else the distorted image of its racial makeup would remain unchallenged. "In the TV era," one commissioner argued, "nearly a generation of minority youths has grown to adulthood with the vision of a world in which material benefits and comforts are solely for those with fair skins." Thus, the commission questioned industry representatives on both equal employment and the racial images that they projected in their work.[27]

Charles Markham, the EEOC director of research, began the day with a quantitative analysis of white-collar employees in what the EEOC defined as the communications industries. He described the employment pattern of the advertising industry as poor. Advertising was the largest employer of the group, but among 64 New York agencies, totaling over 15,000 white-collar employees, there were only 406 blacks, most of whom were in clerical positions (Table 1).

TABLE 2. NEGRO PARTICIPATION: OFFICIALS AND MANAGERS BY INDUSTRY PERCENTAGE

City Average	1.3%
Book Publishing	1.0%
Radio and Television	0.9%
Advertising	0.7%
Periodical Publishing	0.7%
Newspaper Publishing	0.1%

Source: Equal Employment Opportunity Commission, *Hearings before the United States Equal Employment Opportunity Commission on Discrimination in White Collar Employment* (Washington, D.C.: GPO, 1968), 335.

At the management and executive levels, the areas of greatest concern to the EEOC, advertising fared somewhat better, but the figures were still below the citywide average (Table 2) and the city average itself was very low.

Even more alarming to Markham was the concentration of black employees among a small number of agencies. Within the twelve largest advertising firms, just three agencies accounted for over 30 percent of all black white-collar workers and 40 percent of all other black employees. Markham did not identify these agencies by name, but he noted that they also accounted for most of the recent increases in black agency employment. To him, the actions of these few firms demonstrated that some agencies were taking the issue of equal employment seriously and making tangible strides but that most were not. Markham finished his remarks with arguments similar to those used by civil rights activists earlier in the decade. Specifically, he reminded the commission that failure to racially diversify the communications industry had "consequences more serious than in any of the others because of these employers' great responsibility as the opinion and taste makers in a grave period in our national history."[28] Blacks who sought agency employment echoed Markham's sentiment and provided tangible descriptions of racial discrimination in agency employment.

Emmanual Robinson, a black man with a broad range of advertising experience, related his hiring battles to the commission. Despite his expertise in the trade, he felt that hiring managers repeatedly denied him a permanent job because of his race. For example, he was not hired because the office manager felt that more than one black face in the office was "excessive." At a separate company, an executive refused him because the job required client contact, and he was unwilling to take the chance of offending the client's racial sensibilities. Summarizing his own experience, he said, "The reality is that the blame for the low proportion of Negroes in white-collar jobs lies in the history of conscious exclusion of Negroes from these jobs by employers and not in some fancied lack or deficiency or shortcoming among Negroes themselves." Although training programs, recruitment efforts by individual agencies, and the work of the AAAA proved that progress was not impossible, he believed that most agency leaders continued to assume that no qualified blacks were available. He implored the commission to work in concert with civil rights groups to police the industry rather than leave policy changes up to voluntary actions.[29]

Another black witness, Saundra Sharp, echoed Robinson's testimony and broadened it with a description of a black woman's experience. Sharp had several years experience in radio and television production but when searching for an agency position had only received offers for secretarial work. Thus black women not only faced limitations on finding agency jobs, but when jobs were offered they were outside the professional ranks. In fact, Sharp pointed to problems of gender discrimination within agencies, but the commissioners did not explore that aspect of her remarks. Sharp allowed that advertising was a difficult industry to enter, but she and Robinson agreed that racism meant limited opportunities for blacks far exceeding those of other groups. Further, although not part of the testimony, the experiences of both Robinson and Sharp mirrored the description David Sullivan enunciated in his open letter to AAAA president John Crichton almost four years earlier and demonstrated that, at least in the minds of some black professionals, precious little real change had occurred at the hiring level. Backed by Markham's employment statistics and information from the two morning witnesses, the commission eagerly awaited the testimony from industry representatives.[30]

John Devine, a vice president from J. Walter Thompson (JWT), and Richard Scherzer, director of personnel at Grey Advertising, appeared on behalf of advertising agencies. Devine began by recounting JWT's recent history on black employment. In 1963, at the urging of the company chairman, Dan Seymour, the firm began efforts to increase the number of black employees. As a member of the board of directors of the AAAA, Seymour had firsthand knowledge of the demands of civil rights activists. In response, he voluntarily initiated a process of encouraging JWT management to identify and recruit qualified minorities to the company. This action was more than simply a public relations effort; it was an effort by upper management to develop a cadre of black professionals. Accordingly, Seymour refused to lower standards for employment or job performance and, instead, developed a program to create black professionals in the agency. To do so, JWT recruited blacks for clerical positions with plans to then train them in the skills to become copywriters, account representatives, or media researchers. The agency also recruited blacks in various ways, including sponsoring recruitment seminars, recruiting black college students, advertising in equal employment directories, contracting with black employment agencies, working with civil rights groups to find qualified candidates, supporting AAAA efforts to increase black employment, and encouraging current black JWT employees to recruit others to the agency. So far the measures had proved successful. Most blacks recently recruited to the agency were still with the firm and several had received promotion into the professional ranks. In the New York office alone, the percentage of black employees had gone from 0.6 percent in 1963 to just under 5 percent in 1968. "We felt then and still do that a true measure of success would depend upon our ability to develop writers, artists, account representatives, researchers and media specialists—in other words, the key jobs in our business," Devine concluded.[31]

Commissioners' remarks displayed an appreciation for the leadership JWT displayed to develop black professionals but questioned their use of minorities in advertisements. They specifically asked Devine about what group, among agencies, advertisers, and the television and print media, bore responsibility for increasing the use of minorities in advertisements. Devine immediately responded, "As Mr. Truman used to say, 'the buck stops here.'" Instead of shifting the responsibility to network executives, publishers, or agency clients, Devine candidly admitted that agencies had the most direct influence on what copy and images appeared in advertisements. This was a major public admission for the industry. In prior open testimony to government commissions like the NYSHR or the NYCHR, or in discussions with civil rights activists, executives often shifted blame to clients, publishers, or television networks. For the representative of one of the largest agencies in the country to make this admission was a tacit indictment of practices throughout the industry. Devine stopped short of calling the dearth of minority images a conscious or racist exclusion but instead said that an "affirmative reminder" might be necessary to include them consistently. Commissioners, though cautious, seemed satisfied with Devine's description of JWT's growing efforts on employment and sense of responsibility for improving minority depictions in advertising. They turned their attention to the second industry representative.[32]

In contrast to Devine's account of JWT, Scherzer revealed that Grey Advertising had taken far fewer steps to improve minority employment. After opening with the vague statement that Grey employed anyone with the talent to contribute to the company, Scherzer admitted that most of Grey's black employees were in the clerical area. While this was similar to the status of most blacks at JWT, Grey lacked a similar commitment to training its black employees in professional skills. Also, Grey did not recruit black employees, and the firm had no working relationships with any civil rights organization. In marked contrast to JWT, Grey settled for interviewing the few minority applicants who applied and made no efforts to deepen that pool. But rather than accept even minimal responsibility for the low number of black employees, Scherzer blamed the agency's low starting wages. Further, he reminded commissioners that JWT was a much larger firm than Grey and had more resources to devote to its efforts. In short, to Scherzer, the two firms defied comparison in their treatment of minority employees.[33]

Grey represented what commissioners felt was the predominant attitude within the industry, and they aggressively pressed Scherzer to account for his firm's abysmal record of minority hires and lack of any plans for changes. In contrast to their critical, yet amiable, questioning of Devine, they attacked Scherzer for Grey's failure to make any efforts to alter its existing hiring policies or find minority employees. For example, they found it unacceptable that Grey lacked even the smallest measure of an informal program for recruiting, training, or promoting minorities. Scherzer responded that it made little sense to recruit students for jobs that did not exist. Doing so would give the agency the appearance of doing little more than public relations, of presenting an interest in black students but having no positions for them to fill. In response, commissioners suggested that Grey recruit a limited number of students for existing positions and create new positions for students to fill. Although he stopped short of publicly committing his agency to this course of action, Scherzer finished his testimony by admitting the need for greater equal employment efforts from Grey.[34]

The advertising industry testimony ended with a written statement from the AAAA reaffirming its support for equal employment opportunity and describing some of its continuing efforts to ensure its growth. Since 1963, the group had continued to expand its scholastic informational campaign about working in the industry and developed training programs. "It is not easy," the statement noted. "The present talent pool is not large. But the long-term trend makes it essential that we meet more and more of our growing personnel demands with Negroes." Beyond employment, the statement voiced clear support for continuing efforts to improve racial representation within advertisements. The AAAA wanted to make it clear to the EEOC that it had spent the years between its first appearance before a government commission, the NYCHR, and the present with decisive action, rather than foot dragging and recalcitrance.[35]

The hearings closed with a warning from the commission: If the members of the communications industries did not quickly improve the minority hiring record and the use of minority images in their work, individual companies would face government prosecution. To forestall that prosecution, commissioners strongly encouraged companies to increase their training efforts and increase the pool of qualified minority candidates. Training and promotion programs were the single most effective way to reduce the existing problem and to forestall future EEOC attention. Commissioners concluded, "Jobs are a key point and every company, every agency and every person must simply do whatever is needed to bring about a solution to this serious problem."[36]

The commission's emphasis on voluntarism rankled some present at the hearings. Herbert Hill, labor secretary of the NAACP, warned the commission to be even more vigorous in their approach to the problem. Specifically, Hill wanted an immediate prosecution of companies already in violation of existing state and federal antidiscrimination laws. He was fighting an uphill battle. The EEOC had little interest in taking legal steps until it had no other choice. As a result, commissioners decided to allow companies time to move toward compliance with existing laws. Thus, rather than become an active investigator of employment discrimination in the advertising industry, the EEOC only took action when individual cases came to its attention.[37]

With the prominence of the advertising industry in the EEOC hearings, the event received extensive and supportive coverage in the trade press. After the hearings concluded, an editorialist in *Advertising Age* lauded the commission's goal of increasing minority employment. Disappointed by the fact that advertising lagged behind other industries in terms of minority employment, the author argued that the industry would have to greatly increase its efforts to attract minorities. Furthermore, if sufficient numbers of experienced minorities could not be located, advertising agency executives would have to institute training programs to create their own experienced minority pool. Training, the writer reasoned, was the single most effective way to increase the numbers of minorities in the industry as well as to increase the pool of those available to hire. "Jobs are a key point," he argued, "and every company, every agency and every person simply must do whatever is needed to bring about a solution to this serious problem."[38]

Fortunately, government pressure on the advertising industry did not stop with the conciliatory and reactive polices of the EEOC. In the same year that the EEOC examined the industry, the NYCHR renewed its attention to it as well. In contrast to the EEOC, the NYCHR not only held public hearings, but it maintained pressure on the industry for several years afterward.

The City and State of New York Versus the Advertising Industry

After its first involvement with the advertising industry in 1963–64, attention from the NYCHR had shifted to other issues facing the city.

Similar to the experience of other cities, however, the riots and increased militancy of civil rights groups convinced commissioners of the need for more aggressive policies to address employment discrimination. The lack of economic opportunity lay behind much of the unrest, commissioners reasoned, and one way to eliminate that was to focus on jobs. Additionally, the commission was an important political tool for the mayor. As political scientist Gerald Benjamin observed, by taking on issues of job discrimination, the NYCHR gave Mayor John Lindsay additional credibility within the black community. The commission's new, more aggressive stance served as evidence that the city government was taking action to address discrimination in the city. In the "do something" climate of the period, the appearance of action was almost as important as the action itself. Also, an organizational leadership change in the NYCHR invigorated the commission with a new, more proactive role. In 1965, Lowell left the commission to focus energy on his private law practice. His replacement, William Booth, viewed the commission's role to be that of strong advocacy for minority issues. Further, he wanted to develop the commission into a stronger force to pressure employers into developing greater job opportunities for minorities. Therefore, by 1968 the commission's focus once again shifted back to the twin issues of agency employment and racial representation in advertising. This time, rather than giving tentative praise for voluntary industry efforts, the commission consciously moved toward the active enforcement of existing laws. "Discriminators were viewed not as innocents who had wandered from the path of righteousness . . . but as violators of the law who could be made to pay to the full extent for their actions," wrote Benjamin.[39]

Two months after the EEOC's 1968 hearings, the NYCHR held a ten-day hearing into minority employment in radio and television broadcasting and in advertising agencies. Although the EEOC had compiled similar information at almost the same time, there is no evidence that they participated in the NYCHR/NYSHR joint effort. In fact, Benjamin concluded that there was little cooperation between the state and city commissions in New York with any agency in the federal government.[40] Nonetheless, as part of the New York commission's investigations into advertising, they also examined representations of minorities in advertisements. Working with the NYSHR, they had spent the prior year compiling their own employment statistics for blacks and Puerto Ricans in the top fifty agencies in New York. These were the largest two minority groups in the city, and commissioners wanted to compare their percentage in the city's population with their employment in the advertising industry. Michael Vallon, lead council for the NYCHR, termed their findings "appalling" while a reporter described them as "lamentable

TABLE 3. MINORITY GROUP EMPLOYMENT IN NEW YORK ADVERTISING AGENCIES
BY CATEGORY AS OF AUGUST 31, 1967

Category	Total	Black	Percent Black
Account Handling/Client Service	2,222	11	0.49
Administration and General Service	422	4	0.94
Copy	1,450	15	1.0
Publicity & Public Relations	213	3	1.4
Visualization	1,272	22	1.7
Radio-TV Production	906	15	1.7
Media	1,969	36	1.8
Marketing and Merchandising	330	6	1.8
Print Production	379	8	2.1
Accounting, Billing, Checking, Traffic	702	16	2.3
Research	778	20	2.6
Secretaries	3,727	125	3.4
Data Processing	335	32	9.6
All Others (Messengers, Mail Room Clerks, etc.)	1,627	195	12.0
Total	17,967	635	3.5

Source: Maurine Christopher, "Racial 'Imbalance' in Ad Agency Personnel Is Termed
'Appalling,' " *Advertising Age* (March 18, 1968): 1, 86.

and distressing." It was, an NYCHR report decided, "a state of de facto segregation strongly suggesting discrimination."[41] Regardless of the choice of description, the survey proved there were distressingly few blacks and Puerto Rican advertising professionals. In addition, as the EEOC found, the lowest skill categories (clerks, secretaries, and data processors) held most minority employees. Statistics showed that only fifteen blacks were at the level in which they directly worked on a client account. Table 3 summarizes the survey findings.

The report also contained employment statistics specifically for the New York offices of agencies represented at the hearings. The comprehensive findings for all the agencies studied were not released. Table 4 summarizes the survey findings.

None of the agencies under examination had minority employment numbers comparable to the percentage of minorities in the city. While commissioners were impressed that some agencies, like Benton & Bowles and Norman, Craig & Kummel, had large percentages of minority employees, these two firms were unusual in this regard. Backed by these disappointing figures, members of the commission pushed agency representatives to account for the dismal records of their firms. The commission also made it clear before the hearing that it wanted more than simple reports or platitudes about the lack of qualified minorities. Instead, they directed representatives to bring specific suggestions for improvements in minority employment.[42]

TABLE 4. MINORITY GROUP EMPLOYMENT IN NEW YORK ADVERTISING AGENCIES
BY AGENCY

Agency	Total	Black	Percent Black
Gardner Advertising Company	130	0	0
Leo Burnett Company	42	0	0
Cunningham & Walsh	400	3	0.08
William Esty Company	490	2	0.4
Marschalk Company	785	7	0.9
Kenyon & Eckhardt	328	4	1.2
Geyer, Oswald	120	2	1.7
McCann-Erickson	559	10	1.8
Sullivan, Stauffer, Colwell & Bayles	603	12	2.0
Batten, Barton, Durstine & Osborn	1,296	28	2.2
Young & Rubicam	1,897	45	2.4
D'Arcy Advertising Company	237	6	2.5
Ted Bates & Company	1,178	30	2.5
Ogilvy & Mather	799	20	2.5
Warwick & Legler	162	4	2.5
Foote, Cone & Belding	465	13	2.8
MacManus, John & Adams	128	4	3.1
Compton Advertising	651	23	3.5
Ketchum, MacLeod & Grove	136	5	3.7
Dancer-Fitzgerald-Sample	698	31	4.4
J. Walter Thompson Company	1,676	82	4.9
Doyle Dane Bernbach	1,299	68	5.2
Grey Advertising	1,173	68	5.8
Needham, Harper & Steers	195	11	5.6
Norman, Craig & Kummel	245	19	7.8
Benton & Bowles	977	83	8.5
Total	16669	580	3.5 (average)

Source: Maurine Christopher, "No Letup in Push for Minority Hiring: Booth," *Advertising Age* (March 25, 1968): 142.

There appears to have been no link between an agency's current percentage of minority employees and its recruitment or training efforts. Instead, aware of the NYCHR's goals for employment opportunity and fresh off the EEOC hearings, some executives were prescient enough to realize their firm's need for improvement. So, several could answer the NYCHR's questions with descriptions of existing programs and plans for development. Some claimed that their companies upheld antidiscrimination policies but could not find qualified minorities—though it was not for lack of effort. Conversely, other representatives allowed that their agencies had disturbingly low numbers of minority employees and they presented outlines for training and recruiting more. For example, Ogilvy & Mather outlined a plan to train high school students in clerical skills for entry-level jobs. The agency also planned to set up college scholarships and to reserve some existing positions for black graduates. Robert Pruett, vice president with Warwick & Legler, described his company's plans for Operation Ad Start, a program creating a minimum of five permanent jobs for minority high school students or minority Vietnam veterans. Several other agencies, including Kenyon & Eckhardt, Ted Bates, Marschalk Company, and Grey Advertising (perhaps still stinging from its performance before the EEOC), outlined prospective training and recruitment programs targeting black high school graduates and Vietnam veterans. Some agencies, such as Grey Advertising, also created programs targeting the hard-core unemployed to provide them with both educational and agency training. Grey now also awarded employees who found qualified minorities a $50 bonus for each one the agency hired.[43]

After listening to the various responses, the NYCHR took its first steps beyond voluntarism. Commissioners told the agency men that open hiring policies or planned training programs were not enough. Instead, as the NYCHR had in negotiations with contractors and labor unions, commissioners wanted agencies to develop ongoing recruitment programs for minority candidates. In other words, they wanted agencies to develop outreach programs, rather than wait for interested minority candidates to appear in their personnel offices. Instead, noted Vallon, just as agencies used their creative powers to encourage people to switch their brands of toothpaste, they should use those same powers to create an interest in the industry within the black and Puerto Rican communities. Also, in contrast to the first hearing in 1963, the NYCHR now bluntly told representatives they would continue to call attention to the issue until the industry satisfactorily corrected the imbalances. More importantly, they highlighted that, barring change, prosecution under state and federal antidiscrimination statutes remained a distinct possibility.[44]

The NYCHR also reaffirmed its belief in a link between minority employment and representation in advertisements. Specifically, that increasing the number of minority professionals in the industry would positively influence how minorities were depicted in advertisements and by relation their image in the country. Commissioners asked: How could agencies present themselves as able to influence consumers' choice of car or soft drink but not their position on race? Vallon charged, "If you fellows can't change attitudes and create attitudes, then you've been taking a lot of good money from a lot of people under false pretenses. *You can mold opinion* [emphasis mine]." Increasing the number of minorities in agencies and in advertisements improved a firm's capacity to meet the sales needs of the client and the social need of the nation. "The image projected is the vital consideration," Booth reasoned. "The man who gets used to seeing the Negro on TV as a normal part of the scene will be more likely to hire Negroes." Like other government bodies, NYCHR commissioners understood that addressing the current crisis in the nation's cities demanded more than the influence of the government and activists. It also needed an involved business community. Moreover, commissioners were not asking agencies to make specific social arguments within their ads but to include blacks in roles that they already occupied in real life as a way to make their real-life presence seem that much more common. After all, commissioners reasoned, desegregation was leading to more black faces in places and positions where they had never been, and agencies could help soothe some of that tension by showing more minority faces in advertisements.[45]

After the hearings ended, reporters and even some agency executives strongly criticized the industry's performances. Agency leaders, some argued, needed to take a much more involved interest in the issues the NYCHR raised than was obvious at the hearings. Few upper-level executives were present at the hearings. Even among those executives who testified before the commission, one reporter labeled the majority "living examples of poor advertising" in which only "a handful of them showed they had given the matter serious thought." He continued, "For people engaged in the communications business, they seemed surprisingly inept at getting across a point of view forthrightly and affirmatively. Nor were they very impressive as creative minds at work on problem solving. They seemed to vie with one another in confessing that they were ineffective at attracting desirable Negro talent. . . . It seemed an awkward stance for people who earn their livings by counseling clients on tough marketing, merchandising and advertising problems." Rather than agency leaders, most firms sent middle-level managers or personnel directors to the hearings, a situation some viewed as a lack of commitment or interest by agency leaders. "You can't count on personnel directors to set policy, even if they grasp the situation," argued Ogilvy & Mather chairman Jock Elliott. Chief executives had that responsibility, but could hardly do so if they were ignorant of the NYCHR's concerns or asked their personnel directors to establish the agency's directives on equal employment. In fact, during the hearings one personnel director remarked to his counterpart, "We're overreacting to this Negro thing. It's just a virus, and like all viruses it will go away."[46]

Barton Cummings, chairman of Compton Advertising, candidly echoed Elliott's comments, "Corporate policy, never opposed publicly, never denied publicly [has been] administered so as to protect the status quo—and most of us simply let it go at that." Real change demanded real action by corporate leaders, Elliott and Cummings argued. To carry out effective integration efforts, the leadership of each agency had to communicate throughout the company their interest in increasing minority employees. Doing so provided the internal support that allowed for hiring minorities without fear of negative reaction from upper-level managers. In addition, it became evidence of an agency's attempt toward equal employment.[47]

Another trade reporter bluntly asked readers to consider their own racial ideals: "Are Negroes welcome on your account team?" He cautioned readers that the existence of special-markets groups like that at BBDO was hardly evidence of true company integration. These groups were important to a total advertising and marketing program but helped to segregate blacks away from others at the agency. Beyond special marketers, at too many firms a thinly veiled hypocrisy allowed for hiring blacks for internal positions but barred them from jobs that involved client contact—the fast lane to top jobs in most agencies. A few blacks, like veterans Roy Eaton and Georg Olden, occupied such positions, but they were the exception to an established rule.[48]

After completing their examination of advertising agencies, the NYCHR continued the ten-day hearings and shifted their focus to national advertisers. Specifically, they called advertiser representatives to explain why there were so few minorities in commercials. According to the NYCHR's survey, completed during their employment survey of advertising agencies, over a one-year period the companies represented made nearly seventy-five hundred television commercials. Slightly more than three hundred used black or Puerto Rican models, and out of that number fewer than fifteen featured them in a principal role. The representatives were candid in their testimony. Most company representatives stated there was no reason their advertisements could not feature blacks. But casting choices, they protested, were the responsibility of their advertising agencies. And, while their companies had not been proactive in demanding changes, they implied they would accept them if the agency recommended them.[49]

After the conclusion of the hearings, commissions in New York continued to monitor the status of minority employment in advertising, and unlike the EEOC, charged companies in violation of equal employment statutes. In May 1968, the NYSHR charged ten companies, including two advertising agencies, with employment discrimination. These charges against Ogilvy & Mather were surprising. Many observers considered the agency an industry leader in the effort to increase minority employment. In terms of the raw number of minority employees, the agency was near the middle among its peers, and it had existing programs to increase that number further. A member of the NYCHR had even told the agency that its training and recruitment programs should become the model for the entire industry. Further, one of the agency's founders, David Ogilvy, served as chairman of the New York committee for the United

Negro College Fund. And, during the hearings two months earlier, commissioners lauded company chairman Elliott as the leading example of executive involvement to raise minority employment. He was also chairman of the AAAA equal employment opportunities committee responsible for developing programs for the industry. He had also recently told his management staff to move the agency beyond an open-door policy on minority employment and instead aim for "an affirmative program that seeks out minority group employees, encourages their interest and provides development opportunities for them."[50] So, at least on paper, for minority hiring, Ogilvy & Mather appeared as an example of the correct way to go about raising the number of minorities in the industry.

Unfortunately, beyond vague mentions of an "informal" commission investigation of employment practices, the record is silent about why the commission filed discrimination charges against Ogilvy & Mather. Nevertheless, filing charges compelled the company to meet with the NYSHR. During these meetings, the two sides agreed the agency would place help wanted ads in media directed to minorities and continue their program of active recruitment. The amicable meetings between the two groups led NYSHR chairman Robert Mangum to laud the executives for their openness to suggested changes.[51]

Despite the pressure applied by the NYCHR and NYSHR, the number of minorities in the industry improved only slightly by the end of 1968. In early 1969, the NYCHR released the results for its 1968 study. Perhaps foreshadowing a decline in agency cooperation, only thirty-five agencies responded to the commissions request for employment numbers versus forty the prior year. Numbers were up across the board, with the secretarial, media, and radio-TV production areas showing the greatest increases. The areas that were most central to agency day-to-day decision making, account handling and copywriting, were up less than one-half percent. Minority positions in management were down slightly. And, while more secretaries may not have been what activists and commissioners had in mind, by being in an agency they at least offered the possibility for future professional training or other opportunities for advancement. For example, Caroline Jones, one of the top black females in advertising history, started her career in the secretarial pool. Admittedly, entry-level jobs did not immediately increase an agency's number of black professionals, but they offered the possibility of doing so over the long term. Also, though not statistically corroborated, the NYCHR chairman Booth said that there appeared to be more minorities visible in commercials since the prior year's hearings. But he cautiously observed, "There is no room for complacency just because there has been some progress in front of the camera."[52]

During commission hearings in early 1969, Booth suggested that if greater improvements were not obvious by the end of the year, those agencies with the lowest percentage of minority employees would face inquiry. Booth felt that too few executives had gone beyond the vocal support of equal employment and that too many programs were in the planning stages and far too few were in operation. Therefore, the commission recommended a three-point program to raise minority employment numbers:

> The advertising industry [should] examine its insistence on prior experience as a qualification for employment, especially in such positions as account executives, and consider instead how potential ability can be recognized and developed.
> Professional trade unions, such as the American Federation of Television & Radio Artists, [should] try to find ways to enforce the anti-discrimination clauses in their contracts.
> Admen and broadcasters [should] use their sales talents to convince Negroes and others who have become accustomed to having doors closed in their faces that there are opportunities for them in the world of advertising.[53]

Further, the commission told agencies to use their creative skill and aggressively advertise their efforts to potential applicants.

This time, advertising executives began to listen to the commission's warnings. Several agencies increased their recruitment and training programs. Admittedly, some agency executives launched their programs voluntarily. But the timing of most programs suggests that most agencies did so in response to pressure brought by the NYCHR, NYSHR, and EEOC. By raising the threat of both negative publicity and prosecution, the cumulative effect of governmental inquiry and civil rights group pressure helped prod agency executives who lacked the interest or commitment to develop such programs on their own. This combination of internal interest and external pressure led to an explosion in the number of training and recruitment efforts that helped increase the number of minority professionals in the industry. As one observer wryly concluded, "There is something about the threat of prosecution that seems to make voluntary programs work much better."[54]

Do Something: The Development of Training Programs

By the early 1960s, companies throughout the nation could with some justification claim that they could not find any qualified black applicants, that is, any applicants with significant job experience. In contrast to prior years, in which activists could meet that claim by producing a qualified applicant, now they sometimes could not. The broad range of companies seeking black managers or those with technical skills had drained the pool of easily located black professionals. As a result, finding qualified blacks could sometimes be a difficult and time-consuming task. In 1964, the Urban League tried to address this problem by opening the National Skills Bank as a placement center for black professionals, but the number of qualified minorities for various professions remained small. As a result, civil rights activists and, eventually, government commissions realized that if the pool of minority applications was to increase, companies had to go beyond merely searching for qualified candidates and find those with the aptitude to become qualified. Further, activists began to press companies, eventually including advertising agencies, to underwrite the costs of developing the pool of qualified black applicants.[55]

The advertising industry did not exist in a vacuum. Throughout the early 1960s, daily stories of local and national struggles for racial equality confronted its members just as they did the rest of the country. Moreover, to many in the industry, the existence of local, state, and federal equal employment commissions proved that if the industry did not move voluntarily on issues of equal employment the government would force them to do so. Therefore, the leading trade journals for the industry continued to report on the subject. In the mid-1960s, a story on agency hiring catalyzed the development of one of the most effective minority recruitment and training programs in industry history.

THE BASIC ADVERTISING COURSE

In 1966, editors at *Advertising Age* launched a study of mainstream agency employment of minorities. To do so they surveyed major agencies in New York, Chicago, and Los Angeles, requesting a count of their minority employees. The findings discouraged the paper's reporters and editors. Although agencies in New York were ahead of their counterparts in the other two cities, there was clearly a gap between agency rhetoric and action. When queried, agency representatives offered the traditional rationale—there simply were not any qualified blacks available. Conversely, blacks who had sought agency jobs or who ran employment placement firms had a different response. "Sure agencies say they want to hire Negroes, but few of them are making any efforts at all to inform Negroes of the opportunities in advertising," one black employment specialist argued. "And when a Negro is genuinely qualified it's far more difficult for him to get hired than it would be for a white applicant." One employment agency reported that only 10 percent of the candidates they sent for agency interviews found jobs. Agency personnel directors were always friendly and encouraged employment agencies to send them black applicants, but their cordiality and encouragement had translated into few job offers. Further, some agencies, such as J. Walter

Thompson, Doyle Dane Bernbach, and Foote, Cone and Belding maintained aggressive recruitment policies, but they were the exception in
the industry. Reporters concluded that public pressure seemed the only
thing that encouraged other agencies to pursue similar measures.[56]

However, to at least one employment specialist reporters interviewed,
public pressure created little meaningful action. Most advertising executives chose to weather the public pressure by vocally supporting equal
opportunity, but that support led to few actual jobs. Once the protests
stopped and picketers went home, agencies had hired few black professionals or established significant training or recruitment programs.
Instead, in the minds of some blacks, "phonies" and "foot-draggers"
staffed most agencies, and their only desire was to uphold the racial
status quo. Agency executives' and black employment specialists' analyses of the problem were so different, one might wonder if they were
examining the same issue.[57]

The *Advertising Age* study found that Los Angeles agencies had the lowest number of black professionals. Reporters found only one black
advertising professional working at a major firm. Further, the Los
Angeles advertising community lacked even the basic training and
recruitment mechanisms available in Chicago and New York. In Chicago, although civil rights groups and agency leaders periodically discussed minority employment matters, the number of black professionals
remained small. Meanwhile, New York had the largest number of black
professionals. Additionally, agencies in the city had opened their training programs to black applicants and several had extended recruitment
efforts to find black applicants.[58]

Much of New York's lead in the number of black professionals may
have resulted from the pressure brought by civil rights groups and
inquiries from the city and state human rights commissions. Also, the
state passed fair employment laws before both Illinois and California, so
agencies there faced possible legal ramifications for employment discrimination. Reporters also found that representatives of New York
agencies were more open to discussing African American employment
than those in other cities. Representatives in Chicago and Los Angeles
were often more guarded in their comments, did not want their agency
name mentioned in the story, or openly resented the pressure for open
employment. One Chicago executive lamented, "Let's face it, it sticks in
a white man's craw to be told that he has to go out of his way and mount
special programs to give Negroes an opportunity in advertising. Nobody
else is given, or expects, such preferential treatment." This type of
counterargument to the idea of creating special outreach and opportunities for blacks was rarely openly offered. Instead, in interviews,
speeches, and letters from readers published in trade journals, there was

support (at least at the theoretical level) to creating a larger number of black professionals in the industry. In fact, a number of executives admitted that they could do more to raise the number of black employees. "It's probably a valid charge that agencies don't recruit and train enough," one Chicago agency man observed. This same executive went on to note, though, that when he needed to hire someone he did not have time to discuss it with civil rights groups. Those who had pursued consultation with civil rights groups argued they were "difficult to work with" and wanted agencies to place nonqualified blacks into professional agency jobs.[59]

Reporters also surveyed civil rights activists on their opinions of agencies' commitment to hiring blacks. To activists the answer was simple—most agencies had no genuine desire to change employment practices. W. Hampton McKinney, director of the Chicago Urban League's employment department, told reporters that in 1964 the League and the Chicago council of the AAAA had agreed to set up a professional skills training program for blacks, but the effort stalled. The agreement called for the League to send the resumes of black applicants to the AAAA and for the AAAA to select the participants for the program. But after the League sent the AAAA resumes for several prospective students, no training class developed. In response, the AAAA told reporters that the applicants the League sent were too old (late twenties and early thirties) to enter the agency business. Further, some were already earning more than they would get as new agency hires and were unlikely to join the program. "We . . . now know," an AAAA representative concluded, "that it is a mistake to let the Urban League screen the people for our profession. We should have done the screening ourselves."[60]

The disagreement between the Urban League and the AAAA stemmed mostly from poor communication on both sides. League members wanted to use the first batch of resumes to start a dialogue and set up parameters for the referral system. "There was no expectation that the persons represented by the resumes submitted would be included in a training program," McKinney argued. "The question asked was, 'Are these they type of people we should consider?' "[61] But after sending the resumes the only contact from the AAAA was an announcement canceling the training program. To the AAAA, the resumes confirmed that the League's only concern was in supplying black students for the program with no regard for their qualifications. Fortunately for both sides, the story in *Advertising Age* led to them resume discussions about Chicago-based training programs. The result of these conversations was the pioneering Basic Advertising Course (BAC).

While the Urban League and the AAAA agreed on the purpose for a training course, the design of the course fell to Bob Ross and Bill Sharp, a white man and a black man respectively. The two men had known each other professionally for several years. Ross mentored Sharp when he first entered advertising and helped him develop his creative portfolio. Sharp credited Ross, then chairman of the Chicago AAAA, with the initial idea for the BAC. But when he contacted Sharp, he found a willing participant. Unknown to Ross, Sharp and other blacks working in the Chicago advertising industry, including future agency owners Tom Burrell and Frank Mingo, were already discussing ways to increase the number of black employees. These men believed that there were many blacks interested in joining the advertising business and that training could provide them with the skills needed to do so. So, a properly developed and rigorous training course could rapidly increase the numbers of qualified black applicants in the city. Within a few weeks Sharp, Ross, and Vernon Fryburger, chairman of the department of advertising at Northwestern University, designed the BAC. It was up to Sharp, however, to implement the group's plans. The AAAA provided the money and helped secure classroom facilities and Sharp recruited a faculty of black and white advertising professionals from around the city.[62]

Sharp set up the BAC with three goals in mind: First, to equip black students with the tools they needed to earn a professional job in an agency. (There were enough blacks working in the nonprofessional areas and, while janitors and mail carriers performed important roles, increasing their numbers would not further Sharp's or the Urban League's goals.) The challenge was to increase the numbers of black copywriters, art directors, and account executives. Second, he wanted to increase the general pool of black professionals. All students might not go directly into agency work, but the knowledge and experience they gained from the BAC would keep that alternative open to them in the future. To Sharp, the BAC could provide the rigorously trained, motivated people that agency personnel directors said they were looking for. And by increasing that pool, its graduates could help reduce argument that no qualified blacks were available. Third, Sharp viewed the course as a way to bring talented people into the industry who might not have otherwise considered it as a career. "My aim is to bring the very best people I can to this business—people I believe will make a bonafide contribution to advertising—not just to integrate the advertising business," he stated.[63]

To Sharp, blacks were a potential wellspring from which agencies could draw talented people with a perspective different from that of current agency personnel. He felt that blacks' historic struggles gave them a unique vision of the American dream that would help them craft campaigns to better enable agencies to speak to a racially diverse country. He said, "You have an industry that purports to depict America, the real

America, and they can't because they're too limited in their knowledge and experience. Plus they don't feel as though they really need to. Much of it is not malicious, much of it is not because they're prejudiced, much of it is benign. It's an attitude born of 'Oh, we don't need to know that,' or 'I don't need to learn your culture, you need to learn mine.'" To Sharp and other observers, blacks were a source of racial, as well as ideological, diversification of the industry, and they could help spur the development of more effective advertisements.[64]

Students learned about the BAC through either personal recruitment by Ross, Sharp, or others aware of the course or through radio advertisements. Personal appeals to blacks not in the industry were only slightly successful. Most professional-level blacks already earned salaries well over those for entry-level positions and had little interest in moving. For example, one man Ross tried to recruit politely turned down the offer because he was already making three times the $7,000 annual salary Ross quoted him. The radio advertisements Sharp wrote proved far more successful. They explained the course and discussed the opportunities available in the industry to those with talent and the willingness to work hard. Applications for the course stretched into the hundreds. Ross and Sharp personally screened each applicant. "The recruiting revealed to us that there was a plethora of people interested in getting into this business, but most of them didn't know either anything about it or very much about it," Sharp recalled. Both he and Ross scrutinized candidates for their motivation, intelligence, and potential talent, and their standards were tough. Both men knew that the perception of graduates for the first course would likely impact perceptions of subsequent graduates, so they selected the best possible applicants they found. For example, in one class Sharp had to whittle an applicant pool of 165 down to fill eight available slots. He focused on people with high motivation and good oral and written communication skills. All that group of people needed, he believed, was training and an opportunity. "It's amazing just how smart so many black folks are, because you had people who'd never heard of an agency before and they can write, or they can be art directors or they can be analysts for the media department, or they can be assistant account executives," he enthusiastically observed. Once selected, students enrolled in the program free of charge with the only requirement being that they attend each of the thirteen classroom sessions held over thirteen weeks.[65]

The first BAC launched in September 1967, with ten students. Initially, the two-hour classes met at Northwestern University, but subsequent classes met at advertising agencies around Chicago. Courses focused on the media research and planning, as well as creative portions of agency work, the areas Sharp and others believed most appropriate for people with no prior agency experience. Sharp, Burrell, Frank Daughton, and other black professionals taught most of the classes, and white instructors like Bruce Bendinger and Ross sometimes joined them. Outside of the classroom, individual advisors gave students further immersion in agency life via agency visits or other informal arrangements. Student assignments included: crafting new television, radio, or print advertisements; rewriting existing advertisements; or developing a media plan. Even though the students were advertising beginners, Sharp and the other faculty were unsparing in their criticism. There was no reason to coddle the students with criticism less than they would receive as working professionals. Still, Sharp's enthusiasm for advertising and for the prospect of bringing more blacks into agency work translated into his teaching style, an effective combination of jokes, sarcasm, and creativity. The capstone activity before graduation was a formal presentation of each student's creative work.[66]

Sharp wanted to produce BAC graduates who would not require agencies to lower their employment standards. Therefore, course requirements were rigorous, and students who did not follow them could be dismissed from the program. Sharp knew agencies would not tolerate missed assignments, tardiness, or poor quality work, and he refused to do so during the BAC. He required attendance at all classes and students dressed in clothes suitable for an office environment. Sharp and Ross wanted to create advertising professionals, not run a pass-through course that did not prepare students for the realities of the advertising community. Blacks' skin color made them immediately conspicuous before the end of their first day of work, and professional incompetence would make that visibility all the more glaring. If existing black professionals were already under a microscope, Sharp knew that graduates of the BAC would be even more so. "My goal is to have this class looked upon as a gem," he said. "That it develop such a character that people will say, 'Hey, look at the guys coming out of the Basic Ad Class. They're a group of tigers.'" Therefore, the tough course requirements helped ensure that students were ready to meet potential challenges.[67]

In the mock assignments Ross and Sharp designed, students worked on campaigns for the general, rather than black, consumer market. One reason they did so because some large agencies, like J. Walter Thompson and Leo Burnett, agreed to hire a set number of course graduates each year, and the two men wanted students to be able to be professionally flexible. Also, while being a specialist on the black consumer market might help students gain entry into some agencies, Sharp felt that it could also hamper them from branching into other types of accounts. Since there were only a few black-owned agencies, and none had the capacity to absorb a large number of new employees, mainstream agencies were the only practical potential outlet.[68]

But after the first year of the course, Sharp began to have difficulty finding jobs for all the graduates. Those students who did not receive one of the guaranteed positions had to go through the traditional interview process and did not always find agency work. In fact, during interviews several graduates found that their affiliation with the BAC meant little to some personnel directors. While this was not necessarily a function of racism, it discouraged both Sharp and course graduates. Rather than accept the situation, though, Sharp went to the AAAA board of governors and urged them to do more to help blacks, both BAC graduates and others, to enter the business:

They [blacks] don't talk like white folks. They don't dress like white folks. They see life differently and sense life differently. But they're not sick, they're not crippled. Can they build a marketing plan? No. A media plan? No. A research project? No. A new creative concept? No. Kind of reminds me that the young white people we hire—men with a bachelor's degree or a master's degree or even a Ph.D.—are equally innocent of experience in building marketing plans or media plans or research plans or creative plans. . . . I ask only to see young black people given their chance . . . I ask only that you find a new kind of standard to help young black people to get a chance to succeed or fail.[69]

Sharp encouraged the group to guarantee jobs to at least some of the graduates of the BAC or to set up training courses of their own. If they did not, he cautioned, agency employment of black professionals had little chance to increase for the foreseeable future.

Eventually, Sharp's arguments were persuasive and his teaching methods effective. Although not guaranteed jobs before graduation, most BAC students who wanted to work in advertising eventually did so. In early 1970 one report estimated that of the fifty blacks working in a professional capacity in Chicago agencies, approximately thirty were graduates of the BAC. Some graduates worked in advertising for several years, and at least one, Carol Williams, founded and still maintains one of the most successful black-owned agencies in history. The course continued to run for several years even after Sharp briefly left the industry to work in the federal Office of Economic Opportunity. The program achieved many of Sharp's goals. He proved that it was possible to develop a pool of highly trained black advertising professionals, and several course graduates went on to impact the industry in the positive ways he originally imagined. When it ended in the early 1970s, the BAC had helped several dozen blacks earn jobs in advertising.[70]

Sharp later took the lessons acquired from teaching the BAC and self-published a sixty-six-page book entitled *How to Be Black and Get a Job in the Advertising Agency Business Anyway.* The clever title illustrated Sharp's understanding of both the perceived racism many blacks believed was inherent in the industry and the idea that success in advertising meant a loss of black identity. On the subject of racism, Sharp argued that it existed but that blacks could nonetheless find success. Advertising was more than just "white folks business." However, blacks should not forget that they would likely be among the first blacks in an agency. "You can expect to be patronized, parentalized, organized, and scrutinized. And you'll recognize, sometimes, that you symbolize the guilt some White folks have had for a long time," he advised. He reassured those who feared they would be forced to give up their identity as blacks that they did not have to be "Super Nigger" but simply needed to meet existing professional standards.[71]

Despite the success of the BAC, Sharp later felt he made a "major mistake" by not doing more to help students through acculturation to their first agency. He later recognized that getting into the agency was simply the beginning of the process and that students also needed guidance on working within a large white corporation with few other blacks around. Sharp felt that students would have been better able to persevere if they had mentors, as he had in Ross, who could have helped educate them on the unwritten rules of behavior and success that went with agency work. With the support of such mentors or personal contact, he felt the BAC would have been more successful in both getting graduates into agencies and advancing to the professional levels he later achieved.[72]

By the end of 1967, it was evident to industry observers that the numbers of blacks in agencies had increased but were still low. One study by the EEOC found that blacks occupied only 3.7 percent of the white-collar jobs in 13 major advertising agencies. Moreover, agencies accepted blacks for internal positions but not for the jobs that required meetings with clients. Thus, even though the numbers of blacks in mainstream firms were increasing, the specialties that led to professional advancement continued to have precious few black members.[73]

Although the BAC provided a successful model for training minorities, the AAAA did not replicate its structure elsewhere. That speaks less to a failure on the program directors' part than to the large number of training programs in existence in the late 1960s. In the wake of the riots, and especially after the assassination of Martin Luther King, Jr., several agency leaders resolved to "do something" to help address the urban crisis. So by 1968, a plethora of individual agencies, local and regional advertising organizations, and independent groups of industry professionals had developed training and/or recruitment programs. For example, moved by the continuing plight of black citizens in Watts, the Western States Advertising Agencies Association (WSAAA) initiated a course training young blacks for agency positions. This was a unique move because it came voluntarily from agencies that had few black employees and were far removed from the pressures applied by civil rights and government organizations. Around the country advertising clubs in cities like Detroit, Boston, and Cleveland sponsored a variety of independent programs that provided blacks with training for agency jobs. In New York, a group of blacks in the industry set up a program similar to the BAC and provided training for both beginners and experienced professionals. Agency executives had seemingly taken on the recent charge by Elliott and the older calls by David Sullivan to do more than look for qualified minorities but to actually help them become qualified. These programs varied in duration and content, but most trained disadvantaged blacks for the professional areas of agency work. Each of these programs was a small effort, often attracting only ten to fifteen students per session, but they were helping to raise the number of minorities in the industry.[74]

Expanding Training and Recruitment

Although the AAAA did not replicate the BAC course outside Chicago, the organization continued to sponsor discussions about equal employment. For example, it was the primary issue examined at the 1968 AAAA convention. Ogilvy & Mather chairman Elliott chaired a special committee tasked with developing comprehensive minority recruitment and training programs. Elliott eloquently and bluntly encouraged his audience to increase efforts to recruit and develop minority professionals and to take an active interest in solving the urban crisis. He admitted that on matters of employment his own agency was little better than average. But for the industry as a whole, the matter was far worse. "We bring up the rear," he declared. "A hell of a place for people who consider themselves problem solvers, pace-setters, and molders of public opinion." And the low number of minority professionals was not a question of the size of the industry or the need for specialized skills, it was simple apathy. To Elliott, agency leaders, the men and women in the audience, were the ones who had failed to guide their firms beyond their traditional hiring practices. "Nothing will happen in the use of minority group talent unless we set the policy, unless we make that policy known to all our staff, unless we set up the procedures to make it work, unless we cope with the occasional client who drags his heels," he argued. Elliott singled out the Benton & Bowles (B&B) agency for its record on minority hiring and for its number of minority executives. More agencies needed to follow B&B's lead, he said, and do more than have an open door for minority hires but actively seek them out. Elliott failed to mention that at least a portion of B&B's enlightened practices were the results of agreements the firm reached with the CORE/CIS protest in 1966 (see Chapter 3).[75]

Elliott closed by asking executives to set a proactive policy for including minorities as principal figures in advertisements and to make that policy known at all levels of the agency. The executives gathered in the room received Elliott's speech with "prolonged applause." Whether the agency CEOs, presidents, and senior account managers in the room would translate that enthusiasm into systematic changes in agency practices remained in question. These were not the personnel directors that some agencies had sent to early NYCHR hearings but were the ones with the power to lead immediate changes. What would they do, however when the enthusiasm had faded and they returned to the demands of agency life?[76]

Individual Agency Programs

Although not singled out in Elliott's speech, several agencies were already designing programs to develop minority employees. Shortly after the 1968 NYCHR hearings, a full-page advertisement appeared in the *New York Times* with a caption reading; "Who says there are no Negroes in the advertising business? I've heard of five." Crafted by the executive staff at the Daniels & Charles agency, the group had considered running the advertisement for some time but declined because it seemed "too self-serving." But after the assassination of Martin Luther King, Jr., executives decided, "The hell with it; someone has to do something, so let's run the ad." They expressed the feeling of many in the industry and the country whom the assassination shocked into action. Several agencies started training programs in the wake of King's death, including that at Daniels & Charles as well as the JWT Training Program at J. Walter Thompson.[77]

The text of the "Who says" advertisement described the hiring experiences of Laurence Dunst, the agency's senior vice president and creative director. Over the preceding five years, Dunst had hired over one hundred people and interviewed hundreds more. But in that period he never hired a black art director or copywriter because he "never saw one." "And my case is not unusual," he stated in the advertisement. "The facts are obvious. The advertising business is one of the most racially unbalanced industries in America." Although he did not consider advertising personnel to be "bigots or racists," in the ad Dunst accused them of having done next to nothing to relieve the problem. Thus, he and other Daniels & Charles executives agreed to set up a scholarship program enabling black students to attend art or business schools. Still, Dunst did not even consider these efforts to be satisfactory. Therefore, in the ad he challenged both leaders in his agency and others in the advertising industry to do more on the matter. He stated in the advertisement, "We need advertisers to endow more scholarships. We need agencies to set up training programs for every phase of our business that will recruit some members from Harlem instead of Harvard. We need prominent ad men to speak to, or actually help run special advertising courses for Negro high school students." The ad closed with the request for all people willing to "do something" to contact Dunst.[78]

The *Times* advertisement provoked a tremendous response. It appeared in the Monday edition, and by Friday Dunst had received over three hundred letters and phone calls expressing interest and offering support. A few agency executives promised financial and staff support, and some major advertisers offered to make a contribution. Also, at least one "major foundation" pledged financial support for the scholarship program. The program called for agencies to provide scholarships to individual students and then provide employment for that student for at least twelve months. Similar to the BAC, students would take courses enabling them to work in the creative areas because, like Sharp, Dunst believed it allowed novices the best opportunities for advancing to other areas of agency work.[79]

Other agencies followed the lead of Daniels & Charles and developed their own independent training programs. In July 1968, executives at Doyle Dane Bernbach (DDB), with the support of the New York State Employment Service and in partnership with the National Alliance of Businessmen (NAB), announced the creation of a training program for minorities without the basic educational needs for agency work. There were no educational requirements for admittance to the program, and students received coursework in reading and mathematics, as well as in typing and other clerical skills. Targeting the group some believed to be the primary riot participants, the "hard-core unemployed," the joint effort led to a series of recruiting efforts targeting unemployed persons.[80]

Because of the group targeted by the program, leaders decided that all who expressed an interest in participating would be able to do so. This open enrollment policy meant that students who entered the course each came with varying degrees of education. In contrast to the BAC, to graduate the course students only needed to show a tenth-grade reading level. Several students entered the program reading at only the third- or fourth-grade level, but by the end they had met the basic requirements. In the mornings, students attended classes, and during the afternoon they worked in different areas of the agency. After doing

introductory-level work around the firm, students received departmen-
tal placements to continue their training and advancement. As the
design of the course shows, agency executives did not view the course as
a means to increase their professional-level black employees. Instead, in
the spirit of "do something," they hoped to "make a dent" in the overall level of blacks in the agency.[81]

In Chicago, executives at Foote, Cone & Belding created "Operation
College Bound" to introduce area black high school students to the
inner workings of advertising agencies. An added goal of the program
was to encourage students to advance their educations beyond the high
school level and, if interested, eventually work in an agency. During the
eight-week program, students worked throughout the agency in the
mornings and took classes in economics and marketing during the afternoons. Students also had the opportunity to create advertisements for
existing and introductory products, but the program focused on providing instruction on a broad range of subjects. The program accepted only
seven to ten students per summer, but participation in the program convinced several students to go to college and others to work in the advertising field.[82]

In a move similar to that of Foote, Cone & Belding, executives at
Campbell-Ewald set up a program targeting Detroit-area black high
school students. But the Campbell-Ewald program also provided entering students with college scholarships. Therefore, it motivated students
to seek higher education and provided them with a means to get there.
Students worked at the agency during the summer and after graduation
received scholarships to pursue any college major they wanted. Among
minority scholarship programs, the Campbell-Ewald program was
unique because it did not require students to major in areas connected
with advertising. Hugh Redhead, president of Campbell-Ewald, noted,
"We started a scholarship program a year ago to remove economic road-
blocks for Detroit high school graduates with the ability and desire to
attend college." Thus, executives considered the program to be a means
of assuming a higher level of social responsibility and community participation. But they also saw the program as a way to attract more blacks to
the advertising industry. Redhead reasoned the program would help to
"open up opportunities in the advertising business and also to attract
bright young talent in the city to work for us." It is unclear how Redhead
thought the program could open opportunities for minorities because
the program did not require students to work for the agency or promise
them jobs after graduation from college.[83]

The most comprehensive program by an individual agency came from
JWT. In early 1968, the agency president, Dan Seymour, became the
coordinator of the President's Council on Youth Opportunity. His new

position led others within JWT to consider ways in which the agency could further aid members of minority groups. In 1968 the agency launched Program Brother, a series of community-based efforts to aid blacks and Hispanics in New York City. One executive, John Bellini, drafted the idea for a minority youth training program for blacks and Puerto Ricans. The resulting course, the JWT Training Program began its first class in July 1968.[84]

Employment agencies and social service organizations provided applicants for the program. As did Bill Sharp, Bellini selected students for the program only after intensive interviews assessing their interest and aptitude. "These young men must not be treated as poverty victims, but as men, each learning a job that will help him become a professional." All of the fourteen students who eventually enrolled in the initial program were under twenty-six years old and had varying educational qualifications. Some had failed to complete high school, while others had some college or technical training. Regardless of their background, though, they were enthusiastic about the opportunity to work at JWT. One student compared working at JWT with landing in a "gold mine." "We take great pride in our new occupation," one student proudly wrote. "We are no longer 'boys' but men, and soon hopefully, advertising men." Bellini served as the program coordinator while Kathy Solomon became the course's day-to-day instructor. Those students without high school degrees received instruction to help them get their equivalency diplomas, but the primary focus of the JWT program was training for professional-level jobs. Students were in the program for one year during which they spent a month in different agency departments. At the end of each monthly rotation, each student received a progress report from his supervisor. At the end of the first full program, eleven graduates were offered and accepted jobs at the agency. For the three remaining students, two became full-time college students, and the last experienced a significant illness that prevented him from working. Ten black women, who participated in a secretarial program JWT cosponsored with other agencies and advertising organizations, also joined the agency with the eleven new male employees.[85]

Agency executives considered the first class a success, and a second, expanded class attracted fifty-five students. In the morning, students received instruction in history, math, and English. In the afternoon men learned the basics of advertising while women received training in shorthand and typing, a gender separation mirroring that within the larger agency. Despite the fact that there were female vice presidents at the agency and that one, Helen Resor, had sat on the board of directors, the majority of women in the agency were secretaries. The gender division also existed at the professional ranks. Black adwoman Caroline Jones, a former JWT copywriter, recalled that "women writers worked on 'women's' products, men on 'men's' accounts. And, yes, the women wore white gloves and hats to the office and some kept their hats on *in* [emphasis in original] the office." In the early 1960s, JWT only offered existing female employees the chance to become copywriters once per year. All the women at the agency were invited to compete for slots in the agency's copywriter training course. They were given three weeks to complete a copywriting assignment, and those with the best results were placed into a six-week training course. After completing the training they returned to their secretarial positions until a female copywriter position became available. "Lest you think this cruel and unusual punishment, I hasten to point out there were only two agencies in the country, both located in New York City, that offered even this much internal opportunity for women to crawl out of the secretarial ditch into which all of us, college education notwithstanding, were traditionally tossed," Jones stated. Thus, the black women being trained as secretaries were treated differently than the men, but (in a twisted nod to equality) they received the same professionally limited options as other women at the agency.[86]

In the second year of the program one of the overarching goals was to go beyond creating future advertising professionals to encouraging students in an effort to contribute to easing the problems experienced by the underemployed. The broad educational component of the program became envisioned as a way to give students a foundation on which they could be employed in jobs beyond those available just within the advertising industry.

Unfortunately, it is unclear why or even when the JWT Training Program ended. Most likely it was a victim of the advertising slowdown of the early 1970s, when agencies canceled many similar training programs. It would have been hard for JWT executives to justify training new employees when they were laying of existing ones. It was not cheap or easy to run, costing more than $20,000 yearly (approximately $112,000 in 2006 dollars). Also, because many of the instructors were JWT employees, another staff member had to cover lost productivity. When revenues were lean, executives understandably chose to eliminate that kind of inefficiency to maintain profitability. Still, judging by agency evaluations, agency leaders considered the JWT Training Program a success. The program increased the number of minority employees at the agency. Graduates of the first two classes represented nearly 20 percent of all the agency's new minority hires with the other 80 percent coming largely from the agency's ongoing recruiting efforts. In the end, the success of JWT Training Program demonstrated that, while sometimes costly, training programs could lead to a visible increase in an agency's black professional staff.[87]

By 1970, advertising agencies across the country had set up programs to increase minority employment. Lacking their own individual programs, several agencies took part in or cosponsored efforts established by other agencies or advertising organizations. Some executives considered their agency's training programs to be experimental, while others (albeit a smaller number) envisioned them as a permanent part of company efforts. Regardless of the projected duration of the respective program, during the 1960s efforts to raise the number of minorities in the industry occurred at virtually all the major agencies. Regrettably, most of these effective, but costly, programs quietly disappeared in the recession of the early 1970s.

To be fair, most training programs targeting minority candidates represented a marked departure from traditional agency hiring in which laws of supply and demand allowed managers to select the cream of the applicant pool. Training and recruitment programs were an expensive shift in the traditionally successful, but racially restrictive, industry hiring measures. Still, these programs, though short-lived, led directly to an increase in the number of blacks in the advertising industry. Several of these new and veteran black professionals joined to form a training and advocacy group.

THE GROUP FOR ADVERTISING PROGRESS

In 1968, several black professionals in New York City created the Group for Advertising Progress (GAP) to increase the number of blacks in advertising agencies and to be a resource for those already in the industry. There were no racial limits on membership, but to become a member an individual had to be working in some capacity in the advertising industry. Most of the members worked in agencies, but several members were freelancers or in worked corporate advertising and marketing departments. This focused membership criteria allowed GAP to emphasize programs and services for advertising veterans. In contrast to the Basic Advertising Course, which focused on those new to advertising, many of GAP's programs helped blacks already in the industry further develop their skill sets. This was a conscious decision by GAP leaders. By focusing on existing black professionals, they believed they could encourage agency leaders to develop programs to help experienced blacks in the industry advance faster. Further, GAP president Doug Alligood, an account executive at Batten, Barton, Durstine, and Osborn, linked the presence of blacks in the industry to their treatment in advertisements. He believed that if GAP were able to raise the number of blacks in decision-making positions, the stature of blacks in advertisements would naturally follow.[88]

Founded with over one hundred charter members, GAP developed various programs targeting black students as well as working professionals. GAP worked in concert with the AAAA to encourage member agencies to create training programs and further expand those in already in existence. Members of the organization spoke at industry conventions and spoke on subjects ranging from the current state of blacks in the industry to advice on recruiting minorities to agencies. The group also published *Final Proof*, a newsletter that included literary articles as well as technical pieces on items such as television production work.[89]

GAP members also visited high schools and colleges and worked with the Urban League to increase student awareness about advertising careers and to find prospective candidates for training programs. For example, the two organizations and the AAAA organized an advertising training and information program at Howard University and Morehouse College, two historically black universities. A portion of the effort focused on training interested students, but its key thrust was to disseminate information about the industry. As Alligood noted, "Because minority-group people don't imagine they can establish careers in advertising, they do not even consider it in their vocational planning." Instead, blacks with an interest in business or marketing careers majored in traditional business categories. Alligood and others hoped the training program could help develop the colleges into a pool from which agencies could draw future black employees. Beyond the college program, GAP also offered training seminars in account management, creative arts, and crafting television commercials to blacks already in the industry. These courses gave members access to training that increased their knowledge and made them more competitive for promotions.[90]

Despite the working relationship between GAP and other industry groups, efforts to set up joint training programs were only modestly successful. In contrast to the BAC in Chicago, neither GAP nor the AAAA secured job commitments for course graduates. Therefore, when students completed training they had little support in finding a job. As a result fewer than one hundred blacks joined the industry because of GAP programs. Another key problem was that GAP courses often duplicated existing efforts from other advertising organizations and individual agencies. These programs convinced many advertising executives that they already had enough prospective black job candidates. Later, when individual agencies began to reduce their training programs they declined to hire GAP course graduates because of continuing staff reductions.[91]

GAP members actively worked to alter the depictions of minorities within advertisements and television programs. They also developed programs to help blacks in the industry gain the marketable skills that would make them better candidates for advancement and promotion. As part of that effort, they worked with civil rights and government organizations for investigations into racial discrimination in the advertising industry. While the group's efforts at setting up its own training programs for blacks inexperienced in advertising largely failed, its work at helping blacks already in the industry upgrade their skills was successful. Beyond training courses, the group served as a place where blacks could express the frustrations and successes in their careers among those of similar mind and experience. Additionally, along with the BAC, GAP displayed the agency of blacks within the industry to further increase their numbers. Each of the various training and recruitment programs, regardless of size or geographic location, helped achieve that goal. Despite its limited programmatic success, GAP was an important organizational voice keeping the topic of minority recruitment and professional development near the forefront of industry issues. And, while still small in comparison to total industry size, research in the late 1960s showed the number of blacks in mainstream agencies had increased.[92]

Blacks in Mainstream Advertising Agencies

In 1968, Elliott charged advertising executives to "do something" to help create more opportunities for blacks and other minorities. While executives may or may not have been responding directly to Elliott's charge, it is clear from the multitude of efforts that agencies initiated in 1968 and 1969 that several people at least tried to act on the ideas he expressed. Assessing the flurry of activity, one reporter stated, "No one is going to look on these events, individually or collectively, as giant strides toward the solution of the problems to which they are addressing themselves. But they do give a pretty clear indication that there is a great deal of activity, as well as discussion, concerning these major problems, and that there is hope for real accomplishments ahead."[93]

Initially, the optimism borne by people who supported equal employment efforts seemed justified. At large agencies, like J. Walter Thompson and Ogilvy & Mather, the number of blacks in the agency grew steadily after the political and social upheavals of 1968. In agencies in New York and Chicago especially, the number of black account executives, the people who had day-to-day contact with clients, also grew. In most agencies, to reach the level of company officer, one needed to have once been an account executive. Thus, some blacks were at least "in the pipeline" to achieve the level of vice president or higher. Also, the increase in account executives points toward blacks' widening presence in several different areas of agency work. Although some, both black and white, felt that agencies could do even more in their efforts, the overall number of blacks in both nonprofessional and professional areas was rising.[94]

According to a study conducted by the AAAA in late 1969, over a two-year period the percentage of minority employees at the fifteen largest agencies in New York City had more than doubled. In fact, at some agencies the number of black employees had approached 15 percent of the company's total. The study did not list, however, the job categories in which the gains had taken place. During another AAAA speech, Elliott lauded executives for their efforts and urged all agencies to set a target goal of 13 percent minority employees by 1972. Unfortunately, few people were present to hear Elliott's congratulations and target goal. In contrast to his landmark speech just a year prior, Elliott's speech was part of the closing session of the 1969 conference, and his appearance was the "second most poorly attended session" there. As the number of audience members present silently illustrated, interest in training and recruiting minorities had began to wane and the results were far from satisfactory. As BAC director Sharp remarked in a separate meeting of agency leaders, "You white advertising folks are a lot happier about the progress of integration than us black advertising folks."[95]

Still, even in the face of general employment cuts, NYCHR reports confirmed the number of minority employees continued to climb or remain constant. While the actual number of minority employees remained small, there had been impressive percentage gains during the previous two years. The new NYCHR chairperson, Eleanor Holmes Norton, observed that agency executives had made a good-faith effort in their development of training and recruitment programs. There was some reason for Norton's optimism: All of the agencies listed in the report showed a decline in the total number of employees in their New York offices, but every one, except for Benton & Bowles, also showed major gains in their percentage of black employees. Further, within the category the NYCHR defined as "professional," all twelve agencies had increased their number of minority employees. Table 5 summarizes the NYCHR's findings.

Unfortunately, neither advertising agencies nor the NYCHR met Norton's optimism with significant continued action. After the 1970 report, the NYCHR stopped the yearly release of agency employment statistics. Although the commission continued to collect the information, agencies filed their employment numbers voluntarily and knew there was little punishment for not doing so. The fear of pressure from the commission or public condemnation among advertising executives had dissipated. Also, in reality the commission had few serious enforcement

TABLE 5. MINORITY EMPLOYMENT OF PROFESSIONALS IN TWELVE TOP AGENCIES
GAINS OVER A THREE-YEAR PERIOD

Agency	Total Staff	Blacks	% Change in Employment
J. Walter Thompson Company			
1967–68	1,676	82	
1970	1,821	169	106.1
Ogilvy & Mather			
1967–68	799	20	
1970	865	70	250
Young & Rubicam			
1967–68	1,897	45	
1970	1,776	152	237.8
Ted Bates & Company			
1967–68	1,178	30	
1970	1,020	85	183.3
Dancer-Fitzgerald-Sample			
1967–68	697	31	
1970	687	62	100
Batten, Barton, Durstine & Osborn			
1967–68	1,296	28	
1970	1,224	81	189.3
Doyle Dane Bernbach			
1967–68	1,299	68	
1970	1,248	142	108.8
Compton Advertising			
1967–68	651	23	
1970	587	46	100
William Esty Company			
1967–68	490	2	
1970	563	48	2300
Grey Advertising			
1967–68	1,173	68	
1970	945	78	14.7
Benton & Bowles			
1967–68	977	83	
1970	820	62	− 25.3
SSC&B			
1967–68	603	12	
1970	578	30	150

Source: "Dozen Agencies Increase Minority Hiring, Reports N.Y. Rights Unit," *Advertising Age* (May 18, 1970): 96.

mechanisms. The maximum penalty for discrimination was a $500 fine and up to one year in jail. The key weapon in the NYCHR arsenal was public pressure. Agencies and their clients understandably loathed negative public attention and, because there was also intense public support for ending employment discrimination, the commission had a valuable tool. But public attention is a shifting thing. In the late 1960s and early '70s the war in Vietnam continued without visible end, a recession began, and, eventually, the public interest in employment or solving the crisis in the cities shifted to other issues. As a result the NYCHR was unable to maintain continued pressure on the industry, and the government's interest in agency hiring practices ended. Certainly both the NYCHR and EEOC investigated charges of discrimination when brought before them, but they did so reactively and only then in individual incidents.[96]

Conclusion

This important period in the history of the industry proves how dramatically agencies can change hiring practices, increase the number of minority professionals, and develop socially responsible, but economically effective, images of minorities in advertisements. However, it also demonstrates that change only occurs if outside forces push agencies to do so and the agencies are willing to invest financially and act inclusively and creatively. The EEOC and NYCHR moved beyond economic arguments in pressing agencies to feature blacks in advertisements. Nowhere in the records of the hearings is there any consistent emphasis that featuring more blacks in advertisements would improve sales among black consumers. Instead, they called on agencies to hire more blacks and include more of them in advertisements and general media as a distinct way to fulfill their corporate and social responsibility. Commissioners challenged agency representatives to use the latitude that they had to craft sales messages to depict minorities in ways that showed them as common citizens. This was a point echoed across government commissions looking into the media industries in the late 1960s. In 1968 the Kerner commission, the group charged with exploring the causes of urban rioting and violence, asserted, "Any initial surprise at seeing a Negro selling a sponsor's product will eventually fade into routine acceptance, an attitude that white society must ultimately develop toward all Negroes."[97]

But given the impressive gains in black employment numbers within just a few Years' time, we must question why they did not continue to increase during the 1970s in a manner consistent with the rapid growth of the late 1960s. There are three major factors: the organization and costs of the training programs, a reduction in outside pressure, and the recession of the early to mid-1970s. First, after the urban riots from 1964 to 1967, training programs in various industries focused on numbers, rather than on ensuring that students met existing employment standards. The rush to "do something" in the late 1960s resulted in programs that were sometimes too hastily conceived more as social experiments than programmatic efforts to develop a continuing pipeline of black professionals. While it was a necessary and admirable goal to target the hard-core unemployed and develop courses that gave them opportunities for agency work, in the face of declining ad revenues it became hard for executives to justify paying to create a new employee when experienced ones were being dismissed. One advertising executive described agency training as a "3-for-1 proposition." Executives first had to find someone eligible for training; take one of their present employees to teach the necessary classes; and then find someone to replace the person doing the training for its duration. And the high cost of training was an unfortunately common problem for many companies. One survey in 1967 found that 64 percent of over four hundred employers questioned agreed with the statement "Negroes are apt to be less well trained than whites, so hiring many Negroes will either decrease production or increase training costs." The result was another potential employee, but he or she came at the cost of lost productivity for other workers.[98]

But the real challenge came with incorporating blacks into the day-to-day routine of agency life. One unfortunate fact of some training efforts was that most agencies had little idea what to do with black workers once they had left training programs. For example, incorporating African Americans into a previously all-white agency was comparatively different from an automobile manufacturer adding black employees to their thousands of assembly-line workers. Instead, even in larger agencies, blacks became part of small, intimate working groups that (despite the pronouncements of upper management) sometimes did not welcome their presence or made little effort to involve them in ongoing campaigns. While there were no reports of violence or blatant hostility, blacks sometimes found that their rejection came silently, through a neglect that clearly communicated little trust in their contributions to the agency. As one new black professional remarked, "I don't want to be hired as an engineer and then find myself assigned as the company's representative to Plans for Progress or some other government-sponsored program in the equal opportunity bag. Above all, deliver me from presiding over the company table at the annual Urban League benefit dinner." Like the protagonist in Sam Greenlee's novel, *The Spook Who Sat by the Door,* some blacks found that their only utility came when their employer trotted them out to quiet civil rights activists or to display workplace diversity to government investigators.[99]

This experience was not unique to blacks in advertising agencies. Regardless of industry, the first blacks hired in professional or managerial roles, especially in nontechnical professions, found that their primary reason for being with the company was far less operative than ornamental. This gap between blacks' expected and desired professional role with the actual one led to significant frustration. But for these first professional hires, as scholar Steven Gelber recognized, tokenism was the necessary first step to integration. When token hires performed their jobs successfully, they destroyed traditional arguments about blacks' intellectual or professional limits. Also, in all but a few isolated cases, neither white employees nor customers protested the action. The successful integration of African Americans set an important precedent for integration in other departments in a firm, and the success at that firm set the stage for integration of an industry.[100]

However, the AAAA also failed to maintain the most successful training program yet created, the Basic Advertising Course. According to estimates, within three years the BAC was responsible for just over half of the black professionals working in the Chicago advertising industry. Even if we allow that these numbers were not arrived at scientifically, they still indicate that the program had a major impact on the industry in that city. Its proactive recruitment, talented staff, and, most importantly, agency commitments to its graduates strongly suggests that the AAAA should have made a more concerted effort to expand it throughout the country.

The second major factor affecting minority employment in the industry was the rapid decline in government pressure after 1970. The government interest in the advertising industry that began in 1963 was largely over by the mid-1970s. The NYCHR continued, but successive changes in leadership and organization severely hampered its ability to foster change in the industry. As NYCHR historian Gerald Benjamin noted, the commission, which had been the most proactive governmental group investigating the advertising industry, proved unable to maintain long-term pressure on private employers in a variety of industries, not just advertising. The commission had its best results challenging the employment practices in companies with city contracts. Those contracts could be removed if the company did not adequately respond to the commission's inquiries or suggestions for change. These contracts sometimes represented significant income, so their possible loss meant far more to companies facing that possibility than did the $500 fine with which the commission could threaten advertising agencies and other businesses that did not work directly for the city. In addition, the EEOC continued to investigate individual cases of discrimination, but did so on a small, isolated scale rather than in large public hearings. Some civil rights organizations kept an intermittent interest in industry hiring figures, but the focus was nowhere near the intensity produced during the early to mid-1960s. For example, none of the major three civil rights organizations launched a major initiative protesting black employment in the advertising industry. While employment discrimination was still an issue, the sense of immediacy had dissipated, and other social and economic issues led civil rights, government organization, and public attention elsewhere.[101]

Finally, there was the simple matter of timing. Unfortunately, we will never know what long-range impact many of the training programs could have had because of their duration. Because of the recession, most programs lasted less than five years, so there was not time for these programs to move beyond the "experimental" stage to the point where they became a permanent part of an agency's planning or budget. It would be inaccurate to say that agencies then immediately went back to business as usual, because many agency leaders displayed a genuine desire to bring more minorities into the advertising industry. But even as advertising budgets began to increase in the mid-1970s, the training and recruitment programs were not reinstated. It seemed that, as one reporter observed, "Employment opportunities for blacks and Hispanics in the ad world improve only when the spigots are forcibly turned on." While some agency leaders continued to pursue measures aimed at increasing black employees, only the largest agencies or those under investigation for racial discrimination did so. As one black advertising executive noted, "The [racial] revolution on Madison Avenue is dead forever; from now on it's all business."[102]

Still, one major benefit of the training and recruitment efforts was that they led to agency positions for several of the African Americans who later created independent advertising agencies. Just as blacks found greater opportunities for employment in mainstream agencies, they also found more opportunities to become agency owners. Several African Americans, some fed up with tokenism and others in search of entrepreneurial opportunity, used the knowledge they had gained at mainstream agencies to become owners of their own firms. In so doing, these men and women helped launch the Golden Age for blacks in the advertising industry.

Chapter 5

The Golden Age

When they made a flesh-colored Band-Aid, baby, they didn't have us in mind.

—*Godfrey Cambridge, 1970*

Although black comedian Godfrey Cambridge was joking about Band-Aids, a stark truth lay behind his assertion. The makers of the popular but pink-toned Band-Aid overlooked that, in fact, it did not match all flesh tones. His joke encapsulated the long-held belief among black consumers that consumer product manufacturers and their advertisers ignored them in creating and advertising many products. Of course, history demonstrates that being ignored as a consumer group and receiving unequal treatment in consumer spaces were routine experiences for blacks for much of the twentieth century. However, as the consumer-oriented protests of the late 1950s and early 1960s demonstrated, black consumers had grown unwilling to continue to accept such disregard. For the advertising industry, blacks' activism, combined with the public scrutiny from government organizations, necessitated a simultaneous change in both employees and the creation of advertisements.

But in the mid- to late 1960s, concurrent with the shift in emphasis on blacks' employment in the industry—from simply hiring qualified minorities to the development of active recruitment and training—there was also a shift in argument on how to approach the black consumer market. In the early 1960s, the weight had been on the creation of integrated advertisements to be placed in general media. Now, whereas trade journalists once confidently argued that blacks wanted advertisements and marketing approaches that reflected a desire for assimilation into white society, the rising cry of "Black Power" placed those traditional approaches in doubt. Instead, agency executives were increasingly told that black consumers wanted to see unique representations that reflected knowledge of blacks' lifestyle, culture, and aspirations. All of this presented a challenge to advertising executives, who increasingly asked themselves how they could create those representations when they had so few professional blacks on staff and a seemingly limited reservoir of knowledge on which to draw.[1]

Several black professionals saw these pressures, combined with the continued economic growth of the black consumer market (approaching $30 billion annually), as a prospect for entrepreneurship. Additionally, broader acceptance by many advertisers of the new, small, creative "boutique" agencies that were part of the industry's Creative Revolution convinced some observers that other traditional industry practices were beginning to change. As corporations seemed willing to end affiliations with traditional large agencies, the chance to open a small agency and garner large, national accounts appeared to be possible. Thus, beginning in the mid-1960s, black advertising professionals, as well as entrepreneurs from outside the industry, began opening advertising agencies at an unprecedented rate. Combined with the attention of observers both inside and outside the industry devoted to minority hiring, these agency openings helped make the years between 1967 and 1975 a Golden Age for blacks in the advertising industry. Never before (nor, sadly, ever since) had such broad possibilities for blacks and other minorities in the advertising field seemed so feasible, and dozens of African Americans positioned themselves to carve out a space in the industry.[2]

Along with seeking personal success, black agency owners sought to project a different image of African Americans through advertising. In this, they pursued an old ambition of black citizens while drawing inspiration from a new flowering of African American artistic consciousness. The Black Arts movement occurred almost simultaneously with the explosion of black-owned advertising agencies, promoting the idea that black artists should produce relevant art for black people to aid them on their quest for freedom and liberation. Further, that art should celebrate blacks' distinctiveness and at the same time be political. Black poet and writer Amiri Baraka argued, "The Black Artist . . . is desperately needed to change the images his people identify with, by asserting Black feeling, Black mind, Black judgment." As cultural producers, this aesthetic unquestionably affected many blacks working in the advertising industry. Through the images and copy they produced, a number black advertising professionals sought ways to both sell the products of their client and, at the same time, contribute to the uplift Baraka mandated. While blacks in mainstream agencies may have contributed to this aesthetic, its major expression in the industry came from the men and women working in black-owned agencies crafting advertising campaigns directed at black consumers.[3]

Black agency owners in the Golden Age represent the third stage of blacks in the advertising field. In the first stage, mainstream agency pioneers like Leonard Sullivan, Clarence Holte, Roy Eaton, and Georg Olden, along with black agency owners like David Sullivan and William B. Graham, established the first vestiges of a black presence in the industry. In the second stage, training and recruitment programs began to increase the presence of blacks in mainstream agencies, which in turn provided them with the experience to open their own firms. In the third stage—perhaps the litmus test for corporate executives' trust in blacks' advertising competence—African Americans opened their own agencies in the midst of the broader acceptance of black consumers as a legitimate target market.

This chapter examines the development of the black-owned agency niche during the Golden Age. The foundation of this discussion is the model of economic detour. As a theory of African American business enterprise, this model aids in the examination of the historical continuity of experience of black business owners. This analysis pursues a case study approach, examining eight advertising agencies founded during the Golden Age, four of which closed during the period and four that survived. Beyond the exploration of the history of these firms, however, is the question of why some were able to successfully navigate their way through the Golden Age and some were not. That new agencies were opened and closed shortly thereafter was a common occurrence in the late 1960s and early '70s. However, African American business enterprises have often faced business limitations different from those owned by members of other racial groups. Therefore, we must at least question whether the racism and segregation that Merah Stuart, the original theorist of economic detour, identified as hindering black business in the 1930s and '40s similarly affected black-owned advertising agencies in the 1960s and '70s.

The firms examined include Junius Edwards Advertising, Howard Sanders Advertising, John Small Advertising, Zebra Advertising, Vince Cullers Advertising, UniWorld, Proctor and Gardner Advertising, and Burrell Advertising. Blacks set up some of these firms during the years when scrutiny from the Equal Employment Opportunity Commission (EEOC) and New York City and State Human Right Commissions (NYCHR and NYSHR, respectively) crested, and they hoped the attention these groups brought meant opportunities for long-term agency ownership. These were not the only black agencies in existence in the period, but they were the largest in billings and they kept the highest public profiles. Also, among the new black agencies, these firms had the best chances for success, as they were created by individuals with several years' experience in advertising sales, account management, or creative work. In contrast to the small, local black-owned agencies, these full-service firms had the capacity to handle all phases of an advertising campaign for national-level clients. Executives from these firms were the ones who appeared most often at trade conferences, were sought out by reporters for interviews, and had their client gains and losses detailed in the trade press. When larger mainstream agencies planned to open in-house ethnic marketing units, executives from these firms were in the forefront of those questioning the rationale behind their purposes. Thus, the experiences of these owners are representative of the broader black-owned agency segment of the Golden Age. Understanding the reasons behind their establishment and, for some, failure, is key to clarifying not only the history of the black-owned agency niche, but also the racial diversity issues with which the advertising industry struggles to this day.[4]

The story of the third stage of blacks in the advertising industry, like that of the larger mainstream industry, begins in New York. Some black-owned firms announced their arrival with feature articles and interviews with journalists, while others arrived in the industry quietly with a short press release announcing their existence and an outline of their plans for growth. A few years before the start of the Golden Age, Junius Edwards quietly opened an advertising agency in New York City and became one of the first African American professionals to try to establish his own firm in the changing climate of the advertising industry.

Into the Golden Age: Junius Edwards Advertising

Junius Edwards cut quite a figure walking along Madison Avenue. Standing over 6'4", his height and skin color made his presence difficult to overlook. Originally from Louisiana, he went overseas on a tour of duty in the military, during which he earned a degree from the University of Oslo and learned to speak Norwegian. A gifted writer, Edwards won many awards for short story writing and penned a novel entitled *If We Must Die*, which examined black experiences in the South. Like black advertising pioneer Roy Eaton, Edwards went from the military into advertising. When he had written his short stories, he also entered advertising writing contests, and he often won. So he began to study advertising more closely to try to develop theories about why some advertisements worked and others did not. After three months of searching, he landed a job at the Ogilvy & Mather agency as a copywriter. He later moved on to a similar job at Ted Bates and Company and eventually became a copy group head at Norman, Craig and Kummel. After several years of working at these general market agencies, he decided to branch out on his own.[5]

In 1965, Edwards opened the agency that bore his name. Located in New York City, the firm represented his vision of an advertising agency. "I'm not interested in selling black ads only," he remarked. "I don't think there are enough billings in it. I'm interested in diversity. I want as many different and interesting jobs as I can get. The only way to grow is to be a general advertising agency." Edwards did not reject accounts directed at the black consumer market. Instead, he was selective. For example, he refused to accept what he called "goody-goody" ads in which a client simply wanted to communicate its awareness of the black community. Edwards wanted to avoid these kinds of corporate public relations campaigns that he felt did little more than improve a firm's perception among blacks, rather than sell products. Therefore, he focused on accounts that would help meet financial obligations in the short term and also develop into long-term relationships that would help the agency grow.[6]

Like many new agencies, Edwards opened his firm with a single client, Carver Federal Savings and Loan. Executives at Carver, a black-owned bank in Harlem, had grand ambitions but a limited advertising budget. Edwards convinced executives to fund an advertising campaign to reach white clients as well as blacks. He successfully argued that the firm should expand its advertising campaign beyond black-oriented media to also include mainstream media like the *New York Times* and *Wall Street Journal*. As part of the new campaign, Edwards also expanded Carver's advertising throughout the city beyond the boundaries black neighborhoods. He penned a series of advertisements whose headlines read, "What can I do about Harlem?" The copy advised white readers that Harlem residents needed access to capital for mortgages and small business loans. Deposits to area banks were a key way for them to get those funds. Readers were not expected to move all of their accounts to the bank but were encouraged to transfer their "idle funds" there to "help people help themselves." Edwards purchased space on billboards along railroad tracks, challenging white commuters on their way out of the city and into the suburbs to "Do something about Harlem."[7]

The response to the advertisements was tremendous. Executives at Carver credited the $100,000 campaign with producing over $16 million in new deposits. These advertisements demonstrated Edwards's conviction that advertising should appeal to the conscience as well as the intellect. Further, their success reinforced his belief that when making requests for assistance from whites, advertisements should not depict blacks as charity cases, but, instead, as people who just needed some support. As the advertisements carefully explained, blacks would use the deposits that came into Carver to help economically develop Harlem, not as handouts. He presented blacks as ready to do the work to build their community, lacking only some investment from the outside.[8]

Often, the advertisements Edwards created for the black consumer market depicted blacks as an urban population in touch with life in their communities. For example, he consistently showed black couples engaged in activities that suggested a pride in being black: attending concerts by black artists or shopping for African art. He also purposely chose words that illustrated an understanding of blacks' unique vernacular and as an indicator that the company intended the product for blacks. For example, an advertisement for the Liggett and Myers (L&M) Tobacco Company menthol cigarettes featured a young black couple who had just come from watching a "super bad" (meaning excellent) performance. The copy read: "That show was out-of-sight. You can still feel every note. They played hot and hard. They gave you the truth. And now you're both ready for L&M." Edwards believed the use of this style went beyond just a selection of popular words or a listing of a product's qualities. "You have to appeal to the feelings and emotions that interest and motivate them," he argued. The words linked the cigarettes with the couple and the show, both of which were presumably excellent. The dress of the couple presented them as a genuine representation of black youth and physical attractiveness. Arrayed close together, their position implied a personal closeness, but not in a manner suggesting overt sexuality, and it mirrored the general market campaign that depicted couples enjoying "L&M moments."[9]

The success Edwards produced for L&M's menthol cigarettes led to other assignments from the company, including the black consumer advertising for both the Chesterfield and Lark brands. In early 1971, company executives also rewarded him with the responsibility for the black consumer advertising for Eve cigarettes, the company's first cigarette exclusively for the female market and a direct competitor to the leading female cigarette, Virginia Slims. In part because of an impending ban on tobacco advertisements on television, Liggett and Myers executives wanted a broad print media campaign for Eve. The company designed the package with colorful flowers and gave the cigarette a slender form to communicate visually that the product was for women. Because market research suggested that African Americans preferred brands with menthol, advertisements targeted that version of Eve to black women. The advertisements Edwards created appeared in all of the major black media publications and featured attractive black women of different skin tones enjoying the new cigarette. Extending his use of black slang, copy for the ads read, "Eve has the menthol to cool a stone fox." Edwards's ads aligned with the general market emphasis on femininity and independence but with a racially specific creative twist to make the product more attractive to black women.[10]

In spite of his hopes to be a general market agency, Edwards mainly worked on accounts directed to the black consumer market for clients like Liggett and Myers, Accent Foods, and a few local banks similar to Carver Federal. He did secure some general market work for Faberge, but only on a limited basis. Ironically, he was one of the few blacks working at his own agency. Like many mainstream agency executives, he explained in a 1971 interview, he had been unable to find enough qualified blacks to staff his agency. Further, as a small enterprise, he lacked the time and capital to train the inexperienced. As a result, Edwards kept the number of permanent employees on the payroll small, and his agency did not become a significant route through which other blacks entered the advertising industry. Never employing more than ten staff members, he often completed much of the work personally. Further, although he was the first of the new black agencies of the period, competitors proved more effective at winning clients.[11]

Still, Edwards seemed remarkably prescient in his understanding of blacks' potential role in advertising and marketing. In a 1971 interview he foreshadowed the "urban marketing" trend of the 1990s and early twenty-first century. He told a trade press reporter, "White teenagers have long regarded Negroes their own age as fashion trend setters. Fashion starts in the streets and filters up, not merely from youth to age, but from lower economic class to upper." In his analysis, this African American trendsetting also occurred in the areas of music as well as language. Therefore, because of African American's unique cultural leadership in fashion, music, and language, advertisements that included them could effectively reach white and black consumers. Unfortunately for Edwards, there were few takers for his product. His broad conception of the incorporation of African American culture into general market advertising failed to translate into enough billings to preserve his agency. In the mid-1970s, Edwards closed his small firm and disappeared from the annals of advertising history.[12]

Howard Sanders Advertising

One year after Edwards's firm opened in 1965, another black agency started in New York, Howard Sanders Advertising. In contrast to Edwards, Sanders had no advertising agency experience. But he inadvertently gained copywriting experience working as a sales agent for a radio station programming to black listeners. He found that he continually had to change the advertisements submitted to the station to make them more effective with black listeners. He recalled, "I would often have to revise the entire advertising campaign written by the white agency because it was irrelevant to the black community." To Sanders, the choice of words, or particular areas of product emphasis, showed that the agencies creating the ads for the station had little understanding of the station's black listeners. The effectiveness of his reworked advertising promotions convinced Sanders he could be successful with an agency founded specifically to reach the black consumer segment.[13]

Like Edwards and other black agency owners, Sanders initially relied on a series of local accounts. Eventually, however, as Sanders added experienced managers and staff members, the firm gained black consumer accounts for national-level campaigns for companies like Pepsi-Cola, Cutty Sark, Schlitz Malt Liquor, and Kraft Foods, and billings began to rise. Sanders's work came exclusively in the programs directed to black consumers, and he viewed this role as a way to distinguish his agency from other small firms competing for client attention. Additionally, Sanders decided that he would accept account assignments of varying sizes and types, even in the area of corporate image building among the black population. Many other black agency owners shunned most forms of corporate public relations because they considered them short-lived projects that did little to aid their company's growth. In contrast, Sanders believed that he could effectively sell products through this type of advertising, that such campaigns offered him the chance to display the skill of his agency, and that a short-term public relations contract had the potential to expand into a long-term advertising campaign.[14]

In his corporate public relations advertisements, Sanders sought to communicate his client's appreciation for the black community. For example, he created a series of ads for the R. J. Reynolds Company that focused on blacks who worked for the firm. Several Reynolds products were not the leaders among black consumers that they were among whites, in part because of charges of racial discrimination at the company. Therefore, they commissioned Edwards to develop a campaign communicating the opportunities available for blacks at Reynolds. The text of one ad Sanders created for the campaign asked, "What's Franklin Weaver doing in our chemical plant if he's not there to sweep?" The text of the advertisement focused on the important role that Weaver and other blacks played at R. J. Reynolds, the work they did that went well beyond menial tasks. They also conveyed that the company was more than a place where blacks were affirmative action window dressing. Instead, Reynolds was a company that wanted to find qualified black employees and eventually promoted them into the management ranks. The advertisements also projected an image of R. J. Reynolds as a company that wanted the patronage of black consumers. What the advertising series did not stress, however, was products. Therefore, the company's ads may have succeeded in improving the company's image among black consumers, but they gave limited indication of how Sanders's work could increase product sales.[15]

By 1972, the trade press routinely recognized Sanders's firm as the largest black-owned agency in the country. Along with the New York City headquarters, Sanders opened branch offices in Detroit and Philadelphia. Also, he expanded beyond advertising and public relations work to pursue a public service role. In 1971, the firm organized a telethon that raised $300,000 to fight sickle-cell anemia, a disease prominent among African Americans. In addition, Sanders diversified agency work into areas such as the sponsorship of local television programs and movie promotions.[16]

In spite of the growth and apparent success, eventually Sanders proved unable to sustain the momentum. As other black agency owners predicted, the corporate public relations accounts that enabled him to quickly increase the size of his agency also helped lead to its demise when companies canceled them in the face of a growing recession. While he had some traditional consumer-product advertising accounts, the almost simultaneous loss of multiple accounts, both consumer-product and corporate image, left Sanders with little chance of preserving his agency. Even among accounts maintained at the agency, his clients drastically slashed their spending by 80–90 percent. The rapid decline of his agency left Sanders disillusioned with the prospects of starting another one. He later recalled that the experience left him with the belief "that it had become futile to try to continue running a black agency." Sanders stopped short of ascribing his failure to racism, but in retrospect he concluded that many of his clients had more interest in giving him "good will" accounts rather than genuine assignments to increase product sales among black consumers. In 1974, he dissolved the company and invested his earnings in a restaurant venture.[17]

John Small Advertising

After the creation of the agencies by Junius Edwards and Howard Sanders, nearly three years passed before another full-service black-owned agency opened in New York City. In 1969, John Small left a sales position at NBC Television to open an advertising firm. He brought some professional experience to the agency, having worked as a media analyst and buyer at Grey Advertising, but he supplemented his inexperience by hiring three other black men from major agencies. A. Philip Fenty left his position at Ted Bates and Company to become Small's creative director; James Bell left an account executive position at J. Walter Thompson (JWT) for a similar job with Small; and Curt Young, formerly a copywriter with Leo Burnett, also joined the agency. So he began with a level of industry experience within his agency that both Edwards and Sanders had initially lacked.[18]

Small considered himself part of what he called the "third generation" of blacks in the advertising industry. In the first generation, blacks had integrated mainstream firms. In the second, they had opened black agencies specifically to market products to the black consumer. To Small, the third generation represented the point at which "the black man is ready to compete as an entrepreneur on the same basis as whites—on the sales his agency can generate on a national, rather than an ethnic basis." In other words, Small focused on becoming a general market agency from the beginning and he pointedly referred to himself as "the black president of an agency, not the president of a black agency." Like Edwards, he wanted to compete directly with mainstream firms for accounts directed to the general marketplace rather than focus solely on black consumers.[19]

In fact, Small's early emphasis on general-market work extended a practice he had followed as a sales representative. Before he went to work for NBC, he rejected the opportunity to become a representative for a black radio station because he wanted to work in the general market rather than face what he viewed as the limits of being an ethnic specialist. To him, the ethnic-agency route was one that led to limited agency growth, if not outright failure. Therefore, he focused on seeking accounts for the general market rather than those aimed at black consumers. And though he did not actively avoid the black consumer market, he wanted his first accounts to be for the general market. Once the agency developed a reputation in the general market, the black consumer market would become a possible option. It was a logical policy, but also one that turned out to limit his choices. The agency was new, small, black-owned, and, regardless of Small's goals, getting that first client proved difficult.[20]

Over nearly nine months, Small made sixty corporate presentations and failed to win a single account. Each of the companies he met with declined to become his first client, a pattern he attributed to the size of his firm rather than to racial prejudice. Instead, Small believed that he faced problems common to every small or new agency: clients who either did not want to risk the unknown or who assumed the size of the firm made it unable to adequately service their accounts. Additionally, Small refused to accept anything he viewed as corporate image-campaign work rather than a genuine assignment based on the expected contributions of his firm.[21]

In 1970, Small finally landed his first account, a historic one in the black-owned agency field. With limited agency experience and no other clients, Small won the largest single account ever held by a black-owned advertising agency. After several weeks of competition, executives at the Singer corporation awarded Small the account for their home entertainment products division. The campaign was for the general market and had a budget of $1 million annually. Singer executives originally tabbed J. Walter Thompson for the campaign, but that agency marketed a comparable line of products the RCA company, so regulations prevented them from performing similar work for Singer. In announcing the historic campaign, Singer executives carefully pointed out that they had not chosen Small's firm because of a need to fill an affirmative action quota. Charles Manley, Singer's director of advertising, proclaimed that he chose Small's firm "not because of the blackness of the agency executives, but because of the potential greenness their efforts could produce for our company."[22]

Justifiably proud of the new account, Small optimistically predicted that its acquisition would lead to a similar "breakthrough" for other black-owned agencies to handle general-market campaigns. To him, the account showed that in the coming years company executives would judge black agencies on merit rather than race and that blacks would be able to compete on an equal basis for general-market work. Winning the account also led Small to apply for added financing to help expand the size of his agency staff. His former employer, NBC, gave him a line of credit, $100,000 came from a minority small-business investment firm, and he received a $250,000 loan of which the Small Business Administration guaranteed 90 percent. When he opened his agency Small had wisely chosen not to incur any large debts before he had found clients. But while this new infusion of capital helped him expand his firm, paying off these first loans would eventually prove too difficult.[23]

However, this is not to say that Small's agency did not experience success. His firm won accounts from the Peace Corps and the navy, as well as ethnic-market consulting assignments for companies like General Foods. Admittedly these were not the large general-market accounts that he wanted, but they helped the agency maintain a presence in corporate offices and kept open the possibility that greater assignments might result. In fact, despite the decline in responsibilities for Singer, by 1973 Small estimated that his firm was billing nearly $14 million annually. In less than four years Small had taken his agency from having no clients to having an impressive client roster and the largest annual billings of any black-owned agency in the country. Unfortunately, though, Small's rapid success helped lead to his eventual failure.[24]

Ultimately, Small's optimism proved short-lived. The agency, like many other firms black or white owned, fell victim to changes within the client company. By late 1971, Singer began to phase out its home entertainment division. Although Small's agency received more assignments from the company, by mid-1972 it had shifted those responsibilities. After that, the agency received only limited assignments from the company.[25]

Also, other large budget, general-market campaigns had not followed the Singer account to Small's firm. The size of his agency played some role in that, but Small also found that, despite his efforts, few people in either the trade press or within advertising organizations seemed willing to view his company as a general-market agency. When advertising or trade groups invited him to speak, they requested that he talk about the black consumer market, and much of the work that Small received came from companies advertising products for black consumers. For example, when he worked with the Peace Corps and the navy to develop recruitment campaigns, Small's agency directed only the minority-focused portion of their campaigns rather than the entire effort. Small earned some revenue from working with the navy, but a mainstream agency handled most of the advertising, worth nearly $20 million. Also, Small witnessed other black firms like UniWorld and Zebra Advertising growing through handling campaigns for the black consumer market, and he realized that to remain competitive he would have to soften his policies.[26]

In early 1974, the growth in the agency's responsibilities enabled Small to expand his workforce and pushed him to seek more loans to meet expenses. By this time Small softened his public stance on avoiding accounts directed at ethnic markets. He began to openly refer to his firm as a "black agency" and actively pursued accounts directed at black consumers. But he did not pick up significant new accounts. By this time, competitors like Zebra Advertising, UniWorld, and Burrell-McBain had come along and had built relationships with many of the companies interested in the black consumer market. Because Small had refused to actively pursue accounts for black consumer advertising when he opened his agency, he may have squandered the opportunity to dominate the field.[27]

Complicating the matter, he began to lose the accounts that he did have to other agencies. The specific reasons behind the account losses are not completely clear. But based on the complaints of his final clients, Small had become unable to adequately manage his firm's accounts. For example, navy officials pulled their account from the agency after it did not make the advertising placements that they paid for. Their charges of repeated instances of account mismanagement became public knowledge after reports in the trade press detailed the navy's complaints against the agency. Additionally, several publishers of black magazines and newspapers alleged that Small failed to pay for contracted media placements. For example, after Small's agency closed, *Ebony* publisher

John Johnson revealed that he had begun to refuse to allow Small to place any advertisements in his publications unless he paid in cash. Further, it appeared that Small grossly exaggerated his estimate of nearly $14 million in billings in order to make his firm appear larger and more comprehensive to outside observers. The firm lost almost all credibility with its media partners and potential clients.[28]

The loss of the navy account dealt the final blow to Small's agency. Bank officers refused to continue their tolerant polices and called in his loans. In 1975, out of working capital and deeply in debt, Small declared bankruptcy and closed his agency. The public failure of his agency made Small a pariah in the advertising industry, and no agency, black or white, offered him a position afterward.[29]

Zebra Advertising

Among all the African American agencies founded during the Golden Age, Zebra Associates seemed the most likely to succeed. When agency cofounders Raymond League and Joan Murray opened the agency in 1969, their staff included award-winning artists and copywriters such as Caroline Jones, Herb Lubalin, and Byron Barclay. League himself brought significant agency experience after six years at J. Walter Thompson, where he had been an award-winning producer and one of the agency's first black account executives. Also, before joining JWT he had been a successful playwright and director and had owned a public relations firm. League left Thompson because he felt he was approaching a career plateau because of his race. "I was going to hit a glass ceiling soon," he recalled. "Although they treated me well, I knew I was not about to become a vice president." His partner, Murray, also knew the travails of being a racial pioneer. She had been the first black woman hired as a newscaster for CBS. The two wanted to take advantage of the growing interest among large advertisers in black consumers to create successful campaigns that both sold products and that projected a positive vision of African American identity and culture.[30]

In addition to $250,000 in financing, Zebra had three small clients and a racially integrated staff of twelve people when the firm opened. In articles and speeches, League referred to it as the first "totally integrated national advertising agency with black principals."[31] Like Edwards and Small, League could not find enough experienced black professionals to staff the agency. "There were not enough black people around with the experience to do the work that had to be done," he asserted. "And the blacks with experience didn't want to leave their fat white jobs." Regardless of how or why it occurred, though, the racial integration at Zebra drew considerable attention. Feature articles in

Time, Newsweek, the *New York Times,* and *Advertising Age,* and a segment on *60 Minutes* highlighted the racial integration, and stressed that two African Americans owned the agency. Zebra's name and black-and-white motif gave it a unique appeal; photographs showed the staff at work in the company's black-and-white zebra-themed offices decorated with African art. The industry buzz quickly identified the firm an agency on the rise. This publicity did not just naturally happen: League's background in public relations and Murray's connections in the news media gave Zebra a significant advantage over other black-owned firms in crafting the agency's public perception. In truth, several black agencies kept integrated staffs.[32]

Alongside the primary mission of getting clients, three community-centered goals guided the agency. Its first goal was to contribute to the growth of a minority presence in the advertising industry. From its inception, Zebra included a training program for black and Puerto Rican youth. (The agency had one trainee on staff when it opened, and it also retained an employment consultant to find more candidates and refine their training program where needed.) To League, too many of the new training programs at mainstream firms were "big farces" that only provided educational and advertising basics. Those programs "bring in blacks who have no potential, and once they've got them, they don't know what to do with them, he argued." In contrast, League designed Zebra's training program to attract talented people and give them a rigorous education that prepared them to become advertising professionals. He paired trainees with experienced staff members for on-the-job training and gave them increased responsibilities when he thought they were ready. While at JWT, League had joined in the community outreach efforts of Program Brother, though not directly with the JWT Training Program. And in contrast to the gendered division of the JWT program, League and Murray expected Zebra trainees to become more than secretaries or clerical assistants.[33]

Second, League and Murray wanted to use Zebra's resources to help raise the status of black media among advertisers. Shortly after opening the agency, Zebra staff members prepared a white paper analyzing the sales efficiency of black newspapers. League believed that advertisers did not adequately understand the sales potential of the black press and placed advertising there only as a last alternative. Claude Barnett, the erstwhile founder of the Associated Negro Press, who had passed away a short time earlier, would have been proud of their effort. By working from within the advertising industry to promote the efficacy of black newspapers, League and Murray continued Barnett's legacy. League and Murray recognized that the fortunes of any agency targeting the black consumer market were linked to their client's perceptions of the black media vehicles that featured their advertisements. Without that understanding, potential clients might argue that general media sources or magazines like *Ebony* effectively reached black consumers and that black newspapers were redundant and unnecessary. League and Murray hoped that their detailed analysis of the black press would aid them in promoting black newspapers to advertisers as a viable medium through which they could reach black consumers.[34]

Third, Zebra wanted to use their expertise to help the black business community. Since many minority businesses were small they often lacked the money to retain professional advertising services. Therefore, Zebra offered a service in which minority business owners could get professional advertising counseling at a reduced cost. This small business program displayed a sense of community responsibility that made Zebra unique among its peers.[35]

In contrast to John Small, League and Murray presented the Zebra staff as experts on the black consumer market from the beginning. For them race served as a driving factor in understanding the proper tone to use in advertisements to black consumers. "It's hard for a white adman to find out even simple things, like the language people speak in Harlem," Murray emphasized. "I can change from a Pucci miniskirt to dungarees and a sweatshirt and learn from my friends in the ghetto without problems." An agency had to court the black consumer with advertising appeals that were authentic and respectful and that conveyed an understanding of blacks' larger goals and aspirations. An advertisement for the agency communicated this philosophy (Figure 12).

A portion of the copy reads: "Mass advertising is color-blind. It approaches the Black consumer as if he were somebody's fair-haired boy. It offers him great white hopes." In contrast, advertisements from Zebra made race a clear and salient factor. To League and Murray, to do anything less than boldly recognize the importance of racial recognition to blacks would be inauthentic and would also fail to move black consumers to action. Similar to Godfrey Cambridge's joke regarding Band-Aids (which appeared in a promotional film about Zebra) League and Murray identified that "color-blind" too often meant "white." Simply integrating advertisements was not enough, they argued. Instead, mirroring the larger artistic idea that "Black is Beautiful," the duo contended that advertisements had to convey both a sales message as well as be a positive representation of blacks' life, culture, and aspirations.[36]

League and Murray also added the element of class to their palette of advertising expertise. Specifically, they initially positioned the Zebra staff as experts on reaching low-income consumers who lived in urban centers and had annual incomes below $5,000. This was a unique approach. Most agencies targeted middle-class consumers who had the

Mass advertising is color-blind

The most effective communications technique ever devised isn't making it in the $50billion-a-year Black consumer market. The reason is obvious. Mass advertising is color-blind. It approaches the Black consumer as if he were somebody's fair-haired boy. It speaks to him in a foreign language. It offers him Great White Hopes. It pictures him in off-color, unrealistic settings.

Companies aware of this have frantically begun coloring mass advertising black. But the result isn't black. It just looks that way to the people who create it. People whose understanding of Black sensibilities comes out of textbooks and seminars.

If you're an advertiser or agency who wants to talk to the Black consumer in a way he finds acceptable and believable, we'd like to talk to you. We'd like you to meet our black-and-white staff. People whose inner-city experiences, awarding-winning creative talents, and proven marketing skills can help you bridge the gap between white advertiser and Black consumer.

Zebra Associates
Inc. Advertising
1180 Avenue of the Americas
New York, N.Y. 10036

Figure 12. League and Murray wanted potential clients to understand that reaching and selling to black consumers demanded insight and expertise that went beyond changing the skin color of models. Zebra Associates advertisement, *Marketing/Communications* (February 1970): 50.

disposable income to buy the consumer products they were advertising. In contrast, League and Murray tried to entice clients by highlighting the $100 billion in annual income they estimated was controlled by the multiethnic, low-income consumer market. And they pointed out that mainstream agencies should not assume that general marketing plans would work with this population: A Zebra promotional pamphlet stressed, "To be understood in the low-income market you've got to speak inner-city. And you've got to speak it fluently. One poorly chosen subject, one wrong predicate can sentence a whole campaign to Nowheresville." Showing off their fluency, Zebra advertisements deployed phrases such as "Good-lookin' don't shout. Go 'head on. Tell me 'bout it." As Junius Edwards had done before them, League and Murray confidently argued that these linguistic styles resonated with low-income consumers because they were familiar and comfortable.[37]

Of course, whether they could persuade clients that a group of consumers who had an estimated large aggregate income but small individual income was worthy of targeting was another question entirely. The idea that Zebra spoke the language of this group to which they alone were privy was an added way to help the agency stand out from its competitors. Where Edwards argued for the occasional insertion of proper slang terms into advertisements, in agency advertisements and speeches to trade groups, League and Murray presented inner-city residents as an almost separate people. Similar to the "city within a city" constructions popular among newspaper representatives and trade reporters in the 1940s, League and Murray were attempting to construct an isolated multicultural community that they could guide advertisers in colonizing. It seems as though League and Murray were trying to capitalize on the broader attention being paid to the nation's inner cities. As a former account executive, League knew that most potential clients had little interest in reaching a group of consumers who earned individual average incomes that fell below the poverty line. Further, he was in a position to know that many potential clients had enough difficulty agreeing to spend money with the black consumer market, something that had been a regular feature in the trade press since the end of the Second World War. To expect that those same clients could then be persuaded of this newly discovered low-income and inner-city market seems an unlikely step. Thus, rather than emphasizing their expertise with low-income, inner-city residents, League and Murray eventually began stressing their expertise at reaching black consumers.[38]

Although client acquisition went slowly, by the end of the second year Zebra was billing over $2.5 million yearly. The agency handled both regional and national-level accounts for clients such as Coca-Cola, Clairol, Spectrum Cosmetics, and the Peace Corps. Staff members also consulted with mainstream agencies working on campaigns to reach black consumers and handled public service advertisements for the National Urban League. League and Murray upheld the public image of the firm by appearing at advertising conventions and talking about black and low-income consumers. League also eyed advertising opportunities in Liberia, and his visit to that country in 1970 brought the agency a small tourism promotional account. So Zebra Associates appeared to be developing into a successful firm. In fact, though, all was not well within the agency.[39]

The first evidence of problems within Zebra came near the end of 1971. Although billings at the firm continued to grow, the creative director, Caroline Jones, resigned. She had been with the agency since the beginning and had a good reputation in the larger advertising community. During her tenure at the agency, Jones represented Zebra on a number of trade panels, helped expand the creative department from two to ten people, conducted training programs, and spoke to trade groups about black consumers. Publicly, the agency presented Jones's departure from Zebra as a move to a higher-level position with another firm, a common practice in the industry. But Jones's private resignation letter signaled that there were reasons that propelled her away from Zebra as much as her new position attracted her. She argued there had been a steady decline in the working and production standards in Zebra's creative department. A draft of the letter in her personal note-book shows that she also sensed a climate of racial discrimination at the agency. "I have always fought against racist policy when it applied to blacks," she wrote, "and my conscience will not allow me to ignore the reverse practice within the Zebra family." She had witnessed account managers prevent white staff members from openly working on accounts for black-owned companies. Additionally, managers sometimes kept whites away from working on campaigns aimed at blacks, such as the agency's Clairol account. Jones believed that League already knew about the instances she described and refused to curb the practice. As a result, rather than continue in an uncomfortable position, Jones left the agency for a position at Kenyon and Eckhardt. While her departure left a creative and administrative void, the firm did not lose any clients because of her resignation. Soon, though, problems also emerged within the agency's executive management.[40]

Citing reasons of ill health, in 1973 League resigned as Zebra's chair-man and president. Bill Castleberry, formerly a senior account executive at Young & Rubicam, took over League's position. On Castleberry's arrival, Murray said that she was "absolutely delighted that a man of [his] caliber and integrity is moving into this position." Her early enthu-siasm proved to be short-lived. When Castleberry took the position, the financial picture of the agency was already precarious. The agency had debts over $500,000 and, making matters worse, the working relation-ship between Castleberry and Murray slowly decayed.[41]

As with the departure of Caroline Jones, Zebra lost no client accounts in the wake of League's resignation. In fact, under Castleberry's direc-tion the agency continued to pick up new clients and the firm appeared to be steadily growing. At the start of 1975, the agency was one of the largest black-owned firms in the country with billings over $5 million annually. Assessing the dismal financial position of other black agencies, Castleberry confidently stated, "Downturn in the economy? Not here!" He went on to predict that within the year Zebra billings would crest $5 million. On that prediction he proved correct, but the firm also had substantial debts that were increasingly difficult for Castleberry to manage.[42]

During his short tenure, Castleberry reduced the debt load of the firm by over 60 percent. With the agency's rising account billings, he believed he would have the time to reduce that figure even further. But public attention on the failure of John Small Advertising placed a strain on many black-owned agencies, especially Zebra. Small had not just gone out of business and disappeared, as commonly occurred in the industry. Instead, the trade press splashed stories about the collapse of his agency across the front page. Because there were so few black-owned agencies, the demise of Small's agency tarnished the others by mere implication. For Zebra, Small's failure directly affected the firm's relationship with its creditors. After Small declared bankruptcy, Zebra's creditors refused Castleberry's request for more time to restructure the agency's debts. As a result, in 1976, the financial burden forced him and Murray to close the firm.[43]

The story of Zebra Associates did not end there. Instead, the growing hostility between Murray and Castleberry led to one of the most bizarre stories of the year. Murray openly blamed Castleberry for Zebra's demise. In her judgment, before Castleberry's arrival, Zebra's existing and potential future clients had positioned the firm for future growth. She believed that Castleberry's business and financial decisions hindered Zebra's continued growth. Further, she believed Castleberry had hidden the true nature of the firm's relationship with its existing creditors from her until it was too late for her to work out a solution. Privately, Murray also accused Castleberry of having stolen money from the agency. A few weeks after Zebra's closure, Murray's frustration nearly turned to physical violence. In a story reminiscent of the blaxploitation films of the era, Murray allegedly hired two men, "a cab driver and an unemployed karate expert," to kill Castleberry and throw his body from a window. The alleged plot unraveled when, instead of killing Castleberry, the pair tried to extort money from him and police captured them. Although prosecutors charged her with conspiring to have Castleberry murdered, Murray pleaded guilty to a lesser charge and served no time in jail. Unhurt, Castleberry briefly ran another advertising agency, and Murray never returned to the advertising industry.[44]

Behind the Closure of African American Advertising Agencies

Despite the sensational end of Zebra Associates, black agencies did not close because executives conspired to have one another killed. Instead, they faced an array of problems similar to those of many new agencies of the period: declining revenue, a resulting inability to repay loans, and a difficulty in keeping a client base. Additionally, nearly every new agency faced the challenge of size. Clients with sizable advertising budgets were hesitant to believe that a small agency could handle the work, or they preferred to wait until an agency had a proven record of performance. But a new agency could not grow unless it had billable accounts. Further complicating matters, the interest clients once devoted to the small, boutique agency during the Creative Revolution did not survive the reduced advertising spending common in the early 1970s. As a result, several new agencies were casualties of the recession of the 1970s, not just those owned by African Americans. But additional issues specific to the African American agency segment also limited blacks' success.[45]

Despite their experience as agency employees, most of the men and women who founded the agencies examined above were first-time business owners. In fact, of the five agency owners or co-owners only Raymond League had operated his own business prior to opening up an advertising agency. Therefore, we must allow that the inexperience common to all new business owners may have impacted the development of some black-owned agencies. At a minimum it is apparent that by the time it failed, Small's agency had developed serious problems maintaining account services. In a relationship and service-oriented business like advertising, a reputation for poorly handling client services is anathema to an agency's health. Further, because there were few blacks with experience as agency owners, there were few possible mentors for the new entrepreneurs to go to for advice on handling clients, financing, or employment issues. Also complicating matters was the gradual disappearance of training and recruitment programs from mainstream agencies. As these programs were canceled at mainstream firms, those firms started to poach experienced personnel from black agencies. Like the experience of black insurance firms, black advertising agencies were a fertile source for experienced black professionals, and mainstream agencies eagerly recruited their employees to enhance their staffs and meet affirmative action requirements. "As fast as we train a man," League lamented, "he's stolen by a white agency." Admittedly, moving from smaller to larger agencies was admen's traditional approach to professional advancement in the industry. But this tradition proved difficult to overcome for some black agencies.[46]

Beyond ownership experience, executives at black agencies also quickly found that, despite their appeals for work in the general market, clients perceived them to only have expertise in the black consumer market: a classic example of an economic detour. This both sustained their firms for a time and limited their growth. Of the four companies examined above, only League and Murray's Zebra and Howard Sanders's agency started out with the marketing premise of an ability to speak to black or low-income markets. And when the others (Edwards and Small) began working in the black consumer market as well, they used the same marketing rationale as other black agency owners. To prove their expertise in the black consumer market arena, owners of the four agencies emphasized that they had special insights into the black consumer behavior because they were black, an argument that clients accepted. The logical reverse corollary of that argument, however, was that they did not have the ability and insights to reach white consumers. As one black agency owner bitterly recalled, "You can't survive on ethnic business, and yet they won't accept you on your merits as an advertising agency." Some agencies did secure assignments for general-market work, but they were usually small accounts that did not lead to more work in that market. Without the option of competing for general-market accounts and with the increasing competition within the black-owned agency niche, the four black agencies examined above reached an untenable position and were forced to close.[47]

In the do-something climate of the late 1960s and early 1970s, some corporate executives might not have questioned the sales benefits of using black-owned agencies and instead gave these firms money not for their professional abilities but to demonstrate goodwill or a stance against racism. These corporate affirmative action accounts, or what one agency owner called "get-off-my-back money," eventually limited the growth opportunities of black agencies. These came from companies eager to improve their perception among minorities but uninterested in maintaining a permanent effort. Too often these accounts came to an agency because of pressure from a corporate affirmative action committee, rather than a voluntary decision of an advertising director. So in too many cases executives chose black agencies for the skin color of their owner and personnel rather than their potential contribution to an advertising campaign. These token accounts had limited lasting value to the agency that serviced them. Although they provided important short-term revenue, in the long run they did more to harm agencies than to help them. Owners like Sanders and Small expanded their firms' size to handle these accounts, but when the recession began in the early 1970s, these campaigns were often the first ones canceled. Certainly these accounts gave black agency owners the chance to prove the skills of their agencies. But in contrast to the black agencies that survived past the Golden Age, for the nonsurvivors clients did not supplement the initial assignment with more work. In other words, with the four nonsurviving firms, clients did not follow the "guilt" assignments with enough work that allowed them to sustain growth. As one black executive perceptively remarked, "On a long-range basis, you can't build a business on the white man's guilt."[48]

Additionally, the pressures from civil rights groups and government agencies to use black-owned services had largely ended by the mid-1970s. Therefore, corporations would not pay any penalty for not using black agencies. Jesse Jackson expanded the range of Operation PUSH (People United to Save Humanity) and succeeded in getting corporations to invest more dollars with minority suppliers, and some black agencies benefited from his efforts. However, a broader push against advertisers and agencies, like that which occurred during the 1960s, did not occur. Instead of being faced with actions by three major civil rights organizations, advertisers now faced a significant, but still individual, civil rights group. As a reporter remarked, "Corporate advertisers, now that the gun is no longer at their heads, are not exactly beating the doors down to buy specialized services."[49]

Changes in federal advertising laws also hampered black agency growth. By 1972, new federal laws restricted cigarette companies from using radio and television as a location for advertisements. Since the birth of Negro radio in the 1940s, radio had been a key medium to reach black consumers. Without that valuable media source no longer available for a key advertiser, an already limited client list shrank even further. Cigarette executives were among the groups most interested in reaching black consumers, and billings from their companies were an important revenue source for black firms. Although the print medium was still viable, the prohibition on radio advertisements led to a significant decrease in the billings to some African American agencies.[50]

A few black advertising executives believed that the trade press also played a role in limiting black agency success. Specifically, they argued that reporters did not consistently cover enough of the advertising campaigns created by black agencies or the industry activities of black agency executives. Zebra Advertising received extensive coverage, but they were the exception. Black executives especially criticized the coverage of *Advertising Age*, the newspaper of the advertising industry. In a letter published shortly after the closure of John Small's agency, UniWorld owner and founder Byron Lewis wrote, "Black agencies do not seem to get much attention from *Advertising Age* except when adversity strikes or an agency collapses . . . I can clearly advise you that UniWorld Group Inc. is one black-owned-and-operated agency that is financially sound, pays its bills and provides real, imaginative service for its clients." This was a serious issue, because advertising agency executives and corporate advertising directors read the paper. These men and women decided which agencies to select for advertising work, and limited coverage led to limited awareness of the work by black agencies. Further, the lack of positive coverage to balance the negative left readers with the impression that all black agencies did substandard work and mismanaged client accounts. Therefore, Lewis pressed reporters to cover both the successes and the failures of black agencies. Speaking for black agency owners, Lewis concluded, "We believe *Advertising Age* could render a significant service by providing more frequent coverage of positive business activities in the minority advertising and marketing sector." Balanced coverage, he noted, would allow black agencies to have the same chances for success as other agencies throughout the industry.[51]

Advertising Age published an editorial several weeks after Lewis's letter that addressed some of his points. It argued that the recent closing of several black-owned agencies "must never be interpreted to mean that approaches to urban markets are clearly best left to whites." But the closing point of the editorial evidenced a quiet prejudice its author failed to recognize. For after expressing hope that the staff members of closed black agencies could find jobs either at mainstream firms or in surviving black agencies, the piece decided that black agencies had a place in the industry "for as long as marketers perceive the importance of a dual approach to urban markets." In other words, the role of black-owned agencies was to serve the black market only. Once marketers no longer felt they were valuable in reaching black consumers, their owners would close them down, and mainstream agencies would handle campaigns to reach all groups of consumers.[52]

Fortunately, the demise of the four agencies examined above did not close the story of the African American effort to develop a presence as agency owners. Instead, another group of black entrepreneurs, facing many of the same conditions as the agency owners examined above, were able to survive the spate of black agency closings of the early 1970s. These survivors demonstrated not only the strength of black entrepreneurship but also blacks' ability to create and develop agencies that produced effective, award-winning work emulated throughout the industry.

The Survivors: Black Advertising Agencies That Survived the Golden Age

In the mid-1970s in New York City, black advertising firms closed at a distressing rate. "It is apparent now that the years of struggle to develop a solid cadre of black-owned and operated advertising agencies in New York City has failed," one reporter declared.[53] Had that reporter extended his vision further west (or even more broadly around New York), however, he would have found that the African American agency niche was far from dead. In Chicago, three black-owned firms were in operation and gaining client accounts. A fourth agency, based in New York City, was also growing under the trade press radar. The owners and personnel of these four agencies made significant contributions to the development of advertising to the black consumer market. In addition, their survival showed jaded observers that blacks could in fact develop successful agencies with a client roster that valued their contributions more than their color.

Vince Cullers Advertising

Vince Cullers entered the advertising industry following a stint in the military during World War II. After working as a freelance artist and as an art director for *Ebony*, he founded Vince Cullers Advertising in 1956. It was not until mid-1960s, however, that his agency achieved national prominence. Before this point, Cullers's agency survived on various local and regional accounts. As the social and political changes advanced in the 1960s, Cullers became one of the leading figures in crafting advertisements for black consumers. After creating a series of advertisements for the Lorillard tobacco company, Cullers became widely recognized for the ability to "speak Soul" through advertisements. In contrast to Zebra's marketing idea of speaking "inner city," Soul marketing incorporated the black middle class, a key socioeconomic category that advertisers actively sought. Through his work in the Soul market, a subset of the black consumer market, Cullers tapped and communicated an understanding of the changes ongoing among African Americans. In the process he helped create a niche within a niche in which his firm became a recognized leader.[54]

In a 1969 article a writer for *Sales Management* proclaimed Soul marketing as "the biggest, most dynamic thing in today's Negro Market." The article also contained an excerpt from a Soul dictionary to inform interested advertisers of the words currently in vogue:

> Boss—The ultimate in compliments.
> Burn—To improvise superlatively, in music or in life.
> Dap—Impeccably dressed.
> Fox—A beautiful woman.
> Gig—A job. Synonyms are "slave" and "hustle."
> Hog—A very large automobile.
> Jive—A persuasive talker but one prone to lies or excuses.[55]

The writer cautioned readers not to use the words without the advice of a black consultant, lest they do so in the wrong context and offend black consumers. The Soul market cut across socioeconomic lines and included areas such as food, music, movies, theater, clothing, social activities, and advertisements. Soul food restaurants began appearing in cities, and manufacturers rushed to produce and label various products with Soul. Broadly defined, adherents described Soul as a "feeling." Historian William Van Deburg argued: "Soul was the folk equivalent of the black aesthetic. It was perceived as being the essence of the separate black culture. If there was beauty and emotion in blackness, soul made it so. If there was a black American mystique, soul provided much of its aura of sly confidence and assumed superiority. Soul was sass—a type of primal spiritual energy and passionate joy available only to members of the exclusive racial confraternity. It was a 'tribal thing,' the emotional medium of a subculture." To advertisers, then, Soul conveyed to blacks a sense that advertisers recognized them as special and welcomed their patronage. "Check your brands to see if they are *soul satisfying* [emphasis in original]." Or, as an *Ebony* advertisement insisted, "You can't really define 'soul.' But when it's there, you know it. In an ad it's the difference between saying, 'My product is for everybody.' Or, 'My product is for you!'" Soul marketing was the commodification of an aesthetic, expressed in the Black Arts movement that provided greater target marketing for a segment of the black consumer market eager for creative work that recognized their unique racial identity. While true that this expression of Soul came through a commercial medium, the calls and letters of support as well as requests for reprints of advertisements testifies to how well they were received by some in the community.[56]

The development of Soul marketing also exemplifies how Cullers and other black professionals highlighted divisions within the black consumer market. Soul marketing was not applicable to every person but instead was something that mainly appealed to young blacks involved in the Black Power movement, those who "viewed themselves as foot soldiers in a cultural revolution against historic white supremacy." Therefore it could not reach every piece of the black consumer market; indeed, it would sometimes alienate blacks from a product. Soul was a tool to reach a segment of the black community rather than the entire black community, and it could transcend racial lines and reached young whites. As Junius Edwards implied, Soul was a black aesthetic toward which young whites gravitated to for a feeling of "cool." A writer asserted, "Since black is a feeling, not a color, many other areas are open for new product expansion. White girls should not be neglected either. They are just as receptive to the black feeling as Negroes." While this writer may have crossed uncomfortable racial boundaries in his assessment, he nonetheless clearly understood, that, as Junius Edwards argued, advertising appeals directed to blacks could attract and sell whites as well. So, alongside the scenes of integration in some advertisements, images implying black independence or Black Power appeared. Soul marketing did not replace the aforementioned scenes of integration but appeared simultaneously to appeal to a different demographic target in the evolving black consumer market.[57]

In 1966, black activist Stokely Carmichael argued, "We have to stop being ashamed of being black. A broad nose, a thick lip and nappy hair is us and we are going to call that beautiful whether they like it or not." Several of the advertisements Cullers created during the Golden Age visually represented Carmichael's argument. For example, an advertisement for Afro Sheen products featured a group of African Americans of

Figure 13. Without the guiding hand of experts like Cullers, occasionally some manufacturers' efforts to introduce "soul" into a product were less than subtle. Soul Brother advertisement, *Ebony* (February 1969): 96.

varying ages and skin tones. The copy read: "A beautiful new product for a beautiful new people." This advertisement and others in the series were a rejection of the idea that black was "ugly" but instead used the theme of "Black is Beautiful." Other advertisements continued his use of blacks of various skin tones from the very light to the very dark. He used blacks who were identifiable as blacks in central roles, and his choices contrasted with the traditional use of black models who were "Caucasian looking." Additional advertisements featured images of blacks in family settings or pictures of fathers and sons, and some of his advertisements even contained copy partially written in Swahili. Cullers's primary goal was to sell his client's products, but within that action (and by means of it) to encourage blacks to accept their natural beauty and to identify with African culture and traditions.[58]

In much of his advertising, Cullers tried to tap the developing sense of pride among blacks. In his work, blacks were a middle-class, urban population who had a clear sense of their African history and culture. Afros, dashikis, African languages, and scenes that conveyed an understanding of black militancy were part of the Cullers tradition. For example, a radio advertisement for Newport cigarettes featured a black man talking to black smokers over audio from a black militant rally: "Brothers," a voice declared, "you've been hand-picked as the boldest brothers in the country." The task: To sample Newport cigarettes in order to test their level of Soul. After various men sampled the cigarettes and voiced an agreement to switch brands, the announcer declared: "Back to your cities, brothers. Put out the word to every bold soul." Thus the cigarettes were not for everyone but were only for those who had the fortitude to attend a rally and change habits, if only their choice of cigarette. The print advertisement for the cigarettes, known as "The Brother in the Blue Dashiki," became one of Cullers's most recognized advertisements of the Golden Age. It featured a bearded black man crowned with a large Afro. He wore a blue dashiki with beads around his neck visible through an opening that also displayed his bare chest. Arrayed on a white background next to a large pack of the cigarettes copy read, "Bold, cold Newport . . . A whole new bag of menthol smoking." The linguistic and visual representations represented Cullers's vision of the new black man, someone who was proud and aware of his heritage—and who also smoked Newport cigarettes.[59]

Further, by combining black militancy with a brand of cigarettes, the advertisements made Newports an expression of militancy even to consumers who did not adopt a militant lifestyle. Some black activists recognized the commodification of black militancy inherent in some Soul marketing. Black Panther Party leader Huey P. Newton argued, "If you want to be 'black and proud' they put Negroes in advertising campaigns and have all the Negroes fighting for the right to drink Coke rather than Pepsi." As a result, the broader issues activists were fighting for became reduced to a brand argument. Yet while it was an advertising tool to sell products, it communicated black pride within the context of an advertisement. Thus, Soul marketing was both a commodification of blackness and a part of the liberation movement. Cullers grasped that current of black consciousness, history, pride, and African identification that was part of the cultural context of the Golden Age and used it appropriately and successfully in his advertisements. Therefore, while Newport cigarettes were "bold" and "cold," the advertisements also communicated that those who smoked them were part of the effort to uplift African Americans.[60]

Soul marketing became part of what scholar Jannette Dates called the "defiant response" of black cultural producers in the media industries. This response positioned blacks in a way that enabled them to contribute to the vision of black liberation, to reject a vision of blacks as ugly but instead present them as beautiful. In so doing it was the heir to the utilitarian vision of advertising demanded by black activists in the early 1960s. Those activists had sought to use advertising to educate the country about blacks' larger contributions and in support of integration efforts. Cullers and other blacks now sought to use advertising as a tool of uplift and pride by speaking directly to African Americans. He recalled, "All this was not only part of how we felt about ourselves . . . but the ads reinforced what Black people were really trying to do in those days. . . . We were kind of spearheading that . . . it was kind of an interesting beautiful kind of period."[61]

Vince Cullers Advertising was the leading agency for the Soul market, in large part because it helped invent the niche. Cullers's emphasis on black pride was a creative and financial success for the agency and its clients, and it supported his vision of his advertising agency's purpose.

He stated on several occasions that he had limited interest in seeking accounts for the general market and preferred to craft campaigns for black consumers in which he could present positive images of them. It was not that Cullers did not want or need the revenue that came from general-market campaigns. Rather, he believed that if advertisers developed greater appreciation of the black consumer market they would increase their billings to agencies like his. Ultimately, the increases Cullers's hoped for did come to the black consumer market niche, and Cullers, until his death in 2003, remained a strong advocate of black-owned advertising agencies.

Despite Cullers's leadership in Soul marketing, however, other agencies eventually surpassed its growth and billings. To the east, even as other black New York agencies fell by the wayside, UniWorld advertising

Figures 14 and 15. Cullers routinely combined images of black families, pride, and heritage to advertise his clients' products. Afro Sheen advertisement, *Ebony* (September 1971): 35; Afro Sheen advertisement, *Ebony* (July 1972): 137.

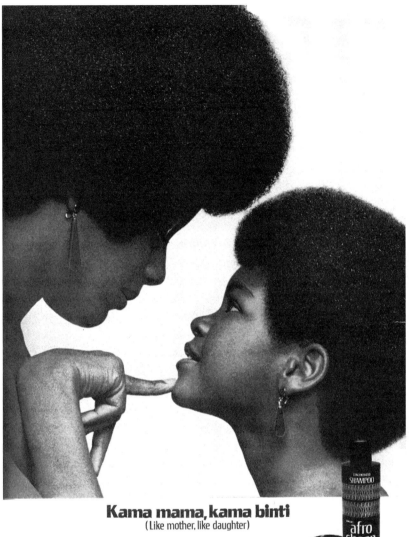

Kama mama, kama binti
(Like mother, like daughter)

Kama mama, kama binti is poetry in Swahili. And your little girl's natural is proud poetry in velvety rings and curls.
Such beauty deserves the same loving care as your own crowning glory. Naturally, we mean Afro Sheen® concentrated shampoo and Afro Sheen® conditioner & hair dress. The best for both of you.

wantu wazuri use afro sheen®

JOHNSON PRODUCTS CO., INC., CHICAGO, ILLINOIS 60621

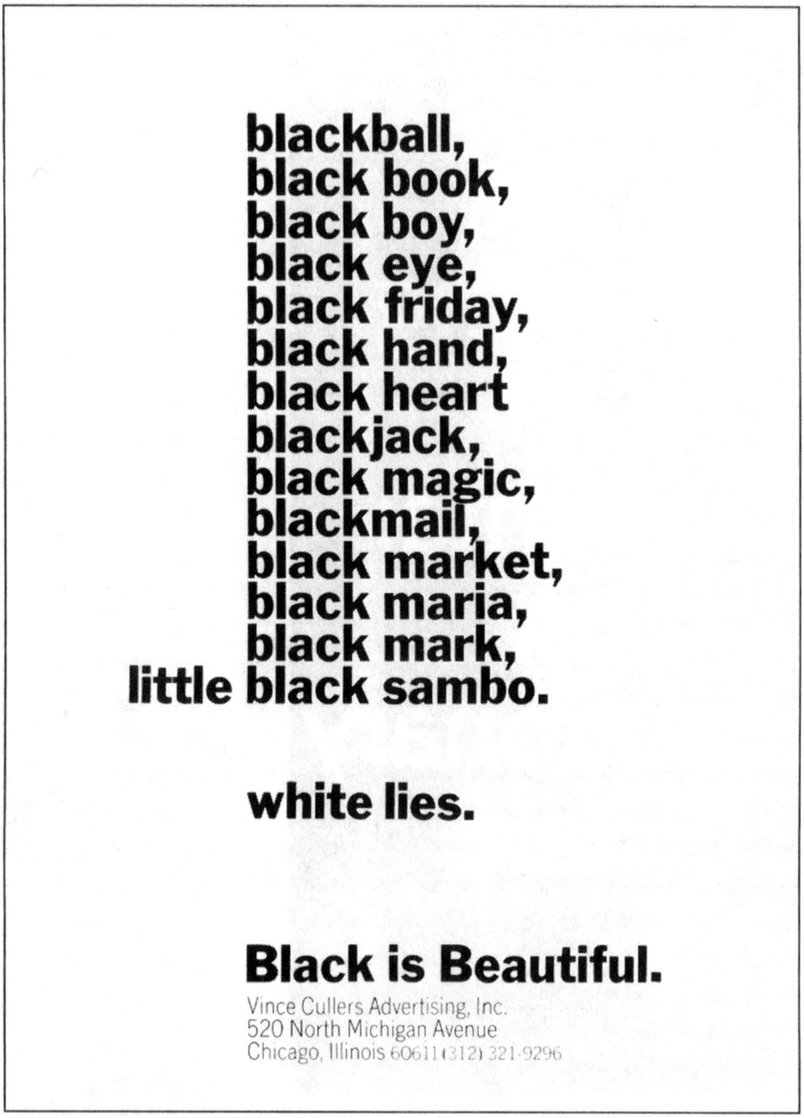

Figure 16. Advertisements for Cullers's agency illustrated his disdain for traditional assumptions about African Americans. Lowell Thompson, "The Invisible Man in the Gray Flannel Suit," *Print* (January/February 1993): 65.

soon proved that blacks could set up and maintain successful agencies at the center of the advertising universe.

UniWorld Advertising

Like Howard Sanders, UniWorld founder Byron Lewis came to the agency business with limited prior experience. In 1953, he graduated from Long Island University with a journalism degree but was unable to find work at a mainstream newspaper. He joined a black newspaper as an advertising-space salesman and later helped to create a literary magazine, *Urbanite*. The magazine had an impressive list of contributing authors, including James Baldwin, Langston Hughes, and Lorraine Hansberry, but low advertising revenues forced it to cease publication after only a few issues. He later worked as a space representative for black advertising pioneer Leonard Evans, Jr., who now published a newspaper supplement, *Tuesday* magazine. The experience at *Urbanite* and *Tuesday* magazine stirred Lewis's curiosity about advertising because it represented the revenue the two magazines so desperately needed. Lewis decided that if an advertising agency could better link potential advertisers with black-oriented media and their consumer base, that agency might make substantial revenue and benefit black-owned media at the same time. As a result, in 1969 Lewis founded UniWorld. His priority was to develop advertising accounts for the black consumer market. But the name of the agency also communicated his vision that the firm might eventually become active in various markets and geographical locales.[62]

With $250,000 from venture capitalists and his network of connections from his time as a space salesman, Lewis opened UniWorld with a staff of five people. He focused on building UniWorld into the leader in the black consumer niche, but initially he found accounts hard to come by. He had a network of associates to contact among corporate advertisers, but few were willing to take a chance on an agency whose owner had no experience in creating advertising campaigns. Lewis shrewdly decided to give the agency a broad financial base by diversifying beyond consumer-product advertising into other areas of promotional work. In 1971, the agency became the first black firm to handle the promotion and advertising work for a major motion picture—*Shaft*. The movie, an action thriller about the adventures of a black private investigator in Harlem, was typical of the blaxploitation film genre of the 1970s. Posters developed by UniWorld depicted the lead character, played by Richard Roundtree, stylishly dressed and firing a pistol as he clung to a rope with his other hand. The picture and posters appealed to black audiences in search of a black hero who not only solved the problems of his community but also refused to bow to whites. Radio advertisements for the movie illustrated UniWorld staffers understanding of black humor and language. The announcer boomed, "If you want to see *Shaft*, ask your momma." The line made reference to both the adult nature of the film and aspects of traditional black humor, such as playing the dozens or the verbal jousts in the black community in which "momma" jokes were key. Referring to the advertisements, a UniWorld executive remarked, "We understand our sense of humor and whites never will." The film and accompanying posters and advertisements were a hit with black audiences. The success of the film showed not only the possibilities of the black movie going market but also the efficacy of a black agency in movie promotions. Its success also prompted two sequels for which the agency handled the advertising and promotion.[63]

UniWorld's client base for product advertisements soon included companies such as Eastman Kodak, Ford Motors, AT&T, and Kraft Foods. Most of the accounts came to the agency because of its positive reputation and creative work. However, some accounts also resulted from pressure applied to a company by civil rights organizations. One such account, Avon cosmetics, came to the agency in the early 1970s because of pressure brought by Reverend Jesse Jackson's Operation PUSH. After a series of meetings with Avon executives, the company agreed to place more advertisements in black-owned media and to contract with a black-owned advertising agency. Avon executives turned to UniWorld to create advertisements for the youth and African American market. Specifically, they wanted advertising that would help in their broader promotional effort to alter the traditional image of the Avon lady. Executives found that younger consumers considered the Avon lady as part of their mother's generation and had began to avoid the company's products as a result. Through a series of advertisements that tied into the company's general-market campaign, UniWorld's work spoke of Avon's new "hip shades" and told viewers and listeners the new Avon lady belonged to the younger generation. In radio advertisements, UniWorld used the traditional "Avon calling" tagline, but listeners learned the Avon lady "Must be more together than I thought." Further, the advertisements conveyed Avon's desire for greater numbers of black Avon representatives. Winners of the Miss Black America pageant also appeared in sales promotions, and Avon also created the Shades of Beauty product line specifically for African American women. In contrast to companies who ended their relationship with black agencies when outside pressure dissipated, the successful advertisements crafted by UniWorld led to Avon becoming a long-standing client.[64]

Besides product advertising and movie promotions, UniWorld also handled promotions for tourism and created some political advertisements. Moreover, it became the first black-owned agency to provide consultation services for black political candidates, providing advertising and public relations support for the successful campaigns of Mayor Kenneth Gibson of Newark, New Jersey, and Mayor Richard Hatcher of Gary, Indiana. Lewis also added a regional office in Washington, D.C., to help develop government advertising accounts. His long-range goal was to expand UniWorld to a level that allowed him to be competitive with executives from mainstream agencies for general-market accounts. He noted, "We feel that the black thing—ethnic advertising—is only the beginning."[65]

Despite his wish to expand into the general market, in the mid-1970s Lewis ran into a significant financial problem. Although the agency continued to gain clients, expenses began to outpace revenues, and in 1974 Lewis nearly ran out of working capital. But in contrast to other agencies like John Small and Zebra Advertising, Lewis developed a mechanism to keep his agency in operation. On the precipice of closing the agency, he developed a radio soap opera, *Sounds of the City*, oriented toward black listeners. The program, which Lewis later called his "creative hustle," was a fifteen-minute syndicated program with black characters that gave Lewis a media vehicle through which to approach potential clients. Eventually Quaker Oats became the program sponsor and helped to produce UniWorld's first million dollars in gross sales. The soap opera provided Lewis the solid financial foundation on which to further grow the agency, and the presence of a blue-chip client on his roster gave him a strong point of departure from which to approach other clients.[66]

By the end of 1975, the closures of John Small, Junius Edwards, and Zebra Advertising left UniWorld as the major black-owned agency in New York City. Lewis had successfully maneuvered the firm through the various problems that had doomed other black agencies. Although the economic crisis of the early 1970s certainly limited agency growth, it did not force him to close the agency. He diversified his firm beyond product advertisements and had gained some small advertising campaigns for the general market. Further, in all of his advertising work, like other black agencies, Lewis and his staff consciously endeavored to present a positive image of African Americans. Early on in the life of the firm, Lewis had established a policy of rejecting ads that placed blacks in stereotypical situations. "I evaluate and carefully examine a product before we decide to take on a client. I would not want this agency to contribute to the social and economic ills already facing our communities," Lewis stressed in an interview. While this philosophy may have resulted in not pursuing some client accounts, the firm continued to grow. In 1976, the AAAA elected UniWorld to membership, a status held by few other black agencies, and in so doing signaled the firm was on the way to financial and industry success.[67]

But, while Byron Lewis and Vince Cullers were pioneering figures in the advertising community, one year after Lewis's firm opened in 1969, a black woman prepared to take a historic step for the advertising industry. In 1970, Barbara Proctor turned her expertise and industry recognition into something no other black woman had ever attempted —ownership of an advertising agency.

Proctor and Gardner Advertising

Even before she entered the advertising industry, Barbara Proctor experienced success in several creative occupations. After having been a successful freelance writer, journalist, television writer, and record company executive, Proctor decided to try her hand at advertising. One of her first job interviews came at the Leo Burnett agency in Chicago, but the firm declined to hire her because she was "overqualified" for the positions then available. Undaunted, she continued to interview and eventually joined Post-Keyes-Gardner as a copywriter, one of the first blacks in this capacity in Chicago. Although she began as a novice, the more Proctor learned about advertising the more successful she became. By the late 1960s, she had won several creative awards and become one of the best-known black women in the industry; reporters sometimes labeled her the "black Mary Wells" after the famed white female copywriter and agency owner. Still, the longer Proctor worked in the industry, the more concerned she became about her prospects for advancement. Like Raymond League, Proctor believed if she remained an employee, she would hit a professional glass ceiling. Although she entered the industry before the late 1960s rush to find and develop black professionals, she thought little of the opportunities most firms offered to blacks. She thought that most mainstream agencies did little more than hire blacks to fill affirmative action quotas rather than give them, as they gave new white hires, the opportunity to learn and advance through the professional ranks. Rather than face any limits on her own advancement, she struck out on her own, reasoning, "They loved my work when I worked for someone else. Let's see how much they love me now."[68]

With an $80,000 loan from the Small Business Administration, Proctor shrewdly chose to combine her married name, Proctor, with her maiden name, Gardner, so prospective clients would assume she had a male partner. She believed that sexism might limit business opportunities before she ever got the chance to present her ideas, unless people believed there was a "man around the house." Located in a small office set over a restaurant, it took nearly seven months for her to land her first account, Jewel Food stores. While the gap between agency opening and her first client made her nervous, Proctor resolved not to quit. She had been successful at nearly every professional endeavor she had tried and vowed that running an agency would be no different.[69]

After gaining the first client, Proctor's billings rose steadily. The agency handled regional and national accounts for clients such as Sears-Roebuck, E. J. Gallo Winery, and Alberto Culver, as well as work for Democratic political campaigns. What surprised her about her client list, however, was the fact that she received only accounts directed at the black consumer market. This reversed her experience in mainstream agencies, where she had worked only on accounts directed at the general market. Like other black agency owners, Proctor continued to compete for accounts directed to both the general and black consumer markets. Eventually, she won some small accounts for general-market work, but they never reached a level equaling those she had worked on as a mainstream agency employee.[70]

However, she tried to combine her knowledge of the general marketplace with that of the black consumer market to argue that campaigns featuring African American models or cultural cues could effectively sell products to white consumers. Like Junius Edwards, she argued that cultural tastes within the United States originated in the black community and then spread to the rest of the nation. Therefore, advertisements could use black musical styles, slang, and fashion habits and efficiently sell products to all consumers regardless of color.[71]

Proctor also conscientiously selected the types of accounts she would accept. She refused to accept advertising assignments for products that reinforced stereotypes about blacks. "I have the opportunity to show the strength, beauty, humor and family respect that is a very proud tradition in the Black experience," she emphasized. Like Cullers and other black agency owners, she believed that advertising could be a mechanism for effecting changes in the image of African Americans. Thus, she refused to handle campaigns for alcohol and tobacco, products she considered unhealthy. Her determined stance cost her agency lost billings, but she chose to run her firm based on her own standards of corporate and social responsibility.[72]

Proctor also supported protecting and developing black-owned businesses, especially the black-owned agency niche. She repeatedly argued that corporate advertisers should use black-owned agencies to reach black consumers. Further, she viewed the establishment of ethnic cells or special marketing departments within mainstream agencies as an attempt to drive black agency owners from business. She believed that black agencies should receive the largest share of advertising dollars directed at black consumers. Doing so would help both black agencies in their growth efforts, as well as provide an important boost to black-owned media organizations.[73]

In 1974, Proctor's advocacy and efforts to support black business erupted into controversy after she announced that she would begin selecting the media for advertising placement based on the race of the owner. She stated that she would no longer place advertising where there was "flagrant exclusion of blacks from the revenues we generate." To counter this practice, she planned give priority to black media owners over white ones. When white-owned media was the only alternative, she would ask that a black representative service the account whenever possible. Further, she emphasized that the new policy had the "100 percent" support of her clients.[74]

The decision to aggressively support black-owned media aligned with Proctor's broader support of black-owned business. What is unclear, however, is why she chose to announce publicly this policy shift rather than simply institute it in practice at her agency. Regardless, the announcement created a firestorm. Reader letters in *Advertising Age* savaged Proctor as a black "racist—pure and simple." Reporters characterized her as embodying the discriminatory decision-making pattern the civil rights movement had ostensibly fought to changes. They also criticized her clients for supporting her decision. In deference to the criticism, Proctor eventually announced that she would choose media on a nonracial basis.[75]

Because of her success as an agency owner, her creative work, and her candid personality, Proctor was one of the leaders of the black advertising community. Many groups cited her creative work for awards, and she received several individual awards for service to the advertising industry and the public. In 1974, the Women's Ad Club of Chicago chose Proctor as Adwoman of the Year. By the end of the Golden Age, Proctor and Gardner's billings were more than $5,000,000 annually and the agency was one of the few surviving full-service black-owned agencies in the industry. Throughout the 1970s, Proctor's creativity and drive helped her agency to be a strong competitor for other black-owned firms.[76]

One year after Proctor and Gardner was opened, a second new black agency was founded in Chicago. In contrast to many other black agency owners, however, one of the principals of this new agency, Tom Burrell, had long been interested in an advertising career.

BURRELL ADVERTISING

Tom Burrell first thought about working in the advertising industry when he was sixteen years old. Scores on aptitude tests revealed that the young man had a talent for persuasiveness and creativity. Having little idea what that meant for occupational potential, he learned from his teacher that they might make him a good advertising copywriter. Burrell later recalled that he had no clear idea what an advertising copywriter was other than that few of his friends knew of the occupation and that it gave him a goal to work toward. After high school, Burrell attended and graduated from Roosevelt University with a major in English and a minor in advertising. His advertising career started in 1960 when he learned of a unique opportunity to join the Wade Advertising agency of Chicago.[77]

That was the year that executives at Wade Advertising decided to hire a black employee. This decision was a major step for the agency, because it had no blacks working in any capacity at the firm. They had no interest in having their new integration policy broadcast throughout Chicago and so, rather than working with the Urban League or other civil right organizations, Wade executives used their contacts with *Ebony* magazine. At that time John Johnson's legion of *Ebony* sales agents were among the only black faces visible in downtown Chicago offices, and Wade executives knew that working through a Johnson employee assured them a measure of discretion. Thus, the *Ebony* salesman who worked with Wade, Ron Sampson, served as a conduit to get the firm's hiring decision into the community.[78]

Wade executives asked Sampson to stress that the first position would be at the lowest employee level. Like executives in other service industries integrating African American employees, they feared a black professional might offend current personnel or clients. Further, as one of the largest three agencies in the city, the actions at Wade were certain to attract attention. "It was a major step because there were no African Americans working in any capacity in any advertising agency in the city of Chicago," Burrell recalled. Hiring an African American, therefore, seemed bound to cause enough local attention; hiring one at the professional level would draw unwanted national attention, something executives clearly wanted to avoid. So the few black professionals in the city turned down the opportunity to apply to the firm, and the prospective interviewee pool was small. In fact, when Burrell learned of the opening through Sampson's brother-in-law, he was the only person to interview. The firm wanted to make certain of the personality and character of the individual they hired, so even though the position was low in rank, Burrell interviewed with upper-level executives.[79]

To their credit, although Wade executives hired Burrell as a mailroom attendant, they planned to gradually move him into the firm's professional ranks. Burrell, though, had different ideas about exactly how long he wished to toil as an in-house mail carrier. "From the day that I started working in the mailroom, I set out to demonstrate to everybody around me that I had no business being in that job, but that I should be in an executive's job." He leveraged his position as a carrier of information into an asset to his goals. As a mail carrier, he had access to the firm's internal memorandums, and he read them to keep abreast of current issues and problems. After learning in this way of a creative problem within the agency, Burrell decided to take a calculated risk. He confidently went to the creative director and told him that it made little sense to have him working as a mail clerk when he could be helping the firm solve advertising problems. Whether it was the boldness of the young man's actions or a belief in his potential, two weeks later the director made Burrell a copywriting trainee. After completing the training courses, Burrell began working on television and print campaigns for the firm, one of the few blacks in Chicago to do so.[80]

And as a black copywriter in the early 1960s, Burrell was one of the few blacks working in any professional position in a mainstream Chicago ad firm. He worked on accounts aimed at the general, rather than black, consumer market. Still, he could only grow so far professionally at Wade because it had a limited roster primarily made up of packaged-goods companies. To broaden his expertise, Burrell knew that he needed to move to a larger agency. The pressure from civil rights and government organizations, combined with his experience, opened professional choices to him that would have been unavailable just a few years before. In 1964, he left Wade Advertising to join the Leo Burnett agency as a copywriter. After nearly three years with Burnett, he moved to a similar position with Foote, Cone & Belding and later to a copy supervisor post with Needham, Harper & Steers.[81]

In under ten years, Burrell had made significant professional progress in the advertising industry. He had worked in a variety of agencies in the United States and had even spent some time abroad working in the European offices of American agencies. Yet he recalled that he had tired of "thinking in reverse" about how to sell to the general market and that he wanted to create campaigns to reach black consumers. In contrast to League and Proctor, who foresaw a professional glass ceiling, Burrell realized that he had no desire to even reach the executive level of a mainstream agency: "I realized that even if I had the opportunity . . . I would not want it. I wouldn't like the transformation I'd have to go through—racial, yes, but also corporate. I wanted something to shape the way I wanted it to be." Therefore, after ten years in mainstream agencies, Burrell left Needham, Harper & Steers to try his hand at developing an advertising agency to market products to black consumers. By specializing in the black consumer market, he believed his firm would have a marketing angle over other new agencies. However, like every other black agency owner of the Golden Age, he imagined that he would eventually begin to earn accounts for general-market accounts.[82]

In 1971, with partner Emmett McBain, an award-winning artist and former employee of Vince Cullers Advertising, Burrell opened Burrell-McBain Advertising. In fact, this was Burrell's third attempt to form an agency. The other two groups he organized had been unable to secure clients, and his would-be partners had withdrawn from the ventures. In fact, even this third effort had lost a partner, Frank Mingo, who left the original triumvirate before the agency opened. In contrast to other black agency owners, the Burrell-McBain agency began without the support of bank loans. Instead, with pooled savings of the two principals, with one administrative assistant, Carol Boston, and with no clients, the agency made a quiet entry into the advertising fraternity. Burrell recalled, "We had no secretary, one telephone and three old desks which we painted red, green and orange." The sparse accommodations and quiet opening were part of a disciplined plan of growth. Burrell and McBain focused on getting clients rather than creating attention. "All I need to start up is a mailing address, a telephone, and a little bit of money to get where the potential client is," Burrell reasoned. Therefore there was no need to fill office space with employees simply because the space existed. One month after opening, Burrell landed the first account for the agency—a nightclub promotion that paid a mere $1,000 per month.[83]

From the beginning, Burrell refused to accept significant amounts of corporate public relations accounts. Early in his career as an agency owner, he received an important lesson in how some advertising directors viewed black advertising agencies. In the early 1970s, Burrell met with the advertising head of a large consumer-products company. The man was white, and Burrell desperately wanted to land his new firm's first big account. During his presentation Burrell told the executive of the various ways he could help his company better target African American consumers. Interrupting the presentation, the executive replied that his company did not want any added help in market penetration, but he told Burrell that his company wanted to help the new agency. He offered to give Burrell "a full fourth of what we pay agencies who do *real work* [emphasis mine]." Without hesitation, Burrell responded that one of the two of them was clearly at the wrong meeting, and he gathered his things and left. This early rejection of guilt or conscience money became an important standard for the agency. By refusing to accept money for doing nothing he unmistakably established that he was serious about setting up an advertising agency. Burrell did not want a client to select his firm because his skin color could help someone soothe his conscience or meet an affirmative action quota. Instead, he wanted clients to choose Burrell-McBain on the basis for what it was able to do for them. "Our basic philosophy is, if you don't think we can do anything for you, then we don't have anything to talk about," he offered. He correctly predicted that conscience money could help a firm stay in business but eventually would prevent it from growing. Although the principled stand led to some lean times, the agency soon began attracting clients and by the end of the first year in business was billing nearly $500,000.[84]

After the initial struggle to find accounts, the firm's client list began to grow. In 1971, a group of black McDonald's franchisees asked the parent corporation to hire a black agency to create ads for black consumers. Because several of the franchisees had already met the young agency man, the group convinced the parent company to choose his firm. After studying the slogan for McDonald's, "You deserve a break today," Burrell decided it was ineffective in reaching blacks. He believed the theme presented McDonald's as being a "special treat" that families used sporadically. In contrast, his research suggested that McDonald's restaurants were a part of many blacks' daily experience. Therefore the idea that the restaurants were only useful when one needed or wanted a break was meaningless to blacks. In place of the original slogan, he suggested the theme "McDonald's is good to have around" for the black consumer market. The new slogan and accompanying advertising campaign were a hit among black consumers. From that point onward, McDonald's remained one of the agency's largest clients.[85]

Beyond changing McDonald's slogan for the black community, Burrell also created ads that conveyed his vision of black life. In one commercial for the chain, entitled "A Family Is," the scene centered on a strong black woman who was clearly the matriarch of her family. The setting was a joyous family reunion that was also a bit sad because her son was absent. As she gazed wistfully on his picture, the scene shifted to the young man riding home on the bus. There was no suggestion what he was returning from, but it was obvious the family missed his presence. The commercial ended as he and his mother embraced in a tearful reunion. Burrell's advertisements for McDonald's often showed scenes of black families enjoying a meal together or black children playing together. Studies suggested that blacks were particularly responsive to scenes that featured a black male as head of the household and sharing in family life, so Burrell used that as a central feature in much of his advertising work. He argued that the large number of black homes without a father made it important to "present an image to them, not of what is, but of what could and should be." The advertisements were a success. In fact, they were so effective that executives assigned the firm a large share of company marketing efforts to black consumers, and the two companies have maintained a working partnership into the twenty-first century.[86]

Along with the McDonald's account, Burrell's other early major client breakthrough came in 1972, when he received an ethnic-marketing account for Coca-Cola. The firm had done work promoting the Fanta brand for the Chicago Coca-Cola bottler, but the new assignment came from the national company. The current Coke general marketing theme was "Look up, America, and see what you've got." Burrell argued the theme was inappropriate for the black community because blacks were not yet at a point where they could take pride in the American experience. As an alternative, he counseled executives to use the theme "For the real times, it's the real thing." The reworked theme tapped into blacks' current social reality and offered Coke as a welcome respite from the demands of the times. The campaign proved so effective that Burrell's agency eventually handled all Coca-Cola advertising to black consumers.

Additionally, one commercial for Coke, "Street Song," showed the crossover appeal of facets of black life and culture. In the commercial a group of young black men sit on the steps of a townhouse and sing the Coca-Cola jingle a cappella. The commercial was a creative hit in the black community, and Coke executives eventually began using it to reach white consumers as well. It also received critical acclaim and a Clio award, the advertising industry's equivalent of the Oscar award. The commercial illustrated what Junius Edwards and Barbara Proctor argued, that advertisements could use elements of black culture, thoughtfully and carefully, to sell products to white consumers as well as black ones.

Work for both McDonald's and Coca-Cola gave Burrell access to work on television commercials, an option that few other black-owned agencies had. The television work helped to distinguish Burrell's agency from his contemporaries in the black-owned agency niche and gave the firm a competitive advantage. Combining that advantage with a strong research and creative focus enabled the young agency to win several major clients within its first few years of existence.[87]

Another early client acquisition was the Philip Morris Company. Executives approached Burrell because the overall best-selling cigarette, Marlboro, was not the number one brand among blacks. Burrell and McBain concluded that the central figure of the advertisements, the Marlboro Man, was the cause for the low sales. They argued that, although whites considered the Marlboro Man a "hero," blacks considered him a "loser." Research suggested that blacks defined manhood as "a man who took charge of family, lived in the city, [and] was involved with people in a responsible role." Where the cowboy was an individual,

Figure 17. Burrell's combination of client products with realistic scenes of African American life proved effective among black consumers. Coca-Cola advertisement, *Ebony* (June 1974): inside back cover.

a black man was with his family or friends; where the cowboy was alone, a black man was active in his community. Therefore blacks' definition of manhood was an almost complete reversal of that of both the white and black individualistic cowboys prevalent in Marlboro ads. The advertisements created by Burrell and McBain (who had been part of creating the "Brother in the Blue Dashiki" advertisement while at Vince Cullers Advertising) featured a black man as the central figure, located in urban settings, involved with his community, and on the move. The images conveyed the sense the black Marlboro Man was someone who had places to go and that wherever he went was the place to be.[88]

Despite an increase in Marlboro sales among blacks, however, Philip Morris stopped the urban Marlboro Man series. A bystander photographed in the background of one the ads threatened to sue Philip Morris for the use of his image. He was an antismoking advocate and objected to a tobacco advertisement that included his image. After Philip Morris settled the case out of court, a few other bystanders threatened to sue the company as well. Also, executives at Leo Burnett, the general market advertising agency for Marlboro, objected to the new urbanized version as a distortion of the brand image they had struggled to establish. While early in his history, men in various occupations had represented the Marlboro Man, but by this time his image was firm: he was a cowboy and he was white. Nonetheless the advertising series displayed Burrell-McBain's creativity, showcased the agency's ability to improve sales, and further solidified its reputation.[89]

Another reason behind Burrell's early and continuing success came from his promotion of the advertising philosophy of "positive realism." Rather than using images of blacks either at alternate extremes of the wealthy black celebrity or the destitute ghetto dweller, he tried to depict the vast middle part of black America, the people "dying to see themselves as they really are." He actively used positive images of blacks in settings and activities that he believed were worthy of emulation. Like early black advertising leaders Claude Barnett and David Sullivan, he reasoned that to reach black consumers, advertisements had to reflect positively on them as a group and on the product in question. "We felt that by showing people in a positive way, unlike the way they had been shown before, it was going to be effective—it was actually going to sell product," he recalled. As a result, many of his advertisements portrayed blacks in everyday situations, such as brushing their teeth, washing their cars, or doing their laundry. By doing so, his advertisements reinforced the idea that a black person did not have to be a celebrity to be worthy of respect or emulation. Burrell argued that black consumers were "not just dark skinned white people" but a group that advertisements had to approach in a unique and creative manner that incorporated African

American life and culture. Images of loving black families, Sunday-morning church activities, black children playing Double Dutch, and again, of black kids singing the Coke jingle a capella on a tenement stoop all proved effective in both selling the client's products and communicating a positive image of African Americans.[90]

Also, as had been the case with the black Marlboro Man, much of his work featured strong black males as central figures. He actively used the imagery and copy within his advertisements to portray blacks as fathers and leaders. For example, an advertisement for Crest toothpaste pictured a father adjusting his son's tie with copy that voiced his wish to be as "involved with my son as much as I can." In television spot for Crest, a black businessman declares that his life and priorities have changed since he had children. Rather than working late at the office, the commercial ends with him leaving to see his son play the cymbals in a school concert. The voiceover then asks, "Aren't your kids worth Crest?"[91]

Burrell's work also penetrated the general market through ads found to have crossover appeal. Advertisements for Coca-Cola, Martell Cognac, and Procter & Gamble effectively reached both black and white consumers and led to further advertising work for the company. He stated, "In many cases, the work that had the African-American folks in it, that had this whole African-American slant to it, had higher recognition, awareness, and likeability than the spots targeted to the non-African-American market."[92]

Burrell's advertising and business philosophy proved effective. Although Emmett McBain left the agency in 1974 to pursue a full-time art career, the firm remained financially and creatively strong. The agency kept a steady rate of billing growth throughout the Golden Age, and in 1975 the AAAA elected the agency to membership status as it would UniWorld the following year. Burrell was also active in some efforts to increase the presence of blacks in the advertising industry including the Basic Advertising Course as well as a series of less-publicized efforts to keep blacks in the agency business. The agency's work also had won several industry creative awards, and it maintained a roster of clients whose longevity with the agency proved their belief in its importance to their advertising strategies.[93]

In the late 1970s, Burrell's advertising career came full circle when he recruited Ron Sampson to join his agency. In the nearly twenty years since Sampson first made Burrell aware of the opening at Wade Advertising, Sampson had gone on to become one of the highest-ranking African Americans in any major agency in the country. Burrell convinced Sampson to leave his management supervisor post at Tatham, Laird, and Kudner and incorporate his experience and network of contacts into Burrell Advertising, to help it be more competitive for general-market accounts. Sampson's hiring confirmed to industry observers not only the health and growth potential of Burrell's agency but also that not all black-owned agencies were going out of business. By the end of the 1970s, the agency had become the second-largest black-owned agency in the nation and its presence assured potential clients that blacks could indeed establish and run successful firms outside New York City. With the presence of Vince Cullers and Proctor and Gardner advertising, Burrell helped make Chicago the center of the black advertising agency universe.[94]

Defending the Black Agency Niche

The growth in the ethnic segment (which by the mid-1970s increasingly included the Hispanic market) of the consumer marketplace, while small, drew the attention of some mainstream agencies. In the cost-conscious early 1970s, when clients were reducing advertising budgets, agency executives looked for ways to maintain revenues from any possible source. As a result, several agencies, including industry leader J. Walter Thompson, studied the viability of internally based ethnic marketing and advertising units. Only one major agency, Young & Rubicam (Y&R), created an ethnic unit, though, and the move caused immediate controversy.[95]

In late 1972 Y&R executives formally set up an ethnic-marketing unit. Agency leadership considered the cell a wise decision because it allowed them to offer "ethnic services" to their clients rather than see them divide their accounts among multiple agencies. Further, it was an easy move to make, as it only centralized work the agency was already doing. One report estimated that Y&R was billing $15 million yearly in ethnic-based advertising. Therefore, setting up a formal group to focus on the African American and Hispanic markets might lead that figure to increase. What Y&R executives had not allowed for, however, was the widespread controversy that followed.[96]

In 1973, the executive board of the Group for Advertising Progress (GAP) called for and received the resignation of the organization president, James Harold. Harold, an account executive at Y&R, had agreed to head the black section of the new ethnic unit. He argued the position was a natural extension of his present responsibilities. Further, Harold had worked at Zebra Associates and J. Walter Thompson and felt his qualifications, rather than color, led to his selection by company leaders. But GAP members argued the unit was a blatant attempt to segregate black advertising professionals within the agency. The existence of the cell would limit blacks at Y&R to working solely on accounts for the black consumer market. Further, GAP leaders argued that Y&R intended for the ethnic cell to take business away from black- and Hispanic-owned agencies. Harold did resign from GAP, and the new president Doug Alligood warned mainstream agencies that, if widely duplicated, Y&R's ethnic unit could negatively impact the careers of black professionals throughout the industry. Like others in GAP, Alligood believed that it was Harold's responsibility to refuse leadership of the ethnic cell and instead use his position in the agency to see it dismantled. "What we need is full opportunity for blacks," Alligood continued, and "integration at the supervisory level and some account supervisors who have empathy with specialized markets."[97]

In contrast to GAP leadership, several individuals, black and white, lauded the creation of the ethnic cell as a way to open more job opportunities in agencies for minorities. "We think it would be good for everyone if the Y&R unit grows and opens new jobs," an *Advertising Age* editorial stated. Further, it argued that the ethnic cell was a way to aid in the "de-ghettoization" of advertising through providing important research figures and marketing programs to help draw the black and Hispanic consumer markets further into the mainstream. Y&R, its proponents argued, had the resources to develop much needed innovative research programs into ethnic markets that would aid all agencies, whether black- or white owned. One white advertising executive argued the cell was "an admission that you need specialists in specialized areas—as I think agencies have recognized with women over the years."[98]

The problem, GAP leaders contended, was that if other agencies adopted Y&R model, ethnic cells might eventually become the *only* areas in which minorities could work. Rather than receiving the salary increases and promotions that came from greater experience, minorities in ethnic cells would soon face a glass ceiling. Alligood and other GAP leaders firmly believed that ethnic-unit positions would quickly become synonymous with being "black jobs" and the only areas in which agencies employed black professionals. In other words, while these special cells could be a point of entry into the profession, they more likely would serve as a kind of internal economic detour that limited the careers of black professionals. Indeed, this had already been the experience of some of GAP's leaders and members who had started their careers as Negro-market specialists. Many felt the positions actually hindered their professional advancement. As ethnically focused specialists they had been outside the traditional routes to advancement in their respective agencies. Also, because so few agencies had accounts that specifically targeted black consumers, they lacked job mobility. Any racially motivated limitations on professional mobility conflicted with GAP's organizational principles. This is exactly why GAP focused, like Bill

Sharp's Basic Advertising Course, on creating "Negroes who are special-ists in marketing—marketing in general, not Negro market specialists." Thus agitation against the creation of the Y&R ethnic cell was a natural extension of GAP's organizational purpose.[99]

On the issue of the cell being an unfair competitor to the small, but growing, black agency niche, several observers criticized GAP for trying to artificially protect them from the natural laws of competition. Instead of unfair competition, the cells were an admission of the potential impact of such agencies, a point highlighted by black agency owners. "White agencies fear black agencies getting a foot in the door with part of an account because it could be a 'stepping-stone to havoc in the agency' with other portions of the account going to other ethnic agen-cies," said one such owner.[100] The ethnic cell was a clear indication that the rationale behind the existence of black agencies was sound and that the black consumer market was a valuable segment to pursue.

Although GAP's protest failed to eliminate the ethnic unit at Y&R, the controversy illustrated changing perceptions in the industry of blacks' role in mainstream agencies. In 1952, observers had hailed BBDO for hiring Clarence Holte to head its special-markets group. Twenty years later, black professionals in the industry labeled a plan to develop a simi-lar unit as an attempt to "pigeonhole" blacks and to create "career dead ends." If ethnic cells were to exist, they said, it would have to be in a manner that fully incorporated them into the agency. Promotions for those in ethnic cells needed to be consistent with that throughout the agency.

Trade journal descriptions of the ethnic unit offer no evidence that Y&R executives planned the unit in the kind of comprehensive manner GAP and other blacks in the industry may have found acceptable. There-fore the agency drew the ire of the black advertising community as both an affront to black agency ownership as well as a potential limitation of blacks' roles in mainstream firms. Executives at Y&R apparently never understood that black professionals wanted their career paths linked with the general market because that presented the best route for advancement. The black consumer market was an option, of course, but the general market gave them a broader base of experience and the best choices for job mobility and salary increases. The African American mar-ket was a necessity for black-owned firms searching for a unique niche but not necessarily for an individual seeking to advance outside those agencies. In the end, the ethnic unit at Y&R lasted roughly five years. In 1977, executives integrated the African American portion of the unit into other agency operations. Ironically, after leading the protest against Y&R's ethnic cell, several years later Alligood went on to head BBDO's special-markets unit focusing on black and Hispanic consumers.[101]

Behind the Success of African American Agencies

What allowed Vince Cullers, Byron Lewis, Barbara Proctor, and Tom Burrell to be successful where other agency owners were not? There is no single reason or checklist of items that guaranteed success or failure, no absolute consistency of practices across companies. Burrell had a policy against accepting large numbers of corporate public relations accounts, but Lewis and Proctor were not as rigid. Also, Junius Edwards had a similar policy, but it did not save his agency. The four agencies did create some outstanding and award-winning advertisements, but so too did some of the agencies that perished. What the four surviving agencies did have in common was that each continually demonstrated their ability to increase product sales, and each had a strong roster of clients with a genuine interest in the black consumer market. Staff members of the surviving black agencies compiled extensive research on black consumers' buying habits and motivations. They proved that they were able to communicate with and sell to black consumers and, most importantly, they found national-level clients like Quaker Oats, McDonald's and Coca-Cola that were committed to *investing* money to target black consumers rather than just *giving* conscience money to black-owned agencies. As a result, when the smoke cleared at the end of the Golden Age, the remaining black-owned agencies were meeting the needs of existing clients and were well prepared to attract additional business.

Additionally, each of the four agency principals would likely say that they each experienced that indefinable quality known as good luck in which they or a member of their staff was in the right place at the right time to land a client account. For example, Burrell's preexisting relationship with black McDonald's franchisees placed his agency near the top of the list when the parent company hired a black firm. Then, based on the successful work his agency created, he cemented a lasting partnership with the company. Or when UniWorld stood on the brink of closure Lewis developed a radio program that he then successfully sold to Quaker Oats. Both Burrell and Lewis were able to demonstrate their advertising acumen and then convince a major corporation to enter into a working relationship with their agencies.

An Economic On-ramp or Detour?

By the close of the Golden Age, the experience of black-owned advertising agencies suggests that Stuart's definition of an economic detour—a racially based limitation on black business development—had begun to be applicable. It is clear that white clients were content to work with a black Burrell or Proctor on white accounts while they were at white mainstream agencies but were sure that these former executives could only work on ethnic markets when they became agency owners. At the same time, it is also true that black agency owners made claims based on their own racial background about their special expertise or insight into the black consumer market. Of course, most owners only meant this to be an initial marketing angle, an economic on-ramp, not a detour. But some of the responsibility for the rigidity of the limitations on black agencies rests on the shoulders of their owners. In creating their unique position and rationale for existence, black agency owners provided clients with reasons to *not* employ them to reach white consumers. After all, a marketer who heard Lewis declare that "It is difficult for white marketers to anticipate black purchasing decisions if they are not black," could be forgiven for making the leap that the reverse was true for blacks anticipating white buying decisions. These assertions, when reported as sound bites from interviews or speeches, limited appreciation for the data mining, consumer research, and creative insights that were the foundation of black agencies' success at selling products to black consumers. Instead of understanding that the success of black agencies rested on the same kinds of in-depth work as mainstream firms, these declarations made it appear as though blacks' advertising strategies were derived from their skin color alone. As a result, like black insurance and beauty products companies in the mid-twentieth century, the surviving black agencies found steady growth but at the same time found themselves limited mainly to the black consumer market.[102]

Still, the fact that some black agencies, including UniWorld and Burrell Advertising, secured some significant general-market assignments at least offered the possibility that black agencies could expand beyond the black consumer market in the coming years. Also, the growth of "crossover" advertising, in which advertisements developed for the black consumer market were used to reach the general market also presented black agencies with greater hopes of gaining more general-market assignments.

One issue the existence of black advertising agencies or special-markets units within agencies uncomfortably raised to some in the industry was whether these organizations formed segregation in reverse. If mainstream agencies did not incorporate black professionals into the fabric of company life, or black agencies primarily crafted advertising to black consumers, some argued, the pattern of segregation had simply evolved to a different form. In response, black advertising professionals argued that targeted marketing and advertising programs extended the individualized consumer attention that African Americans had spent much of the twentieth century demanding. Rather than segregation in reverse, they said, these campaigns were helping incorporate blacks into the fabric of consumer society.[103]

Dividing the mass market into smaller, more efficiently targeted pieces made logical sense, and it had the support of both the changing emphasis of the civil rights movement from integration to nationalism as well as developing marketing theories that legitimized its use. Certainly, race comprised one aspect of the divided marketplace, but it was no less valid than developing a marketing program for women, teenagers, or almost any other division that allowed for greater advertising efficiency. In addition, critics of the practice seemed to overlook the fact that the exclusion of blacks from advertisements (even within black-oriented publications) for much of the twentieth century represented the actual segregation in advertising. In fact, opposition to racially specific marketing says more about the way in which divisions based on race make people uncomfortable than it does about the efficiency such targeting allows. Also, while laws as well as social custom had begun to break down the many of the barriers separating the races, much of society itself remained segregated in many ways. Thus, advertising campaigns specifically for the black consumer market were not a segregation of advertising. They were an evolution and maximization of it.[104]

Conclusion

Many blacks aspiring to a career in advertising welcomed the presence of black-owned advertising agencies. These agencies provided them with a place to express their vision of the black experience in America. This was in contrast to how some viewed blacks working in mainstream agencies where they "often turn into white Negroes creating white commercials," observed one black agency owner. Or, as one black with mainstream agency experience forcefully described, "We have to be black Anglo-Saxons to make it. If you let your hair grow out, you're Rap Brown. Speak out and you're coming on too strong. We're kind of [like] house niggers." In contrast, a black agency was a place where others did not question their talents and creativity or, at a minimum, a place in which one did not have to immediately prove that one belonged in a professional position; instead others assumed their talent and competence until experience proved otherwise. Further, some blacks acknowledged that there was a kind of cold comfort in knowing that, if fired, it was not because they were black.[105]

Black adman Arthur Mitchell argued that black advertising agencies would use their access to media to "portray a more honest picture of the black man" through advertisements than whites had done. Mitchell also argued that in his position as an agency owner he was "not so much interested in making money as in changing images." While he may have had few adherents to promoting images over profit, he alluded to an important part of the mission of black agencies. As Dates noted, once blacks had achieved decision-making positions they worked to challenge the images that had previously existed and contribute to the development of a more positive and realistic image of African Americans.[106]

Because most black agencies worked on accounts directed to black consumers, staff members and potential employees viewed them as places that offered them an opportunity to communicate their sense of black identity. Working in these firms allowed blacks to embrace their culture and work with the freedom of calling on their own backgrounds and experiences. They could then use those experiences to craft successful campaigns using their visions of African American life and culture, as well as that of the role of black adman or woman. Certainly not every black creative person sat at their desk and consciously thought "I want to show black people in a positive light," just as not every white creative consciously said, "Hey, let's show some Uncles and Aunties and have them speak in dialect." Instead, at a minimum, blacks sought to present blacks realistically. After all, their own lives showed them that blacks were not all one anything. Instead, there was a range of experience in the community that advertisements could and should express. This is not to say the secondary discourse of the advertisement, the image projected, took precedence over meeting the needs of clients. But black agencies created advertising that was equal to the responsibility of selling products and improving the images of black Americans.

Black agency owners successfully convinced many corporate executives to approach black consumers in the same way that they approached white consumers—with well-researched and carefully developed campaigns. Black agency owner Frank Mingo wrote, "It is no longer enough to run full-page corporate ads referring obliquely to Crispus Attucks, Sojourner Truth, W. E. B. DuBois and stating what a good liberal company you are or boasting of the handful of black employees (complete with pictures) you have managed to hire."[107] Leaders of surviving agencies encouraged corporate executives to discard their corporate public relations campaigns and replace them with genuine appeals for black consumer patronage. Although the Golden Age proved costly in terms of the number of agency closures, the companies that remained active in the black consumer market gave surviving black agencies a strong base from which to grow in the coming years.

Black-owned advertising agencies were the outgrowth of nearly five decades of work by black media figures like Claude Barnett and John Johnson, as well as that of the Brown Hucksters. These pioneering men and women had proven to many in corporate America the value of the black consumer market through their work as special marketers in American corporations. These individuals consistently argued and explained and illustrated that African Americans were a distinct market with unique consumer needs and habits that could be more effectively reached through targeted advertising campaigns. Combined with civil rights organization and government pressure to develop opportunities for black professionals in the 1960s, their arguments provided an essential foundation to the emergence of black-owned advertising agencies. Further, the training and recruitment programs emerging that developed in the 1960s and '70s provided valuable experience for many of the blacks who went on to become agency pioneers. Although the recession in the early 1970s helped speed the demise of several black agencies, those that survived were in stronger position to better influence the corporate appreciation and development of the black consumer market.

Epilogue

Why can't an agency founded to do black advertising do more than black advertising if it's doing it well?
—*Ron Sampson, 2004*

The recession that hit the advertising industry in the 1970s effectively brought an end to the Golden Age for blacks in the industry. Advertising agencies ended most of the training programs that had increased the numbers of minorities in agencies, and the few remaining programs expanded from their focus on minorities to include all talented beginners. Agency executives had to ask themselves why they should underwrite programs to increase minority employees when they were laying off existing staff members. In the face of declining revenue, financial demands trumped social outreach.

There was a silver lining to this cloud. In the consolidating black-owned agency segment, the surviving agencies were in a stronger position to bid for new accounts. Fewer experienced agencies in the segment meant less competition, and some former members of now-defunct agencies joined the surviving firms and strengthened their pool of employees even further. In mainstream agencies, some blacks who had survived the layoffs now began to move into decision-making positions. Eager to maintain and increase revenues, a growing number of corporate leaders wanted to learn of areas and consumer groups that might help add to their revenue. Companies began to develop spending plans that suggested their serious interest in the black consumer market, rather than running corporate image campaigns or giving conscience money. In turn, this interest sparked the emergence of new black agencies, media vehicles, and spokespersons, helping raise the visibility of black consumers and the black agency segment even further.

Beyond the Recession: Closing Out the 1970s

When the smoke cleared after 1975, UniWorld stood as the only major black-owned agency still in existence in New York. (While there were smaller black firms still in business, they existed on local accounts and were below the radar of the trade press.) Several in the press assumed that the effort to set up black agencies in the heart of the advertising world was over. "It is apparent now that the years of struggle to develop a solid cadre of black-owned and operated advertising agencies in New York City has failed," *Advertising Age* reported. Emerging to prove such skepticism misguided, though, were another group of black advertising professionals who had cut their teeth on major market accounts at mainstream agencies. New agencies like Adworks Advertising and Lockhart & Pettus appeared; among them, Mingo-Jones quickly became the largest and most recognized of the immediate post-Golden Age black agencies.[1]

MINGO-JONES ADVERTISING

Originally founded in 1977 as Mingo, Jones, Guilemenot, the agency had at its inception three principals: Frank Mingo, Caroline Jones, and Richard Guilemenot. Each of them brought impressive industry experience from years of work at the executive levels of mainstream agencies. Mingo left a position as a vice president and management supervisor at McCann-Erickson, where he had recently overseen the product launch of Miller Lite beer. This was Mingo's second foray into agency ownership. He had originally partnered with Tom Burrell and Emmett McBain, but at the last minute had chosen the financial security of being an employee over the risk of ownership. Jones had served as a vice president at BBDO, where she had been the first black woman to hold that position at any mainstream agency. She had also been on the staff of the recently defunct Zebra Advertising and had briefly partnered with Kelvin Wall to set up the Black Consulting Group to guide companies on advertising and marketing campaigns to African Americans. For his part, Guilemenot had been an executive at Ted Bates and Company. But Guilemenot remained part of the new firm only for a few years, and when he left the firm shortened the name to Mingo-Jones.[2]

The firm garnered some early attention because of an unusual relationship with Interpublic, a white-owned advertising agency holding company. Mingo described the link between the two companies as an "affiliation" in which Interpublic handled functions like media payment, accounting and billing, and media buying for Mingo-Jones in exchange for fees. This setup gave the new agency the advantage of being able to provide a broad range of client services, without making extensive initial investments in personnel. Intimately familiar with the role that financial resources had played in the demise of other black firms, the principals at Mingo-Jones viewed the link with Interpublic as a temporary, but necessary, step to provide their firm a solid financial foundation. Some blacks in the industry decried the relationship between Mingo-Jones and Interpublic as one in which Interpublic secretly controlled the new agency from behind the scenes. "They're working on Interpublic's plantation," black advertising executive Sanford Moore charged. But Interpublic had no say in the agency's business decisions, and Mingo-Jones remained an independent agency. Rather than being a plantation relationship (with the dominant/submissive arrangement such a description suggested), the affiliation gave Mingo-Jones a solid base from which to build. Further, it offered the opportunity to avoid the financial straits that doomed firms like John Small Advertising and Zebra Advertising.[3]

Like other black agency owners, the principals at Mingo-Jones wanted to set up a general-market agency. They carefully worded their press release to acknowledge their racial identity (which would signal their interest in the black consumer market) as well as these broader ambitions: "A new independent general ad agency, owned by blacks, was introduced to the press yesterday." The new owners recognized that confining their accounts to the black consumer market would limit their growth, "We are very pleased to do black consumer advertising," Jones told an interviewer. She continued, "Someone has to do it on a professional level, and we think we can do it better than anyone else. However, we will never be a really big successful company unless we get general-market accounts as well." Each of the three principals had worked on major general-market accounts during their years at mainstream agencies, but (like so many of their colleagues) when they became agency owners they found that some clients now questioned their expertise. "It was hard to swallow the fact that, although I had handled $100 million accounts for big agencies, some people were inclined to question my ability to handle a $3 million account because I have a black face," Mingo said. The three principals focused on clients that would help build the agency and avoiding the "token" accounts that had little long-term value and that helped limit the growth other black agencies. Such accounts did not demonstrate a client's belief in their advertising services or a genuine appreciation of the role of the black consumer market in their sales. As a result, they had little chance of developing into a lasting agency/client relationship. Fortunately, as former agency executives each of the partners had a network he or she could access to help build the agency's client roster. Additionally, the agency had one initial client, a $1 million account with Miller Brewing that targeted black consumers and that gave it a foundation from which to begin. The new firm quickly developed a roster of blue-chip clients interested into developing the black consumer segment of their respective businesses.[4]

One of the firm's earliest successes resulted from an account for Kentucky Fried Chicken (KFC). Assigned with the task of improving sales in the New York region, Jones's research found the existing slogan of "It's so nice to feel good about a meal" to be ineffective. Specifically, it did not suggest anything about the product among its heavy users, black and Hispanic consumers. To stress the qualities of the product, Jones and other creatives at the agency developed the slogan "We do chicken right" and began using singer Gladys Knight as the spokesperson. Through billboard and radio advertisements in the regional market, the new slogan had an immediate positive impact on sales. Eventually it proved so successful that KFC executives adopted it for their national advertising campaign.[5]

The agency soon became one of the recognized leaders of the black agency segment. Mingo devoted his energies to expanding the agency's client roster and acquiring other firms to expand its overall capabilities. For example, in 1978 reports emerged of a proposed merger between Mingo-Jones and UniWorld. The deal fell through after it became obvious that some of UniWorld's major clients disliked the idea, and Byron Lewis canceled the deal. Undaunted, Mingo continued to pursue merger options and eventually incorporated a few smaller firms into Mingo-Jones, expanding the agency into public relations and advertising work in the Asian and Hispanic markets.[6]

By the early 1980s, over 40 percent of the agency's billings were for

Figure 18. Although the slogan developed by Mingo-Jones for Kentucky Fried Chicken was widely recognized by consumers and used for the national campaign in all markets, responsibility for the national account remained with KFC's primary agency. Bernice Kanner, "Two-year-old Mingo Shop Came Ready for Success," *Advertising Age* (May 7, 1979): 85.

general-market accounts and Mingo called the creative work of the firm "general first, black second." The agency ended the association with Interpublic in the early 1980s as Mingo-Jones had grown large enough that the relationship was no longer necessary. Through work for clients like Miller Brewing, Disney, and Kentucky Fried Chicken, Mingo-Jones showed that black agencies could in fact succeed in New York and develop campaigns that would reach consumers of various racial backgrounds. Unfortunately for the firm, Caroline Jones left in 1986 to pursue the opportunity to open her own firm. Just a few years later in 1989, Mingo died suddenly from a heart attack. The new leader, Samuel Chisholm, led the firm through several years of continued growth in the 1990s, but by the early twenty-first century mounting debts led him to declare bankruptcy and close the agency.[7]

REACHING BLACK CONSUMERS

As the 1970s closed there was a visible increase in the number of black athletes and entertainers acting as national product spokespersons. To the delight of consumers, precocious five-year-old Rodney Allen Rippy starred in commercials for the Jack-In-The-Box fast food chain and struggled to bite into one of their giant hamburgers. Black sports and entertainment stars like football great O. J. Simpson flew through airports for Hertz rental cars, boxing champion Muhammad Ali knocked out roaches for Raid, and comedian Bill Cosby touted the benefits of Jell-O products. In a testament to blacks' growing popularity as product spokespersons, *Advertising Age* named Simpson and Cosby the Presenter of the Year in 1977 and 1978, respectively.[8]

The world of black-oriented media got bigger, and new black publications such as *Essence,* a magazine targeting black women, and *Black Enterprise,* for blacks in white-collar occupations, were also vehicles for advertisers to reach black consumers. The days of *Ebony* magazine as the only viable national print alternative for campaigns to the black consumer market were over. Additionally, the television shows directed to black audiences, including *Good Times, The Jeffersons,* and *Sanford and Son,* gave advertisers an even greater range of choices to reach blacks. All of the new media choices allowed advertisers to effectively target different parts within the black consumer market. Combined with special programs, such as the highly successful *Roots* miniseries documenting the fictional experience of enslaved Africans, there were more images of blacks within programs and advertisements than at any other point in history. Moreover, the success of these programs and advertising campaigns for both black and white consumers provided evidence that, contrary to the concerns of some, white consumers would not abandon products featuring or pitched by African Americans. Thus, although the racial revolution in advertising had ended and many agencies had closed, those blacks still in the industry had reason to be optimistic as they viewed the coming decades.[9]

New Challenges: The 1980s and '90s

The release of the 1980 census showed that important black statistical indicators were improving. The number of blacks enrolled in college in 1980 was over 90 percent higher than the number in 1970. The black population had increased over 17 percent, nearly three times the increase among whites. Though most blacks continued to live in urban areas, figures indicated that many were moving into the suburbs. The number of blacks working in white-collar occupations had risen almost 40 percent. Though blacks still earned less than whites on average, accompanying the occupational shift was a rise in black income of nearly 200 percent.[10]

Nonetheless, by the mid-1980s racial progress in the advertising industry stalled. Some major advertisers that once used black-owned agencies turned to mainstream firms to handle campaigns to black consumers. As a result, black agencies had to refine their marketing efforts even further and continue to look for ways to strengthen their links with clients. In mainstream agencies, both statistically and anecdotally, the numbers of minorities in advertising agencies was declining. An Equal Employment Opportunity Commission study found the number of professional blacks in New York agencies had declined to 1.7 percent, down from 2.5 percent in the late 1960s. "Agencies are in a regressive mode. Race is not even an issue on their list," said one black agency owner. "Blacks are not going up in advertising; they're going out," agreed another.[11]

On the governmental front, Illinois congresswoman Cardiss Collins introduced legislation to increase billings to minority agencies: two bills called for the Defense Department to set aside part of its advertising budget for minority firms, and a third measure would remove tax deductions for advertisers found to have discriminated against minority-owned advertising agencies. However, all three measures failed to secure the necessary votes. While laudable, her efforts lacked the public attention or depth of inquiry that characterized those of the 1960s and early '70s, and few other legislators followed her lead. Thus, what little change resulted from public pressure outside the industry came from the activities of civil rights organizations.[12]

Jesse Jackson's organization, Operation PUSH (People United to Save Humanity), used public pressure to meet with major advertisers (like Coca-Cola, Anheuser-Busch, and Ford) and to secure agreements with them to increase their advertising budgets with black advertising agencies. Although representatives from both black agencies and national advertisers publicly denied that the agreements led to specific changes in their advertising program, after the meetings a few black agencies did receive increased advertising billings from the targeted companies. For example, after PUSH met with Coca-Cola, Burrell Advertising received increased billings from the soda giant. UniWorld received a similar increase from Burger King and Hueblein Inc., after company executives had met with Jackson. Still, despite the similarities of the government and civil rights organization efforts to those of the 1960s, their overall impact was much lower. Public attention and energy toward racial issues in the 1980s paled in comparison to that of the earlier decades. Neither national advertising organizations nor the trade press took up the issue and, though some agencies experience increased billings, the lack of wider attention limited the overall impact of the efforts by Operation PUSH.[13]

Beyond the attention that Jackson brought to the black-owned agencies, civil unrest once again led to concerns about the number and role of blacks in the broader advertising industry. After the six days of rioting that accompanied the 1992 Rodney King verdict, there was a brief spike in interest in the topic of minority employment within the industry. The topic of blacks' employment in advertising agencies became the topic for major stories in newspapers, trade journals, and business magazines. In *Advertising Age*, reporters concurred with black adman Jo Muse's description of the industry's poor record on minority hiring as its "dirty little secret." An editorial in the paper one week later charged that it was "time for agencies to re-focus their priorities and address the race problem with more resolve . . . [and] rededicate themselves to this vital task [increasing the number of minority professionals] today." Reporters outside the trade press also took up the issue. An article in *Black Enterprise*, the leading black-oriented business magazine bluntly asked readers to consider, "Are ad agencies serious about hiring African-Americans?"[14]

Some blacks in the industry also developed their own programs to try to draw attention to the issue. In Chicago, black adman Lowell Thompson became a leading figure publicizing the industry's poor record on hiring and retaining black professionals. In addition to drawing attention through articles he composed for the trade press, he also developed mechanisms to assist existing black professionals in finding employment. For example, working together with Don Richards, a black executive at the Leo Burnett agency, Thompson organized an exhibition of the work of minority artists and photographers to show that there were minority professionals available for agency work. Additionally, he later helped set up a Minority Talent Hotline that agencies could use to locate minorities for freelance work or permanent jobs.[15]

Unfortunately, coinciding with the King verdict there was an overall decline in employment numbers in the industry. With experienced people losing their jobs, agency executives could not justify programs to attract minority employees, even given the urban unrest. "With so many people out on the street it's hard to look people in the eye and say, 'We need to make this industry attractive to another 12 or 13 percent of the population,'" noted one executive. Further, in comparison to the cumulative effect of four years of urban unrest between 1964 and 1967, the effect of the Los Angeles riots on the public consciousness was minor. Thus the powerful demands from the general public, civil rights organizations, and the government to do something that led to significant changes in the industry in the late 1960s was not equaled in the early 1990s. As a result, despite the efforts of individuals like Thompson, or the disillusionment among blacks and well-intentioned hand-wringing among whites, the King verdict had little tangible impact on blacks' employment numbers in mainstream agencies.[16]

Within this climate of analyzing minority employment, both blacks and whites around the industry began to ask what had happened to all the blacks encouraged to join advertising agencies in the 1960s. The rising presence of black sports and entertainment figures selling various products from Nike shoes to Pepsi-Cola and the use of black music in advertisements made the dearth of black employees even more striking. Certainly some blacks had left the industry as the result of natural attrition or the various economic downturns, but what of those who had persisted and struggled through? Some were now working in mainstream agencies, reporters found, but they also found a sense of disillusionment among them, a feeling that they had to be superior to their white colleagues just to keep pace for promotions. One black professional bitterly admitted, "We believed in the dream because we came up during that era. And now comes the '90s, we're all pawing at the door of vice president and executive manager and the doors are not opening and all sorts of excuses are made so you can't get in."[17]

In fact, an *Advertising Age* survey completed after the Los Angeles riots confirmed that in many mainstream agencies there were few blacks even in position to try and achieve promotions. Editors questioned 470 randomly selected people, nearly 94 percent of whom were white with the remaining 6 percent a mixture of races. They found that almost 57 percent of the people worked with no blacks that were in "non-clerical" positions and almost 17 percent worked with only one that fit that description. The results were alarming to be sure. However, nearly 65 percent of those surveyed also said their agencies should hire more African Americans, and almost 40 percent agreed that it was "extremely or very important" for agencies to maintain recruitment and hiring efforts among minorities. Although the pool of survey respondents was small, its findings were confirmed by a government study that found that only 2.1 percent of the personnel in "marketing, advertising, and public relations" that were managers or professionals were black.[18]

Although the overall number of blacks in the industry did not noticeably climb in the wake of the King verdict, for their part black advertising agencies continued to grow during the '90s. Along with Mingo-Jones, other large black agencies began to receive more billings for accounts directed at the general market. UniWorld Advertising won responsibility for general-market work for clients like Burger King and M&M/Mars. In Chicago, Burrell earned control of the Martell Cognac account after the slogan it developed for the black consumer market, "I assume you drink Martell," tested stronger than the one developed by the mainstream agency. Further, blacks launched two major new agencies during the decade: in Oakland, Carol Williams, a graduate of Bill Sharp's Basic Advertising Class, opened Carol H. Williams Advertising (CHWA), and in Detroit former Burrell Advertising staff member Don Coleman opened Don Coleman Advertising (later renamed Global-Hue). These new agencies not only fed on the viability of the black consumer market but also showed that black agencies could thrive in cities not traditionally considered part of the advertising mainstream. Further, due to their successful work and the commitment of their corporate clients, these agencies, along with their smaller counterparts, have helped maintain the visibility of the black consumer market.[19]

Back to the Future: The NYCHR in the Twenty-first Century

In 2006, the New York City Commission on Human Rights (NYCHR) returned to the issue of minority employment in the advertising agencies. The commission began gathering data in 2004 and, based on its findings, subpoenaed the leaders of fifteen New York-based advertising agencies to testify at public hearings. However, just before the launch of public hearings, the agencies signed private agreements with the NYCHR. The commission did not release the specific details of the agreements, and published reports only referred to their content in vague terms, including setting goals for finding minority employees, retaining them, and advancing them through the professional ranks.

It is too early to assess the effect of this latest round of investigations and agreements. Still, the fact that they needed to be held at all demonstrates the industry's disturbing lethargy at tackling issues of racial diversity. And even at this early stage of these hearings, some managers have eschewed the kind of public accountability to fulfill the agreements. "I don't want my accountability to be public," said Gunnar Wilmot, chairman and CEO of Gotham Advertisinig. "I have every intention of making the goals, but if I don't make them, I want to preclude your calling me [on it]."[20] It has primarily been the kind of accountability and external pressure that Wilmot rejects that has driven changes in the employment of African Americans by mainstream firms. Similar to blacks' experience in other white-collar professions like accounting, evidence shows that the advertising industry has dealt proactively with issues of race only when public pressure forces it to do so. The increasing use of black popular culture in advertisements that started in the 1970s makes the hesitancy in employment and limited opportunities for black-owned agencies to gain more general-market accounts all the more glaring. Throughout history, without the outside pressure of the black consumers, civil rights organizations, the government, or clients, the advertising industry has undertaken limited voluntary action to address racial diversity in employment and alter its traditional practices. At best these policies have been racial nepotism, the employment of people from similar social, educational, or financial backgrounds. At worst they have been institutional racism.

Unfortunately, what racial changes have occurred within the agency business have advanced in fits and starts. There has not been a linear progression from the pressure brought by black consumers and civil rights groups to an advertising agency world in which blacks no longer face underrepresentation. Instead, agencies have responded with short-term solutions that, while they have made some impact, have limited viability in the long term. Thus, starting in the mid-1960s a fifteen- to twenty-year repeating cycle of pressure and response began that lasted through the end of the twentieth century. During this time, other areas of business enterprise, such as financial services, consumer products, and the automotive and insurance industries, have successfully incorporated racial minorities in positions of responsibility and leadership. But the advertising agencies they hire have failed. That an industry so adept at solving the problems of client companies could fail so miserably to solve this pressing internal issue speaks poorly of just how seriously the advertising community has taken the issue of racial diversity.[21]

The responsibility for the historic and continued underrepresentation of African Americans in advertising lies primarily at the feet of individual agencies. Throughout the twentieth century, agency executives engaged in an elaborate shell game of blame and finger pointing. When pressed in the 1960s on their lack of black employees in professional or decision-making positions, agencies alternatively pointed at racist clients, consumers, or media outlets, while executives figuratively threw up their hands and protested, "It's not our fault." Later, when studies of media executives and consumers found that they would accept blacks not only in advertisements but also as creators or directors of advertising campaigns, agency executives fell back to the last point of retreat and argued that they simply could not find suitably qualified blacks. Such arguments are disingenuous for a business whose raison d'etre is to find the smallest increment or area of difference that will increase the effectiveness of an advertising campaign. As Michael Vallon, counsel for the NYCHR during the hearings in the late '60s argued, if advertisements can persuade consumers to change their toothpaste, their makers can certainly develop creative ways to recruit, train, and promote minority employees. Further, black agency owners have been able to effectively train and develop a cadre of black professionals while facing the same employment pool, and with fewer resources, than mainstream firms. Further, mainstream agencies have easily found black employees during times of external public scrutiny (that is when executives actually made the effort to do so). Over a decade ago black adman and chief creative officer for BBDO Phil Gant asked, "Why is it that black images are good enough and black music is good enough, but a black writer and art director maybe aren't?"[22] The advertising industry has yet to answer.

The Future for African Americans in the Advertising Industry

As the recent NYCHR hearings demonstrate, the percentage of blacks in the advertising industry remains small. However, the number of blacks and other minorities in the industry is far exceeded by their importance to its future health. The involvement of minorities in mainstream agencies provides an important reminder of the need to project images of a racially diverse America through advertisements. Because the population of the United States is only becoming more racially diverse, the presence of blacks and other minorities not only in ads but also in mainstream advertising jobs is more than a moral imperative or social responsibility, it is an economic and social necessity. History suggests that an advertising industry devoid of blacks and other minorities would likely picture that daily workplace environment in advertisements: a racially homogenous, whitewashed image of America. Would these ads be the result of conscious racial prejudice among those in the industry? No. Instead, my interviews with advertising personnel reveal a belief that most advertising creatives, regardless of racial background, tend to reproduce what they see. As Bill Sharp perceptively observed, "You have an industry that purports to depict America, the real America, and they can't because their too limited in their knowledge and experience. Plus they don't feel as though they really need to. Much of it is not malicious, much of it is not because their prejudiced, much of it is benign it's an attitude born of 'Oh, we don't need to know that' or 'I don't to learn your culture, you need to learn mine.'" Historically this insensitivity and lack of diversity within mainstream agencies has led to gaffes, oversights, insults, and the production of advertisements that are as white as many of their creators' neighborhoods. Black admen have known this for a long time. As one black agency executive said, "There are a disproportionate number of white people in commercials because there are a disproportionate number of white people at advertising agencies and a disproportionate number of white people making advertising decisions." If the mainstream advertising industry is to be successful in reaching the American population over the next century, its traditional apathy in addressing the hiring, retention, and promotion of minority professionals cannot continue.[23]

However, this is not to say that there has not been progress. A few blacks are now at or near the top of leadership positions in mainstream agencies. Renetta McCann heads the Starcom Media Group and Ann Fudge led industry giant Young & Rubicam. These historic appointments not only broaden the range of possible leadership options for all blacks within the industry, but they also help display the possibilities of advancement and success to minorities outside the industry. However, if agencies do not enhance these individual appointments with broader inclusion of minorities throughout all levels of employment, conditions may stay much the same.[24]

Still, the because of the foot-dragging of mainstream agencies, because of the rising diversification of the population, and especially because of their skill, insight, and creativity at developing advertising, independent black agencies still play an significant role in black employment and in the creation of diverse advertisements. They project creative, uplifting images that both sell products and encourage a nonstereotypical view of African Americans. While various factors have sometimes limited the creative expression from black agencies, including the need to fit into existing general-market campaigns or client conservatism, black agency employees often perceived their creative latitude as being greater than at mainstream firms. "Your success in a big general market agency depends on how much you can be like a white male," said one black professional. Therefore, these agencies continue to serve a valuable role in developing the next generation of African American advertising professionals.[25]

What does the future hold, then, for black-owned agencies? Some argue that the black agency whose primary mission is to market to black consumers will disappear in the next two decades, that the economic detour that black firms entered in the 1940s will eventually come to an end. "With the exception of a couple of regional and niche players, [only] the top four or five black agencies will likely survive the changing dynamics," predicted Chuck Morrison.[26]

It is more likely is that black firms will continue to successfully adapt to their changing environment. For example, in the 1970s and '80s, black agencies primarily described their work as black or ethnic marketing. But recently they have found that clients are more receptive to expressions of urban, lifestyle, or multicultural marketing in which African American music and culture are a part but not the whole and they have adapted their services accordingly. Some black-owned agencies have also expanded their abilities to include public relations and event planning capabilities. Also, today a sizable portion of the focus once directed solely to the African American market has expanded to include the Hispanic market. While that has meant the loss of some billings, it has also presented some agencies with the opportunity to expand their services to include multicultural advertising and marketing services. Among black-owned agencies, GlobalHue has led the black-owned agency niche in service diversification and may well point the way for similar agencies to grow in the future.[27]

Another opportunity for growth may be through strategic partnerships. Some black-owned agencies, like many other once-independent firms, have become part of one of the major advertising holding companies. Similar to the trend of black-owned insurance companies merging together, or independent firms being bought or absorbed by white-owned companies, the top black agencies formed strategic partnerships to maintain growth and stability. For example, near the turn of the century the some of the leading black agencies—including Burrell, UniWorld, and Don Coleman Advertising—entered partnerships in which large agency holding companies like Publicis, WPP Group, and Interpublic held 49 percent ownership. While some condemn the sale of portions of black companies to white corporations, these partnerships, pioneered by the now-closed Mingo-Jones firm, give black agencies much needed opportunities for continued growth. Thus, in contrast to black insurance companies, these partnerships have allowed the largest three companies to grow in billings and clients in a manner commensurate with the broader industry. In fact, as of 2006, among the largest four black agencies, only CHWA remains independent.[28]

However, although the black-owned agency niche is unlikely to fully disappear, there may be a significant number of agency closures and consolidations not unlike that during the Golden Age. In 2005, the combined estimated revenue from the four largest black-owned firms—GlobalHue, Carol H. Williams, Burrell Communications, and UniWorld—was more than double that of the next six black-owned agencies combined. These four firms also employ 60 percent of the employees in the top fifteen black-owned agencies. So it is likely the future direction taken by these four agencies in their strategic partnerships, range of service offerings, and advertising creations will dictate the future of the black-owned agency segment.[29]

As we move onto the next generation of blacks in the advertising industry, it is clear that change is unavoidable. Several of the pioneers from in and around the Golden Age have either passed away (Vince Cullers, Frank Mingo, and Caroline Jones) or retired (Tom Burrell). Only one black-owned agency, Mingo-Jones, successfully made the transition to a new management team after the loss of its original founders, even though Frank Mingo's death came suddenly. The most recent agency to face this leadership change is Burrell Communications. Tom Burrell planned the transition to a new management team at the Burrell Communications Group well in advance. The new management team of Fay Ferguson, McGhee Williams, and Steve Conner, while an experienced and outstanding group, must now prove that an African American agency can effectively move to a second generation of management and flourish without its original founder at the helm. From here it will be up to those who take over these enterprises to decide on their future direction and both continue and expand on the legacy the creators of these agencies provided.[30]

Notes

Introduction

1. Kathy DeSalvo, "Minority Hiring: New Solutions," *Back Stage* (August 14, 1992): 40.

2. On black images in advertisements, see Anthony J. Cortese, *Provocateur: Images of Women and Minorities in Advertising* (Lanham, Md.: Rowman & Littlefield Publishers, 1999); Marilyn Kern-Foxworth, *Aunt Jemima, Uncle Ben, and Rastus: Blacks in Advertising Yesterday, Today, and Tomorrow* (Westport, Conn.: Greenwood Press, 1984); William M. O'Barr, *Culture and the Ad: Exploring Otherness in the World of Advertising* (Boulder, Colo.: Westview Press, 1994). On blacks in the advertising industry see Jannette L. Dates, "Advertising," in *Split Image: African-Americans in the Mass Media*, 2nd ed., ed. Jannette L. Dates and William Barlow (Washington, D.C.: Howard University Press, 1993), 461–93; Stephen Fox, *The Mirror Makers: A History of American Advertising and Its Creators* (New York: William Morrow and Company, 1984), 277–84; Meyer L. Stein, *Blacks in Communications: Journalism, Public Relations, and Advertising* (New York: Julian Messner, 1972), 153–69; Juliet E. K. Walker, *The History of Black Business in America: Capitalism, Race, Entrepreneurship* (New York: Twayne Publishers, 1998), 349–52; Robert Weems, Jr., *Desegregating the Dollar: African American Consumerism in the Twentieth Century* (New York: New York University Press, 1998), 96–99; Gail Baker Woods, *Advertising and Marketing to the New Majority* (Belmont, Calif.: Wadsworth Publishing Company, 1995).

3. The labels of self-identification used by African Americans have varied throughout the twentieth century. The terms "Negro," "Colored," "Black," "Afro-American," "Black American," and "African American" (with or without the hyphen) have been used in different periods. Because the dividing lines between these periods are at best blurred, I have chosen to utilize the terms "black" and "African American" throughout the text except in cases where another term was used specifically. On the black middle class, see E. Franklin Frazier, *Black Bourgeoisie: The Rise of a New Middle Class in the United States* (New York: Free Press, 1957); Bart Landry, *The New Black Middle Class* (Berkeley: University of California Press, 1987); and Charles T. Banner-Haley, *The Fruits of Integration: Black Middle-Class Ideology and Culture, 1960–1990* (Jackson: University Press of Mississippi, 1994).

4. Fox, *The Mirror Makers*, 50.

5. Ronald Berman, *Advertising and Social Change* (Beverly Hills: Sage Publications, 1981), 150; Roland Marchand, *Advertising the American Dream: Making Way for Modernity, 1920–1940* (Berkeley: University of California Press, 1986), 60–65. Estimates for African American consumer spending power in the early twentieth century are unavailable. However, an article entitled "How Negroes Spent Their Incomes, 1920–1945", estimated black spending power in 1920 to be in excess

of $3 billion. Thus, African Americans did have a considerable amount of available spending capital, had advertisers chosen to recognize them as consumers. On the political, social, and economic conditions of African Americans in the early twentieth century, see Rayford W. Logan, *The Negro in American Life and Thought: The Nadir, 1877–1901* (New York: Dial Press, 1954).

6. Charles McGovern, "Consumption and Citizenship in the United States, 1900–1940," in *Getting and Spending: European and American Consumer Societies in the Twentieth Century,* ed. Susan Strasser, Charles McGovern, and Matthias Judt (Cambridge: Cambridge University Press, 1998), 46; "Kanter, Wall Blast Advertising to Blacks, Mexican-Americans," *Advertising Age* (March 16, 1970): 124; Charles McGovern, "Consumption and Citizenship in the United States, 1900–1940," in *Getting and Spending,* ed. Strasser, McGovern, and Judt, 37–58. The broadest historical treatment of the link between citizenship and consumption is Lizabeth Cohen, *A Consumers' Republic: The Politics of Mass Consumption in Postwar America* (New York: Alfred A. Knopf, 2003).

7. Cortese, 2; Evelyn Brooks Higginbotham, "African-American Women's History and the Metalanguage of Race," *Signs* 17 (1992): 252.

8. Grace Elizabeth Hale, *Making Whiteness: The Culture of Segregation in the South, 1890–1940* (New York: Vintage Books, 1999), 167; Varda Leymore, *Hidden Myth: Structure and Symbolism in Advertising* (London: Heinemann, 1975); Fath Davis Ruffins, "Reflecting on Ethnic Imagery in the Landscape of Commerce, 1945–1975," in *Getting and Spending,* ed. Strasser, McGovern, and Judt, 379–406; Kern-Foxworth, 62–63.

9. Quoted in Dawn E. Reno, *Collecting Black Americana* (New York: Crown Publishers, 1986), 1; Kern-Foxworth, 29–49. On the stereotypical images of African Americans in advertisements and elements of popular culture, also see Hale, 121–95; Kenneth W. Goings, *Mammy and Uncle Mose: Black Collectibles and American Stereotyping* (Bloomington: Indiana University Press, 1994); and Patricia A. Turner, *Ceramic Uncles and Celluloid Mammies: Black Images and Their Influence on Culture* (New York: Anchor Books, 1994).

10. Ruffins, 383–86; and Hale, 167–68.

11. James Avery, "African-American Pioneers in the Corporate Sector," accessed on February 19, 2005 from http://www.mgmtguru.com/pioneer.htm; Weems, *Desegregating the Dollar;* Virag Molnár and Michèle Lamont, "Social Categorisation and Group Identification: How African-Americans Shape Their Collective Identity Through Consumption," in *Innovation by Demand: An Interdisciplinary Approach to the Study of Demand and Its Role in Innovation,* ed. Andrew McMeekin, Ken Green, Mark Tomlinson, and Vivien Walsh (Manchester: Manchester University Press, 2002), 88–111; Lizabeth Cohen, "Encountering Mass Culture at the Grassroots: The Experience of Chicago Workers in the 1920s," in *Consumer Society in American History: A Reader,* ed. Lawrence B. Glickman (Ithaca, N.Y.: Cornell University Press, 1999), 147–69.

12. On the importance of consumption and the symbolic breakdown of segregation and also its implications in the definition of citizenship, see Hale, 151–97; Lizabeth Cohen, "Citizens and Consumers in the Century of Mass Consumption," in *Perspectives on Modern America: Making Sense of the Twentieth Century,* ed. Harvard Sitkoff (New York: Oxford University Press, 2001), 145–61; McGovern, "Consumption and Citizenship," 37–58.

13. Langston Hughes, "The Negro Artist and the Racial Mountain," *The Nation* (June 23, 1926).

14. Jannette L. Dates and William Barlow, eds., *Split Image: African Americans*

in the Mass Media (Washington, D.C.: Howard University Press, 1993), 3, 523–28. My thanks to Linda Scott for helping me develop the link between blacks' invisibility in advertisements and the sophisticated criticism of them that developed as a result of their marginalization.

15. Joseph M. Winski, "The Ad Industry's 'Dirty Little Secret,'" *Advertising Age* (June 15, 1992): 16, 38.

16. Jennifer Scanlon, "Advertising Women: The J. Walter Thompson Company Women's Editorial Department," in *The Gender and Consumer Culture Reader* (New York: New York University Press, 2000), 201–25; Fox, 284–89.

17. On the struggle to develop educational standards for advertising, see Quentin Schultze, "An Honorable Place: The Quest for Professional Advertising Education, 1900–1917," *Business History Review* 56 (Spring 1982): 16–32.

18. Merah Stuart, *An Economic Detour: A History of Insurance in the Lives of American Negroes* (New York: Wendell Malliet and Company, 1940); Joseph Pierce, *Negro Business and Business Education* (New York: Harper & Bros, 1947), 18–20.

19. Stuart's and Pierce's analyses has been extended by recent scholars; see John Sibley Butler, *Entrepreneurship and Self-Help Among Black Americans: A Reconsideration of Race and Economics* (Albany: State University of New York Press, 1991), 74–76. Also Judy Foster Davis recently examined black-owned advertising agencies through an application of Stuart's model; see Davis, "Enterprise Development under an Economic Detour? Black-Owned Advertising Agencies, 1940–2000," *Journal of Macromarketing* (June 2002): 75–85. On black-owned insurance firms, see Robert Weems, Jr., *Black Business in the Black Metropolis: The Chicago Metropolitan Assurance Company* (Bloomington: Indiana University Press, 1996). On black beauty companies, see Mark Silverman, "Black Business, Group Resources and the Economic Detour: Contemporary Black Manufacturers in Chicago's Ethnic Beauty Industry," *Journal of Black Studies* 30, no. 2 (1999): 232–58.

20. Davis, 75–85.

21. Theresa A. Hammond, *A White Collar Profession: African American Certified Public Accountants since 1921* (Chapel Hill: University of North Carolina Press, 2002); Weems, *Black Business in the Black Metropolis*.

22. Walker, 364–71.

23. Molnár and Lamont, 88–111; Cohen, *A Consumers' Republic*.

24. Marsha Cassidy and Richard Katula, "The Black Experience in Advertising: An Interview with Thomas J. Burrell," *Journal of Communication Inquiry* (Winter 1990): 100; Kern-Foxworth, 170.

25. Michèle Lamont and Virág Molnár, "How Blacks Use Consumption to Shape Their Collective Identity," *Journal of Consumer Culture* (June 2001): 31–45.

26. Kern-Foxworth, 118.

27. David M. Potter, *People of Plenty: Economic Abundance and the American Character* (Chicago: University of Chicago Press, 1954), 177.

Chapter 1

1. Rayford W. Logan, *The Betrayal of the Negro: From Rutherford B. Hayes to Woodrow Wilson* (New York: Da Capo Press, 1997).

2. On the economic and geographic impact of the Great Migration, see Allan H. Spear, *Black Chicago: The Making of a Negro Ghetto, 1890–1920* (Chicago: University of Chicago Press, 1967), 181–85; Florette Henri, *Black Migration: Move-*

ment North, 1900–1920 (Garden City, N.Y.: Anchor Press, 1975), 158–64; and Joe William Trotter, *Black Milwaukee: The Making of an Industrial Proletariat* (Urbana: University of Illinois Press, 1985), 80–93.

3. Jannette L. Dates, "Print News," in *Split Image: African-Americans in the Mass Media*, 2nd ed., ed. Jannette L. Dates and William Barlow (Washington, D.C.: Howard University Press, 1993), 369–418.

4. Dwight E. Brooks, "In Their Own Words: Advertisers' Construction of an African American Consumer Market, The World War II Era," *Howard Journal of Communications* (October 1995): 32–52; Robert E. Weems, Jr., *Desegregating the Dollar: African American Consumerism in the Twentieth Century* (New York: New York University Press, 1998), 7–30.

5. Linda J. Evans, "Claude A. Barnett and the Associated Negro Press," *Chicago History* (Spring 1983): 44–46.

6. Claude A. Barnett, *Fly Out of Darkness* (unpublished manuscript), 6–7, Claude A. Barnett Papers (hereinafter referred to as the Barnett Papers), Box 406, Folder 5, Manuscripts Collection, Chicago Historical Society, Chicago, Illinois; Lawrence D. Hogan, *A Black National News Service: The Associated Negro Press and Claude Barnett, 1919–1945* (Rutherford, N.J.: Fairleigh Dickinson University Press, 1984), 42–43.

7. Evans, 46.

8. Evans, 44–49; and Barnett, *Fly Out of Darkness*, 9.

9. Evans, 46; Barnett, *Fly Out of Darkness*, 9. On the field of black cosmetics companies, see A'Lelia Perry Bundles, *On Her Own Ground: The Life and Times of Madame C. J. Walker* (New York: Scribner, 2001).

10. Quoted in Barnett, *Fly Out of Darkness*, 9.

11. Kashmir advertisement, *Chicago Defender* (August 31, 1918): 10.

12. Evans, 46; Barnett, *Fly Out of Darkness*, 10–12.

13. Barnett, *Fly Out of Darkness*, 12.

14. On the Associated Negro Press, see Richard Beard and Cyril E. Zoerner, "Associated Negro Press: Its Founding, Ascendancy, and Demise," *Journalism Quarterly* (Spring 1969): 47–52; Evans, 52.

15. Evans, 52–53; Nile Queen advertisement, *Chicago Defender* (November 26, 1921): 11.

16. Evans, 46–53; Claude Barnett to F. B. Ransom, January 30, 1929, Barnett Papers, Box 262, Folder 4; Claude Barnett to Annie M. Malone, February 8, 1929, Barnett Papers, Box 262, Folder 6; Claude Barnett to C. C. Spaulding, April 24, 1929, Barnett Papers, Box 131, Folder 6. On the effect of segregation on black-owned business, see Juliet E. K. Walker, *The History of Black Business in America: Capitalism, Race, Entrepreneurship* (New York: Twayne Publishers, 1998), 182–224.

17. On effect of urbanization on African American consumer spending, see Weems, *Desegregating the Dollar*, 7–21.

18. Stephen Fox, *The Mirror Makers: A History of American Advertising and Its Creators* (New York: William Morrow and Company, 1984), 76–77.

19. Quoted in Barnett to Robert Park, Barnett Papers, Box 132, Folder 2. On Barnett's advertising philosophy, see Evans, 52–53; Tom Pendergast, *Creating the Modern Man: American Magazines and Consumer Culture, 1900–1950* (Columbia: University of Missouri Press, 2000), 201–3.

20. Associated Publishers' Representative, Barnett Papers, Box 131, Folder 6; Evans, 52–53.

21. Claude Barnett to J. B. Bass, August 24, 1929, Barnett Papers, Box 131,

Folder 6; Claude Barnett to *East Tennessee News*, August 30, 1929, Barnett Papers, Box 131, Folder 6; Claude Barnett to James H. Kerns, July 30, 1929, Barnett Papers, Box 131, Folder 6; Pendergast, 201–3.

22. Robert Balderston to Claude Barnett, July 6, 1931, Barnett Papers, Box 132, Folder 1.

23. Evans, 53.

24. Claude Barnet to Robert R. Moton, September 22, 1930, Barnett Papers, Box 131, Folder 6; Claude Barnett to Albon Holsey, September 11, 1931, Barnett Papers, Box 131, Folder 6.

25. Quoted in Hogan, 186.

26. Claude A. Barnett to Robert R. Moton, September 22, 1930, Barnett Papers, Box 131, Folder 6. On Barnett's concerns about the impact of segregation on black-owned business, see Hogan, 186–200.

27. "Ziff-Davis," *Tide* (December 15, 1943): 48, 52.

28. On the Ziff company's hold on the black press see Vishnu Oak, *The Negro Newspaper* (Westport, Conn.: Negro Universities Press, 1948), 112–13; and Armistead S. Pride and Clint C. Wilson, *A History of the Black Press* (Washington, D.C.: Howard University Press, 1997), 240–43.

29. *The Negro Market* (Chicago: William B. Ziff Company, 1932); letter to the editor, *Tide* (August 3, 1951): 13; On Depression-era advertising in the black press, see Oak, *The Negro Newspaper*, 113.

30. *The Negro Market*, 24.

31. *The Negro Market*, 38.

32. Quoted in an unsigned letter to Edgar McDaniel, September 19, 1930, Barnett Papers, Box 262, Folder 7. On Vann and Ziff, see Andrew Buni, *Robert L. Vann of the Pittsburgh Courier: Politics and Black Journalism* (Pittsburgh: University of Pittsburgh Press, 1974), 134.

33. Buni, 134.

34. Mary Alice Sentman and Patrick S. Washburn, "How Excess Profits Tax Brought Ads to Black Newspapers in World War II," *Journalism Quarterly* (Winter 1987): 773, 867.

35. U.S. Department of Labor, *Monthly Labor Review* 29 (July 1929), Washington, D.C., U.S. Government Printing Office. On the NNBL, see Walker, 184–87.

36. Weems, *Desegregating the Dollar*, 20–23.

37. H. A. Haring, "Selling to Harlem," *Advertising & Selling* (October 31, 1928): 17–18, 50–53; Weems, *Desegregating the Dollar*, 20–21.

38. H. A. Haring, "The Negro as Consumer," *Advertising & Selling* (September 3, 1930): 21.

39. Haring, "The Negro as Consumer," 20–21, 67–68; Weems, *Desegregating the Dollar*, 21.

40. Paul K. Edwards, *The Southern Urban Negro as a Consumer* (New York: Negro Universities Press, 1969); Weems, *Desegregating the Dollar*, 22–27.

41. Paul K. Edwards to Claude A. Barnett, October 13, 1932, Barnett Papers, Box 132, Folder 2.

42. Paul K. Edwards to Claude Barnett, October 25, 1932; Paul K. Edwards to Claude Barnett, December 15, 1933, Barnett Papers, Box 132, Folder 2.

43. Claude Barnett to Paul K. Edwards, October 18, 1932, Barnett Papers, Box 132, Folder 2; Paul K. Edwards to Claude Barnett, December 15, 1933, Barnett Papers, Box 132, Folder 2.

44. Paul K. Edwards to Claude Barnett, December 31, 1932, Barnett Papers, Box 132, Folder 2; "Business Enterprise," *Opportunity* (December 1933): 385.

45. Drake and Cayton, 439.

46. Quoted in T. Arnold Hill, "The Negro Market," *Opportunity* (October 1932): 318. On DBWYCW campaigns, see Walker, 226–30; "Survey of the Month," *Opportunity* (May 1930): 155; T. Arnold Hill, "Picketing for Jobs," *Opportunity* (July 1930): 216. On African American consumer activism, see also Lizabeth Cohen, *A Consumers' Republic: The Politics of Mass Consumption in Postwar America* (New York: Alfred A Knopf, 2003).

47. "Overlooking Diamonds," *Chicago Defender* (September 18, 1937): 16. On black purchasing power, see Eugene Kinckle Jones, "Purchasing Power of Negroes in the U.S. Estimated at Two Billion Dollars." *Domestic Commerce* 15 (January 10, 1935): 1; Brooks, 57–58; Weems, *Desegregating the Dollar*, 28–29.

48. On the organization of Interstate United Newspapers see Buni, 223–224, 312–313; Weems, *Desegregating the Dollar*, 35–36.

49. "Interstate Names Black," *Advertising Age* (February 24, 1941): 6; "Negro Press," *Tide* (September 1, 1944): 84–86, 90; Weems, *Desegregating the Dollar*, 35–36. On the excess profits tax, see Sentman and Washburn, 769–74, 867.

50. IUN Advertisement, *Advertising Age* (October 30, 1944): 48; Weems, *Desegregating the Dollar*, 36–38; Oak, 119–20.

51. *City Within a City*, Barnett Papers, Box 132, Folder 7; Weems, *Desegregating the Dollar*, 36–38.

52. *City Within a City*.

53. "Ads By Royal Crown Cola to Feature Negroes," *Chicago Defender* (November 13, 1943): 7; Sentman and Washburn, 769–73; Oak, 113.

54. "The Negro Market: An Appraisal," *Tide* (March 7, 1947): 15–17; Sentman and Washburn, 773–74, 867.

55. Pendergast, 243–44.

56. "'*Ebony*' Marks 5th Anniversary of Publication," *Advertising Age* (October 23, 1950): 49.

57. Pendergast, 244–50; Jason Chambers, "Equal in Every Way: African Americans, Consumption and Materialism from Reconstruction to the Civil Rights Movement," *Advertising and Society Review* (Spring 2006), accessed on December 16, 2006 from http://muse.jhu.edu.proxy2.library.uiuc.edu/journals/asr/v007/7.1chambers.html .

58. "'*Ebony*' Marks 5th Anniversary," 49. Advertisement, *Printer's Ink* (September 22, 1950): 108.

59. Ben Burns, *Nitty Gritty: A White Editor in Black Journalism* (Jackson: University Press of Mississippi, 1996), 121–26; John H. Johnson and Lerone Bennett, *Succeeding Against the Odds* (New York: Warner Books), 61.

60. Derek Dingle, *Black Enterprise Titans of the B.E. 100s* (New York: John Wiley and Sons, 1999), 15.

61. Pendergast, 252–53.

62. Johnson, *Succeeding Against the Odds*, 185–89. "Dollar Value of General Magazines 1948 and 1947," *Advertising Age* (February 28, 1949): 20.

63. Quoted in Johnson, *Succeeding Against the Odds*, 230. See also "Johnson Publishing Launches Merchandising Program for 'Ebony,' 'Tan' Advertisers," *Advertising Age* (October 22, 1951): 23.

64. "Publisher of Three Successful Negro Magazines Got Start with $500 Loan," *Printer's Ink* (October 27, 1950): 100.

65. "Why Negroes Buy Cadillacs," *Ebony* (September 1946): 34.

66. "Why Negroes Buy Cadillacs," 34.

67. "Why Negroes Buy Cadillacs," 34.

68. "Why Negroes Overtip," *Ebony* (July 1953): 96. On Johnson, see Dwight Ernest Brooks, "Consumer Markets and Consumer Magazines: Black America and the Culture of Consumption, 1920–1960" (Ph.D. diss., University of Iowa, 1991), 153–55; Pendergast, 248–49.

69. Quoted in "Selling the Negro Market," *Tide* (July 20, 1951): 43.

70. "The 1950 Census," *Ebony* (April 1950): 31–38; "The Negro Market Grows," *Tide* (March 3, 1950): 39–40; "Census to Disclose Big Negro Gains, *Ebony* Reports," *Advertising Age* (March 6, 1950): 55.

71. "The 1950 Census," 31–38; "The Negro Market Grows," 39–40; "Census to Disclose Big Negro Gains," 55; "In 14 Cities, Marketer Must Have Strong Negro Sales to Dominate Market: Johnson," *Advertising Age* (December 10, 1956): 24.

72. *Ebony*, advertisement, *Advertising Age* (October 9, 1950): 7.

73. "U. of Chicago Tells Nonwhite Population Gains in Big Cities," *Advertising Age* (February 18, 1952): 26; "Negro Families in New York City Average 3.8 Members 'Amsterdam News' Reports," *Advertising Age* (November 10, 1952): 2; "Improved Negro Status," *Tide* (November 28, 1952): 11; "America's Mushrooming Market," *Tide* (December 12, 1952): 57–58, 62–66; "Publishers Told Negro Market is 'One of Richest,'" *Advertising Age* (June 29, 1953): 133; "'Ebony'-'Jet' Study Finds Negro Market Likes Good Liquor," *Advertising Age* (September 7, 1953): 56; "'Chicago Defender' Studies Negro Market," *Tide* (September 12, 1953): 23; "Negro Liquor Buyer Spends Up to 3 Times as Much as Comparable White, 'Ebony' Finds," *Advertising Age* (November 18, 1957): 36; "Some Brands Do Top Job, but Negro Market Is Wide Open, Rollins Finds," *Advertising Age* (June 23, 1958): 98; "20% of Negro Families Plan '58 Car Buys: 'Ebony,'" *Advertising Age* (July 28, 1958): 56; Joseph Johnson, *The Potential Negro Market* (New York: Pageant Press, 1952); William K. Bell, *15 Million Negroes and 15 Billion Dollars* (New York: William K. Bell, 1958); Weems, *Desegregating the Dollar*, 41–49.

74. "'Ebony' Survey Reveals Negro Buying Habits," *Advertising Age* (August 28, 1950): 16–17; "*Ebony* Reader Study Shows Brand Liking," *Advertising Age* (March 19, 1951): 69; Brooks, 153–55.

75. "Mrs. Vann Sells Interstate United Newspapers," *Advertising Age* (January 25, 1954): 1; John H. Johnson, "Does Your Sales Force Know How to Sell the Negro Trade? Some Do's and Don'ts," *Advertising Age* (March 17, 1952): 73–75; "'Ebony' Unveils Movie, Continuing Research Program," *Advertising Age* (August 23, 1954): 45; *Ebony*, advertisement, *Advertising Age* (October 17, 1955): 84.

76. *Reaching the Negro Market*, pamphlet advertisement, *Advertising Age* (September 8, 1952): 64; The report was extensively quoted in advertising trade journals, see "'Jet' Lights into Negro Newspapers," *Advertising Age* (September 8, 1952), 3, 6.

77. "'Jet' Lights Into Negro Newspapers," 3. "Cooperation in Negro Field Very Much Alive: Johnson," *Advertising Age* (September 15, 1952): 70.

78. "Negro Newspaper Circulation Is Up, Representative Says," *Advertising Age* (September 22, 1952): 52–53; "Interstate and 'Courier' Head Agrees with Murphy," *Advertising Age* (September 22, 1952): 53.

79. "Negro Progress Spells Success for 'Ebony'—Mirror of the 'Bright Side,'" *Advertising Age* (October 24, 1955): 48; Sentman and Washburn, 769–74, 867. Despite Johnson's' careful response, in later years he admitted that significant professional acrimony existed between his organization and black newspaper publishers; see Dingle, 21.

80. "Negro Newspapers' Circulation Off 12.8%, Lincoln U. Reports," *Advertising Age* (February 24, 1958): 28.

81. "The Forgotten 15,000,000," *Sponsor* (October 10, 1949): 24–25, 54–55; "The Forgotten 15,000,000 Part 2," *Sponsor* (October 24, 1949): 30+. On the importance of radio in the black community, see Barbara Dianne Savage, *Broadcasting Freedom: Radio, War, and the Politics of Race, 1938–1948* (Chapel Hill: University of North Carolina Press, 1999) and William Barlow, "Commercial and Noncommercial Radio," in *Split Image*, ed. Dates and Barlow, 189–264; Weems, *Desegregating the Dollar*, 41.

82. Quoted in "Negro Radio's Growth," *Sponsor* (September 20, 1954): 164. See also "The Forgotten 15,000,000, Part 2," 54; Barlow, 223–235; Weems, *Desegregating the Dollar*, 42–48.

83. "The Negro-Directed Advertiser Gets a Big 'Plus' from Negro Radio," *Sponsor* (September 20, 1958): 35.

84. "The Negro-Directed Advertiser," 35.

85. "Selling to Negroes: Don't Talk Down," *Sponsor* (July 28, 1952): 36–37, 86–87; "Negro Radio: Keystone of Community Life," *Sponsor* (August 24, 1953): 68–73, 78–84; "Tips on How to Get the Most Out of Negro Radio," *Sponsor* (August 24, 1953): 76–77, 93–94; "Negro Radio's Marketing Role," *Sponsor* (September 17, 1956): 3–5, 26–29; Weems, *Desegregating the Dollar*, 42–48.

86. Weems, *Desegregating the Dollar*, 43–48.

87. "Keystone Sets Up Negro Net Division," *Advertising Age* (August 8, 1955): 166; "Negro Radio: Adolescent Heading for Maturity," *Sponsor* (September 17, 1956): 6, 29–38. "NNN: Negro Radio's Network," *Sponsor* (September 20, 1954): 54, 150–52; "Signpost on the Road to Maturity," *Sponsor* (September 17, 1956): 8, 38; "Action People," *Marketing/Communications* (February 1968): 21–22.

88. "Negro Radio—A Hit-and-Miss National Sales Pattern," *Sponsor* (September 19, 1955): 109+.

89. "The Forgotten 15,000,000," 54.

90. Both quotes taken from "Selling to Negroes," 86.

91. Weems, *Desegregating the Dollar*, 45–46.

92. Charles T. Magill, "Jackson Joins Staff of New York Billboard," *Chicago Defender* (January 22, 1921): 5; "Appointments," *Opportunity* (August 1934): 254; Weems, *Desegregating the Dollar*, 49–50.

93. Dwight E. Brooks, "In Their Own Words: Advertisers' Construction of an African American Consumer Market in the World War II Era," *Howard Journal of Communications* 6 (October 1995): 32–50.

94. Ray Shaw, "The Negro Consumer," *Wall Street Journal* (June 30, 1961): 12.

95. Brooks, "Consumer Markets," 144–54.

96. "The Forgotten 15,000,000," 54.

Chapter 2

1. David M. Kennedy, *Freedom from Fear: The American People in Depression and War, 1929–1945* (New York: Oxford University Press, 1999), 766–68.

2. Kennedy, 768–69.

3. Kennedy, 769, 775–76.

4. "The Future of the Negro," *Advertising Age* (July 27, 1942): 12. On postwar market expansion, also see Dwight E. Brooks, "In Their Own Words: Advertis-

ers' Construction of an African American Consumer Market in the World War II Era," *Howard Journal of Communications* 6 (October 1995): 48–49.

5. Merah Stuart, *An Economic Detour: A History of Insurance in the Lives of American Negroes* (New York: Wendell Malliet and Company, 1940).

6. On special-markets men, see "Methods Found Successful in Selling to Colored Population," *Printer's Ink* (July 27, 1922): 130; "The Brown Hucksters," *Ebony* (May 1948): 28–33. On the growing interest in black consumers, see Juliet E. K. Walker, *The History of Black Business in America: Capitalism, Race, Entrepreneurship* (New York: Twayne Publishers, 1998), 350–51.

7. Quoted in James Avery, "African-American Pioneers in the Corporate Sector," http://www.mgmtguru.com/pioneer.htm, accessed on February 19, 2005; "The Brown Hucksters," 28–33.

8. Brooks, 38–46.

9. "A Proposal for the Coca-Cola Company," Moss Kendrix Papers (hereinafter Kendrix Papers), Alexandria Black History Resource Center, Alexandria, Va.

10. "NAACP and Coca-Cola in Race Hassle," *St. Louis Argus* (December 16, 1955): 14; Roy Wilkins to Moss Kendrix, November 23, 1955, Kendrix Papers; Moss Kendrix to Roy Wilkins, December 7, 1955, Kendrix Papers.

11. Moss Kendrix, Personal Memorandum, December 12, 1955, Kendrix Papers; Carter Wesley, "Ram's Horn," *Houston Informer* (December 20, 1955): 15; Moss Kendrix to Roy Wilkins, December 7, 1955, Kendrix Papers; Moss Kendrix to Roy Wilkins, December 14, 1955, Kendrix Papers; Roy Wilkins to Moss Kendrix, December 9, 1955, Kendrix Papers.

12. H. Naylor Fitzhugh quoted in the *NAMD Market Review* (May 1997): 1. On the NAMD, see Robert E. Weems, Jr., *Desegregating the Dollar: African American Consumerism in the Twentieth Century* (New York: New York University Press, 1998), 52–53.

13. James R. Howard III, "What the Public Thinks Counts," *Negro History Bulletin* (April 1956): 3, 6.

14. Weems, *Desegregating the Dollar*, 52–53.

15. Weems, *Desegregating the Dollar*, 52–53; J. R. E. Lee to Moss Kendrix, May 20, 1959, Kendrix Papers; Chuck Smith, interview with author, May 29, 1999, Philadelphia, Pa.

16. Chuck Smith, interview with author.

17. Quoted in "Special Audience Appeals of Farmers, Women, Negroes, Industrial Men Told," *Advertising Age* (March 23, 1953): 86–87; "Role of Trained Personnel in Selling to Negro Market is Stressed to Marketers," *Advertising Age* (May 9, 1955): 57; "Selling to Negroes Without Proper Guidance Could Be Suicide, Says Curtiss' Albright," *Advertising Age* (November 26, 1956): 54.

18. Quoted in *The Negro Market* (Chicago: William B. Ziff Company, 1932), 24; *City Within a City*, Barnett Papers, Box 132, Folder 7.

19. Chuck Smith, interview with author.

20. Weems, *Desegregating the Dollar*, 32–34.

21. David Sullivan, "Don't Do This—If You Want to Sell your Products to Negroes!" *Sales Management* (March 1, 1943): 46–47; Brooks, 37–38; Weems, *Desegregating the Dollar*, 32–34.

22. Sullivan, 46–47.

23. Sullivan, 48–50. See also Weems, *Desegregating the Dollar*, 32–33.

24. Sullivan, 47; Weems, *Desegregating the Dollar*, 33; Brooks, 37–38.

25. "Admen See Larger Negro Market for Post-War Era," *Advertising Age* (June 29, 1942): 15.

26. The Negro Market Organization, Barnett Papers, Box 131, Folder 2; The Negro Market Organization advertisement, *Advertising Age* (February 21, 1944): 54.

27. David J. Sullivan, "The American Negro—An 'Export' Market at Home!" *Printer's Ink* (July 21, 1944): 90–94.

28. "Sullivan Urges Media Research on Negro Market," *Advertising Age* (December 11, 1944): 38; "U.S. Negro Income Hits $10 Billion, Publishers Told," *Advertising Age* (June 26, 1944): 24; David J. Sullivan, "The Negro Market Today and Postwar," *Journal of Marketing* (July 1945): 68.

29. David J. Sullivan, "Selling the Negro Market," *American Brewer* (June 1961): 47 +. Stephen Fox, *The Mirror Makers: A History of American Advertising and Its Creators* (New York: William Morrow and Company, 1984), 278; David Sullivan to John Crichton, February 17, 1964, Papers of the NAACP, Supplement to Part 13, Reel 14, The Ohio State University, Columbus, Ohio; "Specialist on Negro Market Back," *Chicago Defender* (March 7, 1959): 2

30. Marjorie Greene, "The Story of Edward Brandford," *Opportunity* (Winter 1947): 108–10.

31. Wambly Bald, "Another Step Up—First Agency for Negro Models Opens," *New York Post* (July 31, 1946): 28; "Glamorous Harlem Girls Become Professional Models," *Chicago Defender* (November 30, 1946): 9.

32. "First Negro Model Agency Opened in New York," *Advertising Age* (August 5, 1946): 6.

33. "First Negro Model Agency," 6; "Brandford Models," *Advertising Age* (August 19, 1946): 65; photograph, *Chicago Defender* (August 24, 1951): 3; Arnold de Mille, "Judge's Daughter Has Idea, Makes It Work," *Chicago Defender* (February 20, 1954): 12; *Chicago Defender* (May 14, 1949): 2.

34. "First Negro Model Agency," 6; Walker, 350; "New Advertising Agency to Service Negro Market," *Norfolk Journal & Guide* (January 31, 1948): 3; Ed Brandford to Claude Barnett, December 8, 1949, Barnett Papers, Box 127, Folder 6; "Black Image Makers on Madison Avenue," *Black Enterprise* (February 1971): 22.

35. David J. Sullivan, "The Negro Market," *Negro Digest* (February 1943): 60–62.

36. Sullivan, "The Negro Market," 60–62.

37. "W. B. Graham," *Tide* (March 15, 1945): 35.

38. "W. B. Graham," 34–36; Lawrence Freeny, "For Henry Parks . . . More Than Sausages," *New York Times* (April 10, 1977): F3.

39. "A Negro Integrates His Markets," *Business Week* (May 18, 1968): 94; "Joe Louis Punch," *Tide* (August 23, 1946): 20–21; "Soft Drinks," *Tide* (September 12, 1947): 17–19; "Supersalesman Joe Louis Pushes Joe Louis Punch," *Advertising Age* (August 30, 1948): 1, 41; "Joe Louis Punch Boosts Sales, Ads to Dozen Markets," *Advertising Age* (September 29, 1947): 28.

40. Gail Baker Woods, *Advertising and Marketing to the New Majority* (Belmont, Calif.: Wadsworth Publishing Company, 1995), 156–58; Marian J. Moore, "The Advertising Images of Black Americans, 1880–1920 and 1968–1979: A Thematic and Interpretive Approach" (Ph.D. diss., Bowling Green State University, 1986), 156.

41. Woods, 156; Moore, 157.

42. Quoted in Moore, 158–59. On Cullers, see Fox, 278; Juliann Sivulka, *Soap, Sex, and Cigarettes: A Cultural History of American Advertising* (Belmont, Calif.: Wadsworth Publishing Company, 1998), 264.

43. Vishnu Oak, *The Negro Newspaper* (Westport, Conn.: Negro Universities

Press, 1948), 117–18; "Benson-Brooks Will Open in Chicago to Serve Negro Market," *Advertising Age* (January 14, 1957): 40; "Scott and Nash Formed to Specialize in Negro Market," *Advertising Age* (February 11, 1957): 44; Walker, 225–63.

44. "Joe Louis Signs Officer," *Chicago Defender* (November 9, 1946): 10; Philip Shabecoff, "Negro Executive Finds There Is Room at the Top," *New York Times* (July 1, 1962): 79.

45. "Biow Lists 9 Agencies Which Employ Negroes," *Advertising Age* (March 24, 1947): 50.

46. Fox, 172–78.

47. "Action People," *Marketing/Communications* (February 1968): 21–22; "Negro Consumer Actions Analyzed by Agency Chief," *Printer's Ink* (June 7, 1957): 82–83; Roi Ottley, "Ad Executive Studies Negro Market Trend," *Chicago Daily Tribune* (March 2, 1957): C12.

48. "Negro Consumer Actions Analyzed by Agency Chief," 82; Ottley, C12; "Negro Family Group," *Advertising Age* (April 7, 1952): 66; "Leonard Evans, Jr. Heads Ad Campaign for Broadcast Meats," *Chicago Defender* (June 17, 1950): 2.

49. Claude A. Barnett to A. L. Powell, August 10, 1957, Barnett Papers Box 129, Folder 3; A. L Powell to Claude Barnett, August 5, 1957, Barnett Papers, Box 129, Folder 3; "Negro Consumer Actions Analyzed by Agency Chief," 83.

50. Quoted in "NNN: Negro Radio's Network," *Sponsor* (September 20, 1954): 152. See also "Action People," 21–22; "Keystone Sets Up Negro Net Division," *Advertising Age* (August 8, 1955): 166; "Negro Radio: Adolescent Heading for Maturity," *Sponsor* (September 17, 1956): 6, 29–38.

51. Philip H. Dougherty, "Tuesday, Negro Supplement, Gains Today," *New York Times* (May 26, 1968): F17.

52. James Hicks, "Clarence Holte, Market Specialist, Gets Executive Post with BBDO," *Chicago Defender* (June 28, 1952): 5. On the postwar entry of black professionals into white corporate America, see Walker, 340–41, and Steven M. Gelber, *Black Men and Businessmen: The Growing Awareness of a Social Responsibility* (Port Washington, N.Y.: Kennikat Press, 1974), 23–67.

53. Fox, 278; "Clarence Holte's Search into the Black Past," *Ebony* (April 1970): 94–102.

54. Quoted in "The Negro Market," *Tide* (July 25, 1952), 44. See also Fox, 278.

55. Quoted in "The Negro Market," 44. See also Gelber, 47–48, 111–12.

56. "The Negro Market," 44; "Clients Seek Advice on Negro Market," *Sponsor* (July 25, 1966): 40–43.

57. "The Negro Market," 44; Carl Spielvogel, "Advertising: Recognizing Negro Potential," *New York Times* (August 10, 1958): 10F.

58. James Hicks, "Major Ad Agency Hires First Tan Executive," *Baltimore Afro-American* (June 28, 1952): 5; George Schuyler, "Batten, Barton, Durstine and Osborne [*sic*] Makes a Really Sound Move," *Pittsburgh Courier* (June 28, 1952): 7; James Hicks, "Clarence Holte, Market Specialist, Gets Executive Post with BBDO," *Chicago Defender* (June 28, 1952): 5; "BBDO First," *Advertising Age* (October 5, 1953): 81.

59. Schuyler, 7.

60. "Clarence Holte's Search into the Black Past," 94–97; "The Negro-Directed Advertiser Gets a 'Plus' from Negro Radio," 5, 34–37.

61. "Clarence Holte's Search into the Black Past," 94–97; Marilyn Kern-Foxworth, *Aunt Jemima, Uncle Ben and Rastus: Blacks in Advertising Yesterday, Today, and Tomorrow* (Westport, Conn.: Greenwood Press, 1994), 132–33.

62. Claude A. Barnett to A. L. Powell, August 10, 1957, Barnett Papers Box 129, Folder 3; Holte, "The Negro Market," 29–32.

63. Holte, "The Negro Market," 30–32.

64. Pepsi-Cola's special-markets division was established in the 1930s with the goal of increasing the company's market share among African Americans. The firm had gone bankrupt in 1922 and 1932 and at one point company leaders sent inquiries to Coca-Cola executives about purchasing the company. Assuming that Pepsi was destined for failure Coca-Cola executives subsequently refused the offer. See J. C. Louis and Harvey Z. Yazijian, *The Cola Wars* (New York: Everest House, 1980), 49–50; Joseph T. Johnson, *The Potential Negro Market* (New York: Pageant Press, 1952), 138–40. On Pepsi-Cola's program to African American consumers, see Weems, *Desegregating the Dollar*, 50; Adrian Hirschhorn, "Pepsi-Cola's Campaign to the Negro Market," *Printer's Ink* (September 9, 1949): 38–40; "Are You Interested in a Market Worth TEN BILLION DOLLARS," *Pepsi-Cola World* (May 1948): 6–7. On Walter Mack's convention comments, see The Pepsi-Cola Papers, National Museum of American History, Washington, D.C., Series 3, Box 18.

65. "Class Magazine for Negro Market Bows in Chicago," *Advertising Age* (April 13, 1953): 38; "Convention Offers Chance to Tap Negro Baptist Market," *Advertising Age* (March 14, 1955): 64; "Nation Within a Nation," *Premium Practice* (May 1957): 25–47; Holte, "The Negro Market," 29–32; "Clarence L. Holte, "How the Negro Market Thinks . . . and Buys," *Sponsor* (August 1963): 17–18.

66. "Versatile Adman . . . Roy Eaton," *Advertising Age* (June 17, 1957): 70; M. L. Stein, *Blacks in Communications: Journalism, Public Relations and Advertising* (New York: Julian Messner, 1972), 162–163; "Student Recounts Travels in Europe," *New York Times* (September 25, 1949): 28; Fox, 278.

67. Roy Eaton, interview with author, New York, N.Y., August 16, 2004; "Versatile Adman," 70; Fox, 278; Arnold de Mille, "Not a Commissioned Officer But an Important Person Around Camp Dix, N.J. Is PFC Roy Eaton," *Chicago Defender* (May 8, 1954): 19.

68. Roy Eaton, interview with author; Lesley Mitchell-Clarke, "Roy Eaton Brings His Personal Renaissance to Roosevelt Island," *The Wire*, October 10, 1998, accessed on July 21, 2004 from http://nyc10044.com/wire/1903/eaton.html; "Versatile Adman," 70; Stein, 162–63.

69. Roy Eaton, interview with author.

70. "Kent Jingle 'No Musical Insult,'" *Advertising Age* (June 17, 1957): 70; "Master Musician Scores Ad Success," *Ebony* (September 1958): 59; Roy Eaton, interview with author.

71. Roy Eaton, interview with author.

72. "Roy Eaton Leaves Y&R for Music Makers Post," *Advertising Age* (August 10, 1959): 2; Roy Eaton, interview with author.

73. Mitchell-Clarke.

74. "Master Musician," 60; Fox, 278.

75. A. J. Vogl, "A Face for the Invisible Man," *Sales Management* (December 20, 1963): 31–32.

76. *Chicago Defender* (June 7, 1969): 4.

77. Roy Eaton, interview with author.

78. Julie Lasky, "The Search for Georg Olden," in *Graphic Design History*, ed. Steven Heller and Georgette Ballance (New York: Allworth Press, 2001), 115–20.

79. "Video Veteran," *Opportunity* (Winter 1947): 158; Lasky, 118–20.

80. Quoted in "Video Veteran,"158; also see Lowell Thompson, "Behind the Image", unpublished manuscript, 61.

81. "Olden Is an Art Supervisor at Madison Avenue Agency," *Ebony* (November 1960): 80–84; Calvert Distillers, advertisement, *Our World* (October 1951): 5.

82. "Olden Is an Art Supervisor," 80–82.

83. Thompson, 55–58; Lasky, 123–24; "Olden Is an Art Supervisor," 80–81; "N.Y. Ad Executive Designs Black Iron Chain Emancipation Stamp," *Chicago Defender* (May 8, 1963): 9.

84. Lasky, 119; Thompson, 55.

85. "Adman in the News . . . Georg Olden," *Advertising Age* (May 6, 1963): 151; "Olden Is an Art Supervisor," 83.

86. Quoted in Lasky 127–28. Stephen Fox called the movement of ethnic whites into the advertising industry during the 1960s an "ethnic revolution." See Fox, 273–77.

87. Lasky, 126; "Olden Charges M-E with Racial Bias in Firing," *Advertising Age* (February 8, 1971): 57; On Olden's case, see Lasky, 124–26; "Equal Employment Opportunity Commission," *Advertising Age* (July 31, 1972): 8; "Olden Case Raises Issue of Agency Minority Percentage," *Advertising Age* (August 14, 1972): 56.

88. Lasky, 126–28, "Blacks, Whites, and Bum Raps," *Advertising Age* (August 21, 1972): 14.

89. Walter White, "Negro Leader Looks at TV Race Problem," *Printer's Ink* (August 24, 1951): 31; "Selling the Negro Market," 37; Arnold M. Rose, "TV Bumps into the Negro Problem," *Printer's Ink* (July 20, 1951): 36–37, 78; "Classic Comes to Life," *Advertising Age* (July 23, 1951): 49; Inger L. Stole, "Nat King Cole and the Politics of Race and Broadcasting in the 1950s," *Communication Review* 3 (1996): 350–51.

90. Quoted in Kern-Foxworth, 168.

91. White, 31; "Selling the Negro Market," *Tide* (July 20, 1951): 37; Stole, 351.

92. Quoted in William Barlow, *Voice Over: The Making of Black Radio* (Philadelphia: Temple University Press), 28. On the challenges the struggle in Little Rock presented to the advertising industry, see "Marketing and the Integration Fight," *Printer's Ink* (October 4, 1957): 1–4; Royal D. Colle, "Negro Image in the Mass Media: A Case in Social Change," *Journalism Quarterly* (Spring 1968): 55–60.

93. Stole, 360–66.

94. Stole, 365; Nat King Cole, "After a Year on Network TV, Singer Says Prejudice Is Much More Finance Than Romance," *Ebony* (February 1958): 30; Dave Kaufman, "Nat (King) Cole Hits Madison Ave. Resistance to Negroes on TV," *Variety* (September 11, 1957): 2; Cole, 30.

95. "The U.S. Negro, 1953," *Time* (May 11, 1953): 58.

96. Gelber, 24–25, 118.

97. Quoted in Gelber, 81.

98. On black-owned insurance firms, see Robert Weems, *Black Business in the Black Metropolis: The Chicago Metropolitan Assurance Company* (Bloomington: Indiana University Press, 1996).

99. Judy Foster Davis, "Enterprise Development under an Economic Detour? Black-Owned Advertising Agencies, 1940–2000," *Journal of Macromarketing* 22, no. 1 (June 2002): 75–85.

100. Gelber, 5.

Chapter 3

1. Quoted in A. J. Vogl, "A Face for the Invisible Man," *Sales Management* (December 20, 1963): 3. On civil rights groups and the advertising industry, see Marilyn Kern-Foxworth, *Aunt Jemima, Uncle Ben, and Rastus: Blacks in Advertising, Yesterday, Today, and Tomorrow* (Westport, Conn.: Greenwood Press, 1994), 39–41, 115–17.

2. Steven M. Gelber, *Black Men and Businessmen: The Growing Awareness of a Social Responsibility* (Port Washington, N.Y.: Kennikat Press, 1974), 149–53.

3. Harvard Sitkoff, *The Struggle for Black Equality, 1954–1992* (New York: Hill and Wang, 1993), 61–63.

4. On black consumer activism, see Lizabeth Cohen, *A Consumers' Republic: The Politics of Mass Consumption in Postwar America* (New York: Alfred A Knopf, 2003), 185–91; Robert E. Weems, Jr., *Desegregating the Dollar: African American Consumerism in the Twentieth Century* (New York: New York University Press, 1998), 56–59.

5. Cohen, *A Consumers' Republic*, 185–89. On racial encounters in consumer spaces, see Grace Elizabeth Hale, *Making Whiteness: The Culture of Segregation in the South, 1890–1940* (New York: Vintage Books, 1999), 151–97.

6. Jannette L. Dates, "Half A Loaf: Advertising," in *Split Image: African Americans in the Mass Media*, ed. Jannette L. Dates and William Barlow (Washington, D.C.: Howard University Press, 1993), 486; D. Parke Gibson, *$70 Billion in the Black* (New York: Macmillan Publishing Company, 1978), 21–27.

7. Cohen, *A Consumers' Republic*, 185–86, 372–73. On Nat King Cole's charges against northern companies, see Chapter 2.

8. Gibson, 22.

9. Edward Peeks, "Clerics Get 1,000 New Jobs in Philly," *Washington Afro-American* (September 25, 1962): 1; Michael Creedman, "Negroes Step Up Use of Boycotts to Back Drive for Better Jobs," *Wall Street Journal* (January 8, 1963), 1+.

10. Ray Shaw, "The Negro Consumer," *Wall Street Journal* (June 30, 1961): 1; "The Negro Market," *National Bottlers' Gazette* (February 1963): 18; Peter Bart, "Advertising: Negro Market Plays Big Role," *New York Times* (September 24, 1961): 12F.

11. "Marketing to the Negro Consumer," *Sales Management* (March 4, 1960): 36–44; David J. Sullivan, "Selling the Negro Market," *American Brewer* (June 1961): 47–53, 61–62.

12. Robert Weems, Jr., "The Revolution Will Be Marketed: American Corporations and Black Consumers During the 1960s," *Radical History Review* (Spring 1994): 98; "Past Decade Saw the Market Zoom," *Sponsor* (October 9, 1961): 11–12; "Keeping an Ethnic Market Friendly," *Printer's Ink* (January 19, 1962): 53–54.

13. Quoted in "Media Decision: Integrate or Segregate?" *Sponsor* (July 25, 1966): 26. See also "Changing Role of Negro in Market is Challenge: Wells," *Advertising Age* (October 31, 1966): 84; "Fracturing Markets," *Printer's Ink* (June 21, 1963): 64; Cohen, *A Consumers' Republic*, 323–30.

14. Quoted in Cohen, *A Consumers' Republic*, 190.

15. On Johnson, see "Must Project More Realistic Image of Negro, Admen Told," *Advertising Age* (July 27, 1964): 84. On gaining black consumer support, see David Sullivan, "Selling the Negro Market," *American Brewer* (June 1961): 47–54. On consumer products and racial progress, see "To Be Effective in Negro

Market, Ad Must Indicate Heightened Prestige, Johnson Finds," *Advertising Age* (September 16, 1960): 116; "To Sell in Negro Market, Advertiser Must Communicate Respect for People: Fitzhugh," *Advertising Age* (July 24, 1967): 89.

16. On Leonard Evans, see "Negro Marketers Hit White's Claim Market Dwindles," *Advertising Age* (May 23, 1966): 119. On blacks' middle-class aspirations, see Dave Berkman, "Advertising in 'Ebony' and 'Life': Negro Aspirations vs. Reality," *Journalism Quarterly* (Winter 1963): 53–64; Raymond A. Bauer, Scott M. Cunningham, and Lawrence H. Wortzel, "The Marketing Dilemma of Negroes," *Journal of Marketing* 29 (July 1965): 2–3

17. Quotations from "TV: A 'New Force' in Selling to U.S. Negroes," *Sponsor* (August 17, 1964): 45; Mrs. Medgar Evers with William Peters, *For Us, the Living* (Garden City, N.Y.: Doubleday & Company, 1967), 32; and "Hayakawa Appears to Criticize TV Ads for Achieving a Great Civil Rights Breakthrough," *Advertising Age* (September 2, 1963): 62. See also Bauer, Cunningham, and Wortzel, "The Marketing Dilemma of Negroes," 1–3.

18. "Negro Boycott Could Have Serious, Lasting Effect on Sales, Study Shows," *Advertising Age* (September 30, 1963): 3, 110; "Is There a U.S. Negro Market?" *Sponsor* (August 1964): 33.

19. Quoted in letter to the editor, *Advertising Age* (May 6, 1963): 168. See also "Most Negroes in Poll Say They Would Back Boycott of Concerns," *Wall Street Journal* (September 26, 1963): 6; Kern-Foxworth, 37–41, 115–18.

20. Gunnar Myrdal, *An American Dilemma: Volume II* (New Brunswick, N.J.: Transaction Publishers, 1997), 817–18.

21. Quotations from Cultural Committee of the National Negro Congress Statement of Principles, Papers of the National Negro Congress (hereinafter NNC Papers), Part II, Reel 34, Manuscript Division, Library of Congress; Walter Christmas, "Negroes in the Ads," *Negro Digest* (December 1949): 71; and "NNC Cultural Committee Statement of Principles," NNC Papers, Part II: Reel 34. On contemporary charges of racism in advertising, see Christmas, 70–73; "Anglo-Saxon Myth," *Tide* (April 15, 1945): 110–14. On the National Negro Congress, see John Hope Franklin and Alfred A. Moss Jr., *From Slavery to Freedom: A History of African Americans*, 8th ed. (Boston: McGraw-Hill, 2000), 426, 469.

22. "The Negroes Status in Advertising," NNC Papers, Part II, Reel 34; "Biow Lists 9 Agencies Which Employ Negroes," *Advertising Age* (March 24, 1947): 50.

23. Milton H. Biow, *Butting In: An Adman Speaks Out* (Garden City, N.Y.: Doubleday & Company, 1964), 93.

24. Biow, 93.

25. "The Negroes Status in Advertising"; "Biow Lists 9 Agencies Which Employ Negroes," 50.

26. "The Negroes Status in Advertising."

27. Biow, 93–94.

28. "A Report on the Conference for Free Expression in the American Arts," NNC Papers, Part II, Reel 34.

29. "Advice on the Negro," *Business Week* (April 13, 1940): 47; "Business Enterprise," *Opportunity* (December 1933): 385.

30. "Urban League Hits N.Y. Agencies on Racial Discrimination in Employment," *Advertising Age* (April 22, 1963): 1, 96; Fox, 279.

31. Roy Eaton, interview with author, New York, N.Y., August 16, 2004; David Sullivan, "The Negro Market and the Segregation Issue," *Sales Management* (March 4, 1960): 40–41.

32. "Urban League Hits N.Y. Agencies," 96.

33. "Urban League Hits N.Y. Agencies," 96; "Survey Finds Rigid Race Bias in Ad Agencies," *Chicago Defender* (April 17, 1963): 4.

34. "Urban League Hits N.Y. Agencies," 96; Gelber, 130–32.

35. "Discrimination? Personnel Men's Views Vary," *Advertising Age* (April 22, 1963): 96; "Urban League Hits N.Y. Agencies," 96.

36. "Discrimination?" 96.

37. "Urban League Hits N.Y. Agencies," 96.

38. Letter to the Editor, *Advertising Age* (May 6, 1963): 168.

39. "Urban League Hits N.Y. Agencies," 96.

40. "Urban League Hits N.Y. Agencies," 96. On the linkage between grass-roots activism and civil rights organizations see Cohen, *A Consumers' Republic*, 185–91.

41. "Hiring Bias Laid to 10 Ad Agencies," *New York Times* (April 16, 1963): 15.

42. On local CORE activisim, see Gelber, 47; August Meier and Elliott Rudwick, *CORE: A Study in the Civil Rights Movement, 1942–1968* (New York: Oxford University Press, 1973), 310, 379–80. On CORE's nonviolent strategy, see Inge Powell Bell, *CORE and the Strategy of Non-Violence* (New York: Random House, 1968) and James Farmer, *Lay Bare the Heart: An Autobiography of the Civil Rights Movement* (New York: Arbor House, 1985). On the Image Campaign, see "Negroes Step Up Drives on Radio-TV," *Broadcasting* (August 12, 1963): 62–64.

43. "TV: A 'New Force' in Selling to U.S. Negroes," *Sponsor* (August 17, 1964): 45; Evans quoted in "Negro Marketers Hit White's Claim," 52.

44. "Marching on Madison," *Newsweek* (September 9, 1963): 68; "Colgate Next Target in Integrated-Ads Push," *Advertising Age* (August 19, 1963): 8.

45. "Colgate Next Target in Integrated-Ads Push," 8; "Desegregate Ads, TV, Lever Tells Agencies," *Advertising Age* (August 12, 1963): 1, 8.

46. "Top 10 National Advertisers," *Advertising Age* (August 26, 1963): 1; "Colgate Next Target in Integrated-Ads Push," 8, "Desegregate Ads, TV, Lever Tells Agencies," 8; William H. Boyenton, "The Negro Turns to Advertising," *Journalism Quarterly* (Spring 1965): 227–35.

47. "Negroes Step Up Drives on Radio-TV," 62–64; Boyenton, "The Negro Turns," 228–29.

48. "Desegregate Ads, TV," 1, 8; Lawrence R. Samuel, *Brought to You By: Postwar Television Advertising and the American Dream* (Austin: University of Texas Press, 2001), 186.

49. "Two Views of Negroes in TV," 52; Peter Bart, "Advertising: Use of Negro Models Widening," *New York Times* (June 13, 1963): 35; "Use of Negroes in Ads Has Not Hurt Sales: Lever," *Advertising Age* (November 4, 1963): 1, 8; "ANA Grapples with Problems of Integrated Ads, Agency Compensation," *Advertising Age* (November 18, 1963): 3, 105; "It Isn't Whether, But How," *Broadcasting* (November 18, 1963): 52.

50. "Colgate Next Target in Integrated-Ads Push," 1, 8; Harold J. Ashby, Jr., "The Black Consumer," in *New Consumerism: Selected Readings*, ed. William T. Kelley (Columbus, Ohio: Grid, Inc., 1973), 154–56.

51. "Colgate Next Target in Integrated-Ads Push," 1.

52. Ramona Bechtos, "Ads in Negro-Market Media Do Double Duty with Negro Buyers, Zimmer Says," *Advertising Age* (January 13, 1964): 72; Peter Bart, "Advertising: Colgate to Use Negro Models," *New York Times* (August 23, 1963): 30.

53. "Integration of Advertising," *Advertising Age* (August 19, 1963): 20.

54. "P&G is Next CORE Target; Agencies Later," *Advertising Age* (August 26, 1963): 3, 251; "CORE Seeks Cooperation From More Advertisers," *Advertising Age* (February 10, 1964): 91.

55. "Negro Boycott Could Have Serious, Lasting Effect on Sales, Study Shows," *Advertising Age* (September 30, 1963): 110; Maurine Christopher, "CORE Seeks More Integrated Ads," *Advertising Age* (September 9, 1963): 1, 28.

56. Vogl, "A Face for the Invisible Man," 30–31.

57. "40 Major Advertisers Said Ready to Integrate Ads," *Advertising Age* (September 9, 1963): 127; "Integration Proceeds in Advertising," *Advertising Age* (September 23, 1963): 115; Maurine Christopher, "Integration Drive Gains Momentum in TV Industry," *Advertising Age* (September 30, 1963): 105; John M. Lee, "Advertising: Integrated Scene in Boston," *New York Times* (August 7, 1963): 89; "Integrated Outdoor," *Advertising Age* (August 19, 1963): 3.

58. Quoted in Christopher, 105. See also Kern-Foxworth, 39–40; "CORE Seeks Cooperation From More Advertisers," 91; "CORE in Renewed Plea for More Use of Negroes in Video and Print Ads," *Sponsor* (March 23, 1964): 4; "CORE Reports Drive for Negroes in Ads So Far Successful," 14; "CORE Pleased with Advertisers' Attitude in Latest Meeting," *Advertising Age* (November 30, 1964): 46.

59. "CORE Intensifies Drive for Negroes in Ads; Zeroes in on Pepsi-Cola Co.," *Advertising Age* (November 9, 1964): 3, 71; "CORE, Pepsi End Flare-up Based on Misunderstanding," *Advertising Age* (November 16, 1964): 143.

60. Quoted in Vogl, "A Face for the Invisible Man," 87. On the internal organizational challenges faced by Clarence Funnye, see Meier and Rudwick, 379–80. On the development of Black Nationalism within CORE, see William Van Deburg, *New Day in Babylon: The Black Power Movement and American Culture, 1965–1975* (Chicago: University of Chicago Press, 1992), 129–52. On Funnye's death, see "Hunt for Ex-CORE Aide Ends," *New York Times* (September 13, 1970): 71; "Clarence Funnye, Integrated Ads Leader, Dies at 38," *Advertising Age* (September 28, 1970): 114. On the impact of the Image campaign, see Samuel, 187–88.

61. "Next NAACP Stop: New York," *Broadcasting* (July 29, 1963): 91; "NAACP Still Seeks 'Hazel' Hiring, Asks 4A's Meeting," *Advertising Age* (August 5, 1963): 101; "Negroes Step Up Drives on Radio-TV," 62–64; Henry Lee Moon, "Remarks for Workshop on Selective Use of Economic Power," NAACP 51st Annual Convention in Moss Kendrix Papers, Moss Kendrix and the NAACP; "Now a Negro Push on Radio-TV," *Broadcasting* (July 1, 1963): 27–29; David C. Schmidt and Ivan L. Preston, "How NAACP Leaders View Integrated Advertising," *Journal of Advertising Research* (September 1969): 13–16; Boyenton, "The Negro Turns," 228–30.

62. "NAACP Is Listed in the Telephone Book," *Broadcasting* (August 19, 1963): 58; "Negroes on the Sales Force: The Quiet Integration," *Sales Management* (October 16, 1964): 27.

63. "NAACP Tells 4A's of 5-Point Program," 1, 128; Ashby, 171.

64. "NAACP Tells 4A's of 5-Point Program," 1, 128.

65. "NAACP Tells 4A's of 5-Point Program," 1, 128.

66. "The Negro and the Advertiser," *Saturday Review* (November 9, 1963): 67.

67. Roy Wilkins, "Economic Impact of the Civil Rights Struggle," American Association of Advertising Agencies, *Papers from the 1963 Regional Conventions*, JWT Marketing Vertical File, 1940s-1999, Box 22, Hartman Center, Duke University, 4–5.

68. Wilkins, "Economic Impact," 6.

69. "4A's Cover Ad Spectrum," *Broadcasting* (November 11, 1963): 50.

70. Four A's advertisement, *New York Times* (November 11, 1963): 54.

71. "It Isn't Whether But How," 52.

72. "JWT to Interview 117 Negro Job Seekers in 2-Day Talent Hunt, *Advertising Age* (June 20, 1966): 22; "Job Talk," *Advertising Age* (July 11, 1966): 102.

73. Quoted in "Advertisers and the Race Situation," *Advertising Age* (September 30, 1963): 20. See also "Negro Models in TV," *Sponsor* (September 9, 1963): 21–24; Kern-Foxworth, 39–41.

74. Quotations from "Two Views of Negroes in TV: the Adman, the Activist," *Sponsor* (August 17, 1964): 51; Vogl, "A Face for the Invisible Man," 2; "TV Ads, Shows Still Lag in Use of Negro, Other Races: ACLU," *Advertising Age* (April 11, 1966): 128. On the NAACP and integrated advertising, see Preston and Schmidt, 15–16. On advertiser and agency fears of boycotts by white consumers, see J. Fred MacDonald, *Blacks and White TV: Afro-Americans in Television since 1948* (Chicago: Nelson-Hall Publishers, 1988), 41–45.

75. Lawrence Plotkin, "Report on the Frequency of Appearance of Negroes on Televised Commercials," NAACP Legal Defense and Educational Fund, Inc., McGraw-Hill Marketing Information Center Collection, Box 39, File 50:4–3.23, Hartman Center, Duke University; "NAACP Asks FCC to Investigate Bias in Staffing for TV Commercial Spots," *Advertising Age* (August 28, 1967): 3, 240; Maurine Christopher, "NAACP Asks FCC to Eliminate Racism in Ads," *Advertising Age* (October 5, 1970): 29.

76. David Sullivan to John Crichton, February 17, 1964, Papers of the NAACP, Supplement to Part 13, Reel 14, The Ohio State University, Columbus, Ohio. Also see "Breakthrough in Civil Rights in Advertising Applies Only to Use of Negroes in Ads, Ad Job Seeker Says," *Advertising Age* (March 9, 1964): 92.

77. David Sullivan to John Crichton; Fox, 278–79.

78. David Sullivan to John Crichton.

79. David Sullivan to John Crichton.

80. "Consumer Info Services, CORE to Picket B&B," *Advertising Age* (September 12, 1966): 1. "Picketers Propose Benton & Bowles Train Underprivileged for Ad Jobs," *Advertising Age* (September 26, 1966): 2, 170.

81. Flo Kennedy, *Color Me Flo: My Hard Life and Good Times* (Englewood Cliffs, N.J.: Prentice-Hall, 1976), 53; Kennedy, 2; "Picketers Propose Benton & Bowles Train Underprivileged for Ad Jobs," *Advertising Age* (September 26, 1966): 2, 170.

82. "Cut Ads to Subsidize Ghetto Prices, B&B Told," *Advertising Age* (September 19, 1966): 1, 80; Roy Eaton, interview with author.

83. Quoted in "The White Apathy," *Printer's Ink* (January 13, 1967): 54. On reactions to the CORE/CIS campaign, see "Picketing at Benton & Bowles," *Advertising Age* (September 19, 1966): 16; "Calls CORE Picketing of B&B a Form of Extortion," *Advertising Age* (October 3, 1966): 92; "Advertising and Civil Rights," *Printer's Ink* (October 14, 1966): 78.

84. "Keep Militancy Against Madison Ave. 'Oppressors,' Black Adfolk Are Told," *Advertising Age* (March 9, 1970): 3.

85. "Picketers Propose Benton & Bowles Train Underprivileged for Ad Jobs," 170.

86. Kennedy, 52–53; Meier and Rudwick, 374–408.

87. "B&B to Mold Communication Training Program for Minority Group Members," *Advertising Age* (October 3, 1966): 83.

88. "B&B Gets a Mickey Finn," *Advertising Age* (January 2, 1967): 14.

89. "B&B Gets a Mickey Finn," 14; "Advertising and Civil Rights," *Printer's Ink* (October 14, 1996): 78; "General Foods Involves Its Other Shops in B&B-Negro Rights Hassle," *Advertising Age* (January 16, 1967): 3, 36.

90. Henry Lee, "The 4A's John Crichton," *Madison Avenue* (July 1962): 40; "Eastern Four A's Probes Problems Created by Increasing Urbanization," *Advertising Age* (October 16, 1967): 1, 113–14; Philip H. Dougherty, "Advertising: A Plea to Hire More Negroes," *New York Times* (April 26, 1968): 71.

91. "Monitor South—'A Labor of Love' to Be Reckoned With," *Broadcasting* (January 2, 1961): 46.

92. "Use of Negroes in Ads Has Not Hurt Sales: Lever," 8.

93. Cohen, *A Consumers' Republic*, 371–72; Juliet E. K. Walker, *The History of Black Business in America: Capitalism, Race, Entrepreneurship* (New York: Twayne Publishers, 1998), 270–71.

94. Cohen, *A Consumers' Republic*, 355–57. On the frequency of blacks in advertisements, see Kern-Foxworth, 131–45; Samuel, 188–89.

95. Gelber, 3.

Chapter 4

1. Harlem resident quoted in Lizabeth Cohen, *A Consumers' Republic: The Politics of Mass Consumption in Postwar America* (New York: Alfred A. Knopf, 2003), 373; Hughes quoted in Joseph Boskin, "The Revolt of the Urban Ghettos, 1964–1967," in *Roots of Rebellion: The Evolution of Black Politics and Protest Since World War II*, ed. Richard P. Young (New York: Harper & Row Publishers, 1970), 311.

2. Steven M. Gelber, *Black Men and Businessmen: The Growing Awareness of a Social Responsibility* (Port Washington, N.Y.: Kennikat Press, 1974), 139–40.

3. Juliet E. K. Walker, *The History of Black Business in America: Capitalism, Race, Entrepreneurship* (New York: Twayne Publishers, 1998), 269–70.

4. Tom Burrell, interview by author, January 26, 2001, Chicago, Illinois.

5. Gerald Benjamin, *Race Relations and the New York City Commission on Human Rights* (Ithaca, N.Y.: Cornell University Press, 1974), 98, 106–10.

6. Dann quoted in "CBS-TV Policy Paper on Use of Negroes," *Broadcasting* (August 5, 1963): 44. Also see "Agencies Blamed for Race Bias in TV," *Advertising Age* (April 22, 1963): 96. "Sponsors Absent in Washington March Telecast," *Advertising Age* (September 2, 1963): 8; William H. Boyenton, "The Negro Turns to Advertising," *Journalism Quarterly* (Spring 1965): 229.

7. "Agencies Blamed for Race Bias in TV," 96; "Now a Negro Push on Radio-TV," *Broadcasting* (July 1, 1963): 27–29; "Ads Sans Minorities Distort U.S. Image, Says N.Y. Committee," *Advertising Age* (March 4, 1963): 28.

8. "Major Breakthrough in Integrated Ads, N.Y. Committee Says," *Advertising Age* (February 17, 1964): 58; New York City Commission on Human Rights, "Minority Employment and the Advertising Industry in New York City: A Commission on Human Rights Analysis of Compulsory Versus Voluntary Affirmative Action" (June 1978), accessed on September 20, 2006, from http://adage.com/images/random/diversity1978.pdf.

9. "City's Job Panel Asks Industry to Aid in Fight on Prejudice," *New York Times* (December 7, 1962): 27; "Ads Sans Minorities Distort U.S. Image," 28; "Does Advertising Discriminate Against Minority Groups?" *Advertising Week* (March 1, 1963): 11.

10. Richard Scheidker, "Statement to the New York City Commission on Human Rights," American Association of Advertising Agencies (February 19, 1964): 7; Papers of the NAACP (hereinafter NAACP Papers), Part 24 – Special Subjects, 1956–65, Series A, Reel 25, The Ohio State University, Columbus, Ohio; "Major Breakthrough in Integrated Ads," 58; Royal D. Colle, "Negro Image in the Mass Media: A Case Study in Social Change," *Journalism Quarterly* (Spring 1968): 55–60; Joseph Kaselow, "Integration Report—the Slow Strides of Progress," *New York Herald Tribune* (January 21, 1965): 28.

11. Charles G. Bennett, "Job Panel Set Up to Aid Minorities," *New York Times* (August 26, 1962): 1.

12. Gordon Webber, *Our Kind of People: The Story of the First 50 Years at Benton & Bowles* (New York: Benton & Bowles, Inc.), 133.

13. Benjamin, 77–81, 125–29, 256.

14. "Urban League Hits N.Y. Agencies on Racial Discrimination in Employment," *Advertising Age* (April 22, 1963): 1, 96; Benjamin, 228–30.

15. Quoted in Benjamin, 177. See also Benjamin, 127; "Major Breakthrough in Integrated Ads," 58.

16. Scheidker, "Statement to the New York City Commission on Human Rights," 2, 5, 6.

17. Scheidker, "Statement to the New York City Commission on Human Rights," 6.

18. Fred Danzig, "Ad Industry Praised for Efforts in Equal Job Opportunity Program," *Advertising Age* (February 24, 1964): 175.

19. See Chapter 3 for a discussion of Sullivan's letter to Crichton. David Sullivan to John Crichton, February 17, 1964, NAACP Papers, Supplement to Part 13, Reel 14.

20. Danzig, 175. Scheidker did not provide the commission with a description of the areas in which agencies were increasing minority employees. However, given the NYCHR's overarching emphasis on white-collar jobs, it was unlikely that these were janitorial or other menial positions.

21. Scheidker, "Statement to the New York City Commission on Human Rights," 6; Danzig, 1B, 175.

22. Boskin, 318.

23. Quoted in Gelber, 157, 160. See also Gelber, 157, 201.

24. Benjamin, 128–29, 189; Dorothy Cohen, "Advertising and the Black Community," *Journal of Marketing* (October 1970): 3–5.

25. Gelber, 144. Quoted in Gelber, 164.

26. Equal Employment Opportunity Commission, *Hearings before the United States Equal Employment Opportunity Commission on Discrimination in White Collar Employment* (Washington, D.C.: GPO, 1968).

27. Equal Employment Opportunity Commission, 326.

28. Equal Employment Opportunity Commission, 326.

29. Equal Employment Opportunity Commission, 388–89.

30. Equal Employment Opportunity Commission, 14–22.

31. Equal Employment Opportunity Commission, 417; Maurine Christopher, "Agencies, Media Lag in Hiring of Minorities, N.Y Hearing Reveals," *Advertising Age* (January 22, 1968): 1, 72. Commissioners scheduled a third witness as well but deferred to the submission of a written statement to allow more time for witness questioning.

32. Equal Employment Opportunity Commission, 422; Equal Employment Opportunity Commission, 428–29.

33. Equal Employment Opportunity Commission, 431–33.

34. Equal Employment Opportunity Commission, 434–35.

35. Equal Employment Opportunity Commission, 698, 792; "Eastern Four A's Probes Problems Created by Increasing Urbanization," *Advertising Age* (October 16, 1967): 1, 113–14.

36. Equal Employment Opportunity Commission, 793.

37. "Solving Minority Problems: A Start," *Advertising Age* (January 29, 1968): 14; Equal Employment Opportunity Commission, 490–93; "EEOC Head Commends Industry for Integrating Ads," *Advertising Age* (January 13, 1969): 48; "EEOC Sees 'Notable Progress,'" *Advertising Age* (January 13, 1969): 14; Philip H. Dougherty, "Advertising: McCann Bias Case," *New York Times* (July 25, 1972): 40.

38. "Solving Minority Problems," 14.

39. Benjamin, 240, 213–14; "Admen to Testify in Probe of How They Deal With Minorities," *Advertising Age* (March 4, 1968): 2.

40. Benjamin, 217–18.

41. New York City Commission on Human Rights, "Minority Employment," 3.

42. Maurine Christopher, "Racial 'Imbalance' in Ad Agency Personnel Is Termed 'Appalling,'" *Advertising Age* (March 18, 1968): 1, 86; Benjamin, 228–30; New York City Commission on Human Rights, 2; Maurine Christopher, "Impact of N.Y.'s Minority Group Survey Is Being Seen in TV Ads," *Advertising Age* (February 5, 1968): 3, 86.

43. Christopher, "Racial 'Imbalance,'" 86.

44. Christopher, "Racial 'Imbalance,'" 86; Benjamin, 173–76; Robert E. Dallos, "Advertising Jobs Pass Negroes By," *New York Times* (March 13, 1968): 94.

45. "Minority Group Hiring in Agency's Interest: Vallon," *Advertising Age* (December 9, 1968): 32; Maurine Christopher, "No Letup in Push for Minority Hiring: Booth," *Advertising Age* (March 25, 1968): 3; Christopher, "Racial 'Imbalance,'" 86; Kern-Foxworth, 117.

46. "Agency Employment: Still Far to Go," *Advertising Age* (March 25, 1968): 16; "Management Must Lead the Way," *Advertising Age* (May 6, 1968): 14.

47. Barton Cummings, "Address to the Audit Bureau of Circulations," October 22, 1969, Barton A. Cummings Papers (hereinafter Cummings Papers), Box 2, Folder 3, Archives Center, National Museum of American History, Washington, D.C.; "Minorities in Marketing: No Easy Answers," *Marketing/Communications* (September 1968): 14.

48. Carroll J. Swan, "Are Negroes Welcome on Your Account Team?" *Media/Scope* (November 1967): 49.

49. Christopher, "No Letup," 3, 142.

50. Christopher, "No Letup," 3, 142.

51. "Commission Finds Instances of Better Employment Practice," *Advertising Age* (November 4, 1968): 30; "For Advertising, Signs of Change," *New York Times* (January 6, 1969): C129; "Discrimination Charges 'Shock' to Ogilvy, Esty," *Advertising Age* (May 6, 1968): 116.

52. Letter to the editor, *Advertising Age* (January 27, 1969): 42; Maurine Christopher, "Gains in Minority Hiring People Seem Minimal," *Advertising Age* (January 13, 1969): 1, 82; New York City Commission on Human Rights, "Minority Employment," Appendix A.

53. Christopher, "Gains in Minority Hiring," 1, 82.

54. Quoted in Gelber, 181. See also "New York City's Commission on Human Rights," *Advertising Age* (February 11, 1974): 70.

55. Gelber, 131–32.

56. John Feehery, "Negro Has Precarious Foothold in Agency Field, 3-City Survey Shows," *Advertising Age* (October 17, 1966): 3, 44.

57. Feehery, 44.

58. Feehery, 44.

59. Feehery, 44.

60. Feehery, 44.

61. "Urban League Outlines Proposed Referral System," *Advertising Age* (November 28, 1966): 82.

62. Bill Sharp, interview by author, March 17, 2001, Atlanta, Georgia; Tom Burrell, interview by author, January 26, 2001, Chicago, Illinois; "Chicago Four A's Sponsors Ad Course for Negro Students," *Advertising Age* (September 18, 1967): 64; "Chicago Agency Men Train Negroes for Ad Careers," *Advertising Age* (May 13, 1968): 75; Bill Sharp, *How to Be Black and Get a Job in the Advertising Agency Business Anyway* (Bethesda, Md.: Bill Sharp, 1969), 25–30; Barton Cummings, Address to the Fifty-fifth Annual Meeting of the Audit Bureau of Circulations, October 22, 1969, Cummings Papers, Box 2, Folder 3.

63. "Chicago Agency Men Train Negroes," 75.

64. Quoted in "Chicago Agency Men Train Negroes," 75. See also Cohen, "Advertising and the Black Community," 20; Reva Corda, "Commentary," *Marketing/Communications* (March 1971): 29.

65. Quotations from "The Chicago Council's Basic Advertising Course – A Progress Report," *Papers from the 1968 AAAA Region Conventions*, American Association of Advertising Agencies (November 11–12, 1968): 4, in J. Walter Thompson Advertising Vertical File, Box 27, J. Walter Thompson Company Papers (hereinafter JWT Papers), Hartman Center, Duke University; Bill Sharp, interview by author. On the design of the BAC, see "The Chicago Council's Basic Advertising Course," 12; "Chicago Agency Men Train Negroes," 75; Fox, 282.

66. Bill Sharp, interview by author; "Chicago Four A's Sponsors Ad Course for Negro Students," 64; "Chicago Agency Men Train Negroes," 75; Sharp, *How to Be Black*, 25–30; Swan, 49.

67. Quoted in "Chicago Agency Men Train Negroes," 75. On the rigors of the BAC, see Tom Burrell, interview by author; Bill Sharp, interview by author.

68. Sharp, *How to Be Black*, 29–30; Barton Cummings, Address to the Audit Bureau of Circulations, October 22, 1969, Cummings Papers, Box 2, Folder 3.

69. "Ad Field's Efforts to Induct Blacks Is Overrated, Sharp Tells Four A's," *Advertising Age* (May 5, 1969): 3, 122.

70. Tom Burrell, interview by author; Allan Jaklich, "Basic Ad Course Proves Worth," *Chicago Tribune* (March 26, 1970): J8; "Blacks Are Most 'Hidden Persuaders' in Chicago's Billion Dollar Advertising Business," *Chicago Reporter* 4, no. 3 (March 1975): 6. On Carole H. Williams, see Cassandra Hayes, "Not Just an Ol' Boys Club," *Black Enterprise* (June 1999): 180–88. See also "New Graduate Group Ready for Ad Field After Completion of 4A's Basic Course," *Advertising Age* (July 21, 1969): 118; "Blacks Are Most 'Hidden Persuaders,'" 4; "The Chicago Council's Basic Advertising Course"; "Agencies Slate Course," *Chicago Defender* (November 12, 1973): 7.

71. Sharp, *How to Be Black*, 49, 2.

72. Sharp, *How to Be Black*, 2; Tom Burrell, interview by author.

73. "Equal Opportunities Group Sets Hearing in Ad, Media Fields," *Advertising Age* (October 30, 1967): 8; Swan, 49.

74. "Los Angeles Adman Toils in Watts; Directs Ad Class, Paints Houses,"

Advertising Age (August 18, 1968): 79; "L.A. Four A's Group Sponsors Ad Education for Minority Students," *Advertising Age* (August 25, 1969): 3, 244; Howard Lucraft, "L.A. 4A's Agencies Minority Ad Program Alters Students Attitudes," *Advertising Age* (July 13, 1970): 8; "Wayne State, 4A's Plan Ad Course for Minority Groups," *Advertising Age* (March 3, 1969): 60; "Adman Likes View From the Top," *Black Enterprise* (July 1972): 15; "Twelve Minority Students," *Advertising Age* (April 23, 1973): 128; Photograph, *Advertising Age* (October 15, 1973): 18; "Underprivileged Get Ad Training Via Boston Adclub," *Advertising Age* (July 15, 1968): 18; "FATE Works Wonders, Cleveland Adclub Finds, as 7 Negroes Complete Program," *Advertising Age* (April 14, 1969): 20; Gelber, 178–79; "New York City's Commission on Human Rights," *Advertising Age* (February 11, 1974): 70; Tom Burrell, interview by author; Bill Sharp, interview by author.

75. John Elliott, Jr., "A Look in the Looking Glass," *Papers from the 1968 AAAA Annual Meeting,* American Association of Advertising Agencies (April 25, 1968): 6, 7–8, in J. Walter Thompson Advertising Vertical File, Box 27, JWT Papers.

76. "Management Must Lead the Way," *Advertising Age* (May 6, 1968): 14.

77. Daniels & Charles, advertisement, *New York Times* (April 15, 1968): 67; "Agency Ad Aims to Help Negroes With Ad Careers," *Advertising Age* (April 29, 1968): 32.

78. Daniels & Charles, 67.

79. "Agency Ad Aims to Help Negroes with Ad Careers," 32; "Integrating the Agencies," *Newsweek* (April 29, 1968): 29. The duration of the scholarship program is unclear. The effort was not referenced again in the trade press and no mention of the program is made in scholarship lists in the 1970s and '80s.

80. "DDB Training Program for Minority Groups Begins," *Advertising Age* (July 8, 1968): 16.

81. On the National Alliance of Businessmen's efforts following the 1968 rebellions, see Gelber, 170–72. See also "DDB Training Program for Minority Groups Begins," 16; "DDB Sees Its JOBS Effort Aiding With Problems of 'Unemployables,'" *Advertising Age* (November 18, 1968): 22.

82. "Negro High School Graduates Get Two-Month Ad Training at FC&B," *Advertising Age* (August 26, 1968): 222; "Keep Training Minorities," *Advertising Age* (September 2, 1968): 14; "Operation College Bound," *Advertising Age* (September 8, 1969): 102.

83. Redhead quoted in "Campbell-Ewald Gives Scholarships, Summer Work to Inner City Youths," *Advertising Age* (August 18, 1969): 10; "Adman Likes View from the Top," 15.

84. On Program Brother, see *J. Walter Thompson Company News* (August 9, 1968), in JWT Papers, Hartmann Center, Duke University, JWT Main Newsletters, Box 11; "JWT Training Program Guide," Edward B. Wilson Papers (hereinafter Wilson Papers), Box 2, Hartman Center, Duke University, unpaginated.

85. "JWT Training Program Guide," Wilson Papers, Box 2; "Members of the JWT Training Program," *J. Walter Thompson Company News* (June 6, 1969): 8, in J. Walter Thompson Newsletter Collection, Main Series, Box 11, JWT Papers, Hartmann Center, Duke University; "JOBS Training Program, 1968–1970," Wilson Papers, Box 2.

86. Caroline R. Jones, "Opportunities for Women and Blacks Not Enough . . . But More Than Ever," in *Advertising Career Directory,* 2nd ed., ed. Ronald W. Fry (Hawthorne, N.J.: Career Press, 1987), 34. On the early role of women at JWT, see Jennifer Scanlon, "Advertising Women: The J. Walter Thompson Company Women's Editorial Department," in *The Gender and Consumer Culture Reader,* ed. Jennifer Scanlon (New York: New York University Press, 2000), 201–25.

87. JWT Training Program Guide," Wilson Papers, Box 2.

88. "Recommendation of the Membership Committee," Caroline R. Jones Papers (hereafter Jones Papers), Box 2, Folder 1, National Museum of American History, Smithsonian Institution, Washington D.C.; "Negro Admen Point Finger at GAP," *Media/Scope* (July 1968): 59; "GAP," *Madison Avenue* (July 1968): 27–29.

89. "Negro Admen Point Finger at GAP," 56–57. Group for Advertising Progress Panel Discussion Outline, October 1968, Jones Papers, Box 2, Folder 5.

90. Quoted in M. L. Stein, *Blacks in Communications: Journalism, Public Relations and Advertising* (New York: Julian Messner, 1972), 156; "Four A's Studies 'Minority Gap' in Employment," 1, 8, 87; Letter from Caroline Jones to Doug Alligood, June 16, 1969, Jones Papers, Box 2, Folder 4; John Revett, "Minority Folk Learn TV Ads in GAP Workshop," *Advertising Age* (February 24, 1969): 166.

91. "GAP Finds It Difficult to Get Summer Jobs for Minority Workshop Students," *Advertising Age* (July 7, 1969): 16; "Harry Webber," *Final Proof* (June 1972): 2.

92. John Revett, "Minority Folk Learn TV Ads in GAP Workshop," *Advertising Age* (February 24, 1969): 166; "The Coalition Against Racism and Sexism," *Advertising Age* (January 10, 1977): 8.

93. "Action on Several Fronts," *Advertising Age* (July 8, 1968): 14.

94. Philip Dougherty, "Negroes Are Gaining Account Jobs," *New York Times* (June 22, 1969): sec. 3, 14; Cohen, 4–5.

95. Sharp quoted in "Ad Field's Efforts to Induct Blacks Is Overrated," 3. See also "Hike Minority Groups to 13% of Payroll, Four A's Agencies Urged," *Advertising Age* (November 3, 1969): 3, 103; "How Minority Hiring Fares," *Advertising Age* (November 10, 1969): 14.

96. Benjamin, 223, 228–30. Christopher, "No Letup," 3.

97. *Report of the National Advisory Commission on Civil Disorders* (New York: New York Times Company, 1968), 386.

98. Quoted in Gelber, 132; "JWT to Interview 117 Negro Job Seekers in 2-Day Talent Hunt," *Advertising Age* (June 20, 1966): 22; Gelber, 213–22; Fox, 282.

99. Quoted in Gelber, 130; Ernest Holsendolph, "Black Executives in a Nearly All-White World," *Fortune* (September, 1972): 140–51; Cohen, "Advertising and the Black Community," 3–4. See also Sam Greenlee, *The Spook Who Sat By the Door* (Detroit: Wayne State University Press, 1990).

100. Gelber, 5.

101. Benjamin, 228–30; Walker, 364–65.

102. "Minority Hiring Dips at 7 Shops: Study," *Advertising Age* (June 26, 1978): 85; quoted in Webber, 2; Bob Donath, "Agency Minority Hiring Slow to Rise," *Advertising Age* (October 3, 1977): 2, 91; Gelber, 221–222; "Don't Hide Hiring Data," *Advertising Age* (October 17, 1977): 18; Cohen, "Advertising and the Black Community," 4–5.

Chapter 5

1. Robert E. Weems, Jr., *Desegregating the Dollar: African American Consumerism in the Twentieth Century* (New York: New York University Press, 1998), 75–79; Lizabeth Cohen, *A Consumers' Republic: The Politics of Mass Consumption in Postwar America* (New York: Alfred A Knopf, 2003), 325; Royal D. Colle, "Negro Image in the Mass Media: A Case Study in Social Change," *Journalism Quarterly* (Spring 1968): 55–60. On the development of Black Power, see William L. Van Deburg,

New Day in Babylon: The Black Power Movement and American Culture, 1965–1975 (Chicago: University of Chicago Press, 1992).

2. On the growth of black income levels, see D. Parke Gibson, *The $30 Billion Negro* (Toronto: Collier-Macmillan Ltd., 1969); D. Parke Gibson, *$70 Billion in the Black: America's Black Consumers* (New York: Macmillan, 1978); and Weems, *Desegregating the Dollar,* 70–73. On the Creative Revolution, see Stephen Fox, *The Mirror Makers: A History of American Advertising and Its Creators* (Urbana: University of Illinois Press, 1997), 265–71; Hazel Warlaumont, *Advertising in the 60s: Turncoats, Traditionalists and Waste Makers in America's Turbulent Decade* (Westport, Conn.: Praeger Publishers, 200), 170–72; Janette L. Dates, "Half a Loaf: Advertising," in *Split Image: African Americans in the Mass Media,* ed. Jannette L. Dates and William Barlow (Washington, D.C.: Howard University Press, 1993), 478–79. The term "Golden Age" has been used by other scholars to denote blacks' experience with the media industries during this time; see J. Fred MacDonald, *Blacks and White TV: Afro-Americans in Television since 1948* (Chicago: Nelson-Hall Publishers, 1988), 107–30.

3. Baraka quoted in Darlene Clark Hine, William C. Hine, and Stanley Harrold, *The African American Odyssey* (Upper Saddle River, N.J.: Prentice-Hall, 2000): 547; Van Deburg, 181–88; Dates, "Half a Loaf," 490–91.

4. Judy Foster Davis, "Enterprise Development under an Economic Detour? Black-Owned Advertising Agencies, 1940–2000," *Journal of Macromarketing* (June 2002): 77–78; Merah Stuart, *An Economic Detour: A History of Insurance in the Lives of American Negroes* (New York: Wendell Malliet and Company, 1940).

5. "Black Man on Madison Avenue," *Media Decisions* (February 1971): 38–39, 66–76; "Grey Skies for Black Admen," *Business Week* (October 31, 1970): 81–82; Monroe Anderson, "Black Advertising Agencies Woo the Black Dollar," *National Observer* (November 13, 1971): 11.

6. Anderson, 11; "Grey Skies for Black Admen," 81–82; "Black Image Makers on Madison Avenue," *Black Enterprise* (February 1971): 19–20.

7. "Black Man on Madison Avenue," 66–70.

8. "Black Man on Madison Avenue," 68–76.

9. "L&M Cigarettes Pitched to Blacks as 'Super Bad,'" *Advertising Age* (August 2, 1971): 20; "Black Man on Madison Avenue," 68. On the use of black vernacular as an indicator of black pride, see Van Deburg, 216–19. "L&M Cigarettes," 20; "Black Image Makers on Madison Avenue," 19; Philip H. Dougherty, "Advertising: Eastern Air Alters Course," *New York Times* (January 26, 1970): 88.

10. E. P. Richardson, "Jungle Drums: The Natives Are Really Restless," *Art Direction* (January 1973): 57; Philip H. Dougherty, "Advertising: Eve Cigarette Goes National," *New York Times* (November 30, 1970): 82.

11. "Black Man on Madison Avenue," 71; Philip H. Dougherty, "Advertising: The Story Behind a Telegram," *New York Times* (May 5, 1968): F18.

12. "Black Man on Madison Avenue," 71. On urban marketing, see Melba Newsom and Gerda Gallop-Goodman, "Mad Marketing Skills: Your Guide to Cashing in on the Young, Urban Market," *Black Enterprise* (December 1999): 159–64.

13. Quotation from "Black Image Makers on Madison Avenue," 17. See also Anderson, "Black Advertising Agencies Woo the Black Dollar," 11.

14. "The Black Man in the Gray Flannel Suit," *Time* (June 27, 1969): 76; M. L. Stein, *Blacks in Communications: Journalism, Public Relations, and Advertising* (New York: Julian Messner, 1972), 166–67.

15. Stein, 167.

298 Notes to Pages 214–219

16. Anderson, 11; "Black Ad Agency Opens Philly Office," *Black Enterprise* (April 1972): 12; "Sanders to Handle Movie," *Advertising Age* (March 20, 1972): 54.

17. Quotation from Thomas A. Johnson, "2 Groups Investigating Advertising Agencies in New York City Over Charges of Racial Discrimination," *New York Times* (July 18, 1976): 34. See also Grayson Mitchell, "Black Ad Agencies . . . And Then There Were 13," *Black Enterprise* (September 1979): 44–45; Johnson, "2 Groups," 34; Deborah Bolling, "Then Came Brunson," *Philadelphia Citypaper.net* accessed on January 4, 2007 from http://www.citypaper.net/articles/2003–01–23/om.shtml.

18. "Small Sees Singer Assignment as Breakthrough for Blacks," *Advertising Age* (March 23, 1970): 137; "The Small Story," *Madison Avenue* (June 1972): 19; Leonard Sloane, "Advertising: The Never Land of Promises," *New York Times* (August 24, 1970): 68.

19. Quotation from "Small Sees Singer," 137. See also "Blacks Buy Differently: Adman Small to AAF," *Advertising Age* (June 29, 1970): 2.

20. "The Small Story," 18–19; "John Small Pioneers; Joins WNBC-TV as 1st Negro Salesman," *Advertising Age* (February 15, 1965): 12.

21. "The Small Story," 19; Leonard Slone, "Advertising: The Never Land of Promises," *New York Times* (August 24, 1970): 68.

22. "Small Sees Singer," 137.

23. "The Small Story," 19.

24. "Singer Move to Grey Shows JWT Is Still Having Problems," 1, 97; "Navy Picks Black Shop, 2, 188.

25. "Singer Move to Grey," 1, 97.

26. "Blacks Buy Differently," 2, 8; Photograph, *Advertising Age* (March 15, 1971): 92; "Singer Move to Grey," 1, 97; "Navy Picks Black Shop," Hikes Minority Ad Effort," *Advertising Age* (August 27, 1973): 2, 188; "New York Expert Picked to Get Peace Corps' Message Across to U.S.," *Chicago Daily Defender* (March 22, 1971): 10.

27. "Singer Move to Grey," 1, 97; "Panel on Blacks Agrees Data Lack Hurts Media," *Advertising Age* (April 1, 1974): 10.

28. Bob Donath, "Publishers Say Navy Torpedoed Them, Paid Defunct Agency's Bank for Ads," *Advertising Age* (January 19, 1976): 2, 63; Bob Donath, "Black-Owned Shops Still Seeking Identity," *Advertising Age* (May 16, 1977): 98.

29. Thomas A. Johnson, "2 Groups Investigating Advertising Agencies in New York City over Charges of Racial Discrimination," *New York Times* (July 18, 1976): 34.

30. Quotation from Anderson, 11. On Zebra Associates, see Weems, *Desegregating the Dollar*, 78–79. "Black Image Makers on Madison Avenue," 17–18; "New Ad Agency Specialty to be Selling to the Poor," *Wall Street Journal* (June 20, 1969): 36; "Zebra Associates Working on Accounts Before Agency Opens," June 19, 1969, company press release, Caroline R. Jones Papers (hereafter Jones Papers), Box 1, Folder 1, Archives Center, National Museum of American History, Smithsonian Institution, Washington, D.C; "R.A. League and Associates Adds Two New Staff Members," *Chicago Daily Defender* (October 4, 1961): 14.

31. "Zebra Associates Shop Formed with Negro Principals," *Advertising Age* (June 23, 1969): 103.

32. Anderson, 11; "Zebra Associates Shop," 103; "The Zoo Story," *Newsweek* (January 12, 1970): 49; "Black-Owned Ad Agency Celebrates Second Year," *Chicago Daily Defender* (July 3, 1971): 31.

33. "Whites Fail to Aid Minorities: Don't Speak 'Inner City,' League Charges," *Advertising Age* (June 30, 1969): 93; "Minority Training Program Part of Zebra's Operation," June 19, 1969, company press release, Jones Papers, Box 1, Folder 1.

34. "A Position Paper on Minority Media Being Prepared by Zebra Associates," June 19, 1969, company press release, Jones Papers, Box 1, Folder 1.

35. "Zebra Agency Offers Top Talents to Small Black Advertisers," company press release, Jones Papers, Box 1, Folder 1; Weems, *Desegregating the Dollar*, 78.

36. "Grey Skies for Black Admen," 82; Zebra Associates, advertisement, *Marketing/Communications* (February 1970): 50; "Zebra Associates: Why We Are. . . . What We Are. . . . Who We Are," June 1969, Jones Papers, Box 1, Folder 1, 3.

37. "Zebra Associates: Why We Are," 3; "The Black Man in the Gray Flannel Suit," 76; "Zebra Associates: Why We Are," 1–4.

38. "Zebra," *Madison Avenue* (November 1969): 10–15.

39. "Zebra Associates Gets Fabricators, Wyandotte Division," *Advertising Age* (December 1, 1969): 3; "Zebra Agency Will Handle Spectrum Ads," *Advertising Age* (March 9, 1970): 28; "Schenley Picks Zebra Shop," *Advertising Age* (October 25, 1971): 95; "Agency Profiles: Zebra Associates," *Advertising Age* (February 21, 1972): 122; "How to Advertise to the Black Consumer Market," Jones Papers, Box 1, Folder 1; "Minority Market Is Not So Minor, Ray League Tells Popai Workshop," *Advertising Age* (March 27, 1972): 4; "Black Ad Agency Views Liberia," *Chicago Daily Defender* (November 7, 1970): 31.

40. Caroline Jones, daily notebook entry, October 7, 1971, Jones Papers, Box 2, Folder 3; Caroline Jones to Raymond League, October 14, 1971, Jones Papers, Box 2, Folder 3.

41. Quotation from "Castleberry Is Named New Zebra President," *New York Amsterdam News* (June 9, 1973): C-11. See also "Murray New Acting Chief of Zebra Shop," *Advertising Age* (May 21, 1973): 8; "Five N.Y. Shops Fill Top Positions," *Advertising Age* (June 4, 1973): 33.

42. Quotation from Daniel L. Lionel, "Black-Owned Newspapers Favored by Zebra Agency," *Editor & Publisher* (January 4, 1975): 16. See also "Agency Profiles: Zebra Associates, *Advertising Age* (February 24, 1975): 126.

43. "Agency Profiles: Zebra Associates," *Advertising Age* (February 23, 1976): 100; Donath, "Black-Owned Shops Still Seeking Identity," 98.

44. "Agency Profiles: Zebra Associates," *Advertising Age* (February 23, 1976): 100; Donath, "Black-Owned Shops Still Seeking Identity," 98; "Ex-Zebra Exec Charged with Conspiracy to Kill Her Partner," *Advertising Age* (June 7, 1976): 8; "Hearing Set for Ex-Zebra Exec Murray," *Advertising Age* (January 17, 1977): 70; "Zebra Exec Guilty of Perjury," *Advertising Age* (November 14, 1977): 89. "Castleberry Opens Shop Following Zebra Closing," *Advertising News of New York* (April 30, 1976): 14.

45. Fox, 321; Warlaumont, 172–74.

46. Quotation from "Grey Skies for Black Admen," 82. See also Donath, "Black-Owned Shops Still Seeking Identity," 98; Anderson, 11; "Black Agencies: Their Quiet Demise," 16–17. On the employee drain from black insurance companies, see Robert E. Weems, Jr., *Black Business in the Black Metropolis: The Chicago Metropolitan Assurance Company, 1925–1985* (Bloomington: Indiana University Press, 1996), xv.

47. Quotation from John Revett, "Racial Frustrations Unify Black Communicators," *Advertising Age* (April 3, 1978): 32. See also Fox, 284; Davis, 78–79.

48. Quoted in Donath, "Black-Owned Shops Still Seeking Identity," 3. Tom Burrell, interview by author, January 26, 2001, Chicago, Illinois.

49. Quoted in "Black Ad Agencies . . . And Then There Were 13," 44. Weems, *Desegregating the Dollar,* 98–99; Walker, 351–52, 364–65.

50. "Grey Skies for Black Admen," 81.

51. "Black-Owned Agencies Merit More Attention," *Advertising Age* (February 16, 1976): 28; "Stereotypes Not Fair to All Black Agencies," *Advertising Age* (May 24, 1976): 57; "Black Caucus to Study Ad Agency Complaints," *Advertising Age* (April 19, 1976): 135; "Change Blacks Pushed Out of Ad Business," *Chicago Defender* (August 20, 1977): 4.

52. "Still a Sore Spot—B&W," *Advertising Age* (April 26, 1976): 14.

53. "Still a Sore Spot," 14.

54. "Cullers to Handle Lorillard Brands in the Negro Markets," *Advertising Age* (June 10, 1968): 2; "The Soul Market in Black and White," *Sales Management* (June 1, 1969): 2. On Soul marketing, see Weems, *Desegregating the Dollar,* 76–79, and Van Deburg, 192–247.

55. Quoted in Weems, *Desegregating the Dollar,* 77–78.

56. Van Deburg, 195; *Tuesday* Publications, advertisement, *Advertising Age* (March 10, 1969): 37–38; *Ebony,* advertisement, *Advertising Age* (September 30, 1968): 33. On Soul food and music, see Van Deburg, 202–16. On the use of Soul in marketing, see Weems, *Desegregating the Dollar,* 76–78. "Black Ad Agency Leads Way to Sales for Negro Market," *Chicago Defender* (November 11, 1969): 4.

57. Robert Weems, Jr., "Consumerism and the Construction of Black Female Identity in Twentieth Century America," in *The Gender and Consumer Culture Reader,* ed. Jennifer Scanlon (New York: New York University Press, 2000), 170; "Soul Marketing," *Marketing/Communications* (July 1969): 72; Robin Nelson, "The Rise of the Phoney in Power Markets," *Marketing/Communications* (April 1969): 60–62, 69–70; "The Soul Market in Black and White," 41–42; Kelvin A. Wall, "The Great Waste: Ignoring Blacks," *Marketing/Communications* (February 1970): 42–49.

58. Quoted in Van Deburg, 201; Woods, 157–58; Marian J. Moore, "The Advertising Images of Black Americans, 1880–1920 and 1968–1979: A Thematic and Interpretive Approach" (Ph.D. diss., Bowling Green State University, 1986), 158–60. On the choice of skin tone and facial features of African American models, see Marilyn Kern-Foxworth, *Aunt Jemima, Uncle Ben, and Rastus: Blacks in Advertising, Yesterday, Today, and Tomorrow* (Westport, Conn.: Greenwood Press, 1994), 126. See also "Black Is Busting Out All Over," *Life* (October 17, 1969): 36; Dates, "Half a Loaf," 466; Michael K. Chapko, "Black Ads Are Getting Blacker," *Journal of Communication* (Autumn 1976): 175–78; Ronald Geizer, "Advertising in *Ebony*: 1960 and 1969," *Journalism Quarterly* (Spring 1977): 131–34; A George Gitter, Stephen M. O'Connell, and David Mostofsky, "Trends in Appearance of Models in *Ebony* Ads over 17 Years," *Journalism Quarterly* (Autumn 1972): 547–50.

59. "Black Image Makers on Madison Avenue," *Black Enterprise* (February 1971): 17; Wall, 42–49.

60. Quoted in Elaine Brown, *A Taste of Power: A Black Woman's Story* (New York: Anchor Books, 1994), 280. See also Woods, 157.

61. Quoted in Moore, 160, 163. On the commodification of activist ideals, see Warlaumont, *Advertising in the 60s.* See also Jannette L. Dates, "Split Images and Double Binds," in *Split Image,* ed. Dates and Barlow, 524.

62. Teresa Savage, "Byron Eugene Lewis," in *Encyclopedia of African American Business History* ed. Juliet E. K. Walker (Westport, Conn.: Greenwood Press, 1999): 360–61; Philip A. Dougherty, "How Sole Black Agency Makes It," *New*

York Times (July 27, 1976): 46; Delores Brooks and Lon G. Walls, "Advertising in the Black," *Dollars & Sense* (February/March 1982): 17.

63. Anderson, 11. On the blaxploitation film era, see Weems, *Desegregating the Dollar*, 80–90; Thomas Cripps, "The Film Industry," in *Split Image*, ed. Dates and Barlow, 189–266.

64. Lorraine Baltera, "Avon Lady Is Changing; New Youth, Black Drive," *Advertising Age* (June 5, 1974): 63; Chris Policano, "UniWorld Group Survives Ad Agency Pitfalls," *New York Amsterdam News* (January 15, 1977): C-10; "Dialogue: PUSH and Avon," *Black Enterprise* (November 1973): 42–43; Joel Dreyfuss, "Where Is Jesse Jackson Going?" *Black Enterprise* (October 1974): 23–27; "Business/Commerce/Industry," *The Gibson Report* (May 1977): 4.

65. "Black Image Makers on Madison Avenue," 22; "UniWorld in Wash.," *Advertising Age* (August 15, 1977): 65; "Black Ad Agencies . . . And Then There Were 13," 44–49.

66. Lewis quoted in Policano, C-10. On *Sounds of the City*, see also Savage, 360; Chris Sandlund, "There's a New Face to America," *Success* (April 1999): 39; Cassandra Hayes, "Marketing to the World," *Black Enterprise* (January 1995): 99.

67. Quoted in Woods, 167; "Four A's Taps UniWorld," *Advertising Age* (March 22, 1976): 55; "UniWorld Adds More Gillette," *Advertising Age* (March 7, 1977): 55; "Says UniWorld Success Due to Byron Lewis," *Advertising Age* (May 30, 1977): 51; Philip H. Dougherty, "Ethnic Ad Budgets Holding Up," *New York Times* (December 17, 1981): 87. On Lewis's corporate philosophy, see Woods, 12.

68. Quoted in "Barbara Gardner Proctor," in *African-American Business Leaders: A Biographical Dictionary*, ed. John N. Ingham and Lynne B. Feldman (Westport, Conn.: Greenwood Press, 1994), 566. See also "Barbara Proctor: I Made it BECAUSE I'm Black and a Woman," *Ebony* (August 1982): 143–44; Karen DeWitt, "Black Women in Business," *Black Enterprise* (August 1974): 14–19; "Proctor Takes a Gamble and Hits Jackpot," *Working Woman* (August 1979): 19–20; Lynn Taylor, "Barbara Proctor Wants to Aim at Black and White," *Chicago Tribune* (February 24, 1972): B12; Mara Scudder, "Advertising Executive Speaks Her Mind," *Chicago Defender* (March 9, 1974): 13.

69. "Barbara Gardner Proctor," 565–66.

70. Taylor, B12.

71. "Black Capitalism: The Rarest Breed of Women," *Time* (November 8, 1971): 102; "Chicago Agency Joins Sen. Jackson's Drive," *Chicago Daily Defender* (January 26, 1972): 24.

72. Quoted in "Barbara Gardner Proctor," 568; "Barbara Proctor's Definition of the Ad Function: Helping Client, Consumer Touch Base," *Advertising Age* (March 25, 1974): 106. Proctor was able to maintain her standard of refusing alcohol and tobacco products for the duration of the 1970s. However, as her firm continued to lose billings in the 1980s, she accepted accounts for both alcoholic beverage and tobacco products.

73. "Barbara Proctor's Definition of the Ad Function," 106.

74. "Proctor & Gardner Won't Buy Media If Blacks Excluded," *Advertising Age* (June 17, 1974): 116.

75. "Proctor & Gardner Won't Buy Media," 116; "Black Agency Owner's Practice Is Pure Racism," *Advertising Age* (August 19, 1974): 24; "Barbara Gardner Proctor," 567–69.

76. "Barbara Proctor's Definition of the Ad Function," 106; "Barbara Proctor Selected for Top Advertising Award," *Jet* (May 8, 1975): 16; "Agency Profiles: Proctor & Gardner Advertising," *Advertising Age* (February 23, 1976): 98; Adri-

enne Ward Fawcett, "The Battle for Black Accounts," *Advertising Age* (February 5, 1996): 14; "Barbara Gardner Proctor," 566–69.

77. "Thomas J. Burrell," in *African-American Business Leaders*, ed. Ingham and Feldman,120–21; "Burrell at 25: A Commemorative," *Advertising Age* (June 3, 1996): C2.

78. Ron Sampson, interview with Sean Brewster, April 2004, Champaign, Illinois; Tom Burrell, interview by author.

79. Tom Burrell, interview by author; Adrienne W. Fawcett, "Perseverance Pays Dividend at $128 Million Burrell Shop," *Advertising Age* (June 3, 1996): C-8. On racial integration in white-collar work, see Steven M. Gelber, *Black Men and Businessmen: The Growing Awareness of a Social Responsibility* (Port Washington, N.Y.: Kennikat Press, 1974), 69–85.

80. Tom Burrell, interview by author; "Thomas J. Burrell," 120–21. On Bill Sharp, see Chapter 4.

81. Joseph Winski, "Spotlight: Burrell Success Rooted in Ads Basic to Black Culture," *Chicago Tribune* (April 8, 1981): C1, C10; Tom Burrell, interview by author.

82. Burrell quoted in "Burrell at 25," C4. See also Tom Burrell, interview by author; "Thomas J. Burrell," 126; "Burrell at 25," C2-C3.

83. Quotations from Ken Smikle, "The Image Makers," *Black Enterprise* (December 1985): 44, 45–52; Lawrence J. Tell, "Burrell's Focus on Black Consumers Reaps $10 Million in Billings; Largest Black Ad Agency's Expertise Pays Off in Client Loyalty," *Chicago Reporter* (June 1978): 2. See also Brooks and Walls, 17–18; "Thomas J. Burrell," 125–26; Roi Ottley, "Russians Get Look at Negro's Art," *Chicago Daily Tribune* (February 7, 1960): S7.

84. Quotations from Joseph M. Winski and Kathy Lanpher, "He Said 'No Thanks!' to Handouts," *Advertising Age* (March 1, 1982): M2; "Black Ad Agencies . . . And Then There Were 13," 44. See also Smikle, 44–52; Brooks and Walls, 17–18; "Burrell at 25," C1; Winski and Lanpher, M2-M3.

85. Woods, 26, "Thomas J. Burrell," 125; Winski and Lanpher, M2.

86. "Thomas J. Burrell," 120; Tom Burrell, interview by author; "Burrell at 25," C8.

87. Tom Burrell, interview by author; "Thomas J. Burrell," 124–25; Woods, 26; "Fanta Target . . . ," *Chicago Daily Defender* (February 12, 1972): 32.

88. Tom Burrell, interview by author; Behavioral Systems, Inc., "Appendix B —'The Marlboro Image Revisited': An Exploration of the Masculinity Concept Among Black Urban Male Cigarette Smokers," June 1971; Bates: 2023045830–2023045889 accessed on December 30, 2006 from http://tobaccodocuments.org/pm/2023045830–5889.html; Lynn Taylor, "Black Ad Agencies Look to Future," *Chicago Tribune* (February 23, 1972): C12; "Black Firm Awarded Big Account," *Chicago Daily Defender* (May 5, 1971): 27.

89. "Burrell at 25," C6.

90. Winski and Lanpher, M2–M3; Marsha Cassidy and Richard Katula, "The Black Experience in Advertising: An Interview with Thomas J. Burrell," *Journal of Communication Inquiry* (Winter 1990): 93–94; Tom Burrell, interview by author; Kern-Foxworth, 170; W. Franklyn Joseph, "Blacks' Ambition Enters the Picture," *Advertising Age* (March 14, 1985): 26.

91. Pat McGeehan, "The Burrell Style," *Advertising Age* (December 19, 1985): 5.

92. Tom Burrell, interview by author.

93. Winski and Lanpher, M2; Four A's Adds Burrell," *Advertising Age* (Novem-

ber 10, 1975): 91; Martha T. Moore, "Black Agencies Seek Recognition," *USA Today* (July 25, 1994): 3B; "Burrell at 25," C8; Tom Burrell, interview by author.

94. Nancy F. Millman, "Sampson Quits TL&K for Black-Owned Burrell," *Advertising Age* (April 24, 1978): 54; "Blacks Are Most 'HHidden Persuaders' in Chicago's Billion Dollar Advertising Business," *Chicago Reporter* 4, no. 3 (March 1975): 2–4. Some of Burrell's advertisements were also very popular with international audiences. See *Inside Business Today: Marketing to Minorities*, prod. ArGee Productions, 30 min., University of Wisconsin Telecommunications Center, 1983, videocassette.

95. J. Walter Thompson, "Advertising and Black America," J. Walter Thompson Company Papers, Advertising—Target Groups—Ethnic, Hartman Center, Duke University.

96. "Jungle Drums," *Art Direction* (January 1973): 55–57; "Y&R Ethnic Unit: Finding and Reaching Minority Markets," *Broadcasting* (June 4, 1973): 21.

97. Quotation from "Ethnic Units Rapped by Alligood," *Advertising Age* (June 25, 1973): 52. See also "Black Group Drops Y&R Exec in Dispute Over Ethnic Unit," *Advertising Age* (April 23, 1973): 139.

98. "GAP's Rip-off," *Advertising Age* (April 30, 1973): 14; "Blacks, Whites Wrangle Ethnic Cell Controversy," *Advertising Age* (June 4, 1973): 92.

99. "Negro Admen Point Finger at GAP," 58; "GAP's Rip-off," 14; "Group for Advertising Progress Panel Discussion Outline," 1968 Eastern Annual Conference, American Association of Advertising Agencies, Jones Papers, Box 2, Folder 5; Bill Sharp, *How to Be Black and Get a Job in the Advertising Agency Business Anyway* (Bethesda, Md.: Bill Sharp, 1969), 43–44.

100. "Blacks, Whites Wrangle Ethnic Cell Controversy," 92.

101. "Negro Admen Point Finger at GAP," 57–58; Leon Morse, "Consumer Studies Place Emphasis on Young Blacks," *Television/Radio Age* (February 28, 1977): A-11; "BBDO Wants In" *Marketing & Media Decisions* (March 1986): 38.

102. Jack Feuer, "Perspectives on the Black Marketplace: the Myths and Reality," *Marketing Communications* (September 1977): 30; Davis, "Enterprise Development," 82–83; Fox, 284.

103. David Sullivan, "Selling the Negro Market," *American Brewer* (June 1961): 47–53, 61–62; D. Parke Gibson, "Needs of the Negro Consumer," Speech to the Soap and Detergent Association, New York City, January 26, 1967, in J. Walter Thompson Company Papers, Hartman Center, Duke University, Marketing Vertical File, 1940–99, Box 22.

104. Cohen, *A Consumers' Republic*, 325–27.

105. "Black Image Makers on Madison Avenue," 16; "Four A's Studies 'Minority Gap' in Employment," *Advertising Age* (October 28, 1968): 8, 87.

106. Mitchell quoted in Anderson, "Black Advertising Agencies," 11. See also Dates, "Split Images and Double Binds," 524. On racial memory see Van Deburg, 192–94; Donath, "Black-Owned Shops Still Seeking Identity," 3.

107. "Black Ad Agencies . . . And Then There Were 13," 44.

Epilogue

1. Quotation from "Still a Sore Spot—B&W," *Advertising Age* (April 26, 1976): 14. See also Bob Donath, "New Black-owned Agency Hopes for 'General Status,'" *Advertising Age* (March 28, 1977): 85; Mitchell J. Shields, "Small Is Beautiful," *Savvy* (October 1985): 16–17.

2. Philip H. Dougherty, "New Black Owned Agency," *New York Times* (May 6, 1977): 83; "Black Creative Group Formed," *Advertising Age* (August 20, 1973): 55; Beatryce Nivens, "Caroline Jones: Advertising Trailblazer," *Elan* (February 1982): 28–30; "Mingo-Jones Advertising, Inc.," *Better Business* (December 1981): 9–12.

3. Moore quoted in Bob Donath, "Black-owned Shops Still Seeking Identity," *Advertising Age* (May 16, 1977): 96; Dougherty, "New Black Owned Agency," 83; Donath, "Black-owned Shops," 96.

4. Dougherty, "New Black Owned Agency," 83; Nivens, 29; Leroy Pope, "Ethnic Expertise Helps But Black Agency Viability Depends on Non-ethnic Success," *Business Today* (April 6, 1982): 6.

5. "Mingo-Jones: Doing the Colonel Right," *Black Enterprise* (December 1981): 56; Warren Berger, "Caroline Jones Advertising," *Inside Print* (March 1989): 31.

6. Grayson Mitchell, "And Then There Were 13," *Black Enterprise* (September 1979): 49; Evette Porter, "At the Crossroads: The First of a New Breed of Ad Executive Takes Charge," *Emerge* (September 1990): 31–33.

7. Mingo quoted in Joseph M. Winski and Kathy Lanpher, "He Said 'No Thanks!' to Handouts," *Advertising Age* (March 1, 1982): M3. See also Debbie Seaman, "Mingo-Jones Founder Quits for Own Shop," *Adweek* (November 3, 1986): 4; Lee Anna Jackson, "Chisholm-Mingo Closes Its Doors," www.blackenterprise.com (June 4, 2004) accessed on June 16, 2004, from http://www.blackenterprise.com/ExclusivesEKOpen.asp?id=772&sc=be100s; Juliet E. K. Walker, *The History of Black Business in America: Capitalism, Race, Entrepreneurship* (New York: Twayne Publishers, 1998), 351.

8. Louie Robinson, "Rodney Allen Rippy," *Ebony* (February 1974): 100–104; Louis J. Haugh, "O. J. Tops Year's Star Presenters," *Advertising Age* (June 20, 1977): 1, 82; Chuck Wingis, "O. J. Tells How Ads Led to His Tinseltown Success," *Advertising Age* (June 20, 1977): 80–82; John Revett, "Cosby Top Star Presenter of 1978," *Advertising Age* (July 17, 1978): 1, 48.

9. On the emergence of blacks on television, see J. Fred MacDonald, *Blacks and White TV: Afro-Americans in Television Since 1948* (Chicago: Nelson-Hall Publishers, 1983), 149–237; Maurine Christopher, "Black Entertainment TV to Debut in January," *Advertising Age* (November 26, 1979): 22.

10. "Suburban Migration, Education Advances Signal Social Changes," *Television/Radio Age* (February 1982): A3-A4.

11. Tom Delaney, "Minorities in Ad Biz: No Equal Opportunity," *Adweek* (March 18, 1985): 40.

12. "3 U.S. Agencies Facing Action over Hiring Goals," *New York Times* (August 22, 1984): A14; John H. Cushman, Jr., "Minorities and the Ad Budget," *New York Times* (August 21, 1986) A20; Cardiss Collins, "Let's Bring in New Faces," *Adweek* (September 29, 1986): 24; "Will Minority Agencies Get a Shot at the Army?" *Marketing and Media Decisions* (October 1986): 22.

13. Gail Belsky, "Can a Few Black Agencies Absorb PUSH Bounty," *Adweek* (September 26, 1983): 40; "National Advertisers Rediscover the Black Market," *Ad Forum* (January 1984): 35; Amy Saltzman, "New Big Clients Put Black Agency in the Limelight," *Adweek* (February 27, 1984): 28; "Coke Agrees to Shift Brand to Black Shop," *Advertising Age* (August 17, 1981): 75; Lynda M. Hill, "Buying with a Conscience," *Black Enterprise* (October 1981): 75–78; Nancy Giges, "Burrell Now Int'l with Coke Work," *Advertising Age* (January 24, 1983): 3, 74; Judy Foster Davis, "Enterprise Development under an Economic Detour? Black-

owned Advertising Agencies, 1940–2000," *Journal of Macromarketing* 22, no. 1 (June 2002): 80–82.

14. "Make Minority Hiring a Reality," *Advertising Age* (June 22, 1992): 18; Brian Wright O'Connor, "Are Advertising Agencies Serious About Hiring African Americans," *Black Enterprise* (March 1993): 88–92; Adrienne Ward, "What Role Do Ads Play in Racial Tension?" *Advertising Age* (August 10, 1992): 1, 35; Greg Burns, "Few Blacks at Top Chicago Ad Agencies: Survey," *Chicago Sun-Times* (December 11, 1992): 49, 53; Joseph M. Winski, "The Ad Industry's 'Dirty Little Secret,'" *Advertising Age* (June 15, 1992): 16, 38; Robert E. Weems, Jr., *Desegregating the Dollar: African American Consumerism in the Twentieth Century* (New York: New York University Press, 1998), 118.

15. Heidy Steidlmayer, "Affirmative Inaction," *Screen* (June 8, 1992): 2–6; Kathy DeSalvo, "Minority Hiring: New Solutions," *Back Stage/SHOOT* (August 14, 1992): 40–41; Lowell Thompson, "Blacks in Ad Agencies: It Used to Be Better," *Advertising Age* (November 16, 1992): 22; Lowell Thompson, "The Invisible Man in the Gray Flannel Suit," *Print* (January/February 1993): 56–65, 118; Weems, *Desegregating the Dollar*, 119–20.

16. Stuart Elliot, "Advertising," *New York Times* (January 18, 1994): D20. On agency employment, see Martha T. Moore, "Black Images Abound, Black Staffers Don't," *USA Today* (July 25, 1994): 2B. On the decline in overall industry employment during the 1990s, see William W. Ellis, *African American Enterprise: Full Service Advertising Agencies, 1950–1995* (Washington, D.C.: Congressional Research Service, 1995), CRS-15.

17. Krista Kennedy, "'Dream' for Blacks Ends in a Rude Awakening," *Screen* (February 17, 1992): 4.

18. Ward, 1; Winski, 16; Weems, Jr., *Desegregating the Dollar*, 120–21.

19. Lee Server, "UniWorld Crosses Over," *Credits* 2, no. 6 (1984): 30–31; Scott Hume, "Burrell Recalls Roots But Seeks to Branch Out," *Advertising Age* (September 17, 1984): 12; Nanine Alexander, "Women in Advertising," *Essence* (January 1990): 40. On Don Coleman, see Cassandra Hayes, "A Creative Point of View," *Black Enterprise* (June 1998): 164–70; Alan Hughes, "United Colors of GlobalHue," *Black Enterprise* (June 2003): 186–194. On Carol Williams, see Cassandra Hayes, "Not Just an Ol' Boys Club," *Black Enterprise* (June 1999): 180–88; Sonia Alleyne, "The Magic Touch," *Black Enterprise* (June 2004): 188–94; Davis, 80–81.

20. Lisa Sanders, "Human Rights Commission Releases Agencies' Minority Hiring Goals," *Advertising Age*, accessed on January 11, 2007 from http://adage .com/article?article_id=114246.

21. On the experiences of black accountants, see Theresa A. Hammond, *A White-Collar Profession: African American Certified Public Accountants Since 1921* (Chapel Hill: University of North Carolina Press, 2002).

22. Winski, 38.

23. Bill Sharp, interview by author, Atlanta, Georgia, March 17, 2001; Peter Cannellos, "Why Can't Blacks Talk to Whites?" *Back Stage Magazine Supplement* (March 9, 1984): 9M.

24. Lisa Sanders, "Fudge Y&R Posting Lauded as Watershed," *Advertising Age* (May 19, 2003): 4, 143.

25. Brian O'Conner, "Are Advertising Agencies Serious About Hiring African Americans?," *Black Enterprise* (March 1993): 91.

26. "B.E. 100s: Advertising Agencies," *Black Enterprise* (June 2006): 164–68.

27. Tom Burrell, interview by author, January 26, 2001, Chicago, Illinois; Debra Kent, "UniWorld Turns Trends into Crossover Appeal," *Advertising Age* (December 19, 1985): 16, 22; "B.E. 100s," 164–68; Davis, 80–82.

28. Davis, 81–82.

29. On the state of black insurance companies near the end of the twentieth-century, see Robert E. Weems, Jr., *Black Business in the Black Metropolis: The Chicago Metropolitan Assurance Company, 1925–1985* (Bloomington: Indiana University Press, 1996), xvii, 119–24. See also Davis, 80–83; "Top Multicultural Agencies," *Advertising Age*, accessed on January 9, 2007, from http://adage .com/datacenter/datapopup.php?article_id = 108860; "Top 25 Agency Brands by Advertising Revenue," *Advertising Age*, accessed on January 9, 2007, from http://adage.com/datacenter/datapopup.php?article_id = 108857.

30. Winski, 16, 38; Davis, 81–82; Lisa Sanders, "Fudge Y&R Posting Lauded as Watershed," 4, 143; Dahna M. Chandler, "Burrell CEO Steps Down," www .blackenterprise.com (June 18, 2004) accessed on January 10, 2007, from http://www.blackenterprise.com/ExclusivesEKOpen.asp?id = 786.

Index

Acknowledgments

Although only a single name appears on the cover of this book, it would not have been possible without the support of a number of people and organizations.

First, my thanks to Robert Lockhart at the University of Pennsylvania Press for his support and guidance of this project over the years that it has taken to complete. Thanks also to my editor, Laura Helper-Ferris, whose skill, insight, and dedication were exemplary and of great help. I would also like to thank The Ohio State University and University of Illinois at Urbana-Champaign for financial support at various stages of this work's development. Special thanks here to Bill Berry, who located additional research support for me at a crucial stage. Also many thanks to the Advertising Educational Foundation's Visiting Professor Program for enabling me to spend two weeks at the Burrell Communications Group. Many thanks go out to the leaders and staff at Burrell for their insights into both current and historical issues facing the black consumer market and blacks in the advertising industry.

No historical project could ever be completed without the support of outstanding librarians and archivists, and it has been my pleasure to have encountered several such people: Audrey Davis, at the Alexandria Black History Resource Center, home of the Moss Kendrix papers; Ellen Gartrell and Jacqueline Reid at the John W. Hartman Center at Duke University; Fath Davis Ruffins and the staff at the National Museum of American History; the staff at the Chicago Historical Society, and Lisa Romero and the staff at the Communications Library at the University of Illinois. I would also like to thank the staff in the Department of Advertising office at the University of Illinois: Janette Bradley, Cinda Robbins-Cornstubble, and Robin Price, whose skill and dedication made the completion of this project easier.

I am grateful to several friends who have supported me with words of encouragement, advice, or simply offering me a place to stay. Special thanks to Carolyn Walker-Valentine and Gary Bess for allowing me to stay at their homes during research trips to Chicago and Washington, D.C., respectively, and to Leonard Moore, Sherwin Bryant, and Osei Appiah for their encouragement, advice, and wonderful examples of scholarship on history and communications. I am also thankful to George Dillard and Tyrone Lyons for helping me to take a break from this book by joining me on many trips to chase a little white ball around a golf course (at least we had a nice walk).

Several people helped me by facilitating my research among current and former black advertising professionals and special-markets representatives. I am indebted to Tammy Smalls, whose contacts in the advertising industry led me to my interview with Tom Burrell and to Bruce Bendinger for introducing me to several members of Chicago's black advertising community. I am also grateful to Robert E. Weems, Jr., for introducing me to some of the original "Brown Hucksters" still active in the NAMD.

I am also indebted to several of my collegues in the academy including Tom O'Guinn and Linda Scott for taking on extra teaching responsibilities in the fall of 2004 so that I might have time off to focus on this project; Judy Foster Davis for sharing some of her research on *Ebony* magazine; John Burnham and Warren Van Tine for their advice; and Linda Scott and Lizabeth Cohen for reading unpublished portions of this manuscript and offering valuable criticism, advice, and insight.

I also could not have completed this book without the assistance of several outstanding research assistants including (in alphabetical order) Eric Lugo, Linda Manning, Marissa Randle, and Erica Smith. Additional thanks go to Sean Brewster and Nicole Seals for sharing their interview of Ron Sampson with me.

A number of people in the advertising industry took the time to relate their experiences to me, and those conversations strengthened my understanding of blacks' history in the industry tremendously. Many thanks to (in alphabetical order) Bruce Bendinger, Ella Britton, Tom Burrell, Roy Eaton, Fay Ferguson, Alma Hopkins, Linda Jefferson, Don Richards, Ron Sampson, Bill Sharp, Lowell Thompson, and Bernie Washington. I am also grateful to Chuck Smith for sharing some of his experiences as a special-markets representative, as well as Moss Kendrix, Jr., for relating some of the history of his father.

Finally, to my family I say thanks. Mom and Dad, I could not have done this without you, and it looks like all those trips to the library when I was a kid finally paid off. To my sister, Annette Chambers, you have always been there for me, and I love you for it. I am also thankful for the support and love of the rest of my family and my in-laws. Last, and definitely not least, to Sonya Chambers, my beautiful wife, who endured long research and conference trips and did so with more grace and love than I could possibly repay.

To anyone I may have left out, I apologize. Although there are many individuals and institutions listed here, any errors in this work rest solely with me.